WOLE SOYINKA
Politics, Poetics and Postcolonialism

Biodun Jeyifo examines the connections between the innovative and influential writings of Wole Soyinka and his radical political activism. Jeyifo carries out detailed analyses of Soyinka's most ambitious works, relating them to the controversies generated by Soyinka's use of literature and theatre for radical political purposes. He gives a fascinating account of the profound but paradoxical affinities and misgivings Soyinka has felt about the significance of the avant-garde movements of the twentieth century. Jeyifo also explores Soyinka's works with regard to the impact on his artistic sensibilities of the pervasiveness of representational ambiguity and linguistic exuberance in Yoruba culture. The analyses and evaluations of this study are presented in the context of Soyinka's sustained engagement with the violence of collective experience in post-independence, postcolonial Africa and the developing world. No existing study of Soyinka's works and career has attempted such a systematic investigation of their complex relationship to politics.

BIODUN JEYIFO is Professor of English at Cornell University. He is the author of *The Popular Travelling Theatre of Nigeria* (1984) and *The Truthful Lie: Essays in a Radical Sociology of African Drama* (1985). He has written essays and monographs on Anglophone African and Caribbean literatures, Marxist cultural theory and colonial and postcolonial studies and has also edited several volumes on African drama and critical discourse.

CAMBRIDGE STUDIES IN AFRICAN AND CARIBBEAN
LITERATURE

Series editor: Professor Abiola Irele, Ohio State University

Each volume in this unique series of critical studies will offer a comprehensive and in-depth account of the whole *œuvre* of one individual writer from Africa or the Caribbean, in such a way that the book may be considered a complete coverage of the writer's expression up to the time the study is undertaken. Attention will be devoted primarily to the works themselves – their significant themes, governing ideas and formal procedures, biographical and other background information will thus be employed secondarily, to illuminate these aspects of the writer's work where necessary.

The emergence in the twentieth century of black literature in the United States, the Caribbean, and Africa as a distinct corpus of imaginative work represents one of the most notable developments in world literature in modern times. This series has been established to meet the needs of this growing area of study. It is hoped that it will not only contribute to a wider understanding of the humanistic significance of modern literature from Africa and the Caribbean through the scholarly presentation of the work of the major writers, but also offer a wider framework for the ongoing debates about the problems of interpretation within the disciplines concerned.

Already published

Chinua Achebe, by C. L. Innes
Nadine Gordimer, by Dominic Head
Edouard Glissant, by J. Michael Dash
V. S. Naipaul, by Fawzia Mustafa
Aimé Césaire, by Gregson Davis
J. M. Coetzee, by Dominic Head
Jean Rhys, by Elaine Savory

WOLE SOYINKA

Politics, Poetics and Postcolonialism

BIODUN JEYIFO

Cornell University

CAMBRIDGE
UNIVERSITY PRESS

PUBLISHED BY THE PRESS SYNDICATE OF THE UNIVERSITY OF CAMBRIDGE
The Pitt Building, Trumpington Street, Cambridge, United Kingdom

CAMBRIDGE UNIVERSITY PRESS
The Edinburgh Building, Cambridge, CB2 2RU, UK
40 West 20th Street, New York, NY 10011-4211, USA
477 Williamstown Road, Port Melbourne, VIC 3207, Australia
Ruiz de Alarcón 13, 28014 Madrid, Spain
Dock House, The Waterfront, Cape Town 8001, South Africa

http://www.cambridge.org

First published 2004
Reprinted 2005

Printed in the United Kingdom at the University Press, Cambridge

Typeface Baskerville Monotype 11 / 12.5 pt   *System* LaTeX 2$_\varepsilon$ [TB]

A catalogue record for this book is available from the British Library

ISBN 0 521 39486 4 hardback

For my mother
Morounranti Aduke Jeyifous (nee Oyebanji)
(In memoriam: *"ope mi ko i to"*)

For my sons
Okunola Bamidele and Olalekan Babajide

And for their mother
Sheila Walker

My task is to keep company with the fallen, and this word rose in pride above spiked bushes. We must all stick together. Only the fallen have need of restitution.

The Road

Words are mad horses
running hard to collect
recalcitrant debt from my teeming head

I will not tame them.

John La Rose

Any culture contains essential and secondary elements, strengths and weaknesses, virtues, defects, positive and negative aspects, factors for progress or for regression.

Amilcar Cabral

Contradictions are our only hope.

Bertolt Brecht

Contents

Preface   *page* xi
Chronology   xxv
List of abbreviations   xxxiii

1   'Representative' and unrepresentable modalities of the self:
    the gnostic, worldly and radical humanism of Wole Soyinka   1

2   Tragic mythopoesis as postcolonial discourse – critical and
    theoretical writings   41

3   The "drama of existence": sources and scope   83

4   Ritual, anti-ritual and the festival complex in Soyinka's
    dramatic parables   120

5   The ambiguous freight of visionary mythopoesis: fictional
    and nonfictional prose works   167

6   Poetry, versification and the fractured burdens of
    commitment   220

7   "Things fall together": Wole Soyinka in his Own Write   276

Notes   289
Bibliography   307
Index   317

Preface

When one scholar published a book-length study of the writings of Wole Soyinka in 1993 and gave it the title *Wole Soyinka Revisited*, he was reflecting in that title the fact that at the time, there were already about eight other book-length studies or monographs on the Nigerian author in print. Since then, the number of books and monographs on Soyinka has grown steadily to the point that to date, studies devoted exclusively to Soyinka's works number more than a dozen and a half. And this is without reference to important works like Jonathan Peters' *A Dance of Masks: Senghor, Achebe, Soyinka* (1978), Tejumola Olaniyan's *Scars of Conquests, Masks of Resistance* (1995) and Kole Omotoso's *Achebe or Soyinka* (1996) which involve exhaustive comparison of Soyinka's writings with the works of other major African authors or writers from the African diaspora. Moreover, there are at least five collections of critical essays on Soyinka's works, with others planned or projected. Finally, there are several special issues of academic journals devoted specifically to the many facets of Soyinka's works and career.

Given this impressive number of full-length and full-scale studies of Soyinka, it does seem obligatory to explain why I or anyone else should set out to do yet another study of the Nigerian author. One explanation is one which every single author of a study of Soyinka will perhaps henceforth have to invoke: our author has produced a quantitative and, more importantly, *qualitative* body of works which, for a long time to come, is sure to generate diverse revisionary studies and totally fresh works of interpretation and evaluation. While this book has definitely in part been fostered by this factor, there is a more determinate basis for the publication of the study. This arises from the fact that because Soyinka has sustained an almost unbroken literary productivity over the course of the last four decades, his output has generally tended to very quickly outstrip the scope of each successive study of his writings. And on this point, it is important to note that the more substantial of the full-length studies of Soyinka were published nearly a decade ago, leaving a vacuum which has only partially been filled by the plethora of slim monographs on specific genres and themes which has dominated Soyinka criticism in the intervening years, monographs like Tanure Ojaide's *The Poetry of Wole Soyinka* (1994), Tunde Adeniran's *The Politics of Wole Soyinka* (1994), and Mpalive-Hangson Msiska's *Wole Soyinka* (1998). Thus, that another major, comprehensive study of Soyinka's writings is long overdue is an evident fact; that this book aspires to be such a study is a matter that requires a prefatory statement. What follows is an attempt at such prefatory "annunciation."

Sometime in April 1975, Kole Omotoso, the Nigerian novelist and critic, and I visited Wole Soyinka in Accra, Ghana, on a special mission. Soyinka was then in the fourth year of exile from Nigeria. With the fall of the military government of Yakubu Gowon and the assumption of power by General Murtala Mohammed and indications of a probable change to a more open and perhaps even "progressive" military rule, we felt that it was perhaps time for Soyinka to return home. "We" here refers to a group of writers, critics and academics based at the Universities of Ibadan and Ife called the "Ibadan-Ife Group" who had started the journal *Positive Review*. A few members of the group had been Soyinka's students, and all were ardent admirers of his writings. Moreover, we all felt greatly inspired by the courage of his political activism, and by the fact that we saw him as one of two or three of the most progressive writer-activists on the African continent. Omotoso and I represented this group on that mission.

In Accra, we found a Soyinka who was as productive and as ebullient as ever, a man for whom exile was no state of angst-ridden complacency. He was working full-time as editor of the journal, *Transition* (which he had renamed *Chi'Indaba*) and had just released the first issue of the journal under his editorship, an issue which contained an important statement on the exemplary nature of the revolutionary anti-colonial struggle in Guinea-Bissau under the leadership of Amilcar Cabral and the PAIGC. We found also that Soyinka had turned the journal into a very effective forum for mobilizing opposition on the African continent to the brutal, murderous regime of Idi Amin in Uganda. Indeed, his editorial office in Accra was a veritable beehive swarming with the diverse activities of the Nigerian playwright and his small administrative staff: planning future issues of the journal; serving as a port of call for many local and visiting foreign writers, artists, academics and publishers' agents connected with the arts and cultural scene of Africa and the Black world;

coordinating contacts with writers, diplomats, academics and activists, in Accra itself, and throughout the continent in a truly massive effort to isolate Idi Amin and ultimately cause the downfall of his regime. Beside these round-the-clock activities, Soyinka was also busy on a new venture, this being the then newly formed Union of Writers of the African Peoples of which he was the Protem Secretary-General; he was drafting notes and statements laying out his vision of what the organization could be and accomplish. One of these was a drive to make Kiswahili the continental *lingua franca* and in furtherance of this goal, encouragement of all African writers to work for the translation of their writings into that projected continental common tongue.

Our discussions with Soyinka on that "mission" touched on all these Pan-African issues, but ultimately we settled on the realities of the new situation at home in Nigeria. Like us, Soyinka also felt that things were looking as auspicious for "new beginnings" as they had ever been at any other time in the fifteen years of Nigeria's post-independence history. With this in mind, we discussed the details of his eagerly awaited return to Nigeria: what could be anticipated from the new regime in power in Lagos; what was the state of things with various groups and persons in the political and intellectual life of the country; what specific talks or public lectures we could schedule upon Soyinka's return home.

Not too long after this, Soyinka returned to Nigeria, took up appointment as Professor of Comparative Literature at the University of Ife and generally began what could be called the Nigerian extension of the phase of his career which has been described as "post-civil war" or "post-incarceration," a phase of intense political and ideological radicalization which had started in the years of exile. Thus, it was a totally unanticipated development that in this same period, and within a year of his return from exile, a big falling apart developed between him and most leftist writers, critics and academics in the country, a falling apart that was particularly acute between Soyinka and us, members of the Ibadan-Ife Group who had been so eager for his return from exile. Since a lot has been written about the ferocious intellectual and ideological battles that ensued between Soyinka and ourselves, I will give only a brief summary of the issues involved in the controversy.

At the most general level, the "quarrel" centered around our call for the application of a rigorous class approach to the analysis and evaluation of the production and reception of works of art and literature in Africa, especially given the fact that a class approach in African literary-critical discourse was at that time decidedly marginal to the far more dominant racial and ethnic "imperatives." Moreover, we felt that a class approach was definitely appropriate to the work of a writer-activist like Soyinka who is a self-declared partisan of egalitarian and revolutionary possibilities in the desperate historical and social conditions of Nigeria, postcolonial Africa and the Third World. In the light of such perspectives, we felt that Soyinka was often ideologically irresolute or ambiguous in that his works and activities seemed to promote a sort of "bourgeois" radicalism in representing the lower social orders in ways that did not show a belief in their readiness or capacity to overthrow the conditions of their oppression. From this we concluded that Soyinka's political activism was without question often courageous and powerful in protesting specific policies and trends consolidating misrule and inequality, but left much to be desired with regard to the deep-rooted systemic and structural bases of imperialist domination of the Third World and internal oppression of subaltern groups and classes in Nigeria and Africa.

On his own part, Soyinka felt that our positions were too doctrinaire, too dogmatic, and consistent with his genius for satiric phrase-making, he dubbed us "Leftocrats" in a major essay, "Barthes, Leftocracy and Other Mythologies," which is included in his volume of essays on literature and culture, *Art, Dialogue and Outrage.* He was particularly affronted by what he considered the extremely formulaic, textbook derivativeness of our materialist analyses of his use of myth, ritual and other expressive forms which come from the African precolonial past. One of his most serious charges against us was something he called "literary infanticide"; by this he meant that the narrow and dogmatic application of Marxist principles of class politics and ideology by us, as he saw the matter, was extremely destructive to young, aspiring writers. Such fledgling writers, in Soyinka's view, felt intimidated by the "authority" of our claims to be speaking on behalf of the oppressed masses and by our location as university teachers. Writers of his own stature and self-confidence, Soyinka asserted, were completely immune to our brand of extremism, but not the young, budding literary talents of the country.

With one or two notable exceptions, most of those who have written comments on these battles and controversies have been unaware of the fact that even with the staking of positions and views which seemed – and are – far apart in these battles of words and ideas, there continued to be important collaboration between us and Soyinka in furtherance of what continued to be, ultimately, common goals and objectives. One example of such collaborations happened when, in 1983, I adapted Bertolt Brecht's *Herr Puntilla and his Man Matti* for the Nigerian stage. Soyinka

not only accepted the script of my play titled *Haba Director!* for staging by
the company of the Dramatic Arts Department which he then headed,
he in fact made suggestions about incorporating some topical issues into
the play, suggestions which were willingly accepted because of the satiric
bite which they gave to the production.

I have made the foregoing "declaration" because, inevitably, the experience that it narrates does provide a point of departure for this study.
For me, and I daresay for other members of that now sadly moribund
Ibadan-Ife Group, perhaps the most important aspect of Soyinka's works
and activities, the thing that made him so vital to the prospects we then
felt for real meaningful social and economic transformations in Nigeria
and Africa, was a dimension of art, literature and culture that we did
not pay much heed to in those battles with Soyinka, this being what
can roughly be called the *subjective* dimensions of artistic creativity and
cultural politics. Soyinka's proud assertion in the heat of those quarrels
that *he* was personally beyond "coercion" and intimidation by us and
our invocation of the "objective," "determinate" forces of history speaks
to the heart of this matter. Let us recall again the profile I have drawn
above of Soyinka in the editorial offices of *Transition* in Accra in 1975
which shows the writer-activist engaged in those herculean tasks of mobilizing continental and worldwide opposition to the murderous violence
of the regime of Idi Amin, putting in place the machinery for the smooth
and effective functioning of the then newly formed Union of Writers
of the African Peoples, all the while continuing to write in all genres of
literature.

These issues constitute the conceptual foundations of this study and
shaped the methodological choices I have made in organizing the contents of the book. As a deliberate departure from the common trend
in Soyinka criticism of taking his exceptionally strong personality for
granted, I have made it a focal point for exploring his literary corpus in
its own right. Moreover, I have deployed this focus on "subjectivity" to
explore the deep imbrication of Soyinka's writings in the cultural patterns and dominant ideological discourses and representations of what
I call the postcolonial national-masculine "sublime" which, in my view,
decisively shaped Soyinka's own personality and the collective identity of
his generation of artists, writers and critics and indeed an entire period
of postcolonial history in Africa and the rest of the developing world.
For it is no accident of history or circumstance that Soyinka belongs to a
generation of the Nigerian literary intelligentsia whose leading members
like Chinua Achebe, J.P. Clark, Christopher Okigbo and Soyinka himself

have been called "titans." Neither is it of no consequence to the social ramifications of the works of the most prominent writers in this generational cohort that the political life of Africa, from the late colonial period to the first few decades of the post-independence era, was completely dominated by great, larger-than-life figures in the historic projects of nation-building, social reconstruction and collective self-definitions after the formal end of colonialism.

One definitely has to have this broad pattern in mind when one considers the significant fact that in the international arena of the then newly emergent nonaligned movement and the anti-imperialist front, figures like Nehru, Sukarno, Nasser and Nkrumah projected or exuded much vaster power and *presence* than was warranted by the weak state structures and precarious polities which they inherited from the departing colonial powers. Thus, in Nigeria during the first decade of independence, Soyinka's generation of "titans" in literature and the arts confronted an unceasingly crisis-torn lifeworld dominated by the towering, larger-than-life personality of an Azikiwe, an Awolowo and a Sardauna of Sokoto and many others beside these three potentates. Indeed, we now know that in the postcolonial project of fashioning collective identities to displace the erstwhile identities of "natives" and "subject peoples" brought to life in the high tide of colonial rule in Africa, Asia, Latin America and the Caribbean, the figure of the *male* patriarchal leader of legendary renown was deemed to represent the will to freedom of the colonized nation, putatively holding society together around the charisma and mystique of his person. This broad socio-historical process and its representational inscription around the figure of a strong male leader included conservative bourgeois nationalists as it did left-wing revolutionary socialists; and it embraced authoritarian, elitist military putschists as well as leaders of grassroots populist movements. There are many famous names and personalities here: Jawaharlal Nehru, Ho Chi Minh, Gamal Abdel Nasser, Fidel Castro, Che Guevara, Mohammed Zia-ul-Haq, Kwame Nkrumah, Eric Williams, Jomo Kenyatta and Leopold Sedar Senghor. These and many more are the scions of a highly gendered postcolonial national-masculine tradition which provided the pivotal signposts of identity formation and collective self-fashioning in the period of struggle against foreign domination in the former colonies and in the first few decades of the post-independence era. It is a tradition that is clearly in deep, sustained and perhaps terminal crisis. Among other factors, it is in a terminal crisis because of the historically inevitable unraveling of the idealistic or coercive unification it once imposed on the diverse communities and conflicting interests and practices making up the "nation." One important expression of this crisis in the world of literature and the arts, at least in the West Africa region, is the fact that the generation of writers who came into prominence after Soyinka's generation have virtually all made a break with the "big man" view of artistic creation. This generational cohort includes writers like Kole Omotoso, Femi Osofisan, Niyi Osundare, Kofi Ayindoho, Sonny Labou Tansi, Tanure Ojaide, Odia Ofeimun, Syl Cheney-Coker, Festus Iyayi, Atukwe Okai and Funso Aiyejina. They have made what could be described, following Antonio Gramsci, a national-popular ideal the basis of their collective identity, of their situation as engaged writers. And of course by far the most important institutional and ideological expression of the crisis of the national-masculine tradition in literature and critical discourse is the strong female presence of writers and critics in West Africa like Ama Ata Aidoo, Efua Sutherland, Flora Nwapa, Buchi Emecheta, Mariama Ba, Aminata Sow Fall, Calixthe Beyala, Tess Onwueme, Zeinab Alkali, Molara Ogundipe, Chikwenye Okonjo Ogunyemi, Nana Wilson-Tagoe and Abena Busia. Elsewhere on the continent, the national-masculine tradition in the arts, literature and criticism is even more powerfully transcended by the works of women writers, scholars and critics like Micere Githae Mugo, Nadine Gordimer, Bessie Head, Assia Djebar, Nawal el Saadawi, Tsitsi Dangarembga, Yvonne Vera, Rose Mbowa, Brenda Cooper, Rosemary Jolly and many others.

This study locates Soyinka's towering artistic personality in this broad socio-historical context. It does this on the basis of two premises. The first premise concerns the methodological assumption that underlies the analysis of texts in this study, the assumption that nearly all of Soyinka's literary writings stand as remarkable works in their own right. From relatively minor works like *The Trials of Brother Jero* and *The Swamp Dwellers* to the great, ambitious titles like *A Dance of the Forests, The Road, Madmen and Specialists* and *Death and the King's Horseman,* no work of Soyinka's maturity as a writer is reducible to national or epochal allegories. On the basis of this premise, the study approaches all of Soyinka's writings as distinctive works of literature, applying the framing ideas and themes of the study to these works, singly and collectively, very flexibly. In other words, the framing ideas and themes of this study, as indicated in its title, will be found hovering around and mostly merely inflecting the exegetical tasks and the sheer intellectual pleasure of tackling the rich, complex texture of Soyinka's writings against the background of his tumultuous career and the critical reception of his works in the last four decades. Moreover, the tasks of textual exegesis and analysis in this study have been dialectically conditioned by four decades of scholarly and critical commentary on Soyinka's works. In the main, Soyinka criticism in these decades has focused intensively on the alleged "complexity" and "obscurity" of his most important writings, without paying systematic or even sustained attention to one important source of the alleged "complexity" and "obscurity." This is Soyinka's literary avant-gardism, his extensive and defining open and experimental approach to the diverse and contending traditions of formal and linguistic resources available to the postcolonial writer or indeed any writer in our contemporary global civilization. The study is thus conceived in part as a critical response to the influence of critical commentary on Soyinka's works in the last four decades, the purpose being to locate the "difficulty" and "complexity" of his writings in their appropriate linguistic and cultural sources, and to reorient the study of Soyinka as a writer towards a more systematic engagement of his connections to the historic avantgarde movements of the contemporary world.

Beyond this, and supplementary to matters of exegesis and analyses, the second premise of this study relates to issues of interpretation and explanation and pertains to the framing ideas and themes which, as I have remarked earlier, are brought to bear in a flexible manner on the analyses of texts. It is perhaps useful to give a brief elaboration of these ideas and themes.

Among the "titans" of his generation of Nigerian literary artists, Soyinka's career is the closest conscious approximation we have in African literature to the revolutionary or "sublime" expressions, as opposed to the conservative or repressive currents, of the long postcolonial tradition of the "big man" of politics, of trade unionism, of coup making, of popular culture and millennarian religious movements. Typically, this is the "big man," whether of the left or the right, whose claim to power or influence rests on the "sovereign" ability to gather around his person diverse areas of the life and times of the late modern postcolony. But this observation is of more than merely documentary interest, for we must bear in mind that the "big man" in literature in the colony and the postcolony has to enact his capacious subjectivity in, and through language, specifically in *written* texts published in the adopted "world" language of the colonizers. Moreover, even if the "turf" of the "big man" in politics, in trade unionism, in commerce or in military coupmaking is not specifically based in language, all these figures who embody the "great man" theory of postcolonial history and politics necessarily must have a justificatory or celebratory discourse around them, a language which serves as a very important currency of their claims to status, power or influence. This makes language a privileged domain, and the "big man" in language and writing such as Soyinka a powerful prism through which to extricate the ontological and normative truth contents of this national-masculine tradition from its massive socio-economic and ideological overdeterminations. The normative "truth content" has to do with the fact that both in nature and in all forms and at all stages of society, extraordinary concentration of talents, energies and capacities are often lodged in exceptional individuals, taking many forms which, in sum, constitute a permanent source of enrichment to the human community. Moreover, in the nationalist struggles against colonialism and in contemporary struggles in the developing world against local and foreign bases of oppressive social power, exceptionally gifted and endowed individuals have distinguished and are distinguishing themselves as resolute and unwavering agents of progressive change. The "falsehood content" makes us attentive to the fact that because these talents, capacities and energies are "undemocratically" distributed and have often been assimilated to an essential maleness, they often take bizarre forms, forms in and through which individual, group, national or racial claims to exceptionalism or superiority produce unjust, oppressive and alienating social arrangements which, in their most extreme expressions, assume the false "sovereignty" of organized state terror. In the life of the African postcolony, this "falsehood content" has produced in countries like Somalia, Uganda, Liberia and especially Sierra Leone, the inexpressible and ineffable terror of warlords many of whom present themselves as revolutionaries and "saviors" of the nation and gather around themselves marauding boy-warriors of unspeakable barbarity.

Generally, I take the view that it is possible and necessary to identify and hold separate the "truth" and "falsehood" contents of this historic national-masculine tradition. This is made necessary by the fact that in this study I read the positive, heroic currents of the tradition and its negative and pervasive barbarous deformations as the outer limits of the highly gendered postcolonial project of collective and individual self-definition and self-constitution. But I do not ignore the fact that in its appearance as an image, as a representation of the will to human emancipation and the ideal of freedom, the "truth" and "falsehood" contents of the tradition are often inextricably interfused and stir up powerful emotions of excitement, unease or terror incapable of being represented by conventionally pleasing or "beautiful" aesthetic expressions. Thus,

I explore tradition in this study in the figure of the *sublime*, the figure which confronts conventionally "beautiful" and pleasing affects and effects with their inadequacies and infelicities, the figure in short in which the claims of representation, *any* representation including the representation of the will to emancipation, confronts its limits. It is perhaps necessary for me to state that unlike most postmodernists on the concept of the sublime, for me its figuration of the constitutive aporias and limits of representation does not thereby imply an abyss at the (absent) core of representation; rather, it represents a need for representation to reflect back on its processes, means and ends the better to meet the great challenges of progressive cultural politics at the present time.

The highly gendered postcolonial national-masculine tradition of the patrimonial "big man" of national, continental or "racial" destiny is evidently in deep crisis and is indeed in decline, even as it continues to generate regimes and acts of great barbarity. Its inscription in Soyinka's writings and career dialectically involves both positive celebration of the heroic, revolutionary currents of the tradition and at the same time very scathing, ironizing parodies of its pretensions and mystifications, especially in their yield of cycles of catastrophic violence and tyrannical misrule in Africa and many other parts of the developing world. This study engages this little explored but crucial dimension of Soyinka's career not by making sociological allusions to it, but by placing considerable emphasis on the textual constructions of his "personality" by the Nigerian author. Most previous studies of Soyinka have taken this "personality" as simply existent, even when it is admitted that it is a complex personality compounded, like the personalities of many great artists, of heterogeneous and even somewhat contradictory attributes. As in nearly all previous studies of Soyinka's writings and career, the personality of the Nigerian poet, playwright and activist looms large in this study. But while I have not sought to entirely suppress the perspectives of "Soyinka and his times" or "Soyinka's unified sensibility and vision" which have been implicitly or explicitly dominant in Soyinka criticism, as a deliberate departure from this trend, I have emphasized the ideological pressures and ethical choices which have shaped the construction of that personality. In effect, this means that I have been very attentive to the postmodernist call to be wary of the metaphysics of "presence" and intentionalist subject-centeredness in all cultural criticism and literary studies, especially where this involves "strong" individuals. However, unlike the postmodernists, I have not reproduced in this study yet another instance of discourses of the "death of the subject," of the "waning of affect" or of the impersonal regime of the "author effect." In the study will be found a "subject" who is present in his writings and acts in an elaborate mythopoesis of the self and the social as a basis for both self-idealized and self-critical engagements of the often terrifying dilemmas of the life and times of the modern postcolony. What I can state as hopefully a distinctive aspect of the study is a considerable emphasis on the active relationship between Soyinka's textual constructions of his "personality" and his permanent openness to possibilities that might expand the scope of political and cultural freedoms in Africa and the rest of our increasingly globalized world.

These underlying perspectives of this study that I have outlined here perhaps resume, in a *sublated* fashion, the old debates that we had with Soyinka in the 1970s and 1980s. However, in the present study I have tried to combine the values and methodologies of objective scholarship, especially in the exegeses of texts and the arduous tasks of social and historical interpretation, with the sort of passionate ideological partisanship of the experience narrated in the "declaration" through which I have tried to indicate the point of departure for this study. Thus, it will be found that for the first six chapters of the study, I have pretty much stayed within the methodology which I adopted when I collected and edited Soyinka's essays for the book, *Art, Dialogue and Outrage*. This, in principle, was mostly to confine myself as much as possible to explicating objectively the most important ideas and themes of Soyinka's critical thought and the contexts in which they were elaborated. Thus, what I have tried to accomplish in these first six chapters is an expostulation of the construction or "fashioning" of the self in Soyinka's works. This I have done with regard to the fascinating, differential patterns of our author's self-expressions and self-extensions in the genres of drama, prose and poetry. These are the patterns which in the study I have designated "homologies of the self and the social," seeking to explicate them in the refracted light of Soyinka's unique combination of aesthetic innovativeness and political radicalism. It is only in the seventh and last chapter of the study that I have expressed any sustained critique in a manner that may be vaguely reminiscent of those battles of yesteryears with Soyinka, but even in that chapter, I have not been exhaustive in this critique. That kind of critique, it is my belief, belongs in another work of the future which will expand the terms of the exploration of the issues beyond the works of Wole Soyinka. In this respect, the study is intended as a combination of limited ideology-critique and, more extensively, a prolegomenon to a systematic investigation of the intersection of artistic avant-gardism and political radicalism in Africa and the developing world.

No work of course exists in a vacuum or starts *ex nihilo*. Indeed, far from this, this study, in every chapter of the work, is constructed on an assimilation, positively and in some cases by negative dialectics, of the vast body of existing scholarship and criticism on Soyinka's works. In fact the careful reader will very quickly find, by openly acknowledged intellectual debts, which scholars and critics have provided perspectives and ideas without which this study would simply have been impossible. To all such scholars and critics, my gratitude.

The completion of this book was delayed for at least six years by a grave illness that nearly proved terminal in 1994/95. This not only led to a rewriting of the entire earlier draft of the study when I was able at last to resume work on the project with the energy and focus of the years before the illness, it also made me permanently indebted to many friends, family and colleagues whose love or concern saw me through the critical period of the illness. They are too many to name in entirety here. So, if I leave out any names, I give assurance that I will make amends fully at the earliest opportunity. Thus, a great debt of gratitude which I can never hope to repay in full to: Sheila Walker, Okunola and Lekan; to Yemi and Sade Ogunbiyi; to Femi and Nike Osofisan; to John La Rose and Sarah White; to Seinde and Dunni Arigbede; to Eddie and Bene Madunagu; to Emmett and Charlotte Walker; to Ropo and Banke Sekoni; to Lai and Elaine Ogunbiyi; to Akwasi and Constance Osei; to John and Lily Ohiorhenuan; to Winthrop and Andrea Whetherbee; to Yomi and Deola Durotoye; to Chima and Bisi Anyadike; to Elaine Savory and Robert Jones; to Eileen Marie Julien, Anne Adams, Susan Andrade, Michelin Rice-Maximin and Rhonda Cobham-Sander; to Wole Ogundele, Teju and Moji Olaniyan, Priyamvada Gopal, Catherine McKinley and Ken McClane.

Over the years, I have been the fortunate beneficiary of the unwavering support of friends and interlocutors whose contribution, in many intangible but invaluable ways, sustained me in the course of writing this book. For this reason, very special thanks are due to Reginald Selwyn Cudjoe, Odun Balogun, Sope Oyelaran, Niyi Osundare, Kole Omotoso, G.G. Darah, Folabo Soyinka-Ajayi, Odia Ofeimun, Macdonald Ovbiagele, Olu Ademulegun, Lanre Adebisi, Kayode Komolafe, Ike Okafor-Newsum, Dapo Adeniyi and John Onajide for their friendship and encouragement. This group of friends includes the "trio" in France, Christiane "Kenshiro" Fioupou, Etienne Galle and Alain Ricard whose comradeship I shall always treasure and whose many conversations with me on the subject of Wole Soyinka brought an informal but rich "Francophone" dimension to preparatory work on this study. I note also, with deep appreciation, the solidarity of "Comrade Egbon" Molara Ogundipe, "Uncle D" Dapo Adelugba, Omafume Onoge and Tunji Oyelana. In the same vein, I wish to acknowledge here the inestimable comradeship of spirit and intellect of Segun Osoba and Dipo Fasina that began in my years in Ile-Ife and has deepened in the intervening years. And I give special, heartfelt thanks to Hudita Mustafa for her sustaining love and friendship.

The members of the administrative staff of the Department of English, Cornell University, my institutional "home," deserve my thanks for their friendship, their courtesy and their many kindnesses. Marianne Marsh, Vicky Brevetti, Darlene Flint, Robin Doxtater, Jenka Fyfe and Heather Gowe, my warmest thanks to you all. My appreciation also goes to many friends and colleagues in the Department: all the members of the Minority and Third World Studies caucus, especially Satya Mohanty, Ken McClane, Helena Maria Viramontes and Hortense Spillers; Harry Shaw, Paul Sawyer, Tim Murray and Scott McMillin. Parts of this study were written during a two-year period I spent at Harvard in the Afro-American and English departments. For their friendship and hospitality, I am greatly indebted to H.L. "Skip" Gates, Jr. and Larry Buell. I also thank Cindy Fallows of the administrative staff of the Harvard English Department for her warmth, courtesy and kindness.

Of a very special kind of debt is what I owe Abiola Irele, the editor of the series of studies of African and Caribbean authors for which this study was written. His patience, solidarity and encouragement were unstinting. Indeed, but for his steadfast encouragement, this study would have finally been abandoned for other projects after the long hiatus between its earlier incarnations and what began, very slowly and fitfully, to crystallize after my convalescence from my illness. In the last fourteen or fifteen years, I have had intellectual discussions with "Egbon" Irele of a kind which I have had with no one else, with the possible exception of John La Rose and, of course, Femi Osofisan, on diverse subjects and topics touching on, ultimately, the dimensions of the crises and perplexities facing our country, Nigeria and the African continent. If only indirectly and subliminally, these discussions have shaped some of the perspectives which make this book what it is, though in exactly what ways I am unable to say.

The debts to "Kongi" are equally as great, even if they are infinitely more difficult to assess or express. I can only say that I hope the honesty and frankness of the analyses and evaluations of his work and legacy in this study constitute an adequate acknowledgment of these debts which I share with all who have found much profit and inspiration in his writings but which really began about thirty-four years ago when he taught my undergraduate dramatic criticism class and for a brief period acted as supervisor of my studies as a graduate student.

Finally and ultimately inexpressibly, my mother, of unforgettable memory. Pablo Neruda has declared: "There is no space that is wider than that of grief." In bringing this project to completion not before I had experienced that grave illness and slowly regained my strengths, I learnt that great grief can be a psychically sustaining emotion, that it can powerfully bring to consciousness hitherto barely recognized or acknowledged dimensions of the self. But I made this discovery *only* when I was finally able to overcome the great folly of repressing my emotions and could then grieve, really grieve for your loss, Morounranti Aduke.

Chronology

<table>
<tr><td>1934</td><td>Born 13 July, at Abeokuta, western Nigeria, the second child of Samuel Ayodele and Grace Eniola Soyinka.</td></tr>
<tr><td>1944–45</td><td>Attends Abeokuta Grammar School.</td></tr>
<tr><td>1946–50</td><td>Attends Government College, elite high school where he begins writing and wins prizes for his poems.</td></tr>
<tr><td>1950–52</td><td>On graduating from high school works in Lagos as an inventory clerk at a government pharmaceutical store. Has stories read on national radio.</td></tr>
<tr><td>1952–54</td><td>Attends University College, Ibadan.</td></tr>
<tr><td>1954–59</td><td>Five-year sojourn in the UK. Attends the University of Leeds, obtaining the BA English Honours degree in 1957. Begins writing two plays, The Swamp Dwellers and The Lion and the Jewel. Works for some time as playreader at The Royal Court Theatre in London. In 1958 directs the Nigeria Drama Group in The Swamp Dwellers and has an evening of his work comprising poems, songs and a play, The Invention performed at The Royal Court.</td></tr>
<tr><td>1957</td><td>March 6, independence of Ghana, inaugurating the post-colonial era in black Africa.</td></tr>
<tr><td>1959</td><td>Returns to Nigeria, on eve of the country's independence from Britain. Given a two-year Rockefeller research grant to study drama in West Africa.</td></tr>
<tr><td>1960</td><td>October 1, independence. Soyinka completes Camwood on the Leaves, a radio play, and The Trials of Brother Jero, a stage play. Forms a theatre group, The 1960 Masks, and produces A Dance of the Forests which raises questions about the country's future for Nigeria's independence celebrations.</td></tr>
<tr><td>1962</td><td>Appointed a lecturer in English at the University of Ife but resigns in protest when the authorities of the</td></tr>
</table>

University align the institution with the unpopular government of Samuel Ladoke Akintola. General social and political unrest in western Nigeria.

1964   General Strike of Nigeria's trade unions, effective countrywide. Soyinka very actively involved around the Lagos-Ibadan area. Produces *The Lion and the Jewel* in a season of plays in English and Yoruba. Forms a new theatre group, The Orisun Theatre Company.

1965   Produces satirical revue, *Before the Blackout* as political turmoil escalates in western Nigeria. Premieres a major new play, *Kongi's Harvest*, in August in Lagos. Later in the year in London for the Commonwealth Arts Festival in which another major play, *The Road*, is staged and Soyinka reads from his long poem, "Idanre." Appointed senior lecturer at the University of Lagos. Novel, *The Interpreters*, published. Turbulent election in western Nigeria and disputed victory of S.L. Akintola after widespread rigging of the elections. A gunman holds up the radio station of the Nigerian Broadcasting Service at Ibadan and forces the station to broadcast a recorded speech disputing Akintola's victory. Soyinka is later charged for the action, but is acquitted on a legal technicality.

1966   First military coup in Nigeria, January 15, topples the federal government of Tafawa Balewa. Second countercoup in July after May pogroms against Igbos in Northern Nigeria. The country slides irreversibly to civil war.

1967–70   Nigerian civil war pitching federal forces against Biafran secessionists.

1967   *Kongi's Harvest* and *Idanre and Other Poems* published early 1967. With Tom Stoppard, receives the John Whiting Drama Award in London. Off-Broadway productions of *The Trials of Brother Jero* and *The Strong Breed* at Greenwich Mews Theater, New York. Appointed Head of the School of Drama, University of Ibadan but unable to take up the position because of arrest in August by the federal government for activities to stop the war. He is incarcerated without trial for most of the duration of the war and spends most of his time in prison in solitary confinement. Smuggles some protest poems out of prison; later writes

	a book of his prison experience, *The Man Died*, published in 1972.
1968	Receives Jock Campbell-New Statesman Literary Award, London. Publication of *Forest of a Thousand Daemons*, Soyinka's translation of D.O. Fagunwa's classic Yoruba hunter's saga, *Ogboju Ode Ninu Igbo Irunmale*. *Kongi's Harvest* produced by Negro Ensemble Company at St. Mark's Theater, New York.
1969	*Three Short Plays* (new edition of *Three Plays*) and *Poems from Prison* published. Released from detention in October and takes up post of head of Department of Theatre Arts, University of Ibadan.
1970	Directs *Madmen and Specialists* at the Eugene O'Neill Theater Center, Waterford, Connecticut. Plays the role of Kongi, the dictator, in Calpenny Films production of his play, *Kongi's Harvest*. Inauguration of Orisun Acting Editions with Soyinka as literary editor.
1971–75	Years of self-imposed exile from Nigeria, traveling around the world and ultimately settling in Accra, Ghana, where in 1974 he assumes editorship of the journal, *Transition* which he re-names *Ch'Indaba*.
1971	*Before the Blackout*, first title in the Orisun Acting Editions, published. Directs *Madmen and Specialists* at Ibadan. The play published later in the year. Plays the role of Lumumba in Joan Littlewood's Paris production of *Murderous Angels*, Conor Cruise O'Brien's play on the Congo crisis.
1972	*A Shuttle in the Crypt* and *The Man Died* published. Resigns as head of the Department of Theatre Arts at the University of Ibadan. Directs extracts from *A Dance of the Forests* in Paris.
1973	Appointed Visiting Professor of English at University of Sheffield and overseas fellow at Churchill College, Cambridge University. Publication of *Collected Plays*, vol. 1, *Camwood on the Leaves*, and *The Bacchae of Euripides* which is given an unimaginative production by the National Theatre at Old Vic, London. Publication of second novel, *Season of Anomy*.
1974	*Collected Plays*, vol. 2, published. Teams up with the South African poet, Dennis Brutus, to form Union of Writers

of the African Peoples and is elected its first Secretary-General.

1975   Yakubu Gowon overthrown in a military coup. General Murtala Mohammed becomes head of state. Soyinka returns to Nigeria and is given appointment of Professor of Comparative Literature by the University of Ife. *Death and the King's Horseman* published. Edits *Poems of Black Africa*.

1976   Murtala Muhammed assassinated, General Olusegun Obasanjo becomes head of state. *Myth, Literature and the African World* and *Ogun Abibiman* published. Governmental corruption and social inequality intensify in the wake of an oil-boom economy. Soyinka fiercely outspoken in his social criticism and faces intimidation by agents of the military regime. First stage production of *Death and the King's Horseman* at the University of Ife in December.

1977   Administrator of FESTAC (International Festival of Negro Arts and Culture), Lagos. Completes and directs *Opera Wonyosi*, a composite adaptation of John Gay's *Beggars' Opera* and Brecht's *Threepenny Opera* which savages several African military and civilian despots and the values they are entrenching across the borders of African countries. Soyinka is prevented from staging this play in Lagos and he forms a group called Guerrilla Theatre Unit out of the professional company of the University of Ife Theatre. Writes short, biting and highly popular skits attacking governmental hypocrisy, corruption and sadistic policies which are performed by the new group in open-air markets, streets, community centres and school playing fields.

1979   Joins the People's Redemption Party, a social-democratic party whose leadership is made up of the most prominent progressive politicians of the North and the South, and trade union and academic leftists. When the party fragments into conservative and radical factions, Soyinka goes with the latter and becomes its Deputy Director of Research. Directs *The Biko Inquest*, an edited version of the court proceedings of an inquest on the death of Steve Biko in police custody. In the fall he directs *Death and the King's Horseman* at the Goodman Theater, Chicago. Upon successful run at the Goodman, production is transferred to the Kennedy Center in Washington, DC where it is also well received. Shehu Shagari wins federal elections and Nigeria returns to civilian rule.

1981   Appointed Visiting Professor, Yale University. *Opera Wonyosi* and *Aké*, the first part of Soyinka's autobiography, published. Produces satirical revue, "Rice Unlimited" with the Guerrilla Theatre Unit.

1982   *Aké* launched at Aké, Abeokuta in January. Soyinka uses the occasion to lambast the policies of the Shagari government and its "achievements": the plundering of the country's wealth; the massacre of unarmed farmers and peasants at Bakolori in the North; the subversion of the Kaduna and Kano state governments controlled by the People's Redemption Party (PRP); the destruction of the offices of *The Triumph* newspaper owned by the PRP; the storming of an elected legislature by the paramilitary detachment of the Nigerian Police Force controlled by Shagari's government; the deaths of students, athletes, members of the National Youth Corps and ordinary citizens at the hands of the police at the innumerable checkpoints set up by the government to intimidate and cower an increasingly restive populace. Late in the year *Die Still, Dr. Godspeak!*, a play on the influence of the quackery of parapsychologists, astrologers and 'metaphysicians' in Nigeria is broadcast on the African Service of the BBC World Service.

1983   Production of *Requiem for a Futurologist*, stage version of *Die Still, Dr. Godspeak!* Soyinka uses countrywide tour of the production to spread ideas contained in the "Priority Projects," a satirical revue attacking corruption, mismanagement and hypocrisy of the country's political rulers. On the eve of the national elections in August, Soyinka releases the songs from this revue in a record album titled *Unlimited Liability Company*; the album takes the country by storm and is a huge success. Shagari wins the elections which are marked by massive vote rigging, use of the armed services of the state to intimidate opposition parties and their supporters, and widespread outbreak of violent protests and demonstrations. Soyinka flies to London and uses the BBC World Service and the international press to condemn the corruption of the just concluded elections. He predicts revolution or a coup. On the last day of the year, Shagari is overthrown in a coup that brings General Mohammadu Buhari to power.

1984   *Blues for a Prodigal*, Soyinka's film on the elections of 1983 released. In May an unsuccessful production of *The Road* opens at the Goodman Theater in Chicago and in December Yale Repertory Theatre produces *A Play of Giants*. *Six Plays* and *A Play of Giants* published.

1985   August 27, General Ibrahim Badamasi Babangida overthrows the Buhari-Idiagbon junta.

1986   In June, Wole Soyinka, as President of the International Theatre Institute (ITI), is embroiled in an international press and media controversy following the decision of the ITI to drop a dramatization of George Orwell's *Animal Farm* by the National Theatre of Britain from the official program of the *Festival of Nations* in Baltimore, Maryland, USA. (The ITI decision is based on petition by the Soviet Union that the version of *Animal Farm* in the National Theatre of Britain entry is a veiled Cold War-inspired cultural assault on the Soviet state).

In October, the Swedish Academy announces that Soyinka is the year's winner of the Nobel Prize for literature.

1987   *Death and the King's Horseman* produced at Lincoln Center, New York City.

1988   Publication of *Art, Dialogue and Outrage*, a major collection of Soyinka's essays on literature and culture. *Mandela's Earth* published.

1989   *Isara: A Voyage Around 'Essay'*, a fictional account of the author's father and his friends published.

1991   *A Scourge of Hyacinths*, a new radio play broadcast on BBC Radio 4.

1992   *From Zia, with Love*, a stage version of *A Scourge of Hyacinths*, is premiered in Sienna, Italy. The play uses a satirical and farcical exploration of the inner workings of the international traffic in drugs to expose the corruption and hypocrisy of the Nigerian military rulers.

1993   June 12, the victory of Moshood Kashimawo Abiola at the federal elections to return Nigeria to civilian rule canceled by the military dictatorship of Ibrahim Babangida. Massive protests in Lagos, Ibadan and other Nigerian cities, met with brutal force by the army. Attempt by Soyinka to organize a long protest march from the South to the nation's capital in Abuja in the North is aborted by the regime. The country is plunged into constitutional and political crisis as Babangida is forced from office and hands power over to a lame-duck civilian-led caretaker government headed by Ernest Shonekan, a crony of the generals. In August Shonekan is removed from office and General Sani Abacha replaces him as head of state. *The Beatification of Area Boy*, a new play on the revolt of the underclasses of the Lagos slums, is given its world premiere at the West Yorkshire Playhouse, Leeds and is published.

1994   Publication of *Ibadan: The 'Penkelemes' Years – A Memoir, 1945–1965*, the third part of the author's memoirs.

1996   Soyinka forced into exile in the face of threats to his life from the Abacha regime which escalates repression, intimidation and politically motivated assassination beyond anything previously seen in the country. Publication of *Open Sore of a Continent: A Personal Narrative of the Nigeria Crisis*.

1997–2001   President of the International Parliament of Writers.

1997   Soyinka and eleven other pro-democracy members of the internal and external opposition to the Abacha regime are charged with treason and placed on trial *in absentia*. Meanwhile, in association with other members of the external opposition, Soyinka launches "Radio Kudirat" which transmits broadcasts to Nigeria in English and the country's main indigenous languages challenging the legitimacy of the Abacha regime and exposing its isolation in the international community.

1998   On June 8, Sani Abacha dies unexpectedly and is succeeded by General Abdulsalami Abubakar. Two weeks later, on the eve of his release from prison, Moshood K. Abiola dies mysteriously. In September, Soyinka returns to Nigeria, ending his four-year exile.

1999   In January, publication of *Outsiders*, a volume of poetry. In February, Olusegun Obasanjo wins federal presidential elections and becomes civilian head of state in

October. Publication of *The Burden of Memory, the Muse of Forgiveness.*

2000   June 19, meets Mumia Abu-Jamal, the prominent African American death row activist and thinker.

September 5, addresses Roundtable on Dialogue Among Civilizations at the United Nations in New York.

2001   August 31–September 7, attends conference against racism in Durban, South Africa sponsored by the United Nations Commission for Human Rights.

July-August, unpublished play *King Babu* premiered in Lagos and tours a few Nigerian cities.

October 19–21, International Conference on Soyinka's theatre at the University of Toronto, Canada.

2002   In mid-March Soyinka and five other writers representing the International Parliament of Writers make goodwill visit to Palestine and Israel in furtherance of peace in the Middle East.

October 12, reads old and new poems in the distinguished Readings in Contemporary Poetry of the DIA Center in Manhattan, New York.

Abbreviations

ADO 1	*Art, Dialogue and Outrage*, Ibadan: New Horn Press, 1988
ADO 2	*Art, Dialogue and Outrage*, New York: Pantheon, 1994
CP 1	*Collected Plays, vol. 1*
CP 2	*Collected Plays, vol. 2*
DKH	*Death and the King's Horseman*
IOP	*Idanre and Other Poems*
ME	*Mandela's Earth*
MLAW	*Myth, Literature and the African World*
OA	*Ogun Abibiman*
SOA	*Season of Anomy*
TBE	*The Bacchae of Euripides*
TI	*The Interpreters*
TMD	*The Man Died*

CHAPTER I

'Representative' and unrepresentable modalities of the self: the gnostic, worldly and radical humanism of Wole Soyinka

In one sense then (there is) a traveling away from its old self towards a cosmopolitan, modern identity while in another sense (there is) a journeying back to regain a threatened past and selfhood. To comprehend the dimensions of this gigantic paradox and coax from it such unparalleled inventiveness requires . . . the archaic energy, the perspective and temperament of creation myths and symbolism.
> Chinua Achebe, "What Has Literature Got to Do With It."

The language in which we are speaking is his before it is mine. How different are the words *home, Christ, ale, master,* on his lips and on mine! I cannot speak or write these words without unrest of the spirit. His language, so familiar and so foreign, will always be for me an acquired speech. I have not made or accepted its words. My voice holds them at bay. My soul frets in the shadow of language.
> James Joyce, *A Portrait of the Artist as a Young Man.*

Ori kan nuun ni/Iyato kan nuun ni
(That is one person/That is one difference)
> From a Yoruba *Ifa* divination chant

All the book length studies, the monographs, and the innumerable essays on Wole Soyinka's writings and career take as their starting point his stupendous literary productivity: some thirty-five titles since he began writing in the late 1950s, and a career in the theatre, popular culture and political activism matching his literary corpus in scope, originality and propensity for generating controversy. Soyinka had been writing for about five years when his first serious and mature works were published in 1963 and, in the words of Bernth Lindfors, "he became – instantly and forever – one of the most important writers in the English speaking world."[1] It is significant that this observation comes from Lindfors, who, almost alone among students of Soyinka's writings, has been obsessed with his literary juvenilia, hoping therein to find materials to prove that

Soyinka was once a rookie writer, a neophyte artist, even if his rise to fame seemed instantaneous and meteoric. Bearing in mind the fact that Chinua Achebe's much-heralded emergence had taken place in the late 1950s, Soyinka was unquestionably the most talented entrant to the field of modern African literature in the 1960s, that first decade of the post-independence period in Africa. And it was an emergence etched with verbal élan and uncommon wit. His famous quip on Négritude – the tiger does not go about proclaiming its *tigritude* but merely lives and acts it – was complemented by innumerable phrases and lines from poems, short dramatic skits and essays which achieved instant fame for their memorableness, their "quotability," the best of these being the mock-serious jokes and conceits of the more substantial writings of the period such as *The Interpreters* and *The Road*.[2] Indeed, within the first few years of that decade, Soyinka quickly emerged as the *enfant terrible* of the then "new" postcolonial African literature; moreover, he also quickly became that literature's most vigorous literary duelist, his targets and adversaries including not only corrupt officials and politicians, but also other writers and critics, his satirical review of J.P. Clark's *America, Their America* being only the most famous of his quarrels with fellow writers on matters of vision, craft and sensibility.[3] Thus, the recognition at the very start of his career that Soyinka's literary voice and presence were unique and distinctive was very widespread; such recognition is aptly captured in the following plaudits from an influential London theatre critic, Penelope Gilliat, on the occasion of the staging of his second major play, *The Road*, at the 1965 Commonwealth Arts Festival:

Every decade or so, it seems to fall to a non-English dramatist to belt new energy into the English tongue. The last time was when Brendan Beehan's "The Quare Fellow" opened at Theatre Workshop. Nine years later, in the reign of Stage Sixty at the same beloved Victorian building at Stratford East, a Nigerian called Wole Soyinka has done for our napping language what brigand dramatists from Ireland have done for centuries: booted it awake, rifled its pockets and scattered the loot into the middle of next week.[4]

There are important issues of imperial literary history and colonialist discourse buried in this genuinely excited praise for the freshness and vitality of Soyinka's literary English. The allusion to the "brigand dramatists from Ireland," within whose ranks the critic places Soyinka, sets up a silent, non-conflictual opposition between "our napping" language and "their" revitalizing appropriation of it, an opposition which is rendered with poignancy in the second epigraph of this chapter, the passage from

James Joyce's classic fictional autobiography, *A Portrait of the Artist as a Young Man*. The location of Soyinka's writing in this "brigand" school of literary Englishness – which implicitly suggests "writing back" from (ex)colonial outposts to an imperial metropolis – opens up for our consideration some crucial aspects of both the distinctive features of Soyinka's literary art and, on a far more general level, the world-historical context in which his writings – and the writings of his generational cohort of West African Anglophone writers – emerged as an important body of twentieth-century literature in the English language. It is necessary for our purposes in this chapter to give a profile of the biographical and socio-historical contexts of these buried aspects of an otherwise remarkably perceptive commentary by this London theatre critic on one play in Soyinka's literary corpus.

In 1959, the year before Nigeria's independence, Wole Soyinka returned to the country after a sojourn of about five years in Britain. The year 1960 was a "bumper" year for decolonization on the African continent when sixteen countries gained their political freedom from the European colonial powers.[5] Ghana had of course become the first black African country south of the Sahara to gain its independence three years earlier in 1957, which itself was exactly ten years after India's independence.[6] The first few years of Soyinka's early career as a playwright and university lecturer saw more countries swell the ranks of the new independent African nation-states; by the end of the decade, it was clear that though there was a number of countries in western and Southern Africa yet to gain their independence, the era of formal colonization in the continent was gone forever, to be superseded by the then cognitively uncharted world of the modern African postcolony.[7]

As a student in Britain, Soyinka had come to political maturity in strongly internationalist circles of students, academics and writers; he had been a passionate partisan of the African anti-colonial struggles, especially in the settler-dominated East Africa region and in the bastions of apartheid in Africa's own deep south; and he had participated in the big protests and demonstrations in Europe of the late 1950s against the arms race and for a nuclear-free world.[8] Thus, although his sojourn in Britain had evidently provided him with an acute awareness of the great anti-colonial stirring of African peoples and other colonized societies of the world, Soyinka's return home in that portentous moment for his country and continent meant for him both an "awakening" to his own unique skills and sensibilities as a writer-activist and a "return to sources" linking him with other African writers and artists. Any evaluative analysis of this phase of Soyinka's literary career has to be especially mindful of the challenge of simultaneously seeing these aspects of his early career both in their distinctiveness and their inevitable interrelatedness. This is all the more necessary given the fact that the presence that unfolded as Soyinka's unique personality was expressed in imaginative writings that drew attention to themselves as very original works of literature as well as enacted through a passionate political activism whose acts and expressions startled many in the new Nigerian nation by the unprecedented nature of their radical nonconformism. This point requires careful elaboration.

Before Soyinka arrived on the scene from his five-year sojourn in England on the eve of the country's formal independence, there was an older "pre-independence generation" of writers and artists already active in Nigerian literature, theatre and the visual and plastic arts and laying the foundations of the Nigerian "renaissance" which was to reach its apogee with the generation of Achebe and Soyinka. This in itself was only a national expression of a general cultural and political "awakening" in the twilight of colonialism in the West Africa region with important counterparts in countries such as Senegal and the Cameroon, Ghana and Sierra Leone.[9] In Nigeria, the most prominent writers and artists of this "pre-independence generation" included figures like D.O. Fagunwa, Hubert Ogunde, Ben Enwonwu and Fela Sowande. And among Soyinka's own generation, his irruption on the scene was preceded by the ground-breaking fiction of Chinua Achebe and, to a lesser extent, Amos Tutuola; and it coincided with the crystallization of the powerful presence of figures like Christopher Okigbo, John Pepper Clark, Demas Nwoko, Duro Ladipo, Kola Ogunmola, Erabor Emokpae and Bruce Onabrakpeya, all of whom were splashing big waves of originality and vigor in diverse areas of the literary, performance, visual and plastic arts. And in figures like Abiola Irele, Ben Obumselu and Michael Echeruo, with crucial help and some guidance from expatriate patrons and fellow-travelers like Ulli Beier, Martin Banham, Molly Mahood and Gerald Moore, the foundations of a homegrown literary-critical discourse was already in place by the time Soyinka published his first critical essays. The brilliance and energy of members of this group – as well as their mostly idealistic but often self-absorbed and confused involvement at the margins of the political life of the new nation – are imaginatively rendered by Soyinka himself in his portrait of the group of artists and intellectuals who act as a collective protagonist in his first novel, *The Interpreters*. Robert Wren has tried to capture and celebrate the milieu and the social and cultural forces which produced these "titans" of modern Nigerian literature in his posthumously published book, *Those Magical Years: the Making of Nigerian Literature at Ibadan*, 1948–1966. And elsewhere in West Africa, that first decade of the post-independence era saw the increasing visibility and importance of writers like Ousmane Sembene, Cheikh Hamidou Kane, Kofi Awoonor, Mongo Beti, Abioseh Nichol and Efua Sutherland, and also of Ama Ata Aidoo and Ayi Kwei Armah of a somewhat later generation.[10]

With the advantage of historical hindsight and a lot of critical commentary on the collective situation and individual careers of these writers who may be described as the "independence generation" of modern Nigerian literature and criticism, it is relatively easier now than it would have been at the time to tease out the complex connections between their creative writings and their politics. In varying degrees, each writer came gradually to a sense of their collective identity as a cultural elite, an emergent literary intelligentsia whose international renown was at variance with the great gap which separated them from the vast majority of their countrymen and women, literate and non-literate. Achebe, Soyinka, Okigbo and J.P. Clark gradually emerged as perhaps the most talented and self-assured writers; and these four also seem to have been the most concerned to think through the contradictions of their elite status within the ambit of broadly left-identified, progressive views and perspectives.[11] Two things marked Soyinka's unique location within this "quartet." First, there was the extraordinary versatility and prodigiousness of his literary output: Achebe achieved world class status as a writer primarily as a novelist, though he also wrote very influential essays as a cultural critic and thinker; Okigbo produced a small but very distinguished body of work exclusively in poetry; Clark wrote some plays and produced a work of monumental scholarly research, but achieved fame as a poet; Soyinka wrote prodigiously in all the literary forms and genres. Second, and more portentously, Soyinka occupies his distinct place within the "quartet" on account of his propensity for taking very daring *artistic* and *political* risks in furtherance of his deepest political and ethical convictions, risks which often entailed considerable peril to himself and also profoundly challenged, but at the same time complexly re-inscribed the determinate elitism of his generation of writers. The articulation between the political and artistic risks is one of the most fascinating and complex aspects of Soyinka's career.

Soyinka is certainly not an isolated figure with regard to the prominent role that writer-activists collectively play in the public affairs of his country and continent and more generally, in the developing world. In Nigeria alone, there is a large group of writers, artists and musicians who have played prominent roles in placing the arts at the forefront of the nation-building, democratic struggles of the last five decades. The group includes, among others, Ola Rotimi, Fela Anikulapo-Kuti, Sunny Okosun, Molara Ogundipe, Femi Osofisan, Femi Fatoba, Niyi Osundare, Festus Iyayi, Bode Sowande, Iyorwuese Hagher, Funso Aiyejina, Tunde Fatunde, Esiaba Irobi, Olu Obafemi, Tess Onwueme, Salihu Bappa and Ogah Abah.[12] This list can be considerably widened to embrace the role that a highly visible and articulate radical intelligentsia has played in the political life of the country. Indeed, some figures here have created public profiles for themselves almost as visible as Soyinka's public persona as a permanent intellectual dissident of the post-independence system of misrule and inequality: Yusufu Bala Usman, Bala Mohammed, Beko Ransome-Kuti, Gani Fawehinmi, Mokugwo Okoye, Ola Oni, Eskor Toyo, Segun Osoba, Omafume Onoge, Eddie Madunagu and Dipo Fasina.[13] What distinctly marks Soyinka out in this formation is precisely the degree to which he has consistently been prone to taking political and artistic risks most other writer-activists and the whole phalanx of radical academics and intellectuals would consider either totally unacceptable or quixotic, even when they applaud the courage and originality underlying such propensity for risk taking. Because the exceptionalism that this suggests has often led to distorted accounts of Soyinka's political activism, in what follows both artistic and political risk-taking by Soyinka will be placed within a profile which, while highlighting this aspect of his career, will nevertheless embrace the more "mundane," more typical acts of political and artistic radicalism that have linked Soyinka with the national and continental community of progressive, activist writers and academics.

The political risks are much better known, though some of Soyinka's experiences in this particular matter are little understood beyond rumor, speculation and gossip, even within Nigeria. For example, not much has been written on Soyinka's "fire fighting" interventions in the violent electoral and electioneering politics of the 1960s through the 1980s which often fetched a literal price on his head. Much more widely known and discussed are the famous radio station "happening" of 1965, and the near-fatal contretemps of the so-called "Third Force" phenomenon in 1967. In the radio station episode, sometime in October 1965, a young man managed to slip past units of the armed Nigerian mobile paramilitary police stationed at the Ibadan buildings of the Nigerian Broadcasting

Service. Making his way into one of the studios for live broadcasts in the complex, he held up the startled and frightened duty officers in the studio at gun point and then proceeded to force the dazed controllers of the station to broadcast a prerecorded message which, on behalf of "free Nigeria," repudiated the electoral victory which had been fraudulently claimed by the vastly unpopular and repressive regional government of western Nigeria. At the end of the swift operation, the young "desperado" who carried out this action still managed to slip out of the station unharmed. Soyinka was later arrested and tried for this action, but he was acquitted on the grounds of a legal technicality.[14] Barely two years after this incident, on the eve of the Nigerian civil war, Soyinka made contact with elements within the Biafran secessionist leadership, making no secret of this visit to Biafra if not of the details of what transpired with his contacts there, even though at this particular time such action was considered highly treasonous by the Nigerian federal military regime, with its large clutch of fractious, rabidly anti-Biafran military and civilian zealots. Soyinka later described his action as one of a series of interventions planned by a group, the so-called "Third Force," of which the playwright was apparently a key member and whose objective was to avert war by neutralizing the equally compromised and reactionary leadership of the "federalists" and the "secessionists."[15] Apprehended for this action but never formally indicted or tried, Soyinka was held in gaol for the entire duration of the civil war, most of this in solitary confinement.

Unquestionably, the most widely discussed aspect of Soyinka's public personality is that of his fame as one of Nigeria's most uncompromising and vigorous human rights campaigners, and perhaps the fiercest and most consistent opponent of the African continent's slew of dictators and tyrants. The sustained and relentless nature of his activism in furtherance of the protection of democratic rights and egalitarian values places him in the ranks of other African writer-activists like Ngugi wa Thiong'o, Mongo Beti and Nawal el Saadawi. However, Soyinka's activism is distinguished by the sheer reach of his involvements as well as the extraordinary resourcefulness that he brings to them. Quite simply put, Soyinka has always conceived of his political activism as appertaining to the *entire* continent of Africa, with his native Nigeria, apartheid South Africa before the inauguration of black-led majority rule, Hastings Banda's Malawi, Idi Amin's Uganda, Mobutu's Zaire, and Macias Nguema's Equatorial Guinea being over the years the most prominent "theatres" of his fiercest campaigns.

From the foregoing account of Soyinka's activities, it is apparent that many aspects of his radical political activism sit rather uneasily with his general reputation as an "obscure" writer, an "elitist" artist who makes no concessions to populist demands for clarity of thought and accessibility of expressive idioms. Perhaps the most "uncharacteristically" populist of his cultural production in the cause of political activism are his effective forays into the domains of popular culture through the use of media like music and film for biting satire against the corruption and brazen brigandage of the Nigeria political class, and for making rousing calls for the dispossessed and the disenfranchised masses to take their fate in their own hands. The film, "Blues for a Prodigal" made in 1983 (but released in 1984) and based on actual events in the maximum use of violence and intimidation by large sections of the ruling party of Shehu Shagari, the Nigerian president, was far less effective than Soyinka's phonograph and audio cassette recording of a composition titled "Unlimited Liability Company." This was a long-playing album rendered in the brisk, mellifluous style of Israel Njemanze, a popular musician of the 1950s who perfected a compositional style for rendering topical issues and common experiences in an essentially apolitical, sentimental manner. In the flip side to this composition titled "Etiko Revo Wettin?," the tuneful, strongly melodic style of Njemanze is retained, but the ballad form is infused with parodic deflations of the "Ethical Revolution" declared by the Shagari administration as a national goal and promoted by "patriotic" jingles on radio and hypocritical, moralizing exhortations for probity in the newspapers and on television. The two sides of this long-playing album literally took the country by storm, many of the verses giving the common man's view of the hypocrisy and venality of the ruling circles:

> You tief one kobo dey put you for prison
> You tief one million, na patriotism
> Dem go give you chieftaincy and national honour
> You tief even bigger, dem go say na rumour
> Monkey dey work, baboon dey chop
> Sweet pounded yam – some day 'e go stop![16]

> (You filch one penny they'll send you to prison
> But steal one million, that's patriotism!
> They'll make you a chief and give you national honors
> And dare to rob on a grand scale, they'll say it's all rumor
> The monkey slaves while the baboon grows fat
> This parasite's paradise – one day it will end!)

Apart from his very skillful use of a modulated "pidgin" English – the national lingua franca of the "common man" in Anglophone West Africa – and the adroit politicization of the received ballad form which, in the hands of its originator, Njemanze, had been basically apolitical, Soyinka derived the forcefulness of the scathing social commentary of "Unlimited Liability Company" and "Etiko Revo Wettin?" from a radical refusal to suffer the misdeeds and follies of the Nigerian political establishment in either silence or with ineffectual, token protests.

One of the high points of the Nigerian writer-activist's career as a public intellectual was certainly his involvement in the countrywide General Strike called by the Nigerian Labor Congress in 1964. Soyinka threw himself into a heady, optimistic promotion of the action in the Lagos-Ibadan sector of the strike. This general strike was a national event that almost led to the collapse of the first post-independence civilian regime in Nigeria and entailed a call for a popular uprising, totally endorsed by Soyinka, to institute a workers' social-democratic order to replace the government of Abubakar Tafawa Balewa. Another high point of Soyinka's political activism and one that marks a genuine conjunctural moment in the life of the country, is the series of crises and popular rebellions leading to the Nigerian civil war, continuing in diverse covert and overt forms of dissent during the war, and mutating into an unprecedented militancy of students, workers and middle-class professionals after the cessation of hostilities. This series of crises and dissent saw, among other things, the incarceration of Soyinka for most of the duration of the civil war; later it led to the one and only time in his entire activist career when Soyinka apparently overcame his deep and abiding suspicion of the usefulness of registered political parties and became a member of the People's Redemption Party (PRP), the most left-of-centre political party to have actually ever won huge electoral victories in the entire colonial and postcolonial history of Nigeria.[17] Finally, one other high point of Soyinka's career as a political activist is worth mentioning here, this being the central leadership role that he played in the external opposition to the Sani Abacha dictatorship between 1993 and 1998. At one point in this five-year period of yet another involuntary exile for Soyinka, the dictator formally and *in absentia* charged the writer-activist and eleven other leaders of this external opposition with treason, an offense that carried the death penalty.

Against the backdrop of the long periods of exile that Soyinka has had to spend outside Nigeria and the African continent, it may come as a surprise to those unfamiliar with the scope and range of our author's

political existence and tactical options that he has in fact periodically
worked within the institutions and structures of the postcolonial state
and in cooperation with its incumbents. The most widely known instance of this pattern entails the patience and dedication with which
Soyinka created and sustained the Federal Road Safety Corps (FRSC)
in the 1970s and 1980s.[18] Similarly, Soyinka worked mightily with the national government in 1977 to avert total failure of the Festival of Arts and
Culture of Africa and the Black World (FESTAC '77) when it became
known at the last minute that the scale of the festival far exceeded the
competence of the bureaucrats responsible for the planning and execution of the event or, indeed, the available infrastructures on the ground.
More controversially, in the mid-1980s Soyinka, in line with a small
minority of progressives in the country, developed a partiality for the
dictator, Ibrahim Badamasi Babangida, praising his openness to radical
ideas and going so far as to volunteer opinions about the good intentions,
the benevolent predispositions of a hegemon who would later annul the
federal elections of June 1993 and plunge the nation into its worst period of crisis and military dictatorship in the entire post-independence
period.

If much in what we have outlined so far as a profile of Soyinka as a
writer-activist has dealt mainly with his political activism, the matter of
his aesthetic avant-gardism, of his propensity for taking *artistic* risks also
demands our attention, especially as it has, to date, generally received
no systematic analysis in Soyinka criticism. The unprecedented experimentation with form and technique – and even subject matter – that
informed Soyinka's early plays like *A Dance of the Forests* and *The Road*, and
works in other genres like *The Interpreters* and many poems in the first published volume of poetry, *Idanre and Other Poems*, quickly established him as
not only a major talent but also one willing to push radically beyond the
existing boundaries of artistic practice, beyond also the scope of readers'
and audiences' expectations. For instance, nothing then in existence in
Nigerian or African literature quite provided anticipation or inspiration
for the sheer audacity, the artistic gamble of a work like *A Dance of the
Forests*, the very first full-length play written and staged by Soyinka. The
press release of the Swedish academy announcing the award of the Nobel
prize for literature for 1986 to Soyinka describes the scope of this play
as follows: "A kind of African *Midsummer Night's Dream* with spirits, ghosts
and gods. There is distinct link here to indigenous ritual drama and to the
Elizabethan drama."[19] Without a preexisting company of professional
English-language actors highly trained in the theatre and with years of

a perfected performance style or staging experience to its credit, "The 1960 Masks," the newly formed company Soyinka put together for that first production of this play, had the odds stacked heavily against it when the company mounted the play in October 1960 as part of the celebrations for Nigeria's independence. With a sprawling plot and a large cast of characters derived in conception from such diverse sources as *The Tempest* and *A Midsummer Night's Dream* and the world of Yoruba ritual drama and cultic masque, as well as the "forest phantasmagoria" of folklore, the play attempted to yoke together into an artistic whole vastly disparate African and Western theatre and performance traditions which had never before then remotely been in contact. And as an item in the new nation's independence celebrations, the play's subject matter also calculatedly set the sights against the euphoria of the moment by insisting on exploring, not the glorious achievements of the past, but its crimes and evils, suggesting thereby that the sort of "new" beginnings touted in independence from colonialism is fraught with unexorcised moral and psychic maladjustments. Neither the contemporary reception of the play and its staged production, nor subsequent critical commentaries on the play indicate that the artistic gamble quite paid off, that "The 1960 Masks" was quite up to the challenge of the play's synthesization of disparate African and Western theatrical and performance styles and idioms, or that the profound moral and political vision of the play found communicable rendition appropriate to the playwright's apparent intentions to confront his nation at a crucial historical moment.[20]

The mischance indicated in the generally confounded audience and critical responses to the artistic gamble of *Dance of the Forests* has not, fortunately, dogged Soyinka's artistic career. More illustrative of the successes that Soyinka has achieved with his avant-garde experiments in drama is the revelation contained in the "confession" of one of the most industrious and knowledgeable scholars of Soyinka's drama, James Gibbs, that until he *saw* and *heard The Road* in performance, he had been in serious doubts as to its power as *performable* theatre, so totally unprecedented were many of the play's extensions of dramatic and theatrical form.[21]

If the picture that emerges from the foregoing profile of Soyinka's career is that of one who acts in splendid isolation and absolutely according to the dictates of his unique and radically autonomous selfhood, this has to be substantially qualified by another crucial aspect of his personality as a writer-activist. This is the fact that more than any other African writer, the Nigerian playwright actually depends, and even thrives, on attracting circles and bands of collaborators, followers and acolytes around himself.

The circle of collaborators and followers has been crucial particularly in Soyinka's work as a dramatist. Each of the theatre companies he has formed and worked with over the years – notably "The 1960 Masks," "Orisun Theatre" and "The Guerrilla Unit" of the University of Ife Theatre – was made up as much of the fiercely devoted friends, followers and admirers of the playwright as of professional and semiprofessional actors and performers. Femi Osofisan has speculated that some day, the story will be told of how much Soyinka relied on his friend, the late businessman and brilliant actor, Femi Johnson, for conceiving and creating some of the great protagonist characters of his plays.[22] This observation can be extended to Soyinka's reliance, over the years, on a corps of actors, musicians and assistants in constructing many of the characters and situations of his plays, and especially in the composition of music and the writing of songs for these dramas. Indeed, over the course of four decades and from early plays and dramatic sketches such as *Kongi's Harvest* and the *Before the Blackout* series through plays of a "middle" period like *Opera Wonyosi* and *Requiem for a Futurologist* to more recent plays like *From Zia with Love* and *The Beatification of Area Boy*, Soyinka has depended heavily and tapped into the particular gifts and talents of a core of devoted collaborators and followers like Tunji Oyelana, Jimi Solanke, Yomi Obileye, Femi Fatoba and the late Wale Ogunyemi for the realization of the roughhewn, streetwise humor and parody in the dramatic action of these plays.[23] The list is long indeed of prominent actors, musicians, broadcasters, civil servants, journalists, critics and playwrights in Nigeria who, at one time or another, were either perceived, or perceived themselves, as part of the band of *awon omo Soyinka* – literally "Soyinka's brood," but better rendered as "Soyinka's circle."

On its own terms, this aspect of Soyinka's career deserves a book-length study, especially in light of the fact that in nearly all of his most ambitious works of drama and fictional and non-fictional prose, there stands in the foreground of the dramatic action or the narrative plot a larger-than-life protagonist surrounded by a band of followers and acolytes. This is indeed a crucial aspect of what this study conceives of, not as a simple artistic reflection of biographical experience or immediate social milieu, but rather as homologies of the self and the social in Soyinka's writings, fictional and non-fictional. Definitely, much of what Soyinka wrote, said and did in the first two decades of his career was deeply influenced as much by his reliance on the "circle" as by his unique talents and his uncommon angle on events and crises. However, since the late 1980s, the logic of mutability has considerably loosened the bonds that bound the members of the "circle" to the writer-activist. Nevertheless, Soyinka has shown a remarkable capability for reinvigorating remnants of earlier formations of the "circle" into new incarnations. At any rate, whether in the earlier decades when the Soyinka "circle" was relatively more cohesive and dominated aspects of middle-class arts and cultural politics in Nigeria, or in more recent decades when it has been more amorphous, the band has always been cast in the mold of the playwright's well-known persona as *okunrin ogun* (man of conflicts, of contentions), collectively embodying the nonconformist and sybaritic propensities of the playwright-activist. In other words, if it is the case that Soyinka and his "circle" have always managed to be in the storm centre of the tumult of Nigerian politics and letters, they have done so in great style, with panache and, paradoxically, with something akin to the cultivated mystique of a monastic order. This last detail relates as much to the playwright's famed interest in mysticism as it does to his passionate attachment to notions of the sacredness of the bonds of friendship and companionship. And this, subliminally, is not unconnected with the "enchanted" nature of the Soyinka "circle," enchantment in this case having a double side to it. One side speaks to the romance, the *joie de vivre* that is recounted in stories and legends in the Nigerian press and national grapevine about the playwright and his nearly all-male circle: the renown of the playwright and his circle as connoisseurs of good wine and food; their fame as purveyors of trendsetting fashion in dress styles that are fashioned out of locally woven cloth and neotraditional motifs, the famous "Mbari" smock being perhaps the most widely popular of these; their much-deserved celebration as passionate enthusiasts of the theatre and the arts who held rehearsals of plays and dramatic skits everywhere, from the regular university theatre buildings to the bars and nightclubs of Ibadan and Lagos in the 1960s and 1970s. At the heart of these stories and legends is the fame of Soyinka's various homes in Lagos, Ibadan, Ife and Abeokuta in the 1960s through the 1990s as unparalleled watering holes for the select circle of his friends, admirers and followers.

"Enchantment" in these stories and legends also entail a peculiarly "Soyinkan" romantic mystique connected, significantly enough, to the symbolic capital of his famous patronym, "Soyinka." Without any elisions, the full spelling of this is *Oso yi mi ka*. Literally, this means "I am surrounded by sorcerers." More idiomatically translated, it means "I am surrounded or sustained by circles of protective shamans." In the light of the symbolic capital inscribed in this patronym, to the extent that the band of collaborators, admirers and followers of the writer-activist are gifted actors, musicians and artists in their own right, they are "sorcerers" in the world of Soyinka's predilection for art that is cathartic, orphic and ritualistic. In this capacity they may be said to have nourished, protected and sustained the deepest springs of Soyinka's decisive artistic and political interventions in the affairs of his crisis-ridden nation in the last four decades, thereby considerably complicating the "big man" syndrome in art and politics in colonial and postcolonial Yoruba culture and society that Karen Barber and Michael Etherton have subjected to careful scholarly scrutiny.[24] We may thus conjecture that this constitutes a sort of composite equivalent of the shamans, sorcerers and diviners who presumably in the precolonial society sustained the life and activities of the ancestor who supplied the patronym "Soyinka" to the family. It is thus no wonder that enchantment and romance, even if they often assume parodic and bracingly tragicomic forms, are powerful currents in Soyinka's writings, just as a strong interest in mysticism and the occult are known to be aspects of our author's private intellectual and spiritual avocations. It is thus a great lacuna in the critical discourse on Soyinka that beyond citation as mere background to the more "serious" issues in the life and career of the dramatist, these aspects of his artistic career and activist public life seldom ever figure in analyses and evaluations of the social impact and ramifications of Soyinka's writings and his activism. This is a point that will be examined in the concluding chapter of this study in the context of the heroic *voluntarism* that seems to overdetermine Soyinka's view of radical art and politics in Africa and the developing world.

The combination in Soyinka's career of political risk taking with a propensity for artistic gambles reveals a convergence of *aesthetic* and *political* radicalism which, apart from Soyinka, we encounter only in a few other African writers. This observation has to be placed in the context of postcolonial West Africa where, as in many other cultural regions of the world, the paths of aesthetic innovativeness and political radicalism seldom ever converge. But while this convergence in Soyinka's work is thus a crucial aspect of his career and legacy, it is important to remember that there are aspects of his works which are indeed not that far from the mainstream of the canon of modern African literature. Certainly, within the compass of what I have identified as the other distinctive mark of Soyinka's literary art – the versatility and prodigiousness of his writing – many of his poems, essays and dramas have been huge critical successes with readers and critics who, on the whole, have been resistant or even hostile to his more "difficult," ambitiously avant-garde works. Expressed differently, this observation is confirmed by the fact that over the years, as the critical controversies have raged over Soyinka's so-called "obscure" works and his radical political activism, a good number of his poems have become not only staples of high school or college anthologies of modern African poetry, they have indeed been some of the most cherished of these collections, often to the Nigerian poet's own dismay.[25] Similarly, a number of his dramas have become favorites of both amateur and professional companies in many parts of the English-speaking world, while some of his productions in popular forms and media like music and street theatre have been phenomenally successful. For students of Soyinka's writings and career, this point indicates a double challenge. First, it entails a call to read the popular, accessible and generally formalistically conventional works in his corpus both in their own right and in relation to the more complex, more ambitious and more avant-garde works. Second, and far more arduous, there is also the challenge to see the more courageous, idiosyncratic and charismatic aspects of Soyinka's career and personality as a writer-activist neither in the simple, uncomplicated perspective of sedulous adulation nor outright, reactionary rejection but complexly, in its uniqueness and its contradictory determinateness.

The nature of this challenge can be stated both concretely in relation to Soyinka's writing and career and, more generally, in relation to the rarity of the conjunction of political with aesthetic radicalism in all the cultural regions of the world, but most especially in the developing world, with notable exceptions like the "boom literature" of Latin America of the second half of the twentieth century, and the radical film, theatre, dance and music of the first two decades of post-revolutionary Cuba. Concretely, there is the crucial fact that there is now in existence in the accumulated Soyinka criticism of four decades an implicit but nonetheless pervasive bifurcation in the reception of his works in Africa and other parts of the English-speaking world. This has inevitably created a great divide between, on the one hand, a large body of writers, scholars and critics who, at best, are cautious or even discretely suspicious of Soyinka's literary avant-gardism, of what can be described as "neo-modernist" expressions and proclivities especially in his drama and poetry and, on the other hand, a smaller body of critics and theorists who are avid and enthusiastic admirers of precisely these very aspects of Soyinka's works and career. Important figures within the former group are Chinua Achebe, Ngugi wa Thiong'o, Bernth Lindfors, Chinweizu and Derek Wright, while the latter group includes within its rank influential writers and critics like Nadine Gordimer, Derek Walcott, Wilson Harris, Femi

Osofisan, Annemarie Heywood, H.L. Gates, Jr., Tejumola Olaniyan, and Ato Quayson.[26] The more general, but related problematique can equally be stated succinctly: the effective audience for the avant-garde, especially in *written* literature, in all parts of the world, is normatively very narrow; in the developing world, its real and potential audience is within the demographically tiny cultural elite, an elite whose historic colonial (and neocolonial) formation has not at all been predisposed to enthusiasm for either political radicalism or aesthetic avant-gardism.

It is my contention that these issues – of the articulation between art and politics, especially within the framework of historic avant-garde movements around the world, and of the problems of the audience for aesthetically radical works in the developing world – have, from the very beginning of his career, obsessed Soyinka to a degree that is without parallel in postcolonial Anglophone literatures. The most persuasive indication of this is the sheer scope of the occurrence of paradigms and figures of radical nonconformism, in art and politics, in his writings, including, very suggestively, all the works of autobiographical memoir. Even more revealing of this structure in Soyinka's writing is the matter of his attitude to language – by which is meant, implicitly, the scope, the contradictions and the limits of literary English for an Anglophone, postcolonial African tradition of writing. Language and signification in Soyinka's most ambitious, most experimental poems, plays and even essays often considerably exceed perceptible function and referent – confoundingly or exhilaratingly, depending on the reader's or critic's predispositions and sensibilities.[27] The implicit, and sometimes explicit, critical refrain in Soyinka criticism on this issue is: Why does a writer from the developing world, an African writer at that, delight so much in displaying his command of the alien English tongue? Sometimes, this assumes a more blithely philistine form such as: "Who is he writing for, the international literary elite of the English-speaking world, academic eggheads in his own society, or the popular masses he claims to be fighting for?"[28] In the present context of a discussion of highlights of Soyinka's career as a radical writer-activist, perhaps the most crucial aspect of these critical responses to our author's attitude to language is the complete critical silence on the countless instances of his extensive deployment of an "excess" of image and sign over obvious referent and function in his writings for the construction of a "self" that is mimetically unrepresentable precisely because its representation, or rather its representability, is beyond the horizon of presently available or formalized linguistic, artistic, generic and ideological frames.

Critical discourses on Soyinka's writings and career in the last four decades have, at best, only skirted the margins of these features of the Nigerian author's literary corpus. Certainly, the controversies over the alleged "obscurity," "difficulty" and "complexity" of his writing have not notably encompassed elucidation and analysis of figures and paradigms of aesthetic and political radicalism within his works, precisely because the matter of the articulation of the political and the aesthetic in our author's writings has largely been located outside the works, in the social ramifications of the writer-activist's most overtly political works. But precisely because of the pervasive inscription of these figures and paradigms in his writings, this articulation of the political and the aesthetic is as much a matter of what happens within Soyinka's works as they pertain to the effects and ramifications of the works in society. Moreover, the matter is compounded by the fact that many of the figures and paradigms of the convergence of aesthetic experimentalism and political radicalism are as much to be found in Soyinka's autobiographical memoirs as in his fictional works, clearly indicating that what we have here is the elaborate project of constructing a self-reflexive radical subjectivity over the course of his entire career and in all the genres and forms of expression in which he has written. Why Soyinka has apparently felt impelled to make this project such a decisive and pervasive aspect of his works is thus a matter of great theoretical and critical interest. Thus, this issue is central to the present chapter of this study of all the writings of Soyinka in its focus on the project of self-constitution or self-fashioning in our author's writings and career.[29]

Commenting on the fact that Soyinka "wears many hats," James Gibbs has asserted that his hope as an interpreter of the Nigerian dramatist's works and life is to demonstrate that even within the diversity and versatility of our author's creations as a writer and of his involvements as an activist, "the reader will feel the current of a life which is not pursuing different courses separated by islands and delta flats, but a strong river, full of eddies and subtle flows, but one stream, one river, one flow."[30] This conception seems central to Soyinka's own self-understanding as an artist, to his conscious self-presentation as an African writer. It is a self-conception that is inscribed in more than a dozen of Soyinka's essays; and it is intricately woven into the very structure and texture of his writings. Moreover, this view of the unified, integrated personality of Soyinka as artist and intellectual seems to have decisively affected the critical reception of his works. Thus, most of Soyinka's sympathetic critics – and we might add, a few of the most insightful – have generally viewed the Nigerian author as protean and multifaceted as an artist, but they also see a fundamentally unified sensibility at work in all his writings and activities. For such scholars, the fact that Soyinka has written in virtually all the literary genres, and the fact that he has sustained over the course of more than thirty years a prodigious output of some eighteen works of drama, six works of fictional and nonfictional prose, five volumes of poetry, a work of translation, three works of critical prose and innumerable pieces of cultural journalism and political polemics, all these facts do not in the least perturb the perception of the unified, integrated sensibility of Soyinka as an artist.[31]

This view involves many methodological and philosophical problems, especially when applied to the historical and cultural contexts of the postcolonial writer. For this reason, it has generated intense critical controversies that the proponents of Soyinka's harmoniously integrated selfhood have not engaged. At one extreme, there are influential writers and critics like Ngugi wa Thiong'o and Obi Wali who have argued that writing in the languages of colonial imposition entails evacuation of an alleged primary selfhood constituted by the indigenous mother tongue, not ignoring the perpetuation of unequal relations between indigenous languages and languages of imperial imposition.[32] In the light of this postulate, there simply cannot be a unified, integrated selfhood for a postcolonial writer who writes in any of the languages of colonial derivation, French, English or Portuguese. At another extreme, there is the view that the postcolonial writer who writes in the "world languages" is a woman or man of two or more worlds, where such presumed linguistic and cultural pluralism is perceived not as a source of alienation and inauthenticity, but as the positive incarnation of the sort of hybrid, decentered subjectivity celebrated by postmodernists. In other words, one view bemoans an evacuated or inauthentic selfhood while the other view celebrates multiple, heterogeneous selves. The insistence that Soyinka's artistic personality is a unified, integrated one, that in "essence" he remains the same sovereign agent of his "speech acts" in whatever genre he chooses to express himself, this insistence flies in the face of such mutually opposed views of the postcolonial writer, and in the face of the massively overdetermining social and cultural contradictions affecting the production, reception and academic study of postcolonial African writings.[33] Thus, it is useful to subject the theoretical foundations of this view to scrutiny before exploring its practical, embodied incarnation in a writer-activist like Soyinka who has made the issue of self-constitution or self-fashioning an abiding feature of his works.

A useful, widely quoted expression of this view, from the standpoint of classical mimeticism, is revealed in the following formulations of Aristotle in the text of *The Poetics* on how the unified construct known as the "hero" is arbitrarily synthesized from the variety and fullness of life:

Unity of plot does not, as some persons think, consist of the unity of the hero. For infinitely varied are the incidents in one man's life which cannot be reduced to unity; and so too, there are many actions of one man out of which we cannot make one action. Hence the error, as it appears, of all poets who have composed a *Heracleid*, or a *Theseid*, or other poems of the kind. They imagine that as Hercules was one man, the story of Hercules must also be a unity. But Homer, as in all else he is of surpassing merit, here too . . . seems to have happily discerned the truth. In composing the *Odyssey* he did not include all the adventures of Odysseus – such as the wound on Parnassus, or his feigned madness at mustering of the host – *incidents between which there was no necessary or probable connection*. But he made the *Odyssey*, and likewise the *Iliad*, to center around an action that in our sense of the word is one.[34]

Even after making the important observation that there are often "no necessary or probable connections" between the variety of incidents and experiences in the life of an individual human life, Aristotle's main point in this passage from *The Poetics* is the suggestion that it is still possible to see in the life of an individual a "unity" or, in our terms, an "essence." But we must note that this "unity" or "essence" which a powerfully distilled characterization in a play (or for that matter, in the biographical textualization of a writer's life) projects is an illusion arrived at only by a process of selection and condensation which thus necessarily leaves out far more than it includes and highlights. In this connection, the "solution" proposed by Aristotle – the illusionary, full self-presence of classical mimeticism constructed around either a single action or a cluster of divergent but carefully selected actions – in fact produces its own problem, this being the absolutely unavoidable exclusions and elisions of vast areas of "life" or experience of a subject. The theoretical limit of this "unity" is thus unavoidable: as soon as the excluded details and incidents are acknowledged and brought into the representational and discursive field, the "unity" is shattered. In other words, the "hero" of the *Odyssey*, or more pertinent to the present discussion, Maren, the protagonist of Soyinka's autobiographical memoir, *Ibadan*, can be represented as a unified construct only by leaving out a considerable number of incidents and experiences between which there are "no necessary or probable connections."

Modern critical theory, especially poststructuralism, would seem to have resolved the problem of exclusions and omissions of classical mimeticism by suggesting that representation, *per se*, is in fact constituted by this "violence" of repressed or excluded terms or elements, that indeed no representation is possible without this violence. From this has come the suggestion that this "violence" of representation is somewhat mitigated if we pose the question of who and what are excluded and omitted in *any* representation, and if we read back into texts the repressions, gaps, exclusions and absences which enable their production in the first place.[35] But this hardly resolves all the theoretical problems thrown up by representation and subjectivity, especially in a colonial or postcolonial situation.

The mitigation of the inadequacies of mimetic representation through the recuperation of excluded or repressed elements is tremendously complicated when such "recuperations" pertain not only to a "represented" self but also a "representative" self who is deemed to be speaking out of, and for a colonized condition or an imperialized society. At this level, the "violence of representation" operates not merely and restrictedly in specific texts, or with regard to the isolated single author, but manifoldly, through cultural archives which work through the constitutive texts of whole institutions and entire societies. In other words, we are confronted at this level by two distinct but interlocking sets of exclusions and omissions: those which enable the crystallization of a unified subjectivity – either of protagonists of imaginary works or of the textual production of the personality of a writer-intellectual in an autobiographical memoir – and those which enable a whole society, culture or civilization to be represented, negatively or positively, as homogeneous and unanimist. This distinction is strongly indicated in the reported response of Soyinka to the initial news of the award of the Nobel prize for literature:

I have not been able to accept the prize on a personal level . . . I accept it as a tribute to the heritage of African literature, which is very little known in the West. I regard it as a statement of respect and acknowledgment of the long years and centuries of denigration and ignorance of the heritage which all of us have been trying to build. It's on that level that I accept it.[36]

It is perhaps undeniable that Soyinka underplays his own individual merits in this statement as an act of gracious acknowledgment of the contribution of other towering figures of modern African literature like Leopold Sedar Senghor, Chinua Achebe, Ousmane Sembene, Ngugi wa Thiong'o and Bessie Head, some of these writers themselves having for years been known to be hot favorites for the Nobel literature prize. But behind the statement is also the more crucial notion of a representative self whose *raison d'etre* is the authority to speak on behalf of a whole collective tradition threatened not only by acts of repression and silencing of non-Western texts and traditions, but also by the acute cultural contradictions of the postcolonial alienation brilliantly analyzed by, among others, Frantz Fanon and Amilcar Cabral.[37] The great tension between the uniqueness implied in the notion of an autonomous artistic selfhood and the notion of representativeness appertaining to a whole tradition has indeed been extensively explored in Soyinka's writings and is at the heart of his project of self-fashioning. At the heart of this tension in Soyinka's writings is the implied recognition that for the postcolonial writer, the claims of unique, autonomous artistic individuation and those of representativeness and solicitude for a threatened culture or tradition are both vigorously contested. For as Ashis Nandy has cogently and powerfully argued in his monograph, *The Intimate Enemy: the Loss and Recovery of the Self Under Colonialism*, in the matter of precolonial, indigenous traditions, there are not one but diverse, conflicting paradigms and matrices for a representative, resisting selfhood available to the writers and intellectuals who, like Soyinka and indeed most writers of the first generation of postcolonial Anglophone literatures, take up the cultural-nationalist project of fashioning individual selves and collective identities against the negations of colonial subject formation.[38] Similarly, in the matter of the chosen, non-indigenous "world language" of expression and its received modes of literariness – in Soyinka's case English – there are equally diverse, multiple and even conflicting paradigms to choose from. This in effect means that in any critical account of the identity of a postcolonial author and the tradition she claims to speak out of or represent, there is a crucial need to be attentive to what is selected and what is omitted in choosing from the range of available paradigms and matrices, both in indigenous traditions and in foreign, metropolitan sources.

These complicated issues lose their abstract and somewhat factitious character once we move into the concrete, embodied expressions that self-fashioning assume in Soyinka's writings. In both his imaginative works and his essays, the reified, anomic, "fallen" world of the African postcolony in particular and modern life in general obtrudes massively and manifoldly on sensitive individuals, on protagonist figures part of whose moral burden is to register – and in some cases resist – the "fallen" state of the world. Indeed, if it is true that in these works we are not exactly in the world of Kafka's totally hapless, lost souls, or the world of the robotized workers of Chaplin's "Modern Times," it is nonetheless true that the search for a coherent, stable selfhood, a selfhood harmoniously integrated into the human and natural environment, is more applicable to "lesser" works like *The Strong Breed* and *The Swamp Dwellers* than to the great dramatic parables like *The Road* and *Madmen and Specialists*. More tellingly, in the autobiographical memoir, *Ibadan*, it is in spite of the collapse, not the redoubtable support, of all the institutions and sources of "home" and "homecoming" that the protagonist struggles heroically with a small band of collaborators against the festering and destructive "penkelemes" of the Nigerian postcolony.[39]

It is part of Soyinka's significance as a postcolonial writer that in his works he has explored these problems of self-writing or self-constitution with a tacit but pervasive understanding that the issues are not beyond commensurable and productive syntheses, that the postcolonial writer can plot her way through the maze of the conflicting claims of the local and the foreign, the autochthonous and the modern, the familiar and the totally unprecedented and unanticipated precisely by the choices and selections of paradigms and matrices from the African and Western traditions, as well as other literary traditions of the world.

In the following concluding half of the present chapter, and on the basis of the critical and theoretical issues outlined above, I subject the textual production of Soyinka's personality to the sort of careful scrutiny it has hardly received in critical commentary on his works, his life and career. In other words, I place the authorial "self" of Soyinka's works and the "self-presentation" immanent in his radical activism under scrutiny, seeking to elucidate its constitution as a process that dialogically moves back and forth between its inscriptions in literary texts and its embodied incarnations in the extraordinary writer-intellectual that the world knows as Wole Soyinka and that his band of acolytes and admirers in Nigeria knows as "Kongi."[40] Concretely, I explore two distinct but complementary paradigms by which Soyinka in his fictional and nonfictional works has sought to negotiate the great tension between the two sides of the problem. The first of these is the paradigm, or arc, of a complexly and subliminally "representative" self whose authority and originality receive their greatest validation from access to the repressed recesses of collective memory, as codified in myths, rituals and other cultural matrices. This paradigm, I would argue, provides the textual and ideological base for Soyinka's great solicitude for the vitality of a collective African cultural and literary modernity. The second paradigm, or arc, is that of a unique, "unrepresentable" self which locates its replete identity in the endless chain of signification and the polysemy of language, especially as these are teased and played out in our author's writings between figures and idioms of both high and low literariness in the Yoruba and English languages. This particular paradigm, in my reading, provides the base for any possibility of an adequate, sophisticated grasp of Soyinka's more daunting, more elliptical and, on many occasions, esoteric use of language, metaphor and image; it also provides a base for apprehending our author's intimate but profoundly ambivalent relationship to important formations of European modernism and the avant-garde. The juxtaposition of these two paradigms allows Soyinka to achieve several important artistic moves or "swerves" simultaneously. These include the construction of powerful strategies to confront the violence and negations of the social conditions and realities of the most oppressed and marginalized groups in neocolonial Africa; the creation of distance from, and a perspective on his deep immersion in his social and cultural milieu; the invention and finessing of an idealized "self" that tries to combine the full self-presence of classical mimeticism with the putative decentered, contingently predicated subjectivity of poststructuralism; a more or less successful negotiation of the dangers of that extremely narcissistic form of self-absorption which seems to afflict great writers and intellectuals, and has produced bizarre distortions in the careers of many important literary artists of the twentieth century like Ezra Pound, Yukio Mishima and V.S. Naipaul.[41]

First then, we turn to the paradigm of the representative self in Soyinka's writings and activities, paying attention to the complex modes of its construction through recourse to and reinvention of the autochthonous myths and rituals of Yoruba culture.

"Ogun, comrade, bear witness how your metal is travestied!" This silent cry of rage which invokes the wrath of Ogun, the Yoruba god of war, creativity and metallurgy, is from Soyinka's prison memoir, *The Man Died*. It comes from the incarcerated author upon his being shackled at the feet after an ingratiating, deceptively "friendly" interrogator had departed from Soyinka's cell. This is only one of the numerous instances in his writings in which Ogun and many other alter egos, surrogates and "doubles" of the self are invoked to give metaphoric or spiritual depth to the conception of the self. For instance, in other parts of this same text, we encounter other personae and incarnations assumed by the imprisoned author such as "Shuttle," "Fox," "Lawgiver" and "Pluto." This pattern of self-textualization in Soyinka's writings through doubles and avatars is, moreover, not confined to the writer in moments of great peril or confinement; rather, it extends in a great expanse which applies to diverse aspects and stages in the life of our author and even embraces the "selves" of others. In other words, it is a pattern that goes to the roots of Soyinka's creative imagination.

It is perhaps useful here to focus on the manner in which this pattern enables Soyinka to remember, encode and reinvent the "self" and its doubles from the earliest childhood experiences to those of the adult, mature artist and public intellectual. This is all the more interesting given the structure of what appears to be an extensive transcoding that operates between the fictional and nonfictional works such that a non-linear evolutionary pattern in the formation of the artist's selfhood is imagined both retrospectively and prospectively. Thus, in one instance of the textual inscription of this structure, in the novel *The Interpreters* (1965), Egbo recollects a childhood incident in which he came up with the ultimate rationalization of his refusal, when greeting his guardian's husband in particular, and all elders and adults in general, to prostrate. Among males, greeting one's elders in full prostration is one of the most important "conduct" rituals in traditional Yoruba culture. This onerous form of rebellious self-assertion against a central protocol of "proper" etiquette is rendered in almost exact details by Soyinka in the nonfic-tional book of *his* childhood, *Aké* (1981). As recounted by Soyinka in this particular text, the incident takes place in the palace of the Odemo of Isara, and in the august company of the author's father's peers, which comprises the chiefly and professional doyens of the town. The event is precipitated when a truculent elder demands, or rather *commands*, the prostration obeisance from the very young, very tiny Soyinka. In *The Interpreters*, Egbo says: "If I only kneel to God, why should I prostrate to you?" (*TI*, 17). In *Aké*, the young Soyinka asks, in the startled company of his father's friends and relatives: "If I don't prostrate myself to God, why should I prostrate to you?" (*Aké*, 127).

By way of a short, necessary gloss on this pair of textual inscriptions of an assertive youthful rebelliousness, it should be noted that it is less a gratuitous transgression of regulatory "conduct" codes that is involved here than the rejection of a prescribed, normative act – flat out, face-down prostration to all of one's elders – whose interpellative objective is to naturalize what the young protagonist in each respective case intuitively perceives to be an over-regulated and degraded selfhood. Thus, what emerges, what is textualized and enters into a vast machinery of exchange and circulation with other situations and contexts in Soyinka's fictional and nonfictional works, is a notion of an inviolable, infrangible self which is, at all costs, to be protected against any and every attempt at its being subdued, even at the grave risk of infractions against central, normalizing societal rules and codes. This, surely, is the "self" that is revealed in the following passage from *Aké* which, in fact, takes us much further back in the author's life than the "prostration" refusal episode:

As I scrubbed myself in the bathroom I felt ill with apprehension. Lawanle's words had merely increased the unease which was lately surreptitiously trans-mitted to me – those sentences that began on mother's tongue, but were never complete, the fleeting disapproval of some privilege extended to me by Essay, the pursing of the mouth as I made off with my mat to his room while Tinu, cousins and all retired to the common mat. *I hated that communal mat, I realized quite suddenly; it went beyond merely feeling special in Essay's room. I hated it with a vehemence that went beyond the fact that some of the others, much older than I, still continued to wet the mat. I simply preferred to be on my own.* (*Aké*, 83) (My emphasis)

As narrated by Soyinka in the passages following this quote, it takes the carefully planned ruses and stratagems of "Wild Christian," his mother, with the covert connivance of "Essay," his father, to "break" the young boy into the world of the "communal mat," but even so the "interpella-tion" is not completely successful:

That following night I lay on my mat in the dark and cried. My transfer was permanent. And there could be no mistaking the rather guilty half-smile con-firmation on my father's face. (83)

The incorporation by Soyinka into his fictional and nonfictional writings of his total rejection of two of the most powerfully normalizing and inter-pellative "conduct" codes and ritualized practices of traditional Yoruba culture for early childhood – the prostration obeisance and the shared communal mat – is made in each case without much commentary by the author. This, I suggest, is deliberate, for their inscription without commentary is far more powerfully encoding than what a gloss might accomplish. Readers able to decode such inscriptions in fact know, by silent registration, that the "self" textualized by these radical refusals is one that would go to the uttermost limits in following its own intuitions, its own proclivities. This reflexive incarnation of the "self" by Soyinka in the mask of radical, dissenting nonconformism is not monolithic, it is highly differentiated and it is this differentiation that provides an expla-nation for the considerable differences in tone, form and impact in the author's three works of autobiographical memoirs, *Aké*, *The Man Died*, and *Ibadan*.

On the surface of things, it seems highly improbable that such textual inscriptions which emphasize singularity and radical individual autonomy could also be integrated with a "representative" self, a self which aspires to speak and act in defense of a whole culture or tradition. This is the central conundrum of Soyinka's project of self-invention, and this is where his appropriation of the brooding, paradoxical myths and legends of the deity, Ogun, constitutes a brilliant strategic move in this project. For in the myths, narratives and ritual dramas associated with this deity, what we encounter, compositely, is the paradox of the rebel as quintessential culture hero, the radical iconoclast as heroic protagonist of supreme ethical, self-transcending communal values. For this intricate signification, Soyinka has had to go back to what might very well be the "ur-text" of Yoruba mythology and cosmology: the myth of the dismemberment of Orisanla. The *locus classicus* of the myth in Soyinka's writings is probably the following poetic description by the narrator in his first novel, *The Interpreters*, of the "canonical" narratives and legends of the gods and demiurges of the Yoruba pantheon, as captured in the ambitious canvas of the painter, Kola, one of the protagonists of the novel, just before the work is opened for exhibition:

And these floods in the beginning, of the fevered fogs of the beginning, of the first messenger, the thimble of earth, a fowl and ear of corn, seeking the spot where a scratch would become a peopled island; *of the first apostate rolling the boulder down the back of the unsuspecting deity . . . and shattering him into fragments which were picked up and pieced together with devotion . . .* of the lover of purity, the unblemished one whose large compassion embraced the cripples and the dumb, the dwarf, the epileptic – and why not, indeed, for they were creations of his drunken hand and what does it avail, the eternal penance of favoritism and abstinence? *Of the lover of gore, invincible in battle, insatiable in love and carnage, the explorer, path-finder, protector of the forge and the creative hands, companion of the gourd whose crimson-misted sight of debauchery set him upon his own and he butchered them until the bitter cry pierced his fog of wine, stayed his hand and hung the sword, foolish like his dropped jaw . . .* of the parting of the fog and the retreat of the beginning, and the eternal war of the first procedure with the long sickle head of chance, eternally mocking the pretensions of the bowl of plan, mocking lines of order in the ring of chaos . . . (*TI*, 224–5) (My emphasis)

This densely cryptic transcription of oral narrative fragments attempts nothing short of a totalized encapsulation of the creation myths, together with the central myths of the principal *orisa* or deities of the Yoruba religious pantheon. The passage thus symbolically amplifies the "character" of the "interpreters," the eponymous protagonists of the novel; each of them has posed for Kola in his execution of the painting, Kola having in the process assimilated the "essential" traits of each of these diverse *orisa* to each of his friends. The first highlighted section of the passage recodes the dismemberment of the supreme deity, Orisanla, by his slave, Atunda, while the second highlighted passage inscribes the bloody myths of Ogun, god of war and creativity, with his complex and contradictory traits: "insatiable in love and carnage, explorer, pathfinder, protector of the forge and the creative hands, companion of the gourd" (of palm wine). Kola's painting assimilates this deity to Egbo, and we have seen earlier that Egbo's childhood rejection of the "prostration obeisance" resonates with the young Soyinka's enactment of the same emblematic refusal as narrated in *Aké*. Thus, apart from *The Interpreters*, other fictional and nonfictional works, as well as theoretical essays of Soyinka, have appropriated aspects of these Ogun motifs for ideal, symbolic constructions of an artistic identity and authority that is fundamentally humanistic but is riven by great contradictions. Of the essays of Soyinka which participate in this vast machinery of self-fashioning, "The Fourth Stage," "Morality and Aesthetics in the Ritual Archetype" and "The Credo of Being and Nothingness" are particularly noteworthy. And imaginative works such as the long narrative poem "Idanre" in the collection *Idanre and Other Poems*, the dramatic mythopoem, *Ogun Abibiman*, and the plays *A Dance of the Forests*, *The Road*, and *The Bacchae of Euripides*, all entail strong thematic and emblematic foregrounding of this structure of self-invention through the Ogun motifs. That these are all part of a vast, complex and dialogical fashioning of a "self" derived from, but paradoxically set against the grain of tradition is clearly indicated in the following conversation between Soyinka and Ulli Beier:

BEIER: Now let us talk about the way in which some of these traditional Yoruba concepts have been used in your plays. If I am not mistaken, it was in *A Dance of the Forests* that you first used some kind of Yoruba symbolism in a play.

SOYINKA: Yes, of course by that time I had written a draft of *The Lion and the Jewel*, but that was a very different thing. It was on a different level . . .

BEIER: The striking thing about *A Dance of the Forests* is the character of Ogun. This image of Ogun has accompanied you through your later writing; but it has been said that the Ogun of your play is a rather personal, "unorthodox" orisa – that in fact, you created a new kind of Ogun.

SOYINKA: Hmmm . . . that is true.

BEIER: But of course, even in purely traditional Yoruba terms, it is quite a legitimate thing to do. Ogun has never been a rigidly defined being; the orisa can only live through people – by mounting somebody's head – you could go so far as to say that when the orisa fails to manifest himself in this way through his priests and worshipers, he ceases to exist. If the priest who personifies Ogun is an unusually powerful "Olorisa', he can modify the image of Ogun. So that even in Yoruba tradition Ogun consists of a number of interrelated personalities. *Any traditional priest would accord you the right to live Ogun your own way, in fact, they would think it the normal thing to do.* You create Ogun – or perhaps, you are sensitive to other aspects of his being. Because Ogun is a very complex being.

SOYINKA: Yes, indeed . . . [42](My emphasis)

Given the pervasiveness of the binary cultural stereotype of what many commentators have called the encounter of a "communalistic" Africa with the "individualistic" West, the powerful cultural sanction that Yoruba culture gives to individuality – as indicated in the highlighted remarks of Beier in this exchange with Soyinka – will come as a surprise to many students of the Nigerian author's writings who have one-sidedly ascribed Soyinka's assertiveness on the individual autonomy of the artist to the influence of Western individualism. What is involved here, I would argue, is the conflation of the distinct processes and coordinates of *individuation, individuality* and *individualism.* To the remarks of Beier in the quote above we should take note of the ringing celebration of *individuality* in the third epigraph to this chapter, the gnostic aphorism from Ifa divinatory lore: *Ori kan nuun ni; iyato kan nuun ni.* (That is one soul/person; that is one difference).

As stated earlier in this discussion, the diverse textual appropriations of aspects of the Ogun myths in Soyinka's works could be said to cohere around what is perhaps the "ur-text" of mythic lore in Yoruba cosmology, that of the Orisanla-Atunda primal confrontation. Let us recall its particular articulation in the narrator's description of Kola's painting of his friends as avatars of the "orisa" in *The Interpreters*:

Of the first apostate rolling the boulder down the back of the unsuspecting deity . . . and shattering him into fragments which were picked up and pieced together with devotion . . . (*TI*, 224)

Atunda (or Atooda in other versions of the myth), rebellious slave and archetypal rebel, rolls a rock down on Orisanla, the father of the gods in the Yoruba pantheon. This act of "apostasy" which dismembers the original Oneness, inaugurates fragmentation and heterogeneity and what Soyinka in "The Fourth Stage" calls "the separation of self from essence." In our author's highly idiosyncratic appropriation of this myth, Ogun is the deity who, among all the gods in the pantheon, accepts fully the

implications of the violence of that inaugurating and individuating dismemberment, as well as the will to gather into himself the largest stock
of that plenitude and multiplicity originally concentrated in Orisanla.
Thus, Ogun, in Soyinka's inventive textual appropriations of the myth,
is the avatar most auspiciously placed to achieve transcendence of the
chasm between self and essence, being and non-being. And because of
Soyinka's insistence that Ogun is an "explorer god," side by side with
his acknowledgment of the deity's bloodthirstiness, the deity as Muse
affords the poet and playwright visionary significations able to link the
pre-modern with the modern, and to meet the violence of modernity,
as experienced through both colonialism and neocolonialism, on a scale
commensurate with their awesome effectivity.

I have argued in another critical context that Soyinka's appropriations
of the admittedly polysemic significations of his chosen muse, Ogun, involves both an over-semiotization and an incomplete secularization of the
cultic and religious roots of this deity's fascinating hold on the imagina-
tions of large segments of African peoples in West Africa and in diasporic
African communities in Brazil and Cuba.[43] But it is incontestable that in
his endless improvisations on the symbolic resonance of this particular
body of mythic and ritual archetypes, Soyinka found and consolidated
a powerful, high-voltage means of persuasively insisting that his own
unique artistic individuation is inseparable from the burdens and responsibilities that the negations, crises, and challenges of the postcolonial age
present to all African writers, indeed to all writers of the developing world.
In an unintendedly ironic, backhanded manner, Isidore Okpewho pays
homage to this aspect of the self-fashioning, self-mythologizing project
that led Soyinka to Ogun and his tragi-existentialist myths and legends:

No doubt that it is becoming increasingly clear to us that the tragic element
which Soyinka sees in the African character has been projected largely through
his own experience, and that in the end the tormented figure of the Yoruba god,
Ogun, which Soyinka has constantly presented to us cannot be separated from
the trouble-torn personality of our poet-dramatist.[44]

This interpretation of Soyinka's obsession with the myths and symbolism
of Ogun goes to the heart of the centrality of the deity and his significations for the writer's project of self-understanding and self-constitution.
But Okpewho misrecognizes Soyinka's intentions. For these are not so
much about rendering a generalized "African character" as they are
about fashioning surrogates, doubles and incarnations of the self as a
visionary artist and as an activist intellectual whose terrain of operation

is an entire continent. Thus, in placing the weight of Soyinka's adoption of this deity on the "trouble-torn" personality of the writer Okpewho makes a useful point, but he nevertheless elides the question of the social and historic context of this literary mythologization. For even at a cursory level of interpretation, it is not difficult to perceive that the "tormented figure" of the god seems appropriate not only to the "trouble-torn" personality of the writer, it is eminently apposite to a trouble-wracked, post-independence Africa. Beyond this sort of direct correlation of archetype and referent is the far more complicated matter of ambiguity and contradictoriness in Soyinka's Ogun, who turns out to be not merely "tormented," as Okpewho says, but is also, among so many others of his attributes, patron god of song and lyric poetry, liberal imbiber of wine, comrade in battle and play, guardian of sacred oaths and therefore bedrock of moral integrity, protector of orphans, the weak and the destitute. However, Okpewho could have more properly charged Soyinka for an ideological male-centeredness that considerably constrains the "representativeness" of his mobilization of the myths and legends of Ogun for the construction of a paradigmatic figure of the modern African artist. For Soyinka has on many occasions spoken of the complex, multifaceted nature of *his* Ogun; one area in which he has stolidly withheld ambiguity and uncertainty from his Muse – his self-reflecting muse, we may add – is that of gender. For no metaphoric or cultural androgyny, the mixing of the "female" and "male" principles and values in the life of a society, remotely obtrudes into the "virility" that Soyinka celebrates in Ogun.

This last point brings us to the other arc, or cluster, of textual inscriptions of the self in Soyinka's works which we have designated the paradigm of the "unrepresentable" self, of an "unfinalizable" subjectivity. In explicating this dimension of Soyinka's self-fashioning project we turn to one of his most complex and ambitious plays, *The Road*, for an emblematic reading of a crucial episode in the play.

"I offer you sanctuary in my tower of words." This solicitude, expressed almost like a sacrament, is directed by Professor, the protagonist of *The Road*, to his retinue of underclass hangers-on at one of their daily evening carousals. Both the solicitude and the context suggest some of the tropes of the Ogun archetype that we have highlighted: liberal enjoyment of wine, protection of the weak and the dispossessed, patron and guardian of those who work in iron. But coming from Professor, this solicitude, though obviously sincerely meant, is dubious, perhaps even absurd. This is because Professor is nothing if not a "lost," mad visionary and there is no apparent "refuge" for himself, not in his "Aksident Store" and, at a first approximation, not in the confounding madness of his torrent of words. All the same, the offer of a "sanctuary" by this awesome figure is a credible promise and herein lies the complexity of Soyinka's exploration of this issue. The matter turns on the fact that Professor, like the most memorable protagonists of the Nigerian author's literary works, indeed like the playwright himself, has a way with words, he impresses with his verbal eloquence, his uncommon, dazzling use of language. Protagonists and characters like Professor who evince an exceptional mastery of the resources of language, and who additionally manifest a solicitude toward other characters who are in one way or another dependent on them, pervade Soyinka's writings. Such characters include Brother Jero of the two "Jero" plays, Baroka of *The Lion and the Jewel*, Dr. Semuwe of *Requiem for a Futurologist*, the Old Man of *Madmen and Specialists*, Sebe Irawe of *From Zia with Love*. Even the author's father, as fictionalized in several episodes in the life of the character of Akinyode Soditan in *Isara*, belongs in this company of masters of language and its vast potential for liberating the imagination and the human environment (*Isara*, 60, 115–16). In all of these characters, the gift of language and the manipulation of verbal rhetoric is so extensive, so often brilliantly executed that these protagonists' presence in their respective imaginative worlds seems predicated on strategies and effects of language usage. And in the way in which they inhabit, and are in turn inhabited by their "tower of words," they seem to embody Heidegger's description of language as "the house of being."[45] So crucial indeed is the predication of the identity and subjectivity of these protagonists on verbal mastery, that each of them, in their respective dramas, is called upon to either literally *talk* their way out of dangerous, potentially fatal circumstances, (Brother Jero, Dr. Semuwe), or into control and manipulation of other characters in the bitter struggles for advantage, preferment or power (Brother Jero, Baroka, Dr. Semuwe, and Sebe Irawe), or, at their most disconcerting, into undermining the last foundations of their auditors' hold on a secure sense of themselves as centered, rational subjects (Semuwe, Professor, Old Man). This general profile of the vital connection of masterful deployment of language and signification to the construction – and deconstruction – of identity and subjectivity as an index of a radical, almost absolute autonomy of the self, provides a context for an emblematic reading of Professor's offer of a "sanctuary," a refuge, in his "tower of words."

The beginning of the concluding Part Two of the play throws a focused light on the dense suggestiveness of the dramatization of these issues in

The Road. Interestingly, this illumination is produced by a clash of views and attitudes concerning writing and its uses. Basically, the scene involves a mini-drama around Professor's act of transcribing into writing the verbal accounts he has been given by Kotonu and Samson, driver and driver's mate respectively of the passenger lorry, "NO Danger, No Delay," concerning an accident they had witnessed and only barely averted on the road. Kotonu and Samson of course can't read or write, but they are obliged to make a statement for the police files, and so they need the services of Professor.

In differing ways all three are heavily emotionally invested in the transaction of converting the verbal account of the accident into writing. Kotonu is going over the accident mostly as a way of dealing with the trauma of having been so close to the terrible carnage wrought by the accident. Samson, for his part, hopes to get the writing of the account of the accident over with quickly so that he and his mate can get back on the highways. Finally, Professor is over-solicitous in getting the two men to narrate their experience in the hope that their closeness to the carnage, their narrow escape from being victims, has mystical intimations that he may somehow be able to read, thus advancing his quest for an understanding of the link between life and death. Thus, what appears on the surface to be a very simple operation in fact entails almost incommensurable valences of intention and desire in the three subjects in the encounter. Soyinka's dialogue brilliantly captures the very *texture* of this incommensurability:

PROF. (bangs on the table): But you bring back nothing at all. Nothing. How
  do you expect me to make out your statement for the police?
SAMSON: Ah, but you always manage Professor.
PROF.: On nothing? You exaggerate your notion of expressiveness in your
  friend's face. Call him here. (Kotonu comes forward. Professor glares an-
  grily at him). It is only a degree of coarseness, that's all. (Rummages among
  the papers). I need a statement form. Here is one . . . now you tell me,
  you who return empty-handed and empty-minded, what do I write! Well?
  What happened at the bridge? You say the lorry overtook you – good.
  [Writes] Lorry was traveling at excessive speed. You see, I can make up a
  police statement that would dignify the archives of any traffic division, but
  tell me – have I spent all these years in dutiful search only to wind up my
  last moments in meaningless statements? What did you see friend, what
  did you see? Show me the smear of blood on your brain.
KOTONU: There was this lorry . . .
PROF.: Before the event friend, before the event. Were you accessory before the
  fact?

KOTONU: Even before the bridge, I saw what was yet to happen.

PROF. (Puts pen down, softly): You swear to that?

KOTONU: It was a full load and it took some moments overtaking us, heavy it was.

PROF.(Writing furiously): It dragged alongside and after an eternity it pulled to the front swaying from side to side, pregnant with stillborns. Underline – with stillborns (*CP1*, 195–6)

Even the very first sentence that Professor writes from the verbal account he is being given by Samson and Kotonu already strains away from a bare, factual transcription, although he boasts that he can indeed write a masterpiece of precise, factual reportage such as "would dignify the archives of any traffic division." The point of course is that for Professor the "real" is not pre-given or easily recoverable by mere reportage, it comes already semiotized with meaning by the mere act of describing it. Thus, we can see from even this short exchange between Professor and Samson and Kotonu that the verbal account of the two men is elaborately embellished and figuratively transmuted by Professor; as the interaction continues, the distance widens between the verbal narrative and the written transcription of it. Thus, by the end of the scene, Professor is indeed writing a version of the account of the accident narrated to him by Samson and Kotonu that radically departs both from the men's own narrative and their notion of the "real" as literal and empirical; Professor has indeed, in *his* version, moved from the *phenomenal* to the *nuomenal*, and he has infused his transcription with a very private, terrifying vision of the "meaning" of the accident:

PROF. (Writing): Below that bridge a black rise of buttocks, two unyielding thighs and that red trickle like a woman washing her monthly pain in a thin river. So many lives rush in and out between her legs, and most of it a waste.

(*CP1*, 197)

There is in Professor's radical departure from functional, utilitarian and "effective" speech – those designated by J.L. Austin in his speech act theory as "felicitous" – an excessive will to self-expression which, at least on the surface, seems to derive from a perverse kind of self-absorption.[46] Indeed, there is an ethically questionable use of literacy here in the fact that the "statement" desired by Samson and Kotonu never gets written, or is written but not exactly as *they* want it, and not as it could be of any functional use to them. But at another level of the uses of literacy and language – the level of visionary projection and even artistic creation – it ought to be acknowledged that the most powerful artistic works do not simply copy or "reflect" nature and society. At any rate, Professor's flights of utterance and metaphor enable him to push far beyond the limits of mimetic representation to thereby gain access to those figural resources of language and signification which, as poststructuralists remind us in their theory of articulation, open up vast and unsettling possibilities of meaning and non-meaning, identity and agency.[47] What is particularly noteworthy here is that Professor not only leaps ecstatically into domains of language use which disrupt and destabilize demarcations between the literal and the figurative, the functional and the ludic, the demotic and the hieratic, he also wrests from this radical linguistic and significatory disruptiveness an identity which the other characters in the play seem willing to validate and celebrate. We see this in the unabashed (and successful) call by Professor for himself to *be* hailed by the other characters as a benefactor through his fantastic flights of language and rhetoric:

PROF.: It is true I am a gleaner, I dare not be swayed by marvels. Stick to the air and open earth, wet my feet in morning dew, glean words from the road. Remain with the open eye of earth until the shadow of the usurping word touches my place of exile. But I broke my habit. I succumbed to the flaunting of a single word, forgot that exercise of spirit which demand that I make daily pilgrimage in search of leavings. I deserted my course, and – rightly – I lost my way. That was the vengeance of the word. (His manner changes gradually, becomes more deliberate, emphatic, like someone giving a lecture. And they listen, attentive, as if to a customary lesson in their daily routine.) But don't we all change from minute to minute? (Turns in his chair, half-facing them) I pick my word only among rejects . . . My task is to keep company with the fallen, and this word rose in pride above spiked bushes. We must all stick together. Only the fallen have need for restitution. (He turns round to his table, waves them off)*Call out the hymn. Any song will do but to restore my confidence make it a song of praise. But mind you don't disturb me. I feel like working.* (Falls straight on his papers as the group sings his favorite praise-song) (*CP1*, 219–20)(My emphasis)

To read this scene allegorically again from Professor's way with language in *The Road*, there are obvious gaps between, on the one hand, his moments of pragmatic, rational discourses on "business" activities to sustain supplies for the "Aksident Store" and, on the other hand, his discourses on "the word" which entail the use of language in very abstruse, elliptical ways, presumably to gain access to the numinous domains of being and consciousness. For it is incontestable that Professor privileges the latter over the former; and he certainly seems to be superciliously unmindful of the fact that his written version of Samson's and Kotonu's account of the road accident has moved decisively from their expectation of an objective transcription to a private, phantasmic vision of what actually happened. This vision is very distant from an empiricist, functionalist conception of the "real" because it is expressed through an excess of signification which taps into vistas of imagined, counterfactual worlds where Professor's subjectivity, his being, finds itself again after its loss in the degraded world, the alienated, intolerable reality of the daily lives of the working class, lumpen and underclass characters with whom he has taken up a precarious abode. And wherein may these counterfactual worlds which "redeem" the violently destructive, "fallen" world around him be found but in, and through language? This is why Professor's quest in this play is a search for the "word." In a "fallen," alienated world the "word" is inevitably lost; only a recovery of the "word" can help set things aright once again. This plays adroitly on one of the most important of Yoruba aphorisms on language, signification and semantics. As the Yoruba metaproverb puts it: "owe lesin oro; t'oro ba sonu, owe ni a fi n wa." (Proverbs or metaphors are the horses of speech; when words are lost and speech lapses into an incommensurable chasm between Being and the event or the moment, proverbs or metaphors lead us back to meaningful words and speeech). It is largely because of this crucial dimension of *The Road* and the philosophically idealist faith of its protagonist in the redemptive, sacramental power of words and language that critics like Elaine Fido and Segun Adekoya, who are particularly responsive to this aspect of the play, have linked its brilliant use of language to issues of spirituality and metaphysics.[48] And this particular structure explains and undergirds Soyinka's reputation as a consistently inventive wordsmith; it also accounts for the pervasiveness of extensive wordplay and elaborate language games in his writings, as much in his nonfictional works as in his plays, novels and poetry. Finally, it is at the root of our author's avantgardist approach to the received conventions of the traditional genres, especially in drama and poetry.

The location of the self in an endless chain of linguistic signification – such as we see in Professor's flights into language and its limitless resources – constitutes a mode of aestheticized self-fashioning as a free spirit, an existential nomad, an ideological anarchist. Not surprising, the "self" of this particular mode of imagining can only intersect in irreconcilable tension with the "self" imagined through the Ogun archetype, for even with that archetype's considerable latitude for contradictory attributes, its mode of construction does presuppose that the "endless" chain of signification can, or should, be constantly "arrested" around either contingent or normative, universal poles of ethical investments and ideological commitments. It is thus a mark of the suppleness of Soyinka's project of self-invention that it seems completely untroubled by this tension. However, what is truly remarkable but very daunting for his critics is the fact that the Nigerian writer-activist can vibrantly appropriate the burden(s) of ethical and political obligations inherent in the Ogun archetype, and at the same time celebrate the principle of the ultimate impossibility of codifying selfhood and experience into an ordered, fixed and stable identity, as the following "mantra" from that tapestry of the Yoruba creation myths in Kola's painting in *The Interpreters* demonstrates:

Of the eternal word of the first procedure with the long sickle head of chance, eternally mocking the pretension of the bowl of plan, mocking lines of order in the ring of chaos (*TI*, 224)

This study takes its interpretive and analytical point of departure from the dialectical interplay of the two paradigms we have outlined in this chapter. In essence this pertains to the centrality of a project of self-fashioning as an African, postcolonial writer in Soyinka's writings and career. To restate them, these are, respectively, the arc or paradigm of a subliminally "representative" self, a self that our author anchors symbolically in the mythic traditions of the god, Ogun; and the arc of an "unrepresentable," unanchored, "ludic" self born of an excess of signification and the unfinalizeability of "meaning." Although basically unanchored, this latter paradigm, I would suggest, strongly resonates with the ritual and mythic traditions of the Yoruba trickster god of chance, mischief and indeterminacy, Eshu, a deity whom, remarkably, Soyinka has largely left out of his extensive appropriations of mythic and ritual materials from Yoruba cultural, expressive matrices. This line of interpretation is all the more compelling given the fact of Soyinka's great predilection for satire and parody, those specific expressive and performative idioms which, within the Yoruba tradition, have been assigned to the patronage of Eshu.[49] Thus, it would seem that with extensive, some would say decisive, use of parodic and satiric modes and idioms in Soyinka's dramatic and non-dramatic writings, Eshu ought now to take his rightful place beside Ogun as the poet-dramatist's composite or double-headed muse. This is indeed a central premise of this study in its reading of Soyinka's literary use of mythic and ritual material. Moreover, it is a hermeneutic strategy that receives support from the fact that Eshu, not Ogun, as shown in the impressive work of scholarship of Ayodele Ogundipe and H.L. Gates, Jr., is the lord of the crossroads and the incarnation of liminality, two associated conceptions which are central elements of Soyinka's mythopoesis.⁵⁰

If the coupling of order and chaos, causality and contingency in the passage quoted above from *The Interpreters* is strongly suggestive of the modernists' veneration of ambiguity, or perhaps even of the poststructuralists' celebration of radical indeterminacy, this should cause no surprise since we do know that the influence of Western aesthetic thought on Soyinka has been quite profound. More than one critic has pointed out that Soyinka's disquisition on the Ogun archetype in his important essay, "The Fourth Stage," and in some of the essays in *Myth, Literature and the African World* bear a very strong resemblance to Nietzsche's presentation of the Dionysian temper and sensibility in *The Birth of Tragedy*.⁵¹ But it is also the case that Soyinka's coupling of order and chaos, causality and contingency is also a derivative of Yoruba cosmological thought since Eshu, as principle of contingency and chance, is always shown in Yoruba sacred iconography by the side of Ifa or Orunmila, the Yoruba god of wisdom and divination, endless fount of gnostic, doxological knowledge.

In bringing our discussion in this chapter to a statement of its pertinence to the organization of the other chapters of this study, it is necessary to return to our emblematic reading of that scene of Professor's rewriting of the account he is given of a road accident by Kotonu and Samson. In this regard, let us recall that we left off at the point at which Professor asks for a "song of praise" from the auditors of his spellbinding discourses, his "tower of words," as he puts it. It would seem that his deployment of his extraordinary linguistic and rhetorical skills, both in speaking and writing, engenders from his auditors divided, heterodox responses. In the scene, most of his listeners submit willingly to, and are transported by the magic and poetry of his flights of speech; some are also enthralled but remain somewhat detached; and not a few, led by Say-Tokyo Kid, are intimidated and hostile. Significantly, no one is indifferent to the presence powerfully constructed by Professor's strange, haunting discourses. This differentiation of responses calls for a scrutiny of its analogical relevance for Soyinka's self-fashioning project, and more generally, for his writings and the pattern of responses they have engendered.

Professor's linguistic skills enable him to minister to the needs of his underclass cohorts; he writes required briefs and reports for them, alters documents which allow them to survive economically in a rigged, corrupt and violent socioeconomic order. For these acts, our man is highly valued and cherished; he does, at least on this count, after all provide a "sanctuary" in his "tower of words" through his considerable ability to manipulate signs and language. What is particularly important here is that Professor's underclass beneficiaries are themselves, in their own ways, accomplished in deploying and manipulating the resources of language – but only in the oral, non-scribal idioms.

Of a very different import are Professor's verbal fireworks in pursuit of "the word." In this particular regard he operates as a "priest," a mystic, a shaman whose linguistic acts are rites of communion seeking to penetrate the mysteries of life and existence, especially its banal but often unanticipated and unexpected tragedies and absurdities. In this particular domain, Professor's invitation to his "tower" of words draws a more ambiguous response from his audience. And this seems logical and unexceptionable since linguistic communication and effectivity in practical matters are more easily measurable, more commensurate with concrete needs, desires and aspirations than with strivings that are eschatological and metaphysical. Thus, Professor's audience seems deeply appreciative of his services as "consultant" and as a forger of licenses; but while they are dazzled by his torrential verbal disquisition on "the word," they feel confounded by what they see as the "blasphemy" in some of these discourses, and for this reason, in their terror they ultimately slay him.

Reading this structure of responses to Professor's language use(s) analogically to Soyinka's writings, one problem that immediately arises concerns the fact that while Professor's underclass auditors in *The Road* insist on making a distinction between language and speech acts which are utilitarian and those which open up disturbing possibilities of (non)meaning, Professor himself – and presumably his creator – in fact sees no such clear and rigid division between the pragmatic, demotic aspects of language use and the hieratic, ritual articulations of metaphysical yearnings. In effect then, what this entails is an insistence that no particular domain of expression and communication, through language and signification, be privileged above others: the solace or "sanctuary" afforded by the artist's "towers of words" involves all genres, modes and forms of communication. Moreover, there is an insistence here that the sensibility of the artist-communicator remains essentially unchanged and indivisible regardless of the genre, form or occasion of expression.

Like the enthralled but somewhat more detached auditors of Professor's profane, spellbinding discourses at the evening carousals in the "Aksident Store," some critics and scholars of Soyinka's literary career see in his vast corpus a variety of emphases, a lot of unevenness, some gaps, and even dissonances and ruptures.[52] It is in the light of this particular critical stance that we can perceive an apparent discontinuity between the aesthetic philosophy of the "early" Soyinka and the more fully elaborated poetics of culture that he began to articulate vigorously in the mid-1970s. Similarly, this insistence on gaps and dissonances in Soyinka's writings and career underwrites a basic contention of this study that while Soyinka may insist that *all* forms and domains of language use and speech acts are equally important and integral to his sensibility, he has in fact both in "writerly" practice and in his aesthetic philosophy, tended to privilege certain domains and modes of expression and signi-fication over others. Indeed, this study is fundamentally predicated on attentiveness to this aspect of Soyinka's creative sensibilities, an attentive-ness to his obsession with the vast possibilities of non-mimetic, elaborately mythopoeic and unconventional dimensions of language and significa-tion, as captured in the following passage from the essay, "The Fourth Stage":

Language therefore is not a barrier to the profound universality of music but a cohesive dimension and clarification of that wilfully independent art-form which we label music. Language reverts in religious rites to its pristine exis-tence, eschewing the sterile limits of particularization . . . and words are taken back to their roots, to their original poetic sources when fusion was total and the movement of words was the very passage of music and the dance of im-ages. Language is still the embryo of thought and music where myth is daily companion, for there language is constantly mythopoeic. (*ADO2*, 31)

Some key ideas and tropes in this passage are worth noting: "myth (as) daily companion"; language as "embryo of thought and music" in such a cultural context; consequently, this enables us to accord a paradigmatic status to the way that language "reverts in religious rites to its pristine ex-istence, eschewing the sterile limits of particularization." The aesthetic and philosophical attitudes to language and signification expressed in these formulations do not exhaust the range of Soyinka's ideas and at-titudes about artistic creation, but they abound in his writings and are particularly central to his most ambitious, most experimental works. At-tentiveness to this pervasive feature of his corpus provides the underlying rationale for the organization of the chapters of this study around the convention-stretching, genre-bending motive force that operates differ-entially and with varying results in Soyinka's writings in the genres of drama, prose fiction and poetry. In other words, while on the surface the study is organized around the traditional boundaries between the genres, "genre" is conceived in this study as the site of great aesthetic, ideological and ethical contestations. This seems only logical in the work of an artist and thinker who not only writes in *all* the genres but does so cross-generically, decisively infusing the sensibilities of a gifted poet into his dramatic works and his works of fictional and non-fictional prose while also incorporating extensive narrative and dramatic modes into his formal verse. To place this in a broader historical and cultural context, for Soyinka genre and form, technique and idiom necessarily undergo complex acts of translation and transformation when they cross real and artificial boundaries separating the literary and cultural traditions of Africa and the West, or of the ex-colonized and the ex-colonizers. For, as Soyinka conceives of the matter, this is the basis of *any* truly innovative and liberatory aesthetic practice and experience in our postcolonial age. Thus, in organizing the contents of this study around the rubric of genre, one works with *and* against conventional notions of genres as bounded formal types, as fixed and distinct aesthetic and cultural codifications of experience. This is why in this study, the chapters on drama, prose and poetry all entail analyses and evaluations of Soyinka's self-expression both within the normative conventions of these genres and, more important, his radical extensions of genre and form to negotiate the conflicting demands of what we have identified in this chapter as the paradigms of the representative and the unrepresentable selves. And this is as much in his most successful works as in the few considerably flawed works in his corpus. Before coming to chapters on drama, prose and poetry, we turn in the following chapter to a comprehensive exploration of a particularly combative and embattled "generic" site of Soyinka's works, this being his critical and theoretical writings.

CHAPTER 2

Tragic mythopoesis as postcolonial discourse: critical and theoretical writings

There are only two ways to go about forming racial concepts: either one causes certain subjective characteristics to become objective, or else one tries to interiorize objectively revealed manners of conduct. Thus, the black man who asserts his negritude by means of a revolutionary movement immediately places himself in the position of having to meditate, either because he wishes to recognize in himself certain objectively established traits of the African civilization or because he hopes to discover the Essence of blackness in the well of his heart. Thus, subjectivity reappears, the relation of the self with the self, the source of all poetry . . .

> Jean-Paul Sartre, "Orphée Noir"

Esu sleeps in the house/But the house is too small for him/Esu sleeps on the front yard/But the yard is too constricting for him/Esu sleeps in the palm-nut shell/Now he has room enough to stretch at large.

> From a Praise-poem to Esu, the Yoruba god of fate, chance and contingency

Considering the fact that there are only three volumes of the published critical and theoretical essays of Soyinka – *Myth, Literature and the African World, Art, Dialogue and Outrage, The Burden of Memory and the Muse of Forgiveness* – Derek Wright's estimate that in this group of our author's writings we have "the substance of over 1,000 pages of critical prose" may seem an exaggeration.[1] But Wright speaks of "substance" and this seems quite valid if, to the three volumes of collected, published essays, we add the large quantity of uncollected but published materials like essays, prefaces by Soyinka to his own plays, innumerable pieces of political and cultural journalism, and, especially, interviews.[2] These published but uncollected pieces, together with the collected volumes, properly constitute the complement of Soyinka's critical prose. Thus, it is necessary to emphasize that there is much else besides the three titles that are of crucial import in taking a full measure of Soyinka as a theorist and critic. To give only a succinct illustration of this point, two early essays of our author, "The Future of West African Writing" and "After the Narcissist?" are not included in any of the three collected volumes; yet the former has the significance of being the first ever published piece of Soyinka's criticism, and the latter contains a major metacritical reflection on the criticism of African writings of the immediate post-independence period.

These facts and aspects of Soyinka's critical and theoretical writings make it possible to offer some general observations on his critical thought. First, we may surmise that if it is the case that Soyinka is first and foremost a poet and dramatist, his claims to consideration as a major theorist and critic are nonetheless quite formidable. This point is demonstrated by the growing body of scholarly work that this body of his writings has attracted.[3] Second, it ought to be noted that Soyinka's theoretical and critical writings have spanned the entire course of his literary career and thus have a close, reciprocal but dialogical relationship to his imaginative works. Third, and in relation to this previous observation, it is fortuitous that there seems to be a sharp divide between the early critical writings of Soyinka and his mature critical thought, a divide which seems, at first glance, to be absent in the corpus of dramas, poetry, fictional prose and biographical memoirs. Since this break did as a matter of fact extend to both the imaginative writings and the theoretical and critical writings, and since it has all but been ignored in Soyinka criticism, it may serve as a point of entry into a critical review of the Nigerian author's critical and theoretical writings.

In the mid-1970s, Soyinka published a number of works that collectively seemed to indicate a radical departure from the direction and tenor of his previous imaginative works and, particularly, his critical writings. At the most apparent level, this rupture between the Soyinka of the late 1950s through the 1960s to the early 1970s, and the Soyinka who began to emerge in the mid-1970s seems so fundamental as to invite comparisons with the alleged radical discontinuity, the *coupure epistemologique* that Althusserians have urged between the early, "humanistic" Marx of say, *The German Ideology* and the mature, "scientific" Marx of *Capital*.[4] Analogically, it seems that while the "early" Soyinka of such works as *A Dance of the Forests* (1960), *The Strong Breed* (1963), *The Swamp Dwellers* (1963), and *The Interpreters* (1965), as well as essays such as "The Future of West African Writing" (1958), "Towards a True Theatre" (1962), "From a Common Back Cloth: A Reassessment of the African Literary Image" (1963), "And After the Narcissist?" (1965), and "The Writer in a Modern African State" (1967) had been vigorously anti-Négritudinist on the subject of race, culture and nationalism, the Soyinka of works of the mid-1970s such as *Poems of Black Africa* (1974), *Death and the King's Horseman* (1975) and *Ogun Abibiman*, (1976), and the essays collected in *Myth Literature and the African World* (1976) evinces an assertive, if extremely complex neo-Négritudinist temper. In the first group of imaginative works and essays, so strong is the critique of the romanticization of African precolonial traditions and the African past that Soyinka escapes the charge of ideological anti-nationalism or cultural deracination only because nearly all of these works and essays also contain powerful, if critical affirmations of the positive, humanistic aspects of that same precolonial past and its cultural traditions. Stated differently, if none of the protagonist characters of these works who embody a searing indictment of tradition can be remotely deemed deracinated or alienated "natives", it is nonetheless true that they do wage ferocious assaults on mystification and complacency toward the ambiguous legacies of the past. In *A Dance*, this role is embodied in Forest Head who organizes the entire sprawling plot of the play around a determination to confront the play's central characters, not with the glorious past they demand of him, but with the corruptions and brutalities which disfigured that past, especially the past of their great empires. *The Strong Breed* and *The Swamp Dwellers* both contain naturalistic versions of the epic, allegorical indictments of *A Dance*; in both plays, official guardians and priestly functionaries on whom the legitimacy of cultural tradition depends are shown to be ruthless and petty-minded toward any questioning, any exposure of their compromised, self-serving manipulation of tradition. The relationship of the plural, collective protagonists of *The Interpreters* to the past and to tradition is more complexly differentiated, but the single-mindedness with which these "interpreters" pursue *their* own appropriations of tradition in defiance of normative, conventional views and practices is entirely consistent with the pattern established by the earlier works. The disdainful musings of the "interpreters," the novel's protagonists, on romantic nationalist myth-making, and specifically on Négritude, is a major part of the ideological discourse of the novel, a discourse that pervades all of Soyinka's early critical essays.[5]

In sharp contrast to this profile, the works of the 1970s and early 1980s are nothing if not neo-Négritudinist in their evaluation of the African past and of precolonial African traditions. In Soyinka's critical writings, the identification and valorization of a distinct "Black World" is first theorized in the Preface to *Poems of Black Africa*; it assumes vigorous thematic and figural inscriptions in *Death and the King's Horseman, Ogun Abibiman*

and, above all, *Myth, Literature and the African World.* Where the protagonists of the earlier group of works strenuously distance themselves from
the normative, customary institutions and practices of precolonial tradition and culture, the protagonist characters in this second group of works
are equally determined to locate themselves in, and celebrate these very
centres and matrices of collective tradition. Thus, that there does seem
to be a gulf between these two bodies of Soyinka's imaginative writings
and essays is a product of both the distance between their respective
ideological discourses and the abruptness of the shift from one ideological register to another. It is indeed a combination of this distance and
this abruptness that suggests an epistemological break between the early
anti-Négritudist Soyinka and the seeming neo-Négritudist theorist of the
second and third decades of the post-independence era.

Although the biographical facts which establish this point about
Soyinka are well known, they do call for a critical review. His early career
as writer and critic closely followed his return to Nigeria after years of sojourn in England, first as an undergraduate and later as a fellow-traveler
in the celebrated revival in the British theatre of the period. Highly conscious of his situation as a "returnee" to the newly independent nation,
Soyinka began a comprehensive research into the indigenous traditions
of theatre in West Africa soon after his return; these years of his early
career saw him traveling extensively in Africa and Europe and these are
reflected in some of the critical essays. More crucial perhaps is the fact
that our author gradually reinvented himself as indeed one who never,
at least mentally, left "home" in the period of his sojourn abroad. And
from this emerged the intricate web of Soyinka's self-presentation as a
cosmopolitan autochthon, an urbane but rooted, centered "returnee"
which is very palpable in his early critical prose and his creative works of
the period. Moreover, the intricacy of this intermixture defies any simple,
uncomplicated links to biography or chronology. Certainly, the sense of
a radical divide in the Nigerian author's critical thought collapses in the
face of a careful reading of the totality of Soyinka's critical prose. In place
of a decisive rupture, what is revealed by such a careful interpretive act is
a body of postcolonial critical discourse which neither avoids nor reifies
the dichotomies of local and metropolitan, African and Western, old and
new precisely because it is remarkably attentive to the changes acting
on these dichotomous categories and reconfiguring them in the course
a tumultuous historical period. Indeed, in one of the few instances of his
own reflections on this subject, Soyinka admits that a shift did take place
in his discourse on race and cultural politics in the early 1970s, but he

implicitly denies the suggestion of a resultant radical divide in his critical thought:

> If I do not exercise great caution, I know that I may end up with no persuasive defense against some kind of declaration by a nettled European critic or artist that, "in the early Seventies, a certain notorious African playwright underwent a crisis of racism". Certainly, I am aware that my pronouncements on Euramerican society and culture have become more abrasive, less compromising, while recourse to the contrast provided by mine has tended, even by the very fact of comparison, to magnify its virtues. I hope I may yet withdraw from the brink – close to which I of course deny ever being (*ADO2*, 40)

This momentous annunciation raises many questions: what explains this seeming shift in Soyinka's critical discourse on race and ideology, and on race and cultural politics, especially as inscribed in his critical and theoretical writings? And if this shift does not amount to a radical break, how are we to read those writings that belong in the anti-Négritudist phase in relation to the dominant neo-Négritudism of the essays of the mid-1970s to the early 1980s? How might we read the shifts and turns in the entirety of Soyinka's critical and theoretical writings in the light of his early prognostications on the future of postcolonial writing, a "future" which his own subsequent creative and critical writings in part helped to produce? And finally: how does the very practice of critique, of critical intelligence operating as an emancipatory epistemic activity in these early essays, compare with Soyinka's considerable antipathy towards critics and criticism in his mature critical and theoretical prose?

These questions are crucial in the light of the fact that the early essays of Soyinka also established some of the idiosyncratic features through which he would, in his latter, more mature essays, elaborate what is perhaps the central element of his entire critical-theoretical project: the elaboration of a distinctively African literary modernity through a poetics of culture and a revolutionary tragic mythopoesis which is also neo-modernist. Some of these constant features of Soyinka's critical prose are the primacy of metaphoric, figural or poetic iteration over expostulatory analysis in his critical and theoretical writings; the pervasiveness of a sort of negative critique by which the positive contents and rubrics of this African literary modernity are established and highlighted primarily by vigorously polemical, deconstructive assaults on diverse local Nigerian and foreign interlocutors and adversaries; and the prevalence of what might be described as self-quotation throughout his critical and theoretical writings as Soyinka repeatedly redeploys and refurbishes motifs, clusters of ideas and tropes – and even entire passages – that have appeared in previous essays.[6]

Against the background of this general profile of the totality of Soyinka's critical and theoretical writings, this chapter identifies and explores three phases of the author's critical thought, but not as completely distinct or disconnected formations. Rather, the purpose in adopting this approach is to highlight an aspect of this body of the Nigerian author's writings that has generally been ignored. This is the fact that there is, even within the similarities and and continuities between the three phases, a discernible evolution, a process of maturation in Soyinka's critical thought that is important to delineate since this has considerable value for historically grounded and contextual readings of Soyinka's works in particular and, more generally, his entire career. It is perhaps useful to give a brief outline of each of these three phases before exploring each one in fairly detailed readings of the essays and books that correspond to each particular phase.

The first phase begins with the vigorously articulated anti-Négritudism of Soyinka's early critical essays and ends with our author's most important essay on tragedy and art, "The Fourth Stage." The ferocious assault in most of these early essays on what our author deems the self-exoticization and provincialism of much of the "new" literature of post-independent Africa marks this phase decisively as that of a "returnee" whose sojourn in Europe at a formative stage in his early career had predisposed to the promotion of an as yet unexamined cosmopolitanism and universalism. "Cosmopolitanism" here means, concretely, a reinvention of many of the characteristic themes and attitudes of the Western post-romantic, post-realist cultural and aesthetic avant-garde, especially in the light of their startling and invigorating prefigurations in many pre-colonial African expressive traditions and representational idioms. This phase is the most combative, the most self-confidently revolutionary of the three phases of Soyinka's critical and theoretical writings, even if the nature and scope of the "revolution" would only very gradually be thought through in the subsequent phases.

The second phase corresponds to the period inaugurated by the "annunciation" that we have identified earlier in the Preface to *Myth, Literature and the African World*. If the neo-Négritudism of this phase is no less assertively and combatively articulated as the anti-Négritudism of the first phase, it remains true that Soyinka is *defensively* combative in this second phase in a manner that he was not, and could not have been, in the first phase. This is because it is an embattled theorist, critic and polemicist that we encounter in this phase. And in this connection, not the least of his objects of attack here are precisely the Western modernist and avant-garde cultural and literary currents that Soyinka had more or less embraced in the first phase. Moreover, race being a central subject of the discourse in this phase, the historic experiences of slavery, colonialism and epistemic racism enter into Soyinka's critical discourse in this phase and not in the first phase.

If the third phase – corresponding to the essays and writings of the late 1980s and 1990s – returns us to the cosmopolitanism of the first phase, it is a neo-cosmopolitanism quite unlike the unexamined and rather abstractly pessimistic universalism of the first phase. Taking our cue from the title of one of the most significant essays in this third phase, "Climates of Art," the "climates" of culture and the arts in diverse regions of the contemporary world are the main objects of analysis and speculation in the discourses of this phase. Even the thematics of "race" and of the elaboration of a "Black world" which includes both the continent and the Diasporas, both of which are dominant topics in the writings of the second phase, are redefined in this third phase in more intellectually rigorous and more ideologically nuanced ways.

Before moving to an elaboration of the anti-Négritudist cosmopolitanism of the first phase of Soyinka's critical prose, a word of clarification is perhaps necessary on the usefulness of dividing his theoretical writings into phases, especially into a quasi-Hegelian triadic movement of "becoming." Famously, Fanon divided the writings of all colonized societies seeking to end their colonization and move into another, more liberated epoch of history into this same triadic movement, this in his greatest theoretical work, *The Wretched of the Earth*.[7] The three phases in Fanon's schema – which have been widely and most uncritically applied to the writings of virtually all formerly colonized groups and societies – are: a first phase of a derivative, imitative literature based on barely assimilated models and influences from the colonizers; a second phase of more or less extreme nativist reaction to, and in many cases rejection of, all models and influences from the colonizers; and a final phase of what Fanon calls a "fighting" literature, a people's literature, a revolutionary literature. It is instructive that while in terms of the movement of modern, postcolonial African literatures the works of Soyinka and his generation collectively straddle Fanon's second and third phases, Soyinka's own critical thought, as the outline given above indicates, defies any direct and uncomplicated assimilation into the schema of Fanon's three phases. Indeed, it would seem that the motive force of the very first phase of the Nigerian author's own critical thought, as we will presently demonstrate, is an obsessive concern that, with few notable exceptions, the writings of his generation, the so-called "literature of rediscovery" – together with the writings of the generation of Senghor and the whole Négritude movement – was bogged down permanently in Fanon's second phase, the phase of a nativist counterdiscourse to Western paradigms and discourses. This point provides a useful bridgehead to our exploration of this first phase of Soyinka's critical and theoretical writings.

By the time Soyinka launched his career as a critic and theorist, the Négritude writers and the critical pundits of the "rediscovery" phase of contemporary African literature, of whom L.S. Senghor and Alioune Diop are major figures, had established what they deemed appropriate, empowering responses to the binarisms of "indigenous" and "foreign," African and Western, "traditional" and "modern" and other questions of the challenge of capitalist modernity to Africa.[8] In the main, and with few but significant exceptions, these responses rested on the thesis of a fundamental clash of world-views, an incommensurable antithesis between African and European cultural traditions, an antithesis thought resolvable only through abstract syntheses of the best attributes and values of both traditions.[9] The critique single-mindedly sustained through virtually all of Soyinka's early critical essays challenged these claims and questioned the validity of their aesthetic ramifications. The essays in question are "Towards a True Theatre," "From a Common Back cloth," "And After the Narcissist?," "The Writer in Modern African State" and "The Fourth Stage." Each of these five essays addressed a specific, different subject, or group of issues or writers, but they all converged upon a sustained and penetrating questioning of the ideas, premises and attitudes which sought to celebrate and legitimate the so-called postcolonial "literature of rediscovery." It should, of course, be emphasized that these essays are in the main in basic agreement with the implied "renaissance" or "cultural reawakening" inherent in the notion of a "rediscovery" after the long night of colonial cultural subjugation; what these essays vigorously contested were the superficialities and the paradoxes of self-negation in apparent self-assertion in the postures, attitudes and ideas of the standard bearers and pundits of "rediscovery."

"Towards a True Theatre" is the most programmatic of these early essays, as the title implies. The "falsehood" negatively suggested in this title is wittily spelt out in Soyinka's dryly sarcastic delineation of the atmosphere of "preciosity" and "sterility" which the author sees as gradually pervading the new "National Theatre" and "Arts Theatre" movements of the continent, especially in East and West Africa. The source identified for this trend is the same everywhere: imitative appropriation of out-moded, cumbersome or incongruous Western theatre forms and prac-tices as symbols of progress or "modernness." And the perpetrators, in Soyinka's view, are amateurs and enthusiasts made up of expatriates and their pseudo-bourgeois local cohorts, as well as the new apparatchiks of state bureaucracies responsible for national policies regarding culture and the arts. "Towards a True Theatre" is Soyinka's shortest critical es-say, but even within this brevity, the critic is at pains to complicate and finesse his call for a spirit of novelty and experimentation in the "new" arts and literature(s) of the continent; specifically, he is careful to point out that beyond the ludicrousness of the imitation of dubious "modern" Western theatrical influences, there is something far more insidious:

I am not of course trying to create a morality for theatrical selectiveness. *The Merry Widow* has its place on the Nigerian scene as a piece of exoticism; the crime is that it is the forces of *The Merry Widow* which have upheld what we may call the Arts Theatre mentality . . . By all means, let us be accommodating – and I say this genuinely – there is room anywhere, and at any stage of development, for every sort of theatre. But when Anouilh and (for God's sake!) Christopher Fry possess audience mentality and budding student talent in traps from which the British theatre is only slowly extricating itself, then it is probably time for a little intolerance against the octopine symbol of the Arts Theatre (*ADO2*, 4–5)

What is at stake, Soyinka argues in this passage, is the misdirection of creative energies – especially of young, talented student actors and fledgling playwrights – through the importation of outmoded foreign models which are touted as symbols of "modernness."

"From a Common Backcloth" considerably expanded the terms of this critique. The "backcloth" metaphor in the title of the essay refers to the stock of ideas, themes and imagery from which the "new" African litera-ture could draw and on which it could legitimately base its identity. This motif of a "backcloth" lends Soyinka much figural play as he argues force-fully for the rejection of both the "imposed back cloth of primitivism" foisted on African writing by supercilious, "primitivizing" foreign criti-cal pundits, and the "wishful backcloth" of an unspoilt African human nature, a presumed closeness to the heart of Being which, as Négritudist theorists averred, will be Africa's special contribution to world civiliza-tion. Indeed, the thrust of the essay is provided by Soyinka's contention that the most powerful individual talents in the emergent African liter-ature had already laid to rest the primitivist and exoticist rubrics still being touted by foreign "promoters" of African literature. Sentiments conveyed by the following observations pervade the essay: "A very long time ago, the discerning African rejected the anthropological novel. Perhaps during the next twenty years his foreign counterpart will do the same." (*ADO2*, 9) Or: "Those who consider the modern imagery of Amos Tutuola a sign of impurity represent the diminishing minority of African primevalists." (*ADO2*, 9)

Given these sentiments, it should hardly be surprising that Soyinka's most severe critical censure in this essay is directed not at the vanishing breed of foreign Africanist "primevalists," but at African writers who seem to invite, and indeed thrive on, foreign critical condescension, and who collude with the concepts of the African as a true, unspoilt innocent. Particularly savaged by Soyinka in this regard are the fiction writers of the so-called "anthropological novel" and those of the related "culture conflict" school, both of which, in Soyinka's view, are varieties of a superficial, self-exoticizing traditionalism or nativism. Against this, the essay identifies a number of African writers, chiefly Alex La Guma, Mongo Beti, Chinua Achebe and Amos Tutuola, who are praised for forging their own unique, exciting and complex "backcloths." We can thus see a sort of proleptic structure to the argument of this essay in which there is a movement from the "imposed" and "wishful" "backcloths" to the unique, individual idioms being fashioned by the most powerful talents through self-confident and complex appropriations from both African oral sources and Western written models, from contiguously local materials as well as materials appropriated from other cultures and traditions.

The sense of this proleptic movement dominates "And After the Narcissist?," "The Writer in a Modern African State" and "The Fourth Stage," but only in a very complex mediation which, moreover, is deeply inflected with pessimism. It is as if in Soyinka's despairing but outraged view, the very cultural and historical contexts of cultural "rediscovery" conspire to entrench in African writing the "imposed" and "wishful" backcloths so reviled by him, so that instead of the self-confident and complex individual talent and vision required, only self-exoticizing narcissists are bred by the dynamics of the self-absorption of a "rediscovered self."

"And After the Narcissist?" considerably refined this critique, proffering in the process some permanently valid and illuminating commentary on exhibitionist cultural narcissism as the inevitable, even enabling ground on which a dangerously racialized poetics takes root. The essay appropriately focuses on poetry, and more specifically on the excessively aestheticized persona of the Négritudist poet. Psychobiographical topoi such as the womb, the navel and the memory of natal security before the pain and "exile" of birth and individuation are deployed by Soyinka as analogues of the escapist poetic landscape of Négritude. Soyinka's own words are much sharper on this point:

> Poets feed first on the self (anyway); it is the extension of "self" into history and mythology, into society and even into contemporary responsibility which is a conspicuous development in the self-consciousness of most African writers, *since it does not appear to correspond to the degree of creative processing*. Narcissism begins when the writer fails to distinguish between self-exploration and self-manipulation. The latter, overburdened with metaphors usually of thinly disguised precon-cepts, is indeed a work of love, motivated by external responsibility. But self-love is self-love and is far more superficial than the bereavement, the curiosity, or the revelation. (Soyinka, 1966, 54) (my emphasis)

The sustained critique of poetic solipsism in this essay perhaps achieves its most telling expression in Soyinka's insistence that the diverse modes and effects of narcissism – exhibitionism, self-exoticization, passivity, im-mobilism – are all linked to a superficial, factitious, externally imposed intellectualism. In the caustic terms of this particular critique, the "self" vigorously asserted in the writings of Négritude and its offshoots is mostly compounded of facile concepts and a "and magnitude of unfelt abstrac-tions" which make of "the common backcloth" or the cultural heritage, a mere racial label, a badge of "authenticity" hardly ever elicited from genuine literary introspection or exploration of events and phenomena. This critique, it ought to be noted, is fine tuned: it is not intellectual-ism in itself that Soyinka finds fatal to the intense self-awareness of the "literature of rediscovery"; rather, it is what he regards as the peculiarly otiose intellectualism which breeds exoticists, self-willed primitivists and "quaintness mongers" among African writers that Soyinka finds particu-larly deleterious, especially since it provides ready rationalization for the paternalism and condescension of the (re)colonizing gaze of European promoters of the new African literature.

One particular expression of this kind of intellectualism which Soyinka relentlessly assailed in this essay – and others as well – is the pervasive Négritude cult of Africans or blacks as the world's last true "naturals" whose great mission is to rehumanize the species and thereby reverse the reified over-mechanization of the human person set in motion by the technological civilization of the West. That mature, "serious" poets and critics could repetitively peddle and recycle this "unfelt abstrac-tion" in the context of the increasing violence of affairs in the new post-independence states of Africa considerably angered the Soyinka that we encounter in these early critical essays. It is thus no wonder that in taking up his critical lances as the nemesis of the Négritude cult of blacks as nature's innocents, Soyinka *appeared* to be going in the extreme opposite direction, that of a rejection, on the basis of an abstract universalism, of any form, or expression, of an African cultural particularism:

The consideration which brings me, personally, down to earth is the thought of the Angolan or South African writer, either in exile or making his last feeble twitches before the inexorable maul of a desperate regime ends him. It is this exercise of trying to read his mind when he is confronted by the operation of the human factor in black states in which he had fixed his sights and which always represented, at the very least, a temporary haven. And he sees, and he understands for the first time that, given equal opportunity, the black tin god a few thousand miles north of him would degrade and dehumanize his victim as capably as Vorster or Governor Wallace. This fact has been ever-present, this knowledge is not new, and the only wonder is that the romancer, the intellectual myth-maker, has successfully deleted this black portion of a common human equation . . . We, whose humanity the poets celebrated before the proof, whose lyric innocence was daily questioned by the very pages of newspapers, are now being forced by disaster, not foresight, to a reconsideration of our relationship to the outer world. It seems to me that the time has now come when the African writer must have the courage to determine what alone can be salvaged from the recurrent cycle of human stupidity (*ADO2*, 19)

Passages such as this abound in Soyinka's early critical prose, and taken out of context – as they have been, in some notable critical instances[10] – they give an entirely distorted view of his positions and attitudes as being one-sidedly and reductively universalistic. For Soyinka is abundantly particularistic in delineating the cultural and social conditions of African writing in his reflections on artistic responsibility in these early essays. In the essay from which this last passage is excerpted, "The Writer in a Modern African State," there is a comparison of the collective situation of black South African writers with that of their East and West African counterparts, there is an extended profile of the transition from colonial to post-independence relations as a backdrop to the formation of the African writer's sense of a public, "continental" mandate, and there is an evocation of the pervasive dislocation of the Nigerian artistic community in the country's slide to civil war. There is even in the essay a harsh indictment of the hypocritical, benign paternalism of Western critics and publishers which had the indirect effect, in Soyinka's view, of fanning the embers of social and political conflagration by their encouragement of euphoria, complacency and irrelevance in this "new" literature from Africa. Taken together, it is the sum of such historicizing and particularizing criticisms in this essay that considerably relativizes the undeniable universalism of the essay and reveals the sharp edge of Soyinka's uncompromisingly astute and courageous unmasking of the reactionary philistinism that the influential ideological and intellectual props of the "literature of discovery" were gradually but inexorably con-solidating in the then newly emergent postcolonial African literature. Who can deny the prescience of the contained, scrupulous *ressentiment* of the following observations on the ideological and spiritual milieu which produced that literature of "rediscovery"?

In new societies which begin the seductive experiment in authoritarianism, it has become a familiar experience to watch society crush the writer under a load of guilt for his daring to express a sensibility and an outlook apart from, and independent of the mass direction. The revolutionary mood in society is a particularly potent tyrant in this respect, and since the writer is, at the very least sensitive to mood, he respects the demand of the moment and effaces his definition as a writer by an act of choice. And in the modern African state es-pecially, the position of the writer has been such that he is in fact the very prop of state machinery. Independence in every instance has meant an emergency pooling of every mental resource. The writer must, for the moment at least (he persuades himself), postpone that unique reflection on experience and events which is what makes a writer – and constitute himself into a part of that ma-chinery that will actually shape events. Let this impulse be clearly understood and valued for itself; the African writer found he could not deny his society; he could however, temporarily at least, deny himself. He therefore took his place in the new state as a privileged person, placed personally above the effects of the narrowness of vision which usually accompanies the impatience of new nations, African, European or Asian. (*ADO2*, 16)

If this passage suggests a sort of coming to terms with the "revolution-ary mood" which sacrifices the aesthetic autonomy of the artist as the price of social progress in the new postcolonial nation, it should quickly be added that Soyinka's views and positions in the early essays were anything but conformist to this "mood." All the early critical essays consistently upheld a critical, vigilant aesthetic individualism as the proper means of self-distancing for the artist from both the statist, elitist apparatus of the nation-state and the "mass direction" of the populace, and as the only antidote to the traps of narcissistic self-absorption endemic to the "litera-ture of rediscovery." Soyinka's astuteness in advancing this view such that it did not constitute a defense of a reactionary aesthetic individualism is one of the most remarkable achievements of his early critical prose. In-deed, in these essays, our author makes such extensive and illuminating commentaries on other African writers and their works that these early essays constitute a sort of vintage Soyinka literary criticism. Moreover, almost in the accents of the historic Western avant-garde in its privileging of the autonomy of the artistic process against the overpowering pressure of a philistine bourgeoisie and the ravages of the marketplace, these commentaries of Soyinka on his fellow writers in his early critical prose approach writers primarily from within, from the autonomous space of the interiority of the artistic process and the subjectivity of the artist. And since the immediate historic context is the first decade of the post-independence era in Africa, Soyinka's passionate solicitude for the autonomy of the artistic process in these commentaries is made with regard to formidable pressure of conformism that the flawed, myopic nationalism of the period imposed on everyone, especially on writers and intellectuals. It is perhaps not overstating the case to observe that Soyinka was almost alone in insisting that the African writer ought to cultivate and protect the uniqueness of his vision and sensibility apart from both the "mass direction" and the conformist nationalism promoted by the pseudo-bourgeoisie. Parallel to this insistence was Soyinka's ferocious assaults against the pervasive "authority" of the loud, and aggressive racial particularisms of the period, especially in poetry and literary-critical discourses, characterized and derided by Soyinka in an early essay as a form of narcissism, a form of self-manipulation and self-exoticization. In place of this the Nigerian author advanced the notion of "indifferent self-acceptance," a sort of lived, unforced racial or cultural identity. The assumption behind this was Soyinka's suggestion that once racial identity becomes a label of a unique black African humanity and a seal of unearned legitimacy, it breeds all kinds of distortions and simplifications.

And yet, in these early essays, in spite of his strictures against provincialism and racial absolutism, Soyinka begins to explore "an African world" of received paradigms and matrices of the artist and the creative process to which the African writer, in his view, must return. But he was careful in these essays to emphasize that this "essence" of the artist was different from the naive intuition touted by the rhapsodists of Négritude; it is an "essence" inscribed in figures like Ogun, the Yoruba god of war, the hunt, creativity and metallurgy, a god whose traditions of praise poetry celebrate for his inquisitive, wandering spirit, his courage, his solicitude for the weak and defenseless of society, and his mastery of diverse arts and skills.

It is also the case that Soyinka in these essays often used the specific, "local" textual exegeses of his literary criticism to elaborate the outlines of a metacritical, "global" theory of artistic responsibility in times of acute social disjuncture. A good illustration of this is perhaps his reading, in the essay "And After the Narcissist?" of Senghor's treatment of the protagonist of his long dramatic poem, *Chaka*. For Soyinka, the splitting in this poem of Chaka the poet from Chaka the politician, together with the celebration of the former, aestheticizes politics in a manner that is symbolic of the excessively naive cultural politics of Négritude in particular and the dominant temper of the "literature of rediscovery" in general:

Senghor's *Chaka* suggests that the poet's answer to antihumanism lies solely in sublime or aesthetic conceptions. The implication is that poetry in itself is not a force for violence or an occasional instrument of terror. That it combats fear by the revelation of beauty is undoubtedly one of poetry's functions; hence the social responsibility of the artist – his "politics", as Chaka would have it – are not in themselves a contradiction of the poet. A true Ogun sensibility that is African, or should be, recognizes this at once and does not seek the negativity of escapism which blasphemes against the very existence of the poet ... Every creative act breeds and destroys fear, contains within itself both the salvation and damnation. And Senghor has impossibly imposed on his Chaka a poetic stratification that is not compatible with the creative stress of a poet in Ogun possession. (Soyinka, 1966, 59–60)

Given the qualities and attributes associated with his cult, Ogun would seem to be the appropriately powerful, nuanced, countervailing metaphoric construct for what Soyinka perceives to be the escapist flight of the (typical) "narcissistic" writer of the "rediscovery" movement from the gathering violence of post-independence Africa, an Africa in which the pattern of coups and countercoups, rampant corruption and arrogant, dictatorial abuse of power that has since become banal in the politics of the continent was then just beginning to crystallize. The phrase "the poet in Ogun possession" suggests that the writer should register this creeping, miasmic violence of the period, but not as pure, mindless, gratuitous force. Rather, Ogun's creative-destructive axis operates like Derrida's notion of the *pharmakon*: artistic signification conceived in the pharmacological metaphor of the poison which could be the saving prophylactic, or the disease inseparable from its cure.[11]

The vital question of violence which is first broached in Soyinka's early critical essays in "And After the Narcissist?" dominates "The Writer in a Modern African State" and "The Fourth Stage," but in quite divergent ways. "What we are observing in our own time," Soyinka observes in "The Writer in a Modern African State," "is the total collapse of ideals, the collapse of humanity itself. Action therefore becomes meaningless, the writer is pushed deeper and deeper into self-insulation and withdrawal; his commitment accepts its own hopelessness from the very beginning" (*ADO2*, 19). Soyinka calls this pessimism a "historic vision" and there is no question that the pessimism of this essay has distinct overtones of the general pessimism of the intellectual currents of post-Second World War Europe.[12] The vision of the "The Fourth Stage" by contrast, is relentlessly metaphysical and trans-historical, and the analogues which Soyinka deploys in this essay for violence and social disjuncture are all drawn from mythic and ritual archetypes:

The persistent search for the meaning of tragedy, for a redefinition in terms of cultural or private experience is, at the least, man's recognition of certain areas of depth-experience which are not satisfactorily explained by general aesthetic theories; and, of all the subjective unease that is aroused by man's creative insights, that wrench within the human psyche which we vaguely define as 'tragedy' is the most insistent voice that bids us return to our own sources. There, illusively, hovers the key to the human paradox, to man's experience of being and non-being, his dubiousness as essence and matter, intimations of transience and eternity, and the harrowing drives between uniqueness and Oneness (*ADO2*, 27)

While "The Writer in a Modern African State" has many concrete, specific allusions to the manifestations of the rampant social and political malaise of the immediate post-independence era in Africa, there is not a single reference in "The Fourth Stage" to any contemporary event or trend in the politics and culture of the continent – or of any other place in the world for that matter. Only by the sheer contiguity of the publication of these two essays are we enabled to see in both essays a common thread of impassioned, vigorous and prescient response to the looming social and political disasters in the affairs of the continent in that decade which started with great euphoria and optimism.

This divergence and complementarity between the "historic vision" of one essay and the relentless recourse to densely symbolic and mythic idioms in the other essay enables us, in making an assessment of Soyinka's early essays, to broach the matter of the simultaneous closeness and distance of Soyinka in these early essays to the Western literary and cultural avant-garde, especially the Symbolists.

As many commentators on "The Fourth Stage" have observed, the language of the essay is considerably difficult and even in many places quite obscure. This derives, it seems, from the elaborately metaphorical quality of the stock of words, images and archetypes deployed in the essay, as well as from the fact that language itself, as idiom and *enunciation*, is thematized as an object of speculation in the essay. These two aspects distinctly recall the Symbolists' categorical distancing of literary language as much as possible from the more "mundane" representational and referential functions that people ordinarily associate with language and their corollary insistence on the non-mimetic, metaphoric resonance of literary language. Moreover, Soyinka's deployment of language to construct what he calls, following the essay's title, a "fourth stage" of experience and phenomena which links the "worlds" of the ancestors and the dead (the past), the living (the present) and the unborn (the future) also strongly recalls the Symbolists' use of densely and allusively metaphoric language to construct bridges between ancient and modern myths thereby abrogating linear, positivist conceptions of temporality. But if in these aspects Soyinka is solidly in the company of Western avant-garde presuppositions and practices, he is also in this essay powerfully insistent on African expressive matrices as the foundations of his deployment and thematization of language:

Language in Yoruba tragic music therefore undergoes transformation through myth into a secret (masonic) correspondence with the symbolism of tragedy, a symbolic medium of spiritual emotions with the heart of choric union. It transcends particularization (of meaning) to tap the tragic source whence spring the familiar weird disruptive melodies. This masonic union of sign and melody, the true tragic music, unearths cosmic uncertainties which pervade human existence, reveals the magnitude and power of creation, but above all creates a harrowing sense of omnidirectional vastness where the creative Intelligence resides and prompts the soul to futile exploration. The senses do not at such moments interpret myth in their particular concretions; we are left only with the emotional and spiritual values, the essential experience of cosmic reality. (*ADO2*, 31)

As I have demonstrated elsewhere in my reading of both this particular passage and the entire essay from which it is excerpted, the view of tragic art elaborated in the passage is coextensive with all rigorously anti-mimetic, antirealist and mythopoeic conceptions of literature and art.[13] But it is also abundantly clear that the inspiration for this approach to literary language derives far less from the documents and practices of the Symbolists in particular[14] and the Western avant-garde in general than from figurations of tragic art in cultic music and mythic ritual in traditional Yoruba expressive idioms and philosophical principles:

It is no wonder therefore that the overt optimistic nature of the culture is the quality attributed to the Yoruba himself, one which has begun to affect his accommodation towards the modern world, a spiritual complacency with which he encounters threats to his human and unique valuation. Alas, in spite of himself from time to time, the raw urgent question beats in the blood of his temple demanding, what is the will of Ogun? For the hammering of the Yoruba will was done at Ogun's forge, and any threat of disjunction is, as with the gods, a memory code for the resurrection of the tragic myth. (*ADO2*, 36)

Among other considerations, it is the idea in this passage of tragic myth as a cultural code in a period of social stress that links the totally abstract-universal conception of the psychic and spiritual coordinates of tragic art in "The Fourth Stage" with the deeply historic vision of "The Writer in a Modern African State": between both essays a surfeit of gloom, but also invocation of the will to action, the will to resistance from the depths of the individual and collective psyche.

It is worth noting that class and gendered identifications are very strong, ineluctable expressions in this phase of our author's critical thought, as indeed in *all* the phases. The class identifications are more indirect, more subliminal, while the imbrications of gendered identifications are by contrast so immanent in Soyinka's critical prose as to be ideologically and discursively constitutive. Of class, there are the vaguely brahminical tones, the lofty pose of hauteur which haunts even the most genuinely egalitarian and radical views and positions in these early essays. For occasionally, these break out into aristocratic disdain of populist aspects of the "literature of rediscovery," the most characteristic being Soyinka's view that "the average published writer" in the "literature of rediscovery" was a mediocre literary artist. If this was a demonstrable fact – and there is little evidence that it was – it is difficult to think of any other writer-critic in Soyinka's generational cohort who could have said it in print!

On the issue of gender, let us merely remark that it says a lot about the relentlessly male-centered nature of Soyinka's critical thought as expressed in his theoretical and metacritical writings in all three phases, that there is no discussion, not even a passing reference, of *any* female African writer in the capacious body of these writings. In this respect the invariable use of the male pronoun for the African writer in all of the Nigerian author's critical prose is more than the generic linguistic sexism lodged at the heart of normative language usage itself; it is entirely coincident with and inscribes a subliminally "national-masculine" vision of African postcolonial writing as essentially a "men only" literary tradition.[15]

These direct and indirect identifications notwithstanding, Soyinka's early critical prose is unquestionably one of the most progressive,

clear-sighted and courageous literary-critical discourses of the immediate post-independence period.[16] Thus, even though the articulation
of an idealistic, responsible artistic identity was achieved by a constant
and invariable infusion of the male pronoun into Soyinka's profiles of
the African writers, his devastating demystification of superficial racial
essences in Négritude poetry and aesthetic constructs is a lasting contribution to African postcolonial critical discourse. This is particularly
evident in the famous last paragraph of "The Writer in a Modern African
State":

> The reconciliation of cultures, this leaven of black contribution to the metallic
> loaf of European culture, is only another evasion of the inward eye. The despair
> and anguish which is spreading a miasma over the continent must sooner or later
> engage the attention of the writer in his own society or else be boldly ignored.
> For both attitudes are equally valid; only let there be no pretense to a concern
> which fulfills itself in the undeclared, unproven privation of the European world.
> When the writer in his own society can no longer function as conscience, he must
> recognize that his choice lies between denying himself totally or withdrawing
> to the position of chronicler and post-mortem surgeon. But there can be no
> further distractions with universal concerns whose balm is spread on abstract
> wounds, not on the gaping yaws of black inhumanity... The artist has always
> functioned in African society as the record of the mores and experience of his
> society *and* as the voice of vision in his own time. It is time for him to respond
> to this essence of himself (*ADO2*, 19–20)

The urgency and eloquence of this passage, addressed in its particular
context to the last gathering of African writers before the outbreak of
the Nigerian civil war, are qualities which pervade all of Soyinka's early
critical essays. The *tone* of his unique, idiosyncratic critical voice was
not of course always this desperate in the essays. On occasion Soyinka
could combine a playful wit with high seriousness, as is evident in the
following now widely savored short take on Achebe's mastery of the art
of narrative:

> It is doubtful if Achebe's forte lies in the ability to spit occasionally, or to laugh
> from the belly when the situation demands it, but he must learn at least to be
> less prodigal with his stance of a lofty equipose. For this has bred the greatest
> objection to his work, this feeling of unrelieved competence... (*ADO2*, 12)

Always in these essays, Soyinka's delineations of the evolving personal
stylistic and thematic signatures of his fellow African writers are sharp,
and often couched in as memorable turns of phrase as the witticism
concerning Achebe's "unrelieved competence." Soyinka pays close, intimate attention to language, the medium of literature, in these essays and

he gives as much attention to matters of craft, technique and the special pleasures of the text, the *literariness* that, in his opinion, distinguishes
"good" writers from the "inferior" literateurs. His enthusiasms for the
former are always expressed in a way calculated to infect the reader, and
there is never any doubt that he has *read* what he writes about and cares
that others should read with the same mix of submission and vigilance
that he brings to the authors and texts under his critical purview. This
purview, as we have seen, comes with an insistence on high, utopian and
uncompromising principles for a "literature of rediscovery." But in another sense, Soyinka insists in these essays that the literature of "young"
nations just freed from colonial domination, is, first and foremost, and
like literature everywhere, its own justification when practiced with skill
and with integrity of artistic vision.

At the end of Soyinka's first collected volume of critical essays, *Myth,
Literature and the African World* (1976), the author makes the following assertion in concluding a wide-ranging critique of Négritude and its responses
to centuries of Western discourses on Africans in particular, and "race"
in general:

(This) problem does not apply to Négritudinists alone. African intellectualism
in general, and therefore attitudes to race, culture, have failed to come to grips
with the very foundations of Eurocentric epistemology (*MLAW*, 136)

Twelve years later, and on two different occasions, Soyinka again returned to this theme of the crucial need for African postcolonial critical
discourse to engage the question of ethnocentric Western epistemologies, of the very conditions and possibility of discourse and knowledge of
Africa and Africans as they have been shaped by Eurocentrism. First, in
the essay "The External Encounter: Ambivalence in African Arts and
Literature" which was delivered at Cornell University, the Nigerian author directs some urgent cautionary remarks to "those African writers
and even would be aesthetic theorists, (who are) blithely unconscious
how their instincts have been shaped by centuries of European historicism and intellectual canons for which the African reality provided only
the occasional, marginal, race-motivated fodder (*ADO*, 234)." This interrogation of "historicism and (other) intellectual canons" is taken up
again, complete with named "culprits," when Soyinka returns to this
theme in his Nobel lecture, "This Past Must Address Its Present":

Gobineau is a notorious name, but how many students of European thought
today, even among us Africans, recall that several of the most revered names
in European philosophy – Hegel, Locke, Hume, Voltaire – an endless list, were

unabashed theorists of racial superiority and denigrators of the African history and being? (Soyinka, 1988, 437)

In these and other essays then, Soyinka repeatedly insists on the enormous impact of the ethnocentric epistemology of European discourses on race and culture, not only on European writers and intellectuals themselves, but more crucially, on Africans and other non-European peoples as well. However, Soyinka is at pains in these essays to avoid a mere inversion of Eurocentrism, he is anxious to recuperate an "African world" whose self-constitution precedes and survives the Eurocentric epistemological onslaught. And because his invocation of this "African world" combines personal testimony with radical-democratic claims, it reads simultaneously like the personal credo of one artist and a brief on behalf of an entire continent before the tribunal of the world's community of letters and culture. This is particularly evident in the following passage from his 1986 Nobel Lecture:

The world which is so conveniently traduced by apartheid thought is of course that which I so wholeheartedly embrace – and that is my choice, among several options, of the significance of my presence here. It is a world that nourishes my being, one that is so self-sufficient, so replete in all aspects of its productivity, so confident in itself and its density that it experiences no fear in reaching out to others and in responding to the reach of others. It is the hearthstone of our creative existence. It constitutes the prism of our world perception, and this means that our sight need not be and has never been permanently turned inward (Soyinka, 1988, 438–9)

This passage illustrates well the radical shift in perspective, tone and subject matter that we encounter between the earliest essays and Soyinka's essays of the 1970s and 1980s. Where the earliest essays, as we have seen, had attacked aggressive racial self-assertions and insisted on "indifferent self-acceptance," where indeed these early essays had implicitly but eloquently problematized any African literary-critical discourse based on *race*, the essays of the 1970s and 1980s – essays of the "middle period" of Soyinka's critical prose – assert the reality and vitality of "a Black world" of Africa and the African diaspora. They also assert the need to recuperate those precolonial, pre-contact traditions that have survived devaluation by foreign waves of conquests, enslavement and colonization and are thus vital for creative adaptation to the challenges of modernity. Correspondingly, Soyinka in these "middle period" essays enters into both a sustained interest in the long history of Eurocentric discourses on African peoples and cultures, *and* contemporary

Euro-American cultural and racial attitudes regarding the non-Western world. And as we have observed earlier, a sort of deliberate annunciation of this shift is indeed contained in the Preface to *Myth, Literature and the African World*, the book of essays intended to launch this project of "the self-apprehension of a race":

> From a well-publicized position as an anti-Négritudinist (if only one knew in advance what would make one statement more memorable that the next!) it has been with an increasing sense of alarm and even betrayal that we have watched our position distorted and exploited to embrace a "sophisticated" school of thought which (for ideological reasons) actually repudiates the existence of an African world! Both in cultural and political publications, and at such encounters as the UNESCO Conference on the Influence of Colonialism on African Culture, Dar es Salaam 1972, the 6th Pan-African Congress, Dar es Salaam 1974, the pre-Colloque of the Black Arts Festival, Dakar 1974, etc., etc . . . we black Africans have been blandly invited to submit ourselves to a second epoch of colonization – this time by a universal-humanoid abstraction defined and conducted by individuals whose theories and prescriptions are derived from the apprehension of *their* world and *their* history, *their* social neuroses and *their* value systems. It is time, clearly, to respond to this new threat, each in his own field (*MLAW*, ix–x)

In order to apprehend fully the terms which frame this shift in racial discourse in Soyinka's critical prose, it is important to note another point of radical departure from the concerns and attitudes of the early essays that the "middle period" essays manifest. This pertains to the general question of the literary phenomenon in Africa and in the world at large at the present time. For where Soyinka in the early essays had focused almost exclusively on writers and writing, the "middle period" essays focus sharply on critics and criticism, on what the Nigerian author repeatedly designates the "sociology of the critic." In other words, where the earlier essays had projected literature and literary criticism as more or less an autonomous discourse, there is in the essays of the 1970s and early 1980s a strong sense of literary criticism and literature as *one* composite discourse in a vast force field of other discourses: professional and ideological discourses; discourses of the colonizers and those of the colonized; discourses based on class, on nationality and ethnicity, and on race. This new emphasis on the discursive contexts of the production and reception of literature involves diverse but related themes: the teaching of literature in the institutional context of colleges and universities and the attendant politics of pedagogy; the politics of language choice and the formation of reading publics in Africa; the emergence of the writings of professional critics of African literary texts as a rather privileged and overextended discourse in the debates on the strategies necessary for building democratic polities in Africa. On all of these issues and discourses, Soyinka's critical prose, beginning in the mid-1970s, has made characteristically idiosyncratic interventions. The following caustic remarks on the subject of critics and writers, from the essay "The Critic and Society," is typical:

We are familiar, probably even excruciatingly bored with the question, "For whom does the writer write?" Very rarely is the same degree of social angst encountered in the case of the critic. Indeed the question is very rarely posed: For whom does the critic write? For Mr. Dele Bus-Stop of Idi-Oro? Or for the Appointments and Promotions Committee and the Learned Journals International Syndicate of Berne, Harvard, Nairobi, Oxford or Prague? Unquestionably there is an intellectual cop-out in the career of any critic who covers reams of paper with unceasing lament on the failure of this or that writer to write for the masses of the people, when he himself assiduously engages, with a remorseless exclusivity, only the incestuous productivity of his own academic – that is bourgeois-situated literature. (*ADO2*, 97)

Within this new emphasis on the institutions, contexts and class basis of critical discourse, it is easy to see that Soyinka's *racial* discourse in these essays is not in a "protest mode"; the intention is far less to blame the Western "Other" than to point out the discursive, representational traps which await any African response to a Eurocentrism that bases itself on the terms initially proposed by Western discourses of, and on, Africans. Thus, because unlike "classical" Négritude it is constructed not as a counterdiscourse to Eurocentrism, it is necessary to carefully apprehend the cultural politics of this neo-Négritudist turn in Soyinka's critical prose.

Notions of an "African world" of spirit, imagination and creativity are not exclusively to be encountered in Soyinka's "middle period" essays. Even in the earliest critical writings, he had expressed the view that much of the imaginative and expressive resources available to modern African art and literature derive from precolonial traditions of creativity and reflection which preceded and survived colonialism and are therefore not to be comprehended *only* as reactions to, or the products of colonization. What is different in the articulation of this view in Soyinka's critical and theoretical writings both in *Myth, Literature and the African World* and other critical writings of the 1970s is that whereas he had urged in his earlier essays an unfussy, "indifferent self-acceptance" in reclaiming the cultural legacies of the past, the subsequent body of essays loudly and assertively enunciate, defend and celebrate the original, pre-contact, cultural

heirloom available to the African writer and artist. Above all else, it
is largely on account of this deliberate act of making very explicit and
even clamorous what had been mostly implicit, mostly taken for granted
in his earlier critical writings that Soyinka's "middle period" critical prose
can be described as *neo*-Négritudist.

Neo-Négritudist: the prefix needs as much emphasis as possible if we are
to gauge accurately the distance between the "racialization" that informs
Soyinka's essays on literature and culture in what we may designate his
"race retrieval" essays and the original views and attitudes of "classical,"
Senghorian Négritude. For one thing, Soyinka in these "middle period"
essays continues the uncompromising and sustained critical assault on
Négritude that he had begun in his very first essay, "The Future of West
African Writing" and reprised in other essays of the first phase such as
"And After the Narcissist?" and "The Writer in a Modern African State."
Indeed, the resumed critique of Négritude in these essays of the 1970s and
1980s now assumes a precise ideological and political expression which
is calculated to widen the gap between Soyinka's concepts of an "African
world" and those advanced by the poets and theorists of Négritude:

The search for a racial identity was conducted by and for a minuscule minority of uprooted individuals, not merely in Paris but in the metropolis of
the French colonies. At the same time as this historical phenomenon was taking place, a drive through the real Africa, among the real populace of the
African world would have revealed that these millions had never at any time
had cause to question the existence of their – Négritude. This is why, even in a
country like Senegal where Négritude is the official ideology of the regime, it
remains a curiosity for the bulk of the population and an increasingly shopworn
and dissociated expression even among the younger intellectuals and literateurs
(*MLAW*, 135)

This particular quote comes from the final, perorative pages of *Myth,
Literature and the African World* wherein Soyinka extends his critique of
Senghorian Négritude to Jean-Paul Sartre's famous "Orphée Noir," the
historic "Preface to Négritude." Almost in the same accents in which
Fanon had famously criticised Sartre's essay on Négritude in *Black Skins,
White Masks*, Soyinka savages Sartre's celebration of Négitude in the
essay as the very quintessence of a Eurocentric, logocentric and ethnocentric "universalism," one that, in "good faith," completely effaces the
historic and cultural specificity of non-Western Others.[17] Significantly,
Soyinka's critique here is not confined to Négritude and its liberal or left-
wing European promoters and cohorts; nothing short of contemporary

"African attitudes to race and culture" is the quarry in our author's projection of the necessity and the scope of his project of "race retrieval." The energy, the vision of the whole book is devoted obsessively to the subject of how African intellectuals have approached the massive historic penetration of Eurocentric epistemologies into Africa itself, into its ideas of itself, ideas of its peoples and societies about their histories and cultures. In other words, *Myth, Literature and the African World* is only tangentially concerned with what Soyinka identifies as the long history of the vehement denials of humanity or worth of Africa and Africans by European philosophers, historians, anthropologists and writers. The central focus of the book is, rather, the effects of this long tradition of Eurocentric discourses, in Africa itself, and on African writers and intellectuals.

Now, on the surface, this focus seems nothing more than a revisiting of the decades old contention of leading figures of intellectual Pan-Africanism like Edward Wilmot Blyden, J.E. Casely-Hayford and Kobina Sekyi that Africa must shake off its presumed intellectual and spiritual indenture to Europe and revitalize "pre-contact," precolonial African orders of knowledge.[18] Also, Soyinka's premises here seem, again on the surface, to be a rather belated discovery, on his part, that in the wake of the colonial conquest, Africa had been colonized spiritually and intellectually, the effects of these particular aspects of colonization being much deeper and more decisive than the economic and political aspects. But this entirely misses the point of Soyinka's premises in *Myth, Literature and the African World* and many of his subsequent critical essays, for his contention is that while the historic fact of spiritual and intellectual colonization had all along been known and in many instances resisted, this awareness and the resistances it generated had, except in a few cases, not gone to the roots of the problem. Even more onerous than this, in Soyinka's view, is the suspicion that the effects of the spiritual and intellectual domination of Africa by Eurocentric orders of knowledge in Africa were being consolidated and deepened in the post-independence period, this time in the name of a new, putatively post-imperial universalism, what Soyinka calls, as we have seen, "a universal-humanoid abstraction." Indeed, Soyinka calls this a "second epoch of colonization" (*MLAW*, x). We can thus surmise that a keen perception of this underlying premise of the "neo-Négritudist" turn in Soyinka's critical writings shows how distant he is from his early essays where one central underlying premise had been the certitude that Africa and Africans had not been as culturally and spiritually orphaned by colonization as the Négritudist poets had lamented, that indeed, colonialism had not been as corrosive of African spiritual self-confidence as the theorists of Négritude had insisted. In the light of Soyinka's reformulation of the issue in this manner, it would seem that his "race retrieval" project is *neo*-Négritudist to the extent that it is a response to this so-called "second epoch of colonization," whereas classical Senghorian Négritude had been a response to the "first epoch of colonization." It is in this response, in its forms, contents and contours, that Soyinka locates what he calls the project of "race retrieval."

In this respect, *Myth, Literature and the African World* represents a turning point in Soyinka's critical and theoretical writings, a sort of sometimes awkwardly articulated, but richly suggestive prolegomenon to the third phase of Soyinka's critical and theoretical writings – his essays of the mid to late 1980s and early 1990s such as "Climates of Art" (1985), "Of Berlin and Other Walls" (1990), "New Frontiers for Old" (1990) and "The Credo of Being and Nothingness" (1991), and in particular his third book of literary and cultural analysis, *The Burden of Memory and the Muse of Forgiveness.*

If no other single book of postcolonial African literary-critical discourse has generated as much discussion as *Myth, Literature and the African World*, with the possible exception perhaps of Ngugi wa Thiong'o's *Decolonizing the Mind*, the explanation for this lies as much in the manner in which Soyinka frames the argument as in the subject matter of the book. For it is almost impossible not to respond to the many memorable rhetorical and metaphoric flourishes of its argumentation. Two of these are worthy of mention, especially as they pertain to the important issue of the ideological and aesthetic distance that, beginning with the writings of this second phase of his critical thought, Soyinka begins to urge between his ideas and constructs of poetics and literary epistemology and Western modernist and avantgarde ideas and practices. First, there is the extended conceit of modern European literary and cultural history as a steam-engine locomotive lurching from station to station of soon-to-be-discarded movements – naturalism, symbolism, surrealism, cubism, expressionism etc. – each of which is however, in successive revisionisms proclaimed as ultimate verities of Experience or Truth (*MLAW*, 37–8). Second, there is the wildly satirical fantasy with which Soyinka ends the last essay in the book in which the ghost of René Descartes, foraging in the African bush of "prelogical mentality" for confirmation of his ratiocinated existence, is bearded by an African "innocent" who overwhelms the Cartesian cogito with "native" wit and logic (138–9). The critical assault on Western humanist and modernist or avantgarde values and practices indicated in these two examples assume considerably more extended expression in two of the most eloquently polemical essays of this second phase of Soyinka's critical prose, "Drama and the Idioms of Liberation: Proletarian Illusions" and "Between Self and System: the Artist in Search of Liberation." It is not fortuitous that both essays have the word "liberation" in their titles since, in different ways and addressed to different contexts, each of these two essays vigorously challenges the revolutionary credentials of the contemporary Euro-American avant-garde in theatre and literature, detailing the faddishness, preciosity and, above all, the lack of rooted, organic links to either cohering communal values or authentic social movements which, in our author's opinion, had drained the Western avantgarde of its revolutionary energies and authentically emancipatory traditions.

The significance of Soyinka's deployment of highly inventive rhetorical "riffs" and conceits noted above in *Myth, Literature and the African World* for negotiating the inescapable dilemma of the project begun in the book – "race retrieval" – is incalculable. This dilemma, simply stated, is the dilemma of *pure anteriority*, a dilemma which involves the near impossibility of eliciting the constitutive elements of an "African world" with its own internal cohering reference points absolutely without recourse to any external sources. Which culture or tradition in the history of human cultural evolution can meet this rigorously *autochthonous* requirement? How far back do you go to "recover" the absolutely pristine values and matrices of the African "racial" heritage in culture? Islam provides Soyinka with his toughest challenge, that is to say, Islamized Africa whose totally absorbed syncretist "integrity" is a basis for an unquestionably positive identity for some of the African writers and intellectuals that Soyinka not only apparently admires but with whom he feels some cultural kinship. Of these, Amadou Hampate Ba and Cheikh Hamidou Kane are particularly formidable. On Kane in particular Soyinka expends some of the most admiring, luminously exegetical prose in the whole book, but without in any way abjuring or qualifying his insistence that "race retrieval" has to go back to autochthonous sources before the syncretist fusion of cultures that is Islamized Africa. This insistence on an absolute point of aboriginal anteriority inevitably often pushes Soyinka toward a purism of cultural essences which he everywhere in the book disavows. One particularly troubled expression of this is Soyinka's apparent quandary that

The intelligentsia of the black world are in ideological disagreement over the question whether enforced exocentricity, as a retarding factor in the authentic history and development of Black Africa, should be appertaining *only to the European world* (*MLAW*, 99) (My emphasis)

It is not part of Soyinka's purpose in this book to inquire into the factors making for, on the one hand, the apparent consensus among "the intelligentsia of the black world" that European-Christian incursion into Africa involved "enforced exocentricity," and, on the other hand, the absence of such unanimity with regard to Arab-Islamic penetration of Black Africa. It suffices for Soyinka's purposes in the book to enlist the voices of writers and intellectuals who take the view that the story of the Arab-Islamic incursion into Africa south of the Sahara entailed as much of an "enforced exocentricity" as that produced by European-Christian colonization. Two of the most powerful textual examples of this view, Yambo Oulouguem's *Bound to Violence* and Ayi Kwei Armah's *Two Thousand Seasons*, provide Soyinka's exegetical efforts with some of the most controversially dehumanizing portraits of Europeans and Arabs and their respective civilizations, and one of Soyinka's moves in *Myth, Literature and the African World* is to square off the "vehemence" of *Bound to Violence* and *Two Thousand Seasons* with the "vehemence" of the racist narratives and discourses on Africa and Africans that were for centuries produced in Europe and the Arab world. At any rate, what concerns Soyinka beyond this violent settling of accounts in Ouloguem's and Armah's writings is the presumed pay off from their iconoclasm against *all* alien gods and matrices: the chance to reconstruct what was and is indigenous to Africa as a necessary component of the reconstruction of Africa in the modern world.

Of the four essays (with the appendix, "The Fourth Stage," an "early" essay) which make up the contents of *Myth, Literature and the African World*, only the last two, "Ideology and the Social Vision: the Religious Factor" and "Ideology and the Social Vision: the Secular Ideal," can be said to effectively demonstrate that many African writers and intellectuals are indeed obsessed by a need to reconstruct, in many diverse ways, a self-apprehended "African world" consisting of indigenously derived traditions of world apprehension, of reflection on history and experience, and with its own unique cultural and artistic sensibilities. In these two essays, Soyinka provides readings of a wide range of African writers including William Conton, Lewis Nkosi, Richard Rive, Dennis Brutus, Tchicaya U'Tamsi, Cheikh Hamidou Kane, Chinua Achebe, Mongo Beti, Yambo Oulouguem, Ayi Kwei Armah, Ousmane Sembene and Camara Laye. These are all, as in his early essays, male writers, and the list is overwhelmingly tilted toward the West African region. Nonetheless, the readings are almost always compelling and recall and repeat the powerful exegeses of Soyinka's literary criticism in the early essays. The readings of Chinua Achebe's *Arrow of God*, Ousmane Sembene's *God's Bits of Wood*, and Ayi Kwei Armah's *Two Thousand Seasons*, are particularly engrossing, even if sometimes they raise more questions than they answer. The case *is* made by Soyinka in these two essays that African writing in languages of external, colonial derivation, at its most accomplished, inscribes an *African* literary modernity, a distinctly African view on modern experience and its challenges and perplexities.

By contrast, the first two essays of *Myth, Literature and the African World*, "Morality and Aesthetics in the Ritual Archetype" and "Drama and the African World-view," deal, not with works of contemporary writers, but with mostly traditional Yoruba mythic and ritual archetypes; the only contemporary artists discussed are the late Duro Ladipo and J.P. Clark. The strain of stretching Yoruba religious and metaphysical traditions, with all their richness and complexity, to fill the scope of a canvas which covers the entire continent exacts much from these essays by way of over-generalization and idealization. Moreover, much that Soyinka manages to establish in these two essays as distinctively African or "racial" paradigms and matrices come into visibility only by way of a constant inverse cross-referencing with European traditions. This leads almost inevitably to a reproduction of the polarity beloved of classical social anthropology of "traditional," "organic," communalistic and agrarian societies which live close to nature, versus postindustrial, highly mechanized and secular societies. Indeed almost everything that Soyinka proffers in these two essays as "essentially" African – non-positivist, cyclical concepts of temporality, pantheistic spirituality, the cult of nature deities, veneration of ancestors, the unbroken integration of all areas of collective life including the religious, the aesthetic and the technico-economic – can be adjudged broadly typical of most pre-capitalist, non-monotheistic and analphabetic societies of the past and present. It is also the case that a central epistemological theme of these essays – that there is an "assimilative" wisdom or logic in African precolonial orders and matrices of knowledge which selectively absorbs "foreign" inputs and accretions while remaining true to its own self-identity – is generally simply asserted and hardly subjected to either vigorous proof or demonstration, or for that matter, counter-propositions. Meanwhile, it ought to be admitted that the big qualification to the point being urged about these two opening essays of *Myth, Literature and the African World* is that Soyinka *is* a poet and a superb mythopoeist and even if these two essays do not seem to contribute much to the elicitation of distinctively African expressive and representational paradigms, they constitute the first extended attempt in Soyinka's critical and theoretical writings to elaborate the poetics of culture and the tragic and sublime mythopoesis which stand at the center of his aesthetic thought.

There is a broad critical consensus among students of Soyinka's writings that this tragic mythopoesis is the central element of his aesthetic thought. This consensus is established by the extensive scholarly commentary on Soyinka's theoretical writings on the relations between ritual and drama, especially on his insistence in the essays of the 1970s (particularly those collected in *Myth, Literature and the African World*) that the myths and rituals associated with "theatrogenic" divinities of Yoruba religion like Obatala, Ogun and Shango whose cults have over the ages fostered a vast legacy of artistic and performance traditions provide vital sources for a tragic aesthetic profoundly different from, and probably richer than classical and modern Western tragic forms and paradigms.[19] Our reflections here derive from the astonishing fact that virtually all of the scholarly essays on Soyinka's critical and theoretical writings are almost exclusively based on his essays of the 1960s and 1970s, most of which deal self-consciously and rather programmatically with the interface between ritual and drama in the elucidation of the aesthetics and metaphysics of tragic expression. Even critics and scholars who take up this subject in quite recent scholarly interventions virtually ignore the critical and theoretical writings of the late 1980s and 1990s, a period which may be properly adjudged the period of Soyinka's "maturity" as a cultural theorist. Together with his most recent book of literary and cultural analysis, *The Burden of Memory, the Muse of Forgiveness*, I wish in the present context to discuss briefly four of the essays of this "third phase," "The External Encounter: Ambivalence in African Arts and Literature" (1985), "Climates of Art" (1985), "New Frontiers For Old" (1990) and "The Credo of Being and Nothingness" (1991). Because these essays are not focused specifically on aesthetic problems but range across the relations between art, society and culture, they cast a powerful reconfiguring light on the writings of the 1970s, especially those collected in *Myth, Literature and the African World*.

"The External Encounter" and "The Climates of Art" may be regarded as companion pieces, not only because they were written and delivered in the same year but because they both constitute the first attempt in Soyinka's critical prose to explore exhaustively African literary and cultural modernity in the context of the forces and institutions acting on the production and reception of artistic works everywhere in the contemporary world. Like most of his essays of the 1980s and 1990s, these two essays make the vastness of this subject matter manageable only by the sheer poetic license of Soyinka's use of extended, elaborate, but also powerfully evocative conceits. In "The External Encounter" this entails the animation of two African sculptural masterpieces – a Bakota ancestral guardian figure and a Nimba mask – as representations of the sensibilities of a different (African) earth "trapped" in an alien space in the museums of Dresden. In this captive alien space, these avatars of a separate African cultural earth watch with supreme self-possession and ironic wisdom their reception by their hosts as quaint, "primitive" objects – until their "discovery" in the explosive impact of African and Polynesian art on the European modernist imagination between the 1890s and the 1920s. Most of the essay is then given to speculations on what these two magnificent African sculptural masks, animated as ancestral presences and "replete" in their own cultural and spiritual be-ings, would say to the changing, divergent patterns of responses to the African cultural heritage from the late nineteenth century to the present, among Europeans and Africans themselves. Among the essay's most enthralling deployment of this extended metaphor are Soyinka's de-lineations of the extremisms in exhibitionism, gratuitous shock effects, racial exclusivism and bizarre fantasies and cults of power and aggres-sion that resulted from some European modernist appropriations of African techniques of image distortion and stylization, as in the cases of the most infamous fascist and sadomasochistic theorists of Futurism and Abstract Expressionism, Filippo Tommaso Marinetti and Oscar Kokoschska. Equally provocative is Soyinka's characterization of those African critics he terms "Neo-Tarzanists," who decry artistic experimen-tation and stylization as "unAfrican." In his acerbic view, these African "Neo-Tarzanists" are the unwitting offshoots of the early, pre-modernist European incomprehension of the world-view and the techniques of composition which produced the African sculptural masterpieces and their parallels in African oral and performing arts. By this extraordinar-ily provocative line of thinking, Vassily Kandinsky, almost alone among the Abstract Expressionists, turns out to be far more "African" than the "Neo-Tarzanists" and "primevalists" among modern African artists and writers:

If African art and philosophy had any truthful, authentic contact point with the Expressionist movement, it is probably through the Russian Kandinsky, not surprisingly perhaps since . . . his theoretical pronouncements appeared

to be tempered by an apparent Russian spirituality, underplaying the super-
man rhetoric in the common onslaught on a reactionary social condition
(*ADO2*, 169)

"Climates of Art" evinces an even more elaborate use of the extended
conceit than its companion piece, "The External Encounter." The ge-
ographical metaphor of the title of the essay is transcoded to cover the
extremely wide and variable cultural "weather conditions" that artists
and their publics have to endure in the modern world. Beyond the well-
known contexts of censorship, repression and terror that define the reality
of many artists and intellectuals in the developing world, the essay is especially poignant in invoking the climate of terror in Idi Amin's Uganda
which consumed so many of the best crop of the country's artists and intellectuals. Against such severely inclement artistic and cultural "weather
conditions," the essay recalls the "climate" of new possibilities and expanded horizons which opened up when the *cordon sanitaire* imposed by
the different colonial empires on their territories began to be lifted in the
1950s and 1960s with the coming of political independence. Indeed, in
sections of the essay where Soyinka gives a personal, anecdotal account of
his own first encounter with black writers and artists from other parts of
Africa and the African diaspora – artists working in a broad spectrum
of media of expression and genres of literature whose existence Soyinka
and his West African cohorts had simply been unaware of – we have
one of the most affecting and graceful evocations in his critical prose of
a "Black World" of shared histories, values and sentiments which arose
out of an indisputably racialized experience, but is nonetheless an integral part of the movement on five continents to give modernity a truly
nonracial, transcultural and radical-democratic vocation. "The outside
world," says Soyinka, "is not so outside" in our contemporary world. If
this seems to be a beguiling view of modern art and its publics, it needs
to be pointed out that this essay is imbued with a deep sense both of the
horrible things that have gone wrong on a global scale in the twentieth
century, and of possible future misuse of the vast capacities now available in modern civilization for instant human self-annihilation or slow,
inexorable planetary entropy. The most sensitive and prescient of the
world's artists, Soyinka suggests, gain access to the human and spiritual
costs of these conditions of modern life often by operating as the unconscious medium of truths and potentialities buried far below the surface
of the visible, empirical world or lying beyond the horizon of predictable
expectations.

This latter point Soyinka renders in an unforgettable metaphoric deployment of the "abiku" phenomenon in some African traditional beliefs concerning a warped transmigration of souls. In Soyinka's reformulation of this motif, it took the "abiku" occurrence of a military *coup d'état* in Greece, the birthplace of Western democracy, for many in the West to see that the barbarians may after all not be outside the gates, but within the heart of the metropolis itself, just as it took the oneiric, ghoulish visions of a Hieronymous Bosch or a Francis Bacon to reveal the malformations and perversities lodged at the heart of an overconfident bourgeois culture and civilization. This, Soyinka suggests, is one face of the "abiku" phenomenon manifesting itself in so many diverse "climates" of art and politics in the modern world. Indeed one of the most subtle rhetorical moves in this essay is enabled by his use of what he terms the phenomenon of "identification parallels" in the reception of works of art from diverse "climates." It is this phenomenon which triggers Soyinka's recognition of an unmistakable "abiku" motif in a particular painting by Colin Garland, an Australian artist, and more pervasively in the paintings of Francis Bacon. As in Soyinka's famous poem on the "abiku" spirit-child, the motif figures as the very essence of ambiguity in "Climates of Art" and it thus suggests itself to our author as perhaps the most appropriate metaphor on the place of creativity in the contemporary world: the spirit child who is born, dies and is born again may be an image either of a cruel, mocking fate, or an inextinguishable spirit of human resilience, though it is the former incarnation which predominates in Soyinka's final cautionary peroration in the essay:

That paradoxical child, *Abiku*, having been successfully snuffed out in Greece, resurfaces, gloating, in spheres as far apart as the coast of West Africa and Latin America, wearing its mask of death and sadism. This malformed consciousness of contemporary power expands without curb, ignored by those whose sleep is too deep or whose roosts are too distant, they think, by its petulant snarls . . . No one ever thought, before the takeover by the Greek generals, that such retrograde event could take place in that birthland of European democracy. Today, the same endangered species insist on believing that it is not taking place in other countries – not even after the experience of Idi Amin. I regret to disappoint you. We inhabit the same climate of terror – only the agents are different (*ADO2*, 198)

"New Frontiers For Old" and "The Credo of Being and Nothingness" perhaps provide the most appropriate of Soyinka's essayistic reflections on problems of contemporary culture and society with which to conclude the exploration of his critical and theoretical writings. Among the essays of the 1980s and 1990s, the former is the most important essay on art and the process of artistic creation while the latter is Soyinka's most important reflection on religion and human spirituality in the closing decades of the twentieth century. The discussion or argumentation in each of these essays is constructed around a central paradox, respectively of art and religious spirituality. A comparison of these respective paradoxes provides an insight into the ambiguities and paradoxes of Soyinka's own artistic personality and his activist vision. Additionally, each of these paradoxes – of artistic creation and religious creeds – builds on the same use of extended conceits that we have identified as a central feature of Soyinka's essayistic *oeuvre*; this time, the particular conceits are elaborated around the terms "frontier" and "credo" in the title of each respective essay.

If allowance is made for a somewhat excessive verbal and metaphoric play on the word "frontier" and its synonyms and analogues in "New Frontiers for Old," it becomes possible to appreciate the fact that the central paradox of artistic creation argued in the essay manages to give old or familiar ideas about art new and startlingly original reformulations. The artist or writer, Soyinka urges, necessarily lives the paradox of, on the one hand, the certainty of frontiers (which operate as effective barriers) and, on the other hand, the insistence that the frontier, the barrier, must be crossed and exceeded. This is highly suggestive of old debates between classical art and the anti-classical, avant-garde revolts it always provokes or generates. In Soyinka's reformulation of this age-old dialectic, the artist who is happy, even exultant, to work within the austere restraints or "barriers" of classical genres and styles does so because she knows that the power of the classics – whose conditions of production have vanished or become attenuated – can only be "answered" by the creation of new, vital forms. This line of reasoning provides Soyinka in this essay with his most powerful and convincing arguments for the appropriation of the "classics" of African art in sculpture, music, performance arts, oral poetic and narrative idioms, and the vast repository of ritual and mythic lore as models which spur the contemporary arts to create new forms approaching or even exceeding the achievements of the masterpieces of the classical traditions. This indeed is the underlying signification of the essay's title – "New Frontiers For Old" – and in a vigorous presentation of the distinction between the worthy, productive "frontiers" of the classics and the unworthy and crippling "frontiers" of pseudo-tradition, Soyinka in this essay provides some very authoritative and knowledgeable commentary on the state of diverse media and forms of artistic expression in contemporary Africa, most notably on painting.

But the most telling and eloquent aspects of the essay derive not from this reaffirmation of tradition and classicism in the arts; rather, they derive from the energetic negative critique that Soyinka launches against the false, sterile frontiers mounted by the determined or un-witting adversaries of art like the "border guards" and "immigration officers" of (African) "authenticity," the purist defenders of supremacist canons who mount prohibitions and anathemas against the assimilation of content, style, genre or medium from alien traditions, the censorship boards which repress artistic creativity through unchallengeable diktats, and their fundamentalist counterparts who operate by divine fiats. Thus "New Frontiers For Old" is perhaps Soyinka's most important and pow-erful defense of artistic freedom, and its scope in this particular regard is truly extraordinary in its social and historical allusions. Ranging across diverse false and constricting "frontiers" imposed on art and artists by institutions like art galleries and museums, criticism, religious orthodoxy and the state, Soyinka makes a passionate plea in this essay for all artists, and especially *African* artists, to be granted the freedom to engage the challenge of the "true" frontiers which are the very condition of artistic creativity. Within the neo-modernist and neo-Romantic aesthetic frame-work of this and other essays of Soyinka of the 1980s and 1990s, reality itself is the most important and productive of these "true," constitutive frontiers and barriers of art:

Who, in short, is truly content with the frontiers of the empirical, against whose constrictions the writer constructs not merely eponymous histories, but elabo-rate assault towers? Like the scientist, is the writer not really upset, irritated, intrigued, and challenged by the arrogant repletion of objective reality and experience? . . . Indeed, paradise can be regained; again and again, the artist does regain paradise, but only as a magical act of transformation of present reality, not through the pasting of a coy, anachronistic fig-leaf over the pudenda of the past in the present (*ADO2*, 223, 226)

In "The Credo of Being and Nothingness" the paradox deployed to structure the essay's long, circuitous reflections on the social and politi-cal ramifications of religious extremism in Nigeria in particular and the contemporary world in general pertains to human spirituality itself. All religions, in Soyinka's view, affirm man as essentially soul or spirit, yet tend to group that "soulfulness" or spirituality hierarchically in terms of its difference, its lack, or its inferiority in religions other than one's own faith. Within the ambit of this view of religion, or, more specifically, the organized monotheistic religions of the world based on a sacred, written

text of revealed truth, one grasps the centre of one's spirituality by reducing the spirituality of religious Others to – nothing. On this topic,
"The Credo of Being and Nothingness" is at once a keen, well-informed
observer's report on the state of religious extremism and fanaticism in
Nigeria and a wide-ranging reflection on the tendency toward regres-
sive, militant fundamentalism in communities dominated by competing
monopolistic monotheisms in the modern world. In this respect, the
essay implicitly but forcefully critiques the unacknowledged theological or doctrinal predisposition toward exclusivism in all the dominant
monotheistic religions of the world, a predisposition which, in Soyinka's
opinion, haunts these religions' efforts at ecumenism and mutual
tolerance.

From the foregoing, it can be readily perceived that "The Credo of
Being and Nothingness" deserves attention as a vigorous restatement of
many of the radical-humanist, intercultural and internationalist themes
of Soyinka's essays of the 1980s. But the essay is also noteworthy in its
articulation of ideas and tropes fundamental to the crystallization of
Soyinka's sensibility as an artist, and of his unique personality as an
activist intellectual. Thus, though delivered as an address to a mostly
Christian group of scholars and students who, moreover, expected a
partisan condemnation by Soyinka of the upsurge of Islamic fundamentalism in Northern Nigeria, "The Credo of Being and Nothingness"
turns out instead to be a deliberate celebration of radical agnosticism
and "pagan," animistic spirituality. Indeed, while for most liberal and
radical intellectuals mobilized against religious extremism, secularism or
atheism constitute the necessary bulwarks, Soyinka in this essay holds up
the model of the poeticized agnosticism of the twelfth century Persian
poet and mystic, Omar Khayyam, who enjoined the liberal enjoyment
of wine as an antidote to the killjoy repressiveness of organized religion
and asserted: "to be free from belief and unbelief is my religion." "Omar
Khayyam," Soyinka observes, "scoffed at the reification of the ineffable"
in the organized monotheistic religions. This idea provides a link with
Soyinka's affirmation in this essay of the value of Africa's spiritual and
religious heritage for the modern world; this African spiritual heritage, in
Soyinka's view, also derives from a radical refusal to "reify the ineffable"
into revealed dogmas which fuel the supremacist myths and salvationist
zealousness of cultures which set out to dominate and colonize others.
Indeed, the concluding words of this essay are worth quoting in the way
in which they seem to sum up Soyinka's ideas on the tremendous residual
capacities in the heritage of spirit and imagination in Africa to meet the

violence and negations of modernity which run through the three phases
of his critical writings:

religions do exist such as on this continent, that can boast of never having
launched a war, any form of jihad or crusade, for the furtherance of their beliefs.
Yet those beliefs have proved themselves bedrocks of endurance and survival,
informing communities as far away as the Caribbean and the Americas.
   Is there, or is there not a lesson for our universe in this? Is there no lesson
here for those dogmatic, over-scriptured and over-annotated monumentalities
whose rhetoric and secular appropriations far exceeded the ascertainable, inner
verities of their spiritual claims? (*ADO2*, 239)

It is a large subject matter that Soyinka engages in the three long essays
which make up the contents of *The Burden of Memory, the Muse of Forgiveness*. This subject is nothing short of the perennially perplexing problem
of what transpires when the historic supports and institutional bases of
extreme domination and servitude imposed by one group on another
crumble and master and slave, exploiter and the exploited are forced to
settle accounts, morally, spiritually and materially, on issues of atonement,
recompense and restitution. This problem is of course of cardinal importance to Africa's experience of modernity, given the centuries-old ravages
of slavery, colonialism, apartheid and racism, together with waves and
cycles of state criminality imposed on their own kind by internal rulers,
tyrants and oligarchs. On the atrocities and traumas experienced by
African peoples in this long chain of oppression, there are few writers to
match the graphic, moving eloquence of Soyinka's prose. He is equally
moving in his account of the always fraught, often terrifying attempts
of the violated and the dehumanized on the African continent to exact
justice from their erstwhile violators and dehumanizers. What is more,
Soyinka's witness-bearing in this book embraces virtually all attempts at
recompense and reconciliation between former oppressors and their victims in the contemporary world, from South Africa to Argentina, from
Chile to Rwanda, and from Cambodia to Ethiopia. In this particular
dimension of the book, *The Burden of Memory* contains some of Soyinka's
most lucid and forcefully eloquent prose writing.
   But the Nigerian author's purpose in this book is not only to bear
witness; it is also to try to understand, to anticipate and to move readers
to action. In these goals, the great classical prose virtues of simplicity and
directness elude Soyinka. Or, more appropriately, they are not his forte,
not his usual rhetorical and discursive weapons of choice. His strengths in
these aspects of prose writing lie in the extensive use of elaborate conceits,

irony, ambiguity and paradox, all figures and strategies which make for deliberate over-elaboration of a theme, for visionary intuition, and for epiphanic insight. Nowhere is this more apparent in the book than in the great demands made on the reader to keep abreast of the bewildering, but ultimately fruitful range of meanings and inflections that Soyinka gives to the two enigmatic terms in the title of the book – "the burden of memory"; "the muse of forgiveness." "Meaning" in both cases is far less a condition apprehensible through isolable facts and realities than a way of being-in-the-world and being-with-others *in extremis*. In this respect, it could be validly argued that Soyinka in this book is responding to the fact that neither "forgiveness" nor "restitution" has ever been a simple matter to work out between former oppressors and their victims.

But beyond this, Soyinka is in this courageous book responding also to what would seem to be two African peculiarities which enormously complicate the settling of accounts between former colonizers and colonized, former slave holders and the progeny of their manumitted slaves – especially their progeny. One of these is the extensively documented fact that perhaps more than any other "racial" group in the modern world, African peoples tend more to forgive their erstwhile oppressors and dehumanizers, foreign and indigenous. The other point is no less portentous: the claims of Africans for restitution and reparations from their historic oppressors are considerably morally compromised by the fact that African tyrants and despots have visited on their own kind atrocities and oppressions almost on the scale of those visited on them by foreign settlers and conquerors. These presumed "African" exceptionalisms defy the equivocations of diplomats, the hypocrisies and expediencies of rulers and politicians, and the opportunisms and simplifications of racial purists and demagogues. For this reason, in arguing against notions of simple forgiveness, statutes of limitation on restitution for slavery, and degrees and forms of enslavement, Soyinka in this book is as uncompromising as his arguments are irrefutable in his denunciation of such rulers, diplomats and demagogues.

Are Africans in particular and Black people generally more readily forgiving toward their historic enslavers and oppressors? And correspondingly, is their memory of oppression, of dehumanization by foreign and local oppressors tragically short? If this is the case, are these the expressions of a unique African psyche, a unique African spirituality? Is love of one's enemy a supreme virtue or the ultimate folly? What is the legacy of reflections on these matters in autochthonous African orders of knowledge and belief systems and what residual contemporary expressions do they take? Finally, what have the writers and poets of the African world written about these issues? These are the daunting questions which Soyinka tackles in this book and this is why the book is a melange of literary criticism, cultural theory, moral philosophy and metacritical speculation.

Bearing in mind that all the writers and poets from all corners of the African world – continent and Diaspora – whose writings Soyinka explores in *The Burden of Memory* are male, this book contains some of the most comprehensively comparatist reflections on world Black writing to date. To his credit, Soyinka does not ignore peculiarities and specificities of hemispheric, national and class differences among these writers of the Black world; there is even an extended comparison between the specific literary and cultural effects of French and British colonialism on the elites of their respective colonies. But ultimately, his concept of this "Black World" is formulated around a rubric of pure, autochthonous anteriority which predates all waves of foreign conquest and domination of Africa. Since, in this book, this notion is considerably amplified and finessed beyond any of its previous incarnations in Soyinka's critical thought – definitely an advance on its expression in *Myth, Literature and the African World* – it is useful to quote at some length from one of his most extensive extemporizations on it:

By this I simply mean that, if we succeeded in leapfrogging backwards in time over the multiple insertions of contending forces of dissension – be they of the West or the Orient, and with all their own mutually destructive schisms and fragmentations – if, by this process, we are able to regain a measure of anterior self-knowledge, it may be possible to regard religio-cultural interventions as possibly no more than disruptive illusions whose ramifications hold the future in thrall. In any case, how recent, in any effective way, were some of these intrusions? Of course, there is no suggestion here that the accretions of all such interventions be abandoned on all fronts, not in the least. . . . Our proposition is simply one of recollection, to go back to our commencing code, memory. The need for the preservation of the material and spiritual properties by which memory is invested. Acceptance of both its burdens and triumphs or – better still – its actuality, the simple fact of its anterior existence and validity for its time. To accept that is to recognize the irrationality of mutual destructiveness on behalf of any values, any values whatsoever, however seductive – cultural, ideological, religious, or race-authenticated – that intervened and obscured or eroded those *multiple anteriorities* – of any kind – from which our being once took its definition. (*TBM*, 62–3) (My emphasis)

It is important to note that Soyinka talks of multiple *anteriorities* here and that this is the very first time that he pluralizes and relativizes the term in his critical thought. All the same, the notion is, I would suggest, more of a poetic conceit than an objectively verifiable historical and cultural referent, even though Soyinka intends it to be simultaneously both! I suggest that the term operates like other similarly elaborate conceits or concept-metaphors in Soyinka's aesthetic philosophy like "the fourth stage," "the vortex of archetypes," "the chthonic realm" and "the dark whirlpool of energies." The crucial importance of these concepts for Soyinka's aesthetic theory makes it necessary, if daunting, for the student of his critical and theoretical writings to attempt an ordering of relations among the disparate, often conflicting categories of his aesthetic philosophy. This is all the more necessary because, with most scholars who have so far applied their energies to the difficult and comprehensive nature of Soyinka's aesthetic ideas, it is as if after "The Fourth Stage" and after the essays collected in *Myth*, Soyinka stopped writing. It is perhaps indisputable that the kernel of his aesthetic philosophy is indeed to be found in these essays, but as I hope to have demonstrated in this chapter, Soyinka's writings of the 1980s and 1990s considerably expanded the scope and the intricacy of both his aesthetic theory and his critical thought.

Let us conclude by observing that the tragic mythopoesis which stands at the centre of Soyinka's aesthetic philosophy is embedded in a poetics of culture rooted in a metaphysics of nature, a "natural supernaturalism," to press the title of M.H. Abrams' famous monograph on European Romanticism into service here.[20] Indeed, Soyinka's deep affinities with the Romantics, with both their revolutionary ideals and their relationship to nature, has been explored by several critics.[21] The fundamental factor which separates Soyinka from the Romantics is less his efforts to ground his aesthetic ideas in African expressive and ideational matrices, as important as these are, than his acute sense of the radical nature of evil. It takes the form of an insistence in his theoretical writings on the terrifying, destructive urgings and promptings which are both forces of nature and the roots of all that is creative in mankind. Soyinka's notion of action and will, indeed his over-valorization of the latter, is based on the model of nature's awesome powers and forces, both external nature and the "nature" within us. Indeed, in Soyinka's ideational system, it is ultimately unproductive if not futile, to separate "external" from "internal" nature since the same life-force, the same secret tropism animates all of nature and gives it its unity of Being. And what is more, the roots of tragedy, in our author's elaborate theorizations on the subject, lie ultimately in the fragmentation – in one individual life, in communal collectivities, in the coming into being of national groups and "races" – of nature's infinite unity:

Man is grieved by a consciousness of the loss of the eternal essence of his being and must indulge in symbolic transactions to recover the totality of being. Tragedy, in Yoruba traditional drama, is the anguish of this severance, the fragmentation of essence from self. (*ADO2*, 30)

This notion of "fragmentation of essence from self" is crucial for grasping the revolutionary and idealistic dimensions of Soyinka's tragic mythopoesis. It also enables us to perceive the crucial fact that the relentless emphasis on fragmentation, disjuncture and alienation, as themes and techniques, places this mythopoesis solidly in a post-Romantic, *modernist* framework. For it is in the cracks and disjunctures generated by this "fragmentation" that Soyinka both locates the necessity and efficacy of ritual and justifies his great investment in actions and expressions of the Will which attempt to bridge the chasms that separate different spheres and orders of experience and reality. One of the central constructs of Soyinka's aesthetic theory, "the fourth stage," is an expression of his attempt to connect this extremely abstract concept with apprehensible temporal and phenomenological referents. For this "fourth stage" is the liminal area of transition between the three spheres of life and experience which Soyinka renders as time past, present and future, or its metaphysical cognates, the "worlds" of the ancestors and the dead, the living and the unborn. Rites – and not only passage rites – are attempts to ford the divides which separate these tragically sundered entities of a presumed original, primal unity of Being and nature; they work to make it possible to pass from one sphere or domain of life to another. Thus, his investment in ritual idioms and his insistence, in the face of powerful critiques, that *his* notion of ritual is entirely compatible with the revolutionary currents of culture and society, all point to the fact that "the fourth stage" acts as a liminal space to more than the formulaic threesome of time past, present and future; it expands suggestively to the "worlds" of the rich and the poor, the exploiters and the exploited, woman and man, the young and the aged, animal, vegetal and mineral life. Philip Brockbank, in a seminal essay on Soyinka's concept and practice of tragic ritual has expressed this idea in an unforgettable formulation:

There were (and are) communities of the oppressors and the oppressed, of the rich and the poor, the torturers and the tortured, the protected and the exposed, the masters and the servants, the knaves and the fools, and the governed and the ungoverned. They are not stable communities either – they shift about, collapse and destroy each other and a man's history can take him into many communities.[22]

This is as accurate as any account in Soyinka criticism of the underlying ethico-ideological conception of the protagonist characters of Soyinka's writings and the frames of reference and enveloping horizons of their agency and vision as prophets or would-be social reformers. To see this is to see the tremendous, non-formulaic flexibility of Soyinka's deployment of ritual idioms as a central axis of his aesthetic theory. Part of this flexibility – and the suppleness of his use of ritual and the corollary sacrificial motif – is the fact that he consistently subjects this ritual matrix to sometimes savagely ironic inspection. These particular aspects of Soyinka's aesthetic theory are extensively explored in the following two chapters of this study which examine the genre of the Nigerian author's greatest aesthetic and ideological investment and accomplishment – drama.

CHAPTER 3

The "drama of existence": sources and scope

Event in literature is experienced according to the scale of its treatment.

Wole Soyinka, *Myth, Literature and the African World*

Drama in particular, no doubt because it is the most social of the arts, provides the site in which this inherent menace is most strident. In whatever country in black Africa that you open the curtain, you will find that in the absence of genuine democracy, the life of drama is lived on the edge of the cliff . . . The stark reality impresses itself upon us: all dramatists with a conscience know that when they play, they play dangerously.

Femi Osofisan, "Playing Dangerously"

Bad playwrights in every epoch fail to understand the enormous efficacy of the transformations that take place before the spectators' eyes. Theatre is change and not simple presentation of what exists; it is becoming and not being.

Augusto Boal, *Theatre of the Oppressed.*

Soyinka's achievement in drama, relative to the other forms and genres of literary expression, is a fascinating combination and synthesis of individual talent and sensibility, formal institutional training and practical theatre experience, and the weight of received, subliminally absorbed cultural tradition. His early work in the British theatre at a time of important aesthetic and political redirection in that theatre has been amply documented, though not critically assessed.[1] So has the influence of the Western theatrical heritage on the Nigerian playwright, especially as codified and transmitted in the works of canonical and non-canonical figures and movements like Euripides and Aristophanes, Shakespeare and Jacobean drama, Eugene O'Neill and Bertolt Brecht, the music hall revue and agit-prop street theatre.[2] But even though the specific African influences on his drama have also been acknowledged, the sheer weight of this influence has not received extended critical assessment.

In one of his most important theoretical essays on drama and theatre, Soyinka has himself eloquently, though indirectly, acknowledged
his enormous debts to the traditions of drama and theatre in Africa.
This is the essay "Theatre in Traditional African Societies: Survival
Patterns,"[3] an essay that is, at the very least, as important as the most
widely discussed of Soyinka's theoretical essays, "The Fourth Stage."
The essay is an authoritative, sweeping exploration of the African theatrical heritage, particularly under the interdiction of Christianity and
Islam, and against the pervasive dislocations of colonialism in general.
What is particularly noteworthy about the essay is the way in which it
departs from the conventional "cultural nationalist" tactic of merely affirming the survival of traditional precolonial theatrical forms against
colonialist and Eurocentric denials of their validity or vitality. Rather
than this simple "indigenist" line, Soyinka adopts the far more challenging Cabralist approach of investigating the emergence and evolution of
modern West African theatre in the context of the complicated dialectics of cultural repression and nationalist resistance under colonial rule.[4]
In the process, the Nigerian playwright locates the areas of density of
theatrical expression in precolonial Africa – Africa's "theatre belt," so to
speak – and the ruses and disguises that the most significant theatrical
expressions in early to late colonial Africa had to assume in order to survive the onslaught of colonial cultural hegemony. Some of these expressions which survived, Soyinka tells us, could only do so in rather bizarre
mutations:

West Africa in this decade (1930s) could boast of a repertoire of shows displaying the most bizarre products of eclectic art in the history of theatre. Even
cinema, an infant art, had by then left its mark on West African theatre. Some
of Bob Johnson's acts were adaptations of Charlie Chaplin's escapades, not
omitting his costume and celebrated shuffle. And the thought of Empire Day
celebration concerts at which songs like 'Mimi the Moocher' formed part of
the evening musical recitals, side by side with 'God's Gospel is our Heritage'
and vignettes from the life of a Liberian stevedore, stretches the contemporary imagination, distanced from the historical realities of colonial West Africa
(*ADO2*, 143)

It should of course be pointed out that the thrust of this essay is not
merely to identify and reject the bizarre hybridity of West African theatre forms under colonialism; rather, the essay's main line of argument
is the identification and affirmation of the most durable forms which
evolved into what we could call a resisting, ebullient hybridity. This is the

sentiment behind the following statement of affirmation of the legacy of one particular hybrid form of theatre in colonial West Africa:

We will conclude with the 'new' theatre form which has proved the most durable; hybrid in its beginnings, the 'folk opera' has become the most expressive language of theatre in West Africa (*ADO2*, 144)

And after documenting the ways in which "the (most) expressive language of theatre" of this "folk opera" was often deployed to oppose the repressive policies of both colonial and postcolonial regimes, Soyinka then gives an account of how one particular dramatist – Hubert Ogunde – evolved his own unique, powerful theatre form out of the diverse currents and forms thrown up by the colonial encounter. This account could very well serve as a profile of the impulses driving Soyinka's own work as a dramatist. For this reason, it is useful to quote from the account at some length:

Hubert Ogunde exemplifies what we have referred to up until now as the survival patterns of traditional theatrical art. From the outset of his theatrical career, Ogunde's theatre belonged only partially to what we have described as the 'Nova Scotian' tradition. His musical instrumentation was all borrowed from the West, movement on stage was pure Western chorus-line, nightclub variety. Nevertheless, the attachment to traditional musical forms (albeit with Western impurities) gradually became more assertive. Encouraged no doubt by the appearance of more tradition-minded groups such as Kola Ogunmola and Duro Ladipo, Hubert Ogunde in the early sixties began to employ traditional instruments in his music; his music delved deeper into home melodies, and even his costumes began to eschew the purely fabricated, theatrically glossy, for recognizable local gear. Rituals appeared with greater frequency and masquerades became a frequent feature – often, it must be added, as gratuitous insertions. Ogunde's greatest contribution to West African drama – quite apart from his innovative energy and his commitment to a particular political line – lies in his as yet little appreciated musical 'recitative' style, one which he has made unique to himself. It has few imitators, but the success of his records in this genre of 'dramatic monologues' testifies to the chord it elicits from his audience. Based in principle on the Yoruba *rara* style of chanting, but stricter in rhythm, it is melodically a modernistic departure, flexibly manipulated to suit a variety of themes. Once again, we find that drama draws on other art forms for its survival and extension. It is no exaggeration to claim that Hubert Ogunde's highest development of the chanted dramatic monologue can be fixed at the period of the political ban of his *Yoruba Ronu*. Evidently, all art forms flow into one another, confirming . . . that the temporary historic obstacles to the flowering of a particular form sometimes lead to its transformation into other media of expression, or even the birth of totally different genres. (*ADO2*, 145)

Only a comprehensive and sympathetic study of the historic conditions which produced the theatre of Hubert Ogunde in particular and, more generally the travelling theatre tradition, could have generated the acuity and precision of the observations and analysis that we find in this quote. This underscores Soyinka's immersion in the vigorous traditions of Africa's "theatre belt" in West Africa, traditions shaped by a history of resistance to colonial cultural aggression as well as a pronounced tendency to make appropriations from, and recombinations of diverse other indigenous and foreign forms and media of performance. These are the fundamental roots of the great technical and formalistic range of Soyinka's dramaturgy, of the scope of his experimentation with a great diversity of literary and nonliterary sources, with elite forms as well as popular idioms, and with both the "legitimate" theatre and its performative "others." In other words, if it is now generally accepted by students of Soyinka's drama that the fashioning of an extremely flexible, eclectic and synthetic dramaturgy is perhaps the ultimate mark of his formal achievement as a dramatist, the roots of this accomplishment are to be found in the precursors in precolonial, colonial and postcolonial performance traditions that Soyinka acknowledges and celebrates in that essay, "Theatre in Traditional African Cultures."

This last observation is particularly relevant to the centrality which has been ascribed to ritual in scholarly discussions of Soyinka's drama. In the fourth chapter of this study we will explore the interface between drama and ritual in Soyinka's theories of drama and theatre and in his most ambitious plays. The present chapter gives a profile of the general features, the accomplishments, and some weaknesses of his drama. To do so, it is useful to first give a sense of the general shape of his dramatic corpus.

Soyinka is best known and celebrated as a playwright and dramatist, even though he has written extensively in all the genres of literature. The plays bulk much larger in his corpus than either poetry or fiction, and Soyinka's greatest critical successes have come from his dramas. The Nobel Prize citation specifically mentions this point: "Who, in a wide cultural perspective and with poetic overtones, fashions the drama of existence." (Nobel citations are usually short, succinct, incomplete sentences). Also, Soyinka's influence on younger African authors has been more decisive, more evident in his plays than the impact of his writings in other genres and forms.[5] Moreover, his dramatic theories have been more favorably received and more seriously engaged by scholars than his general theories on transcultural aesthetic experience in

Africa and the contemporary world. And most important of all, Soyinka's plays are performed throughout Africa and the rest of the world, in the English-language original and in translations into many of the world's major literary languages. Soyinka may indeed be the first non-European, non-American playwright to have achieved this particular status as a dramatist.[6]

The criticisms often leveled at Soyinka's novels give us some clues to the aesthetic factors behind the relatively greater success of his dramas. There has been notable praise for Soyinka's technical accomplishments as a novelist in his first novel, *The Interpreters*, but many critics have noted that the characters and situations in his second novel, *Season of Anomy*, are too abstract, too cerebral to really come alive in ways that engage readers at deep emotional and psychological levels.[7] This is a criticism that no one can validly apply to Soyinka's dramas. Expressed differently, the characters of *The Interpreters*, such as Egbo, Bamidele, or Lazarus, and of *Season of Anomy*, such as Ofeyi, Iriyise or "the Dentist," do not come close to the presence, individuality and memorableness of the characters of Soyinka's haunting creations in dramatic characterization such as we have in the likes of Demoke and Eshuoro in *Dance of the Forests*, Baroka in *Lion and the Jewel*, Jero in the two "Jero plays," Professor, Samson and Say-Tokyo Kid in *The Road*, the Old Man and the mendicants in *Madmen and Specialist* and Elesin Oba in *Death and the King's Horseman*.

Soyinka comes to these two genres – the novel and drama – with the same self-confident aesthetic venturesomeness, the same boldly innovative spirit. What distinguishes his vastly dissimilar accomplishments in each of these genres is perhaps connected to the fact of the dramatic text's links to the medium of stage performance. These links impose obligations of effective communication between the writer and his or her audience that don't exist for the novelist, obligations codified as conventions specific to the genre of drama. Soyinka has shown himself to be more a master and innovator in the manipulation of the conventions of drama and theatre than he has been with those of narrative.

There are several factors responsible for this, some simple and uncomplicated, others more complex. One fairly obvious, incontrovertible and well-documented factor is Soyinka's extensive experience in the theatre in Britain and Nigeria. His formal apprenticeship in the theatre, as well as some of his early work, took place in the British theatre at a time of important, seminal redirection in the art and politics of that theatre. Additionally, his work as a playwright has been tremendously affected by his work with some of the most important English-language

amateur and semiprofessional companies in Africa, some of which the
Nigerian dramatist himself founded and developed. As James Gibbs has
observed in his very well researched and informative book on Soyinka's
drama and theatre, many of Soyinka's published plays were shaped by
the production and reception histories of these companies' performances
of his plays.[8] Moreover, there is the factor of Soyinka being himself an
actor and director, not forgetting the fact that he has also been an educator in the arts of the theatre.[9] Finally, whether as an actor, director
or educator, Soyinka's experience as a practical man of the theatre has
been overwhelmingly in the subsidized, noncommercial theatre. This
last point is indeed one of the main differences in background and experience between Soyinka and Athol Fugard, perhaps the only rival to
Soyinka's claim to being Africa's foremost playwright. This point of the
impact that Soyinka's theatre experience within university theatres and
semiprofessional troupes has had on his dramaturgy is one that we will
return to later in this chapter. Before then, it is useful to get a sense
of the totality of our author's dramatic corpus. And in exploring this
topic, perhaps the most important point to bear in mind is that, in his
dramaturgy, Soyinka has fashioned idioms and languages of communication so eclectic, so exuberantly flexible that he has been able to pursue
diverse, even conflicting objectives, sometimes simultaneously. One of
these, and a central one at that, is his use of the medium of drama for
passionate opposition to political tyranny and social inequities and the
human suffering that they cause, both in short dramatic sketches and
revues and in "weightier" and more ambitious plays.

We get a sense of the richness and diversity of Soyinka's dramatic
corpus if the plays are grouped chronologically, both in terms of their
staging and publication history and their location in the phases of the
playwright's career as a dramatist and political activist, especially as this
parallels and responds to the changing realities of postcolonial Africa.
Using this composite, many-layered approach, several significant and
interesting patterns become perceptible. For instance, Soyinka was at
the most prolific phase of his career as a dramatist in the period between
the late 1950s to the end of the 1960s. Of the seven or eight plays written
or staged in this period, three or four, *A Dance of the Forests*, *The Road*, *Kongi's
Harvest* and *The Lion and the Jewel*, are among our author's most important
and lasting contributions to the art of drama; two other plays from this
period, *The Swamp Dwellers* and *The Strong Breed*, are two of the most
popularly appreciated and produced among his more "conventional"
plays. By contrast, the 1990s constitute Soyinka's "leanest" decade as a

playwright, with a total of three plays, *A Scourge of Hyacinths*, *From Zia with Love* and *The Beatification of Area Boy*, the first two of these titles being in fact versions of the same text, one for the medium of radio and the longer version for stage production. Juxtaposed against this broad profile is the fact that the "middle period" of the 1970s and 1980s – the post-Civil War, post-incarceration period of Soyinka's career – saw the writing and staging of satirical comedies and social dramas considerably more ferocious, and much gloomier in mood than the plays of the earlier period of Soyinka's efflorescence as a dramatist. Indeed, the first play of this post-incarceration period, *Madmen and Specialists*, marks a crucial turning point in Soyinka's dramaturgy; in language, characterization and dramatic action, it seems to be Soyinka's own "flower of evil" in its frenetic literalization of the explosive and strategic anti-aesthetic which the Nigerian dramatist had called for in the very first long interview that he gave after his release from prison:

... a book, if necessary, should be a hammer, a hand grenade which you detonate under a stagnant way of looking at the world ... we haven't begun actually using words to punch holes inside people ... But let's do our best to use words and style, when we have the opportunity, to arrest the ears of normally complacent people; we must make sure we explode something inside them which is a parallel of the sordidness which they ignore outside.[10]

Madmen and Specialists occupies a special place in the evolution of Soyinka's dramaturgy, not because the ferocious wit and bitter social commentary which it deploys are without precedent in the plays of the 1950s and 1960s, but for the important fact that it took these elements to new directions by deploying them as mechanisms for extensive and de-liberate de-formations of language, form and style. In subsequent plays such as *Opera Wonyosi*, *From Zia with Love* and *The Beatification of Area Boy*, Soyinka would attempt a reprise of this deliberate and artful linguis-tic and formalistic implosion to depict and at the same time challenge the deepening political crises in postcolonial Africa and the uncertainty, fear and hardship that these crises imposed both on sensitive individuals among the elites and the vast majority of entire populations. These latter plays do not have the brilliance and power of *Madmen and Specialists*, but they are not unlike that play – and others like *Jero's Metamorphosis* and *A Play of Giants* – in upping the ante in Soyinka's use of dramatic and the-atrical experimentalism to respond to the waves of outrage perpetrated by many of the continent's rulers in the third and fourth decades of the post-independence period in Africa. This particular artistic response by Soyinka became more perceptible as climates of uncertainty gave way to regimes based on terror and the fomenting of small and large bloodbaths to consolidate and perpetuate tyrannical military and civilian autocracies.[11]

The foregoing observations indicate that there is a perceptible correlation between the evolution of Soyinka's dramaturgy and the unraveling of the promises of political independence in postcolonial Africa that Fanon so prophetically predicted in *The Wretched of the Earth*. This evolution seems intelligible in three phases. In the first phase which spans the late 1950s to the end of the 1960s, the Nigerian dramatist establishes his power and talent as a dramatist in the originality of his handling of dramatic form. In plays of this period, Soyinka makes sharp, memorable responses to the violence and creeping social anomie of postcolonial Africa, but these plays do not take his ambivalence about the prospects for change to the depths of the pessimism of the plays of the 1970s and the 1980s. This first period is also the only period in Soyinka's career when he is able to work extensively, almost full-time, as a practicing dramatist, and with amateur and semiprofessional acting companies which serve as laboratories for the generation and staging of his plays before their publication as written texts. Thus, irrespective of the overall moods of the plays of this period in his career, this phase constitutes the glory years of Soyinka's work on the stage of the English-language theatre in Nigeria. Indeed, it is almost impossible to overstate the seminal nature of the influence that this phase of Soyinka's career has had on subsequent English-language drama and theatre in Nigeria.[12]

In the second phase spanning the 1970s and 1980s, Soyinka's work in the theatre is more fitful, less sustained, and this is consistent with the exigencies of the playwright's deepening embroilment in political activism, the occasions of short or prolonged exile, and his final departure from the Nigerian university system in 1985. As has been previously noted, this period produced some of the most pessimistic, the most savagely iconoclastic plays in Soyinka's dramatic corpus. However, it is also the case that unlike the pessimism of the earlier period, it is a fighting, more *activist* despair; even the nihilism that we see in some of the plays of this "middle period" such as *Madmen and Specialists* and *Opera Wonyosi* are anything but defeatist. And relatively speaking, this period constitutes the phase of Soyinka's most self-conscious experimentation as a playwright and theatre director, a fact which seems as much a matter of contingency as it is of deliberate policy, for with less available time for the Nigerian dramatist to work in a sustained manner in the theatre, he had to tailor his plays to the exigencies of the staging and production context, whether at home in Nigeria, or abroad in exile.

The third and most current period has provided the leanest harvest of plays in Soyinka's career as a dramatist. And again, this seems traceable less to a waning interest in the medium of drama than to the overdetermining fact of an enforced near total absence from the theatre due to this being the most intensely activist phase of Soyinka's involvement in the unfolding political crises of Nigeria and the African continent. Indeed, it is symptomatic of this condition that the plays of this period are not only the most intensely ideological and political of Soyinka's plays, they are also notable in being unambiguously partisan on the side of the disenfranchised masses. The ambivalent solicitude of the plays of the two earlier phases toward working class and déclassé, lumpen characters, as individuals and as a social group, is replaced in the three plays of this phase – *A Scourge of Hyacinths*, *From Zia with Love* and *The Beatification of Area Boy* – with a cautious faith in the ability of the urban poor and disenfranchised to liberate themselves from their degraded, intolerable conditions of existence.

Of course, this evolutionary profile only provides a limited interpretive perspective on Soyinka's drama. For the division of the work of major playwrights with a substantial body of plays into phases, though useful up to a point, is nonetheless qualified by its limitation in providing an adequate critical purchase on the subtle continuities and consistencies between the phases. This is as true of the drama of Soyinka as it is of Ibsen, Brecht or Fugard. In this wise, perhaps the most impressive consistency of Soyinka as a dramatist, no matter which "phase' of his work we choose to explore, is the fact that, at its best, his drama is an actors' and directors' theatre. In other words, when his dramatic imagination seizes on a thought, an event, a general social condition, or an intensely private mystical experience, the resulting play – or act, or scene, or moment of a play – provides a powerful technical vehicle for actors and directors to exercise their art and craft. This is as true of relatively "minor" plays like *The Trials of Brother Jero*, *Jero's Metamorphosis*, *The Swamp Dwellers* and *The Strong Breed* as it is of what Annemarie Heywood, in one of the most insightful essays on the challenges to the staging of Soyinka's plays, called the "weighty" plays.[13] These are dramas like *Kongi's Harvest*, *A Dance of the Forests*, *The Road*, *Madmen and Specialists* and *Death and the King's Horseman*. And as these lists of "minor" and "major" plays show, Soyinka's sure sense of what works, what enlivens dramatic characterization, dialogue or action cuts across the generic boundaries of comedy, tragedy, satire or

farce. With regard to the dynamics of stage performance, he is probably
at his most adept in extemporizing on the classic comic and tragicomic
prototypes, as shown in such characters as Brother Jeroboam of the "Jero
plays," Dende and the choral group of the Aweri Reformed Fraternity
in *Kongi's Harvest*, the slew of thugs, touts and layabouts in *The Road*,
and Alaba/Eleazer/Semuwe, the changeling protagonist of *Requiem for
a Futurologist*. But as the memorable protagonists of Soyinka's most disturbing and perplexing plays demonstrate, his dramatic imagination is
truly ecumenical. Even where he falters, or becomes heavy footed on
technical, formalistic grounds, he is able to hold his own as a master
of the medium. Annemarie Heywood's spirited apologia for Soyinka's
dramaturgy makes this point persuasively in her ripostes against Bernth
Lindfors, one of Soyinka's most caustic critics:

The more weighty plays which take their shape from inner dialectic are sharply
criticized by Lindfors. In the progression from *A Dance of the Forests* ("arty structure', 'plotless plot', 'incoherence') via *The Road* (' a definitely difficult play which
makes no compromises to instant intelligibility') to *Madmen and Specialists* ('a
multifaceted cryptograph') he (Lindfors) diagnoses a growing 'tendency toward
meaningless frivolity which robs his work of any serious implication' (about the
very last thing to fault in this profoundly nihilistic exploration of the deadly follies of the political animal) and wonders for whom these plays are written –
'just for Westernized Yoruba eggheads... for a cosmopolitan international
elite... or simply for himself?'
    Whilst attacking the 'histrionic razzle-dazzle' of the basic articulation,
Lindfors concedes that even the plays he condemns make brilliant theatre.
Soyinka, he says, 'can apply a very slick surface to the roughest or least substantial of narrative foundations', and his 'plotless plots... could be enjoyed
as a series of well-paced theatrical happenings' without making much sense.
This is surely not good enough. The difficulty of obscure plays arises from their
idiom, or basic strategy, which is not well served by illusionist production and
'character'-acting inviting empathy. These plays are best plotted for production
as masques or cabaret, with characters conceived as masks, dialogue as choral,
movement and gesture as emblematic. (132)

The last sentence of this defense or apologia for Soyinka's avantgarde
dramaturgy, it would seem, takes things too far. Even the most unconventional, avantgardist plays of Soyinka, with their accentuation of the
radically anti-realist, anti-mimetic modes of theatre and performance
that he calls for in "The Fourth Stage," have substantial sequences of
realistic action and characterization. Correspondingly, Soyinka's early
naturalistic, more or less 'well-made' dramas like *The Swamp Dwellers*,
The Strong Breed, *Camwood on the Leaves* and *The Lion and the Jewel*, all have

such large doses of genre-bending features that their staging as straight-forwardly conventional slice-of-life dialogue-drama would be totally out of order. Thus, a neat division of Soyinka's plays into realist and non-realist groupings is neither possible nor necessary. Indeed, one of the most remarkable features of Soyinka's drama is the degree to which he is able to create powerfully rendered character, language and action in either mode, realist or anti-realist.

Beside chronology, two approaches which have been applied to extrapolating intelligible patterns of differentiation in Soyinka's large dramatic corpus are the approach informed by thematic emphases, and that which is structured by attentiveness to the theoretical and practical interest of the Nigerian playwright in the interface between drama and ritual. This latter approach is perhaps the most widely distributed area of critical and theoretical interest in Soyinka's drama in recent times; it is also, as we shall argue, the most problematic. For this reason, we shall come to a comprehensive engagement of that approach in a separate chapter on Soyinka's most ambitious dramatic creations.

The thematic approach has been the favored methodology of scholars and critics more interested in Soyinka as a writer than as a theatre artist, the prime examples being Eldred Jones, Gerald Moore and Adrian Roscoe.[14] These scholars and critics have thus tended to group the dramas according to themes, subject matter and recurrent motifs. Since such scholars and critics were at one time clearly in the majority among students and enthusiasts of Soyinka's works – at least for the first two decades of the playwright's career – this approach has dominated others in the explication of Soyinka's plays. In the perspective of this particular approach, Soyinka's dramatic corpus reveal that certain themes, ideas and clusters of motifs recur throughout his plays. For instance, in the light of Soyinka's abiding interest in *power*, in its ineluctable, "epiphenomenal" aspects as well as its institutional, material effects and ramifications, we are enabled to see a grouping of plays from all the periods of his career which we might designate "Power Plays." The outstanding, full-blown examples of this category of plays in Soyinka's dramatic corpus are *Kongi's Harvest* (1967), *Opera Wonyosi* (1981), *A Play of Giants* (1984) and *From Zia with Love* (1992). There are also partial or fragmentary dramatic explorations of this theme in plays such as *Dance of the Forests* (1960), *Madmen and Specialists* (1971) and The *Bacchae of Euripides* (1973). And if corruption of power and reactionary violence constitute a common point of thematic focus in these "power plays," they do differ considerably in their underlying conception of dramatic action, theatrical technique, and *tone* and

these in turn inflect the theme of power itself. This observation demonstrates how, on the same basic theme, Soyinka's dramaturgy expresses
itself with great variation in technique, idiom and tone. Three examples
will serve to illustrate this point: *Kongi's Harvest*, *Opera Wonyosi* and *A Play
of Giants*.

The "Kongi" of the title of the play, *Kongi's Harvest*, is a wildly paranoid dictator of the imaginary state of Isma. The central conflict of the
play ranges those with Kongi against the dissidents who are opposed
to him. With Kongi is his elaborate state apparatus comprising bureaucrats, spies, brigades of "loyalist" conscripts in "voluntary" workers and
youth movements, and a conclave of retained intellectuals who write
the dictator's speeches and books, and are also periodically sequestered
from the rest of the nation to "think" for the dictator. At the time of
the first staging of the play, it was widely believed that these particular
expressions of paranoid autocracy and the claim of authorship of books
ghostwritten by intellectual hirelings constituted unmistakable allusions
to Kwame Nkrumah, an ascription Soyinka never exactly refuted, allowing only that his Kongi was a composite of many African dictators
of the period.[15] Against Kongi and this apparatus are ranged a loose
coalition of dissidents comprising Daodu and his lover, Segi, and their
farmers' and womens' producers' collectives. In its mixture of verse and
prose dialogues, music and song, dance and spectacle, *Kongi's Harvest* is
perhaps the liveliest of Soyinka's dramatic explorations of the theme of
corruption of power in the then newly independent African states. There
is a grim, dark moment at the play's climactic denouement with palpable
allusions to the biblical narrative of Salome and John the Baptist when
the decapitated head of the father of Segi, the play's only speaking female character, is presented in a covered bowl to the dictator in place
of the prize yam he expected as the "Spirit of Harvest."[16] (Segi's father,
a veteran political dissident himself, had been shot while trying to escape from political detention.) But the horror of the moment is highly
aestheticized, and it devolves into a bloodless, symbolic "coup de grace"
in which, frothing at the mouth, the mad dictator wordlessly harangues
the crowd gathered at the ceremonies while singing and dancing by
Segi's "women" increase in volume and energy, thereby "festivalizing"
this whole sequence as a mimed, spectacular denouement. The suggestion is that this is a symbolic neutralization of the antihumanism of the
deranged dictator. Indeed, most of the dramatic action of *Kongi's Harvest*
entails a romantic, even elegiac evocation of social and natural forces
of regeneration against their vitiation by the life-denying corruptions

of power represented by maniacal tyrants like Kongi, the dictator of Isma.

Opera Wonyosi, a composite adaptation of John Gay's *The Beggar's Opera* and Bertolt Brecht's *Threepenny Opera*, takes Soyinka's exploration of the power theme into a far more sinister and dystopian universe. The basic performance mode employed is the comic opera, infused with large doses of savage, caustic satire. The targets of this satire, as particularly malevolent examples of the corruption of power in the contemporary African postcolony are the Nigerian military dictatorship of the initial phase of the "oil boom" years (1973–78), and the "empire" proclaimed by Jean-Bedel Bokasa in the Central African Republic in the same period. In the spirit of Gay's and Brecht's parodic inversions of the classical opera, *Opera Wonyosi* deliberately disconcerts with its deployment of raucous but gutsy satirical songs and wild, off-scale oratory in which the boastful and buffoonish tyrants and their henchmen expose, and thereby denounce themselves. It is a hard task that Soyinka sets himself in this play since this involves using, on the one hand, parody to capture the notorious and outlandish performativity of the tyrannical misrule of many post-colonial African dictators and, on the other hand, deploying satire to cut the dictators and their love of pomp and display down to size by subjecting them and their love of display to ridicule. But the satirized realities are so grotesque, so horrific as to be almost neutralized and aestheticized by the parodic excess of the display. These realities, which are given sharp, bracingly parodic expressions in this play, include the notorious "murder of the innocents" when Bokasa personally supervised the brutal torture and resultant deaths of school children who had dared to protest the personal profiteering by the dictator from inflated costs of school uniforms and school supplies; the festive carnival atmosphere at the public execution of condemned robbers at stakes erected at the beaches of the Atlantic sea-front in Lagos; the routine, sadistic floggings of citizens by Nigerian military top-brass on pretexts supplied by real and imagined misdemeanors of the citizenry; the rampant criminal arson perpetrated by corrupt public officials on state buildings to destroy evidence of monumental theft of state funds, often leading to the loss of many lives. Unlike what we encounter in *Kongi's Harvest*, in *Opera Wonyosi* there are no dissidents, no credible opposition to the brutal, decadent tyrannical regimes in Lagos and Bangui; rather, the gross abuse of power and its corruptive influence circulates, in a Foucauldian manner, between and within the rulers and the ruled, the looters and the "looted."

This view of the "disseminated," unfocused and circulatory nature of power to which Michel Foucault and Vaclav Havel have given the most powerful theoretical formulation in the modern European context,[17] informs the dramatic action of *A Play of Giants* in its focused portrayal of four of the most odious African dictators and tyrants in the post-independence era, Idi Dada Amin of Uganda, Jean-Bedel Bokasa of the Central African Republic-turned-Empire, Macias Nguema of Equatorial Guinea, and Hastings Kamuzu Banda of Malawi. Soyinka gives a direct statement of this view of power in his preface to the play:

Power, we have suggested, calls to power, and vicarious power (that is, the sort enjoyed by the politically impotent intelligentsia) responds obsequiously to the real thing. Apart from self-identification with success, there is also a professed love (in essence a self-love) which is perverse, being also identical with the love of the slave-girl for her master. Often, on listening to the rationalizations of this group, I see that I am listening to the slave-girl in a harem, excusing the latest sadisms of the seraglio, exaggerating the scattered moments of generosity, of 'goodness', forgetting that even the exceptions to the rule merely emphasize the slave relations between herself and the master. Our friends professed to find in Idi Amin the figure of a misunderstood nationalist, revolutionary and even economic genius – after all, he did boot out the blood-sucking Asians, and was he not always to be relied upon for a hilarious insult against one super-power imperialist chieftain or another and their client leaders on the continent? (*TBE*, Preface)

According to Soyinka in this same preface, the model of dramatic *form* which he chose to express this "epiphenomenon" of power which entails complex acts of identification of the victims of dictatorial terror with the perpetrators of these monstrous acts is that represented by Jean Genet's play, *The Balcony*.[18] Presumably, Soyinka is responding to Genet's representation of power in that play primarily in terms of the seductive force of its expressivity, the potent but secret aestheticism of its *display* through spectacle, ceremonies, rituals, symbolism. Thus, a large "Genetian" part of the dramatic action of *The Play of Giants* involves a rather extended, static tableau in which the "giants" of the title, Kamini, Gunema, Kasko and Tobum – each respectively serving as very thinly disguised representations of Idi Amin, Macias Nguema, Jean-Bedel Bokasa and Mobutu – talk about and *parade* themselves as incarnations of replete, fulfilled power. However, another part of the play, departing from Genet's model, effectively desacralizes power by dramatizing the relentless loosening of Kamini's grip on power as some of his henchmen either countermand his orders or desert him, while inter-state, multilateral institutions like the

IMF and the World Bank retrench the monetary and diplomatic props of his grandiose, delusionary aggrandizement. The play ends in an explosively anti-Genetian apocalypse: Kamini holds all the other "giants" and representatives of the two erstwhile superpowers, the United States and the Soviet Union, hostage and, taking personal control over a battery of rocket and grenade launchers in the Bugaran embassy, he begins to rain deadly outbursts of these weapons of destruction on the United Nations headquarters. The element of dramatic parable in this phantasmagoric denouement is inescapable, if rather intricate. Soyinka seems to be suggesting that order, civility and legality are often the convenient facades of a fundamental, rampant and self-serving capitulation to the seductions of power; mindless terror and violence follow very quickly when the masks and facades are stripped away, and this can happen not only "out there" in Africa and the developing world, but also right in the heart of the metropole itself.

The thematic approach to the study of Soyinka's dramas is of course not exhausted by the cluster of themes around the subject of power. One book-length study of Soyinka's works, including his plays, is devoted exclusively to the cluster of themes and motifs around healing and regeneration, and rebirth and renewal after death or decay.[19] And there is a highly visible group of feminist critics who have taken Soyinka to task on the theme of gender and its representation in his plays.[20]

And indeed, the world of Soyinka's drama is intensively, normatively male-centered. The typical protagonist of his plays is a driven, visionary *male* who, like Prometheus, is unbound in a cruel, endlessly violent and destructive world, the world of the politics of dictatorship and repressiveness in the African postcolony. There are tough, steel-nerved and also sensitive women in some of Soyinka's plays, the best two examples of this being Iya Agba in *Madmen and Specialists* and Iyaloja in *Death and the King's Horseman*. Amope, the shrewish termagant of *The Trials of Brother Jero* is also sharply delineated, but no single female character in the Nigerian dramatist's plays is molded in the image, or comes in the putative line of the "primal energy" of Ogun that Soyinka in "The Fourth Stage" identifies as the "first actor." Indeed, the two central structural elements of characterization in Soyinka's drama – a strong, self-divided promethean protagonist and the choral group of socially disadvantaged characters ringed around the protagonist – are both typically constructed around an assumed normativity of maleness. Thus, even where there are two or three strong female presences in a Soyinka play, they are usually in the margins of the drama proper which unfurls as an *agon* between male protagonists and antagonists. The following unvarnished assertion of male superiority by Elesin Oba in the final scene of *Death and the King's Horseman* is extraordinary in its explicitness and though it is the *only* such baldly male-chauvinist expression in all of Soyinka's drama, it is nonetheless a metonymic pointer to the place of women in general in Soyinka's plays:

JANE (*hesitates, then goes to Elesin*): Please, try and understand. Everything my husband did was for the best.

ELESIN (*he gives her a long stare, as if trying to understand who she is*): You are the wife of the District Officer?

JANE: Yes, my name is Jane.

ELESIN: That is my wife over there. You notice how still and silent she sits? My business is with your husband.

(*DKH*, 73)

It must of course be appreciated that a protagonist does not reflect an author's beliefs and world-view; moreover, the normative maleness in Soyinka's drama is far more complexly articulated than this instance of crude expression of male chauvinism in one play. Additionally, in light of the larger canvas of the historic conflict between colonizer and colonized in the play, what we have here is the patriarchy of the colonized confronting that of the colonizers, the project of both colonization and the nationalist resistance that it engendered being both essentially male-centered.

More subliminally, normative maleness in Soyinka's drama is inscribed by the powerful currents of homosociality by which the most formative experiences of infancy through young adulthood of individual members of each sex take place away from intimate contact with members of the other sex. In Soyinka's dramas, this takes the form of the relative absence and marginalization of women in the main action of most plays in his dramatic corpus. Indeed much of the energy and élan of many of the playwright's most memorable plays derive from this factor. Such male homosocial bonding is at the heart of the energy and appeal of plays such as *The Road* and *From Zia with Love*, neither of which has a single female character.

The essential point in the foregoing observations on male-centeredness in Soyinka's plays is the point that what he knows best, what he writes most powerfully about is the world of men – in play and in turmoil. When one or two female presences crash that world, like Segi in *Kongi's Harvest* and Iya Agba and Iya Mate in *Madmen and Specialists*, it is mostly as over-symbolized essences representing the nurturing and healing powers of nature, lacking in the vigor, realism and complex contradictoriness of Soyinka's male characters. Soyinka has staunchly defended himself against feminist critiques of his work on this and other relevant issues; in the following discussion with a scholarly female interlocutor, he invokes something close to biological determinism as his ultimate defensive reaction, adding that only women writers can write truthfully and powerfully about women:

DAVID: I have some difficulty in coming to terms with your women characters who seem to combine the bitch and the Madonna. I think your depiction of women is unrealistic.

SOYINKA: Well, that is my attitude to women. Their form, their being, and the fact that they, unlike men, reproduce, cause them to become fused in my mind with Nature in a way that men are not and can never be. I am aware of criticism, especially feminist criticism which has been getting rabid among one or two individuals. There is no compromise for me on this subject. A woman's shape, a woman's reproductive capacity which is unique to the female sex just sets her apart from men. It does not mean that women are not equal to men intellectually, in capacities and so forth. But the figure of a woman, the biology of a woman – for me Nature is biology, obviously – just separates her; and I can never look at a woman in the same way as I can look at a man and when I reflect her in my writings she occupies that position. But you'll admit that there are exceptions. The Secretary, Dehinwa, in *The Interpreters* is obviously an exception because she was not treated as a symbol but as a member of the new generation.

DAVID: Yes, but I wish your women characters were a little more well-realized.

SOYINKA: But that's the role of women. It is the women who must realize themselves in their writings. I can't enter into the mind and the body of a woman. No, let women write about themselves. Why should they ask me to do that?

(David, 212)

The aesthetic, technical ramifications of Soyinka's admission of the deeply gendered nature of normative maleness in the embodiment of his characters are far more portentous for a dramatist than for a writer of fiction since, in a dramatic work intended for stage production, bodily experience is all. This is why, in terms of dramaturgy and the aesthetics of performance, Soyinka is at his weakest when excess of symbolism over referents combines with idealization to more or less efface the "integrity" of bodily experience. This is bad enough when it applies to male characters as with Forest Head in *A Dance of the Forests* and three of the four eponymous "giants" of *A Play of Giants*, Kasko, Gunema and Tuboum, all of whose flatness and one-dimensionality derive from the extreme idealization of their construction as central protagonists in their respective dramaturgic universes. But when idealization attaches to women characters in Soyinka's drama, or even to a specific male-female relationship, the result is a veritable aesthetic collapse. One of the worst dramaturgic solecisms in Soyinka's drama that is traceable to this problem is the scene between Daodu and Segi in the concluding section of Part One of *Kongi's Harvest* as the two lovers prepare themselves for a confrontation with the paranoiac, life-denying dictator, Kongi. The scene is constructed as a prolonged movement of emotional release, the only one such moment in the entire play for the two lovers and would-be revolutionaries. But it is an emotional release heavily overladen with an over-idealized symbolism in which the love between Daodu and Segi is mythicized as the consummation of oneness between the male and female principles and the resultant regeneration of the forces of nature. In the central pages of the dramatic text in which this scene is enacted, dialogue and action falter badly, progressively become inflated and mawkish; correspondingly, the life-affirming values inscribed in utterance, action and gesture in the scene take on an air of pietistic unreality:

DAODU: My eyes of rain, Queen of the Harvest night.
SEGI (*slowly relenting, half ashamed*): I was so afraid.
DAODU: There is nothing more to fear.
SEGI: I will never be afraid again.
DAODU: Two less for Kongi's collection. I am glad the live one is your father.
SEGI: I feel like dancing naked. If I could again believe, I would say it was a sign from heaven.
DAODU: Yes, if we were awaiting a sign, this would be it. It may turn me superstitious yet.
SEGI: I want to dance on gbegbe leaves – I know I have not been forgotten
DAODU: I'll rub your skin in camwood, you'll be flames at the hide of night.
SEGI: Come with me, Daodu.
DAODU: Now? There is still much to do before you meet us at the gates.
SEGI: Come through the gates tonight. Now, I want you in me, my Spirit of Harvest.
DAODU: Don't tempt me so hard. I am swollen like a prize yam under earth, but all harvest must await its season.

                                                              (*CP2*, 97–8)

The dramaturgic and aesthetic faults of this scene come to their apex when Segi's women break in on this romantic-symbolic exchange between the two lovers, robe Daodu in the resplendent costumes of the Spirit of Harvest and with their leader Segi, kneel before Daodu in adoration of, and supplication to his presumed salvational powers. These faults are all the more surprising because this scene comes from a play which, with all its faults, contains some of Soyinka's most sparkling and accomplished verse dialogue. Indeed, the very fact that this verse dialogue – narrated and chanted as paeans to the chiefly and ritual functions of Danlola and his court – contains a heavy freight of formalism and symbolism proves that it is not idealization or abstractionism in itself which proves insuperable for Soyinka's dramatic genius; rather, it is idealization without embodied, lived, acted-upon experience. This is perhaps the secret source of Soyinka's ability, almost without parallel among contemporary playwrights, to make ritual formalism a vigorous, vibrant theatrical expression. And this is so precisely because ritual ceremonialism is, for Soyinka, a lived, embodied experience. The following passage from "Hemlock," the prologue to *Kongi's Harvest*, shows Soyinka's deftness and discipline in giving form and body to ritual ceremonialism as a state of being-together-in-the-world:

(*As the king's men begin a dirge of 'ege', Danlola sits down slowly onto a chair, drawing more and more into himself*)

> DRUMMER: I saw a strange sight
> In the market today
> The day of the feast of Agemo
> The sun was high
> And the king's umbrella
> Beneath it.
> SARUMI: We lift the king's umbrella
> Higher than men
> But it never pushes
> The sun in the face.
> DRUMMER: I saw a strange sight
> In the market this day
> The sun was high
> But I saw no shadow
> From the king's umbrella.
> OGBO AWERI: This is the last
> That we shall dance together
> This is the last the hairs
> Will lift on our skin
> And draw together
> When the gbedu rouses
> The dead in Oshugbo...
> SARUMI: Don't pound the king's yam
> With a small pestle

> Let the dandy's wardrobe
> Be as lavish as the shop
> Of the dealer in brocades
> It cannot match an elder's rags
> DANLOLA (*almost to himself*): This dance is the last
> Our feet shall dance together
> The royal python may be good
> At hissing, but it seems
> The scorpion's tail is fire
> DRUMMER: The king's umbrella gives no more shade
> But we summon no dirge-master
> The tunnel passes through
> The hill's belly
> But we cry no defilement
> A new-dug path may lead
> To the secret heart of being
> Ogun is still a god
> Even without his navel (*CP2*, 67–8)

The linked but disjointed chain of metaphoric signifiers in this passage have their source in the extremely elliptical, gnostic lore of traditional Yoruba divination poetry that Soyinka has on occasion held up as a model of poetic practice against what he deems the literalism and simple-mindedness of the poetics adumbrated by some of his African neo-traditionalist critics.[21] The metaphors all relate to a deep consciousness of the decline of an indigenous monarchical civilization precipitated by, on the one hand, the creeping authoritarianism of the modern nation-state in Africa and, on the other hand, the imbrication of this political process in the larger framework of the dislocations of the capitalist technological-industrial civilization in Africa and the developing world. In other words, these metaphors compositely and astutely link the travails of Oba Danlola and his courtiers to the clash of modes of production and their associated political-administrative forms and lifeworlds. But nowhere in the entire passage is this historic transition from one mode of governance to another directly and unambiguously referenced; rather, Soyinka relies adroitly on dance, cultic music and chant, and cryptic metaphors to give inscriptional depth to this epochal shift. And he is able to do this because of his ability to completely inhabit the world of the Oshugbo cult and of Ifa divinatory lore, the world of ritual dirges and gnostic orality, in the process cannibalizing their hermetic idioms and ventriloquizing these in the concluding section of the "Hemlock" overture to *Kongi's Harvest*.

This ability which can be characterized as embodied, performative mimeticism, is one of the foundational bases of the suppleness of Soyinka's generically and stylistically eclectic dramaturgy. There are innumerable examples of this in his dramatic corpus. In the two "Jero plays," the playwright enters completely into the world of the beach prophets of Lagos Island, with their unique pseudo-liturgical speech habits and expressive behavior which set them apart from other occupational groups and the rest of the population. This is also true of *Requiem for a Futurologist* in which it is the brotherhood of psychics, astrologers, parapsychologists, palm readers and the like who regale us with the elaborate idiolects, world-view, rivalries and foibles peculiar to their world. We may think analogously here of Ben Jonson's memorable ventriloquizing and parodying of the special jargon and world-views of pseudo-scientists, pseudo-philosophers and knights in *The Alchemist*, or of Caryl Churchill's appropriations, in the play, *Serious Money*, of the hermetic newspeak of traders, bankers, stockbrokers and arbitrageurs.

Perhaps the most impressive of Soyinka's feats of entering into, inhabiting and then appropriating the "languages" internal to a particular social group that is distant from his own middle-class background are to be encountered in *The Road* and *From Zia with Love*. In both plays, there is a complete hermeticization of the milieu of the lumpen, semi-employed and working class characters, together with the "world" of their social and demographic neighbors, the criminal underclass of extortion racketeers, jailbird felons and petty crooks. Indeed, on the strength of these two plays alone, not to talk of the two "Jero plays," Soyinka must be ranked with the late Ken Saro-Wiwa as one of the two most accomplished creative translators of West African pidgin English into a highly nuanced literary language. The following scene from *The Road* is as good as any to illustrate this point. It entails the enactment of the bizarre, idiosyncratic views and attitudes of the oil-tanker driver, Sergeant Burma, on such diverse issues as the fierce professional pride of all those who work, live and die on the roads, the ideological formation of West African veterans who fought in the empire's wars as members of "subject" races, and the savage dog-eat-dog morality of most of those compelled to live at the lower depths of the social order. Thus, though the scene contains a powerful distillation of a particularly cynical side of the world-view of the composite social group to which Sergeant Burma belongs, it is also a veritable *tour de force* of mimetic ventriloquism, and its driving power comes from the fact that since Sergeant Burma is dead, it is Samson who reanimates the dead man by the deployment of brilliant mimicry to impersonate Sergeant Burma's voice, gestural mannerisms and personal idiosyncrasies:

PARTICULARS JOE: We were made much of in those days. To have served in Burma was to have passed your London Matric. Sergeant Burma looked forward to retirement and his choice of business came as a matter of course . . . and Professor offered him the business corner of the drivers' haven . . . the Accident Corner.

SAMSON: Wetin enh? Wetin? You tink say myself I no go die some day? When person die, 'e done die and dat one done finish. I beg, if you see moto accident make you tell me. We sabbee good business . . . sell spare part and second-hand clothes. Wetin? You tink say I get dat kind sentimentation? Me wey I done see dead body so tey I no fit chop meat unless den cook am to nonsense? Go siddon my friend. Business na business. If you see accident make you tell me. I go run go there before those useless men steal all the spare part finish.

PARTICULARS JOE: Sergeant Burma looked forward to retiring and doing the spare part business full-time. But of course his brakes failed going down a hill (The group begins to dirge, softly as if singing to themselves. A short silence. Samson's face begins to show horror and he gasps as he realizes what he has been doing.)

SAMSON: (tearing off the clothes.) God forgive me! Oh God, forgive me. Just see, I have been fooling around pretending to be a dead man. Oh God I was only playing I hope you realize. I was only playing.

(*CP1*, 217–18)

There is a superb, if obvious irony in Samson's panic at the end of this scene, an irony that acts as a metacommentary on the entire play, indeed on Soyinka's dramaturgy in general. For the frantic, desperate protestations of Samson that he was "only playing" introduces a dimension of reflexive theatricality to the scene which can only be clarified by juxtaposing this scene to other scenes, other plays-within-the-play in the dramatic action of *The Road*. To the question why playing a dead man by donning his defining accoutments and inhabiting his total persona should inspire such metaphysical dread in Samson, we can only point to the other numerous instances in the entire play in which, consistent with their quasi-animist world-view, we see great psychic investment of the lumpen, working class characters of the play in the sacred values of certain cultic expressive and *performative* idioms. The most important of these is of course the mask idiom of the "agemo" cult which indeed supplies the deeply enigmatic preface poem to the play. But there is also the climatic flashback scene in Part Two of the play which reenacts the day of the drivers' festival when Murano was knocked down by "No Danger, No Delay," Samson and Kotonu's "mammy wagon."

Thus, to an attentive reader or audience of the play, Samson's terrified self-awareness at the end of his powerfully animated impersonation of Sergeant Burma would be one more element in the deep immersion of this play in the imaginative and performative "worlds" of the drivers, professional thugs, unemployed and semi-employed drifters whose lives and foibles, with Professor's colorful, bizarre eccentricities, Soyinka, as a playwright whose social location is the middle class, ventriloquizes to produce the incredible mix of pathos, comedy and tragedy in the dramatic action of the play.

The foregoing discussion opens up for our consideration another important operative principle of Soyinka's dramaturgy. This pertains to the extreme, radical juxtapositions that he applies to the diverse performative and expressive idioms and "languages" that he appropriates from virtually all spheres and "worlds" of a class-divided social order. For, in general, the kind of obliteration of the boundaries between "ritual" and "drama" that we encounter in *Death and the King's Horseman* does not constitute a dramaturgic norm in Soyinka's theatre. Definitely, in plays like *The Road* and *Kongi's Harvest*, ritual idioms, African or Western, animist or Christian, are deliberately kept from blending with mimetic, realistic drama. The effect is thus more aesthetically and intellectually disconcerting, and there is little question that this is deliberately produced by Soyinka. It is indeed an aspect of his theatrical genius which, while in general it has worked superbly on stage, it has nonetheless tended to confound many of Soyinka's *literary* critics. Indeed, in plays such as *Madmen and Specialists*, *Requiem for a Futurologist* and *From Zia with Love* where either a ferocious satire or an irreverent parody predominates in the dramatic action, the heterogeneous idioms and "languages" are set off against one another in dissonant, contrapuntal collisions. This point has been eloquently made by Joachim Fiebach in a comment on the dramatic action of *Madmen and Specialists*:

The drama . . . is a loose montage of performing stunts on the part of the mendicants, of abrupt changes or gradual slippages from events which are presented as the traditional dialogic interaction of established characters' addresses to the audience. Dr. Bero, the system's specialist's claim that the given order is holy, an immutable social system, is constantly debunked by the various mocking activities of his own watchdogs and by his father, the Old Man's irreverent attitudes . . . Absolute contradiction, ambivalence, and constant reversal of attitudes are dominant features.[22]

What this quote demonstrates is the fact that Soyinka's great penchant for parody makes him especially attentive to the discrepant articulations within, and between the "languages" of the social groups and spheres of life that he so extensively appropriates. *Madmen and Specialists* and from *Zia with Love* are particularly illustrative of this point. For in each of these plays, the protagonist functions, unlike the protagonists of plays like *Death and the King's Horseman*, *Dance of the Forests* and *Kongi's Harvest*, as a sort of embodiment of that figure of medieval European folk festivals, Lord of Misrule. Thus, where *Death and the King's Horseman* more or less success-fully fuses and harmonizes ritual with drama by integrating the words, actions and gestures of Elesin Oba as the communicant of the communal rite and as existential hero of the private drama of his vacillating, sub-liminally divided will, Professor in *The Road*, the Old Man in *Madmen and Specialists*, Sebe Irawe in *From Zia with Love*, and Sanda in *The Beatification of Area Boy* all set in motion and orchestrate wild disruptions and inversions of the protocols and practices of "polite" and official languages and id-ioms of power, privilege or tradition. Moreover, within themselves, these four plays differ so markedly that an element common to all the plays – a sort of plebeian, Bakhtinian "grotesque realism" involving extensive car-nivalesque jokes and conceits on bodily appetites and desires – connects differently with other elements like music, dance and spectacle, ritual and ceremonial performative idioms, and propulsive, plot-driven dra-mas of individual destiny. And it is precisely on account of this extensive internal differentiation in idiom and style, technique and performative mode in Soyinka's drama that in our concluding section of this chapter, we now move to analyses of two particular plays from the "early" and "late" periods of Soyinka's career. These are respectively *The Lion and the Jewel* and *From Zia with Love*.

The Lion and the Jewel occupies a unique place in Soyinka's dramas. It is perhaps the only play by him that is written entirely in a comic spirit uncomplicated by a dark, brooding humor or satire. True, it is a satirical comedy, but the satire is of a gentle, good-natured kind. Most of the satirical barbs are directed at Lakunle, the eccentric schoolteacher, and people like him who propose a superficial, naive, and pretentious view of progress, modernity and Westernization as a counter to what they con-sider the unmodern backwardness of African village life. Thus, though Lakunle finds his village compatriots insufferably ridiculous in their "un-sophisticated" rural ways, the laugh is on him: we laugh *at*, and not with him; we laugh at the incongruity between his inflated self-importance and the half-digested, pedantic nature of the "knowledge" he espouses, and between his affectation of superiority and the utter condescension with which everyone in the village, including even his own pupils, re-gards his ineptitude and eccentricity. But compared with the dictators, tyrants, charlatans and hypocrites of Soyinka's more ferocious satires, Lakunle seems to come from another dramatic imagination. Moreover, *The Lion and the Jewel* is the only one of Soyinka's plays to end with an unambiguously happy resolution. The very last stage direction in the play informs us that having been outmaneuvered by the wily Baroka, the "lion" of the title of the play, in the competition for Sidi the "jewel" of the village, Lakunle is seen rallying to the irrepressible impulses of youth and sexuality as he dances after one of the young maidens in Sidi's bridal party.

The plot of the play involves a deliberate inversion of one of the most constant motifs of romantic comedy: a love triangle in which the romance of a pair of young lovers is for a while thwarted and frustrated by an older, often wealthier suitor; but the younger suitor ultimately prevails and the young lovers marry. In this play, it is the older suitor, Baroka, whose suit prevails and who shows far greater vitality and resourcefulness than his young, hapless competitor. This inversion, in which age prevails over youth, entails other important details as well: the "illiterate" protagonist proves more astute and enterprising than his bookish antagonist; the "backward" villager proves more cultured, more enlightened than the citified, would-be sophisticate.

Soyinka has given an account of the origins of this play that shows how his direct observation of life and its surprises provided a basis for the play's inversion of conventional comic motifs:

I wrote the first draft of *The Lion and the Jewel* towards the end of my student days in England. It was actually inspired by an item which said: "Charlie Chaplin . . . a man of nearly sixty has taken to wife Oona O'Neil," who was then about seventeen, something like that. Now no one reading *The Lion and the Jewel* would ever have imagined that this is the authentic genesis of the play from Charlie Chaplin, and again thinking of the old men I knew in my society who at 70-plus, 80, would still take some new young wives – and always seemed perfectly capable of coping with the onerous tasks which such activity demanded of them! I just sat down and that's how Baroka came into existence. I knew that some of these old men had actually won these new wives against the stiff competition of some younger men, some of them schoolteachers who came to the villages. "This girl has got to be impressed by my canvas shoes." Mind you, the younger men didn't speak the language that those girls understood and they were beaten by the old men. That's how *The Lion and the Jewel* came to be written.[23]

The mental leap in this account from Britain to Nigeria, from Charlie Chaplin to randy octogenarians in his own country, underscores the universal quality of Soyinka's dramatization in this play of sexual rivalry between different generations and between men and women. What gives a trenchant, and often uproarious edge to the dramatization of these motifs of age and gender in *The Lion and the Jewel* is the way Soyinka has conjoined them, inverted the usual pattern of their treatment in conventional romantic comedy, and extended their imaginative resonance by making the conflict of generations one between "grandfathers" and "granddaughters" not, as is usual, between "fathers" and "sons."

These important revisions and extensions of conventional motifs of romantic comedy are made even more enthralling by the way Soyinka particularizes the triangular play between Baroka, Sidi and Lakunle. In general, the power and interest of dramatic action come primarily from the force of the personalities of characters and the simultaneous balance and tension between protagonists and antagonists. Though Baroka's vitality, cunning, and wit dominate the play and assure his eventual triumph over Sidi and Lakunle, Soyinka has taken care to invest great dramatic interest in the other two characters as well. Moreover, the play of conflict and opposition is constantly shifting and moves from Lakunle and Sidi to Lakunle and Baroka and finally to Baroka and Sidi. It is also noteworthy that each of these characters, acting either as protagonist or antagonist in the shifting centers of conflict in the play, is able to deploy considerable improvisations of rhetoric that advance his or her personal interests and desires. Additionally, it is these rhetorical improvisations that give the language of the play its very rich, suggestive texture.

The lighthearted, convivial treatment of the battle of the sexes in this play should not blunt our perception of the seriousness of purpose and the layers of meaning that Soyinka manages to infuse into the dramatic action. Each major point in the unraveling of this battle in the plot is used to deepen Soyinka's exploration of the play's themes of generational conflicts, progress versus reaction, and cant versus sparkling vitality. Sidi's visit to Baroka's bedroom to taunt him about his presumed impotence provides both the advantage Baroka needs to consummate his sexual conquest and the occasion for the two characters, across barriers of gender and age, to discover shared values and spiritual kinship. This is indeed why Sidi is able to accept the seduction that makes her the latest addition to Baroka's harem. Similarly, Sadiku's ritual dance of victory over Baroka's "impotence" – which she envisions as a celebration of the symbolic victory of womankind over the male gender – provides the occasion for an encounter with Lakunle, who then reveals the absurdities of his schemes of bringing "progress" and modernity to the village. In this manner deeper layers of meaning and wider frames of reference are brought into what, on the surface, seems a light romantic comedy.

For a play that comes so early in his career, *The Lion and the Jewel* demonstrates Soyinka's great potential as a dramatist and anticipates many of his developed powers of artistic expression and social vision. The artistic dimension is perhaps best seen in the handling of verse dialogue as a medium for the dramatic action. To write effective verse dialogue and avoid awkwardness and artificiality poses a considerable challenge for playwrights, and especially so with comedy. The spirit of comedy is one of spontaneity and freshness; verse tends to constraints, formality and artificiality. What Soyinka has managed to do is combine the best of both: the deliberate, formal structure of the verse idiom sets the sparkling wit, the rhythms and cadences of spoken speech, and the extensive use of figurative language in high, eloquent relief. This quality is captured even in the ironic, satirical register of Lakunle's zealous "modernizing" rhetoric:

> Within a year or two, I swear,
> This town shall see a transformation
> Bride price will be a thing forgotten
> And wives shall take their place by men.
> A motor road will pass this spot
> And bring the city ways to us.
> We'll buy saucepans for all the women
> Clay pots are crude and unhygienic
> No man shall take more wives than one
> That's why they're impotent too soon.
> The ruler shall ride cars, not horses
> Or a bicycle at the very least.
> We'll burn the forests, cut the trees
> Then plant a modern park for lovers
> We'll print newspapers every day
> With pictures of seductive girls.
> The world will judge our progress by
> The girls that win beauty contests.
> While Lagos builds new factories daily
> We only play 'ayo' and gossip.
> Where is our school of ballroom dancing?
> Who here can throw a cocktail party?
> We must be modern with the rest
> Or live forgotten by the world.
> We must reject the palm wine habit
> And take to tea, with milk and sugar (*CP2*, 34)

This is a false rhetoric of modernization not only on account of its utter callowness and naiveté, but also because Lakunle himself is carried away by the rhetoric: it reflects, but at the same time constructs his reality. In contrast to Lakunle's naively unselfconscious rhetoric of "civilization," Baroka deploys a counter-rhetoric of the alienations and shortcomings of progress and modernization that builds on the best elements of tradition; but he retains a detached, self-amused, even manipulative control over this elaborate rhetoric. The verse form of the dialogue provides an effective modulation for this underground contest of rhetorics, and it reaches its finest expression in the play in the final moments of Sidi's seduction:

> For a long time now
> The town dwellers have made up tales
> Of the backwardness of Ilujinle
> Until it hurts Baroka, who holds
> The welfare of his people deep at heart.
> Now, if we do this thing, it will prove more
> Than any single town has done!

(The wrestler, who has been listening, open-mouthed, drops his cup in admiration. Baroka, annoyed, realizing only now in fact that he is still in the room, waves him impatiently out.)

> I do not hate progress, only its nature
> Which makes all roofs and faces look the same.
> And the wish of one old man is
> That here and there

(Goes progressively towards Sidi, until he bends over her, then sits beside her on the bed.)

> Among the bridges and murderous roads,
> Below the humming birds which
> Smoke the face of Sango, dispenser of
> The snake-tongued lightning; between this moment
> And the reckless broom that will be wielded
> In these years to come, we must leave
> Virgin plots of lives, rich decay
> And the tang of vapor rising from
> Forgotten heaps of compost, lying
> Undisturbed ... But the skin of sameness ...
> Masks, unknown, the spotted wolf of progress ...
> Does sameness not revolt your being,
> My daughter?

> (*CP*2, 47–8)

To the concluding question Sidi can only give a sort of drugged, bewildered nod. The persuasive, seductive logic of this view of progress and of its increasing separation from nature and its inculcation of a deadening uniformity overwhelms its charmed auditor. We, the audience, are also "seduced" by the poetry and rhetoric of this speech, and though we may not be in agreement, point by point, image by image, with the view of history, culture, and tradition that Baroka advances here, we feel that weighty issues are involved, even though they are articulated with a self-gratifying intent. Soyinka created a rich layering of dramatic action in this early play, and we can see here the roots of his full powers as a *poetic* dramatist in the far more adroit and self-assured manipulation of verse dialogue in *Death and the King's Horseman*, as we will see in our discussion of the scene of Elesin and the Praise-Singer's trance-dance in the fourth chapter of this study.

The event on which Soyinka based *From Zia with Love*, his most ferocious satire to date on military dictatorship in Nigeria, took place on April 10, 1985. On that day, three condemned drug traffickers, Bernard Ogedengbe, Bartholomew Owoh and Lawal Ojulope, were executed by a military firing squad in Lagos.[24] These men, all in their twenties, had been condemned to death under the so-called Miscellaneous Offenses Decree of 1984, otherwise known as Decree 20 and generally considered one of the most heinous decrees ever promulgated by any Nigerian military regime. By the time the execution took place in April 1985, the regime of Generals Buhari and Idiagbon was already sixteen months in power; and it had clearly established itself as an arrogantly repressive and self-righteously authoritarian military dictatorship. And yet, the whole country was profoundly shaken by the execution of these three young men. Prior to this event, nobody had ever been condemned to death, let alone executed for drug peddling in Nigeria. Armed robbery, murder and unsuccessful coup making were the only crimes punishable by capital punishment. Also "Decree 20" outraged most Nigerians by its being made retroactive to offenses committed before the promulgation of the decree. Thus, most Nigerians expected that the death sentences on these men would either be commuted to life imprisonment or reduced to a long prison term. At any rate many religious, civic and political leaders publicly appealed to the regime not to carry out the death sentence on the three men, not to implement the retroactive punitiveness of "Decree 20." These pleas were simply ignored and the men were quickly executed.

The scope of the expression of outrage which greeted this event was up till then totally unprecedented in the history of military rule in Nigeria. A former Chief Justice of the Supreme Court of the country described

the execution of the men as "judicial murder." Equally strong condem-
nations were made by influential public figures like the Roman Catholic
Archbishop of Lagos, the Patriarch of the Methodist Church of Nigeria,
the President of the Nigerian Labor Congress, and leaders of scores of
professional associations, traders' and market women's organizations and
students' unions. Some of the open-air markets of Lagos promptly closed
upon the execution of the unlucky men, and the butchers of the city closed
shop for a few days out of sympathy for one of their number who was
said to be a relation of one of the executed men. One of the most bitterly
outraged statements of condemnation was issued by Soyinka in a one-
page tersely-worded statement titled "Death by Retroaction." Soyinka
concluded this document with the following ringing condemnation:

How can one believe that such an act could be seriously contemplated? I feel
as if I have been compelled to participate in triple cold-blooded murders, that I
have been forced to witness a sordid ritual . . . I think, that finally, I have nothing
more to say to a regime that bears responsibility for this.[25]

In view of the characters, the dramatic action and the performance
idioms which give *From Zia* its frenetic energy, it would appear that if
Soyinka had nothing more to say *to* the Buhari-Idiagbon regime on this
event of April 10, 1985, he did have a lot more to say *about* the regime
to the country and the world at large in the medium of drama and in a
form which both reflects and artistically transmutes the outrage which
the event generated. For, in the play, the characters representing the three
condemned men, by an ingeniously parodic twist, find that the prison
to which they've been brought is under the suzerainty of a "ministerial
cabinet" comprising the most hardened criminals who regale the rest of
the prison population with chillingly convincing mimicry of the military
junta which has sent the three men to prison to await their execution.
Thus, the prison reflects the nation which in turn reflects the prison.
Commander Hyacinth, the "Head of State," his "No 2" and the other
members of the "Eternal Ruling Council" have thoroughly assimilated
the ethos, rhetoric and style of their real-life models. Much of the dramatic action of the play centres round the "Sit Rep" – military lingo for
"Situation Report" of a field commander – and the "c.v." (curriculum
vitae) that each new inmate to the prison, be he a "politico" or a common
felon, has to stage, with help from the old hands. These "c.v.'s" and "sit
reps" are reenactments of the crimes or, in the case of political detainees,
allegations for which a new inmate is being imprisoned. In an unmistakable allusion to Dante's Hell, a wooden board, with a crudely scrawled

sign, "Abandon Shame All Who Enter Here" hangs over the cell-bars where these reenactments take place. And while all of this unfolds as a grotesque, carnivalesque spectacle, amplified "military" voices incessantly drone out exhortations for patriotism, discipline, civic-mindedness and moral probity from loudspeakers rigged up throughout the prison. These exhortations are the catechism of BAI, the "Battle Against Indiscipline" project of the military regime outside the walls of the prison.[26] These BAI exhortations achieve a particularly potent satiric effect by their juxtaposition with the most stunning of the numerous "c.v.'s" staged by Commander Hyacinth and his cohorts. In this "c.v.," a new inmate, a small-time drug trafficker on the run from his bosses in the criminal underworld, sets out to show that the sermonizing leaders of the "BAI" in the inner core of the "Eternal Ruling Council" operate the state as a cartel of big-time, big-league drug traffickers with relays and contacts around the world, including and especially the Pakistan of General Zia ul Haq. "Decree 20," as revealed in this "c.v.," is really the product of the determination of these military drug barons to wipe out the presumptuous civilians who would dare not only to encroach on the turf of the military drug barons and their Pakistani principals, but actually pull off hefty heists from state protected conduits. Thus, in this wickedly parodic "c.v.," one of the characters is a Wing Commander, one of the military zealots and a member of the "Eternal Ruling Council." He is out on the trail of a stolen diplomatic bag containing a huge shipment of cocaine; unbeknownst to him, his civilian partner in business is the perpetrator of this heist. Gradually and inexorably, through dialogue, songs and dances, the hunter becomes the hunted and this prepares us for the astonishing twist at the end of the play: the three condemned civilian drug traffickers are led off to their execution; simultaneously, the Wing Commander, the scion of absolute power and infallibility, meets a gruesome fate as a late-night victim of a sacrificial ritual at one of the crossroads of the city, a ritual sacrifice calculated to mobilize the powers of the occult to aid the business of running the state – the "business" we have just seen dramatized in the "c.v."

It would be a reduction of the scope of the ferocious antimilitarism of *From Zia* to see its social vision only in terms of the exposure of the hypocrisies and the mental and spiritual emptiness of Nigeria's military dictators. True, this stands out explicitly in the twists and turns of the play's plot and songs, but what is far more telling in the overall impact of the drama is Soyinka's mobilization of the visual, verbal and gestural repertoire of popular festivity and hilarity as sources of resistance to the

authorized, *decreed* languages and culture of impunity of the state, the state
of drunken power and pomp, of obsession with rank and authority, of a
putatively inscrutable and infallible order of governance. Thus, though
Soyinka had said, as we saw in his document, "Death by Retroaction,"
that he had nothing more to say to the military autocrats, *From Zia with
Love* constitutes a response on a scale completely on a par with the depth
of the injustices, deceptions and cruelties unleashed on Nigeria by the
military despots.

The elaborate carnivalesque mode with which the anti-militarism of
this play is rendered puts it in the company of earlier plays of Soyinka
like *Jero's Metamorphosis*, *Opera Wonyosi* and *A Play of Giants*, each of which
also marshals a combination of dialogue, music, spectacle and plebeian
festivity to attack the pretensions to absolute and invincible power by
Africa's postcolonial military dictators. Like these other plays, and like
some of the "shot gun" skits and revues in the "Priority Projects," *From
Zia with Love* derives its ferocious power from a parade, a spectacle of
the excesses and atrocities of militarist barbarism, as boasted about or
directly enacted by power-mongers who are actual military putschists
(Emperor Boky in *Opera Wonyosi* and Kamini in *A Play of Giants*, Military
Governor in *The Beatification of An Area Boy*) or their civilian imitators
(Jero as "General" in the militarization of the hierarchy and titles of
his "metamorphosed" church in *Jero's Metamorphosis*). In this respect, like
these other plays, *From Zia with Love*, is relentlessly context-specific in
its allusions to figures, events and realities in the postcolonial encounter
of Nigeria and its peoples with military dictatorship. For this reason,
the play seems dated, overly localized and nationally "intramural" in
ways that might pose problems of identification, or even intelligibility,
to a non-Nigerian audience or readership. This is clearly evident in the
following set of stage directions and dialogue which together form part
of the performative crescendo that marks the climactic moment of the
play's parade of militarist megalomania:

*Next to invade the platform is a skimpy figure clad only in even skimpier underpants, blowing
an outsize saxophone. He is followed by female dancers doing a 'shinamanic' dance to the tune
of 'Zombie'. The earlier group retreat. The WING COMMANDER stares aghast, recovers,
and breaks into maniacal laughter. His voice overwhelms the music of the intruders, while the
first group resume their motions with greater vigour.*

WING COMMANDER:
Chief Kalakuta priest
we've got him in our sights

> The way we deal with mavericks
> he'll scream for human rights
> So his club was burnt to cinders
> The culprit was unknown...
> This cat's mother fixated
> why the obsessive worry?
> She fell out of the window
> soldiers don't say 'sorry'
> Does he let her rest in peace?
> He tries to deposit
> Her coffin on our doorstep
> – well, that really does it!
> Resurrect her if you can,
> build another Kalakut'
> You'll learn the truth
> of power, Mr. Cool-and-Cute!...

As the saxophonist is overwhelmed, manacled and encased in prison clothes, his entourage disappear one after the other (90–1)

This brief scene contains a wealth of allusions to very specific incidents and realities which only Nigerians, and even more narrowly those of a certain generation, would be capable of identifying, let alone relating to emotionally. For instance, the detail in the stage directions about the "skimpy figure clad only in even skimpier underpants" refers of course to the late musician, Fela Anikulapo-Kuti, with many other details in the quote alluding to both overt and more tacit aspects of his radical, nonconformist lifestyle and the violent clashes of Anikulapo-Kuti and his commune with the military dictatorship. Another detail, that of a "shina-manic dance" in the stage directions alludes to a popular musician from the period, Sir Shina Peters, and the fast, furious and rather manic dance steps associated with his style of music which became the rage of Lagosian socialites in the late 1980s and 1990s. It was a common, but definitely an insider's knowledge that the 'shinamanic' dance style was part of a general militarization of both popular and elite culture in the period. This order of allusiveness to an irreducibly specific time- and place-bound collective experience pervades *From Zia with Love*, paradoxically giving it its frenetic energy and its extremely narrow frame of reference in many parts of its dramatic action. Among the more memorable and telling items of this socially "intramural" allusiveness of the play are the references to the late Hubert Ogunde, especially in his brushes with both colonial and postcolonial censorship and repression; the near-complete infestation of the creeks and lagoons of the Lagos metropolitan area by a species of wild and aggressive water hyacinths in the 1980s which both spelt economic ruin for the fishing villages in the area and for a long time confounded the knowledge and expertise of the country's marine and environmental scientists; and, of course, the big-time entry of Nigeria into the illegal international drug trade.

The strong claim of *From Zia with Love* to being Soyinka's most successful, most powerful anti-militarist play lies in its uniqueness among the playwright's anti-militarist dramatic works. More than the other plays in this particular body of Soyinka's dramas, its deep immersion in topicalities of time and place is underscored by a symbolic framework which gives its deliberately scrappy, pastiche-like lurch from one "c.v." or "sit-rep" to another imaginative coherence. Moreover and equally important, in its deployment of motifs of the grotesque and the macabre, this symbolic framework lifts the actual menace and malevolent ramifications of militarism beyond merely local or even regional expressions to frightening, disquieting intimations of what the playwright deems the constants of power. In its most graphic and perhaps atavistic inscriptions in the play, this symbolic framework revolves around ritual murder and its links to the mobilization of dark, occult forces, either to attain vast concentrations of wealth or power, or to avert the fate of being victims of power sadists in control of the state. In this particular aspect, Soyinka in the play is responding courageously to the rash of ritual murders that scandalized the whole country in the late 1970s and 1980s and, especially constituted a great embarrassment for the middle class elites. But at a deeper level, *From Zia with Love* pushes its graphic depiction of the literally macabre and grotesque to an exploration of the moral and spiritual ramifications of a power lust so extreme in its disregard for human life that it seems that there is no better way in which to imaginatively confront it than through the prism of deities and avatars whose cults require the sacrifice of human lives. Only this conception of totalitarian power as basically cultic and atavistic wherever, and in whatever forms and guises it manifests itself in the modern world, explains why the apologia for militarism by the Wing Commander in the following dialogue has a profoundly disturbing ring of truth about it:

WING COMMANDER: You know what I am talking about! Zia, Zia, Zia! What did he do which you bloody civilians haven't done here? I mean, you are beginning to sound like these University types...

SEBE: Is that my fault? They do business with me all the time, they and their
tiroro children. If the leaf sticks too long to the soap, it will soon start to
froth on its own.

WING COMMANDER: Well, the next time one of them comes here, ask him what
happened to Diallo Telli. Yes, let your acada friends tell you what happened
to the first-ever Secretary-General of the Organization of African Unity.

SEBE: What happened to him?

WING COMMANDER: Tortured to death by Sekou Toure's goons. And Sekou
Toure was not Army. Or Navy. Or Air Force. He was a civilian.

SEBE: All right, all right, I don't know why we dey argue self.

WING COMMANDER: (*flaring up*) We are arguing because I am tired of having everything blamed on us military people. Between Sekou Toure
and General Zia or Pinochet or Arap Moi and Houphouet Boigny and
other one-party African and Asian dictators, tell me, just what is the
difference?

(53–4)

The catch in the veracity of the Wing Commander's rationalizations of
the institutionalization of systematic misrule in many parts of the developing world lies in the fact that his apologia is made in the context of a
dramatic action in which he – and the radically unrepentant militarization of power which he represents – is being gradually and inexorably
ensnared. He is being ensnared in a diabolic plot which will not only
destroy him as a sacrificial victim of the very cult of power which he embodies, but will also expose the "truth" of his assertions as both illusory,
ethically and spiritually untenable. For this, Soyinka deploys the motifs
and the associated cultic traditions of Esu, the Yoruba trickster god of
mischief and contingency. The following dialogue between Sebe, as Esu's
agent and the "hunter" in the diabolic plot, and the Wing Commander,
as his unwitting "quarry," constitutes the *coup de grace* in the rout of the
inflated self-possession of militarist absolutism:

WING COMMANDER: You know something else?

SEBE: What is that, dear partner?

WING COMMANDER: We will make it retroactive.

SEBE: You will make what retroactive?

WING COMMANDER: The campaign of course. The LAW, the Decree, the
penalties. It will show we mean business. And anyway, that's our style.
That's how people recognize who's in charge. That's the difference between
you and us. Civilians can only operate in linear time. We will go backwards
and forwards at will.

SEBE: And in circles. Brilliant! Don't we know it? Your patron god is
Esu. (*Confidentially*) And let me tell you, we must not neglect the little
fellow.

WING COMMANDER: Who? What little fellow?

SEBE: Esu. Small but potent. (*Unveils his Esu shrine*) You know his oriki don't you? He throws a stone today and it kills a man last week. That retroactive twist is just the kind of idea he inspires in men of action.

WING COMMANDER: Look, Sebe, you stick to your superstitions. I will take care of the practical measures...

SEBE: I am a practical man, Commander. I keep a toe in every shrine and a finger in every business pie. Your man is Esu, but you are going modern. Esu only throws stones, but you, you fire bullets. But Esu is broadminded, don't worry. He won't be resentful of your prowess – that is, as long as we give him his due. This exercise enh, you'll see, when you fire a bullet today, it will have hit its target long before you ever took over government. Now, that is real power for you.

WING COMMANDER: (*rapt in the prospect*): You know, the power to act backwards in time...

SEBE: And it was your own idea! You people are trained to think big.

(81, 83)

Because he is so captivated by the vision to act, not only without the constraints of institutional and moral accountability to the ruled, but also outside the natural bounds of temporality, the Wing Commander easily falls prey to Sebe's diabolical plot and becomes a sacrificial victim whose corpse is discovered the next day at one of the city's crossroads. What is grimly ironic about this grisly fate is the fact that Sebe, who pretends to act as Esu's intermediary and goads the Wing Commander into fulfilling his fate as unconscious sacrificial scapegoat, has not the slightest belief in the efficacy of the ritual sacrifice; Sebe acts purely and solely to get the Wing Commander out of the way in order to be finally secure in the success of his heist of the huge consignment of cocaine the hapless military officer and his bosses wish to recover. In this respect, Sebe's unbelief in, or indifference to the metaphysics of sacrificial myths and ritual practices is of one kind with the inverted, demythologizing rites of the prison inmates in their enactments of the elaborate protocols of militarist rule.

With all its dramaturgic scrappiness, *From Zia with Love* is an engrossing parable of both the seductions and the illusions of totalitarianism in the weak state formations of the developing world. The play thus constitutes part of any exploration of the issue of an appropriate scale of artistic response to historical currents and political crises of great moment, an issue that has always been at the base of Soyinka's sense of the social ramifications of modern African literature. It has famously been expressed in his critical writings, especially in such widely discussed essays as "The Writer in a Modern African State," "And After the Narcissist?," "Climates of Art" and "The Credo of Being and Nothingness." And it is particularly relevant, as we have seen in our discussion of *From Zia with Love*, to Soyinka's great dramas and is perhaps the most appropriate frame for the detailed exploration of Soyinka's greatest dramatic creations to which we now turn in the next chapter of this study.

CHAPTER 4

Ritual, anti-ritual and the festival complex in Soyinka's dramatic parables

> In the selection of pretenders, a new 'king maker' takes part, it is ritual legitimation, the ability to rely on ritual, to fulfill it and use it, to allow oneself, as it were to be borne aloft by it . . . Because of this dictatorship of the ritual, however, power becomes clearly anonymous. Individuals are almost dissolved in the ritual . . . (and) it seems as though ritual alone carries people from obscurity to the light of power.
>
> Vaclav Havel, *The Power of the Powerless*

The plays discussed in this chapter are amongst Soyinka's most ambitious and most memorable dramas, but are also the most pessimistic in his dramatic corpus: *A Dance of the Forests, The Road, Madmen and Specialists, Death and the King's Horseman* and *The Bacchae of Euripides*. Moreover, in terms of form and craft, and of language and ideas, Soyinka is at his most resourceful and most vigorous in this group of dark, brooding plays. Because each of these plays deals with, or derives directly from a major historical event or crisis, the dramatist's artistic resourcefulness in the plays seems in turn to be linked to that element in his career as a dramatist that we have identified in Chapter 3 of this study as the imperative of appropriate response. Within the logic of this imperative, an historic event, a widespread socioeconomic trend, or world-historical forces which engender massive individual and collective crises of conscience find Soyinka responding through dramas which, in order to match the instigating event or condition, contain startling or provocative formalistic and thematic expressions. How does this operate in each of these plays?

A Dance of the Forests was written and produced as part of the Nigerian independence celebrations in 1960; appropriate to the historic task of forging a nation out of diverse peoples and communities that the celebrations symbolically entailed, the central action of the play revolves around a "gathering of the tribes" at which the festivities intended to celebrate the glorious past and hopeful future of the assembled "tribes" turns into an unanticipated encounter with monstrous evils in the past and present life of the community. *The Road*, written for, and staged at the Commonwealth Arts Festival in 1965, dramatizes the profound dislocating impact of the forces of technology and social and cultural change on the daily lives of the newly urbanized working poor of West African cities who try to make a living out of professions associated with the roads and the highways. *Madmen and Specialists*, the first of Soyinka's plays written and staged after his release from incarceration during the Nigerian civil war, is in fact based partly on that war; it quite appropriately dramatizes the horrific transference of war psychosis at the battle front into a terminal struggle between the two central characters of the play, a father and his son, both of whom have seen service in the war front. Of all of Soyinka's plays, *Death and the King's Horseman* is perhaps the most event-specific in its derivation; it dramatizes the famous incident in 1946 when the British colonial authorities prevented the carrying out of a customary ritual suicide by an important chief, a ritual suicide intended to officially conclude the funerary ceremonies for one of the most important indigenous rulers in colonial Nigeria, the Alafin of Oyo. In Soyinka's dramatization of this event, the tragic and unanticipated reversals which result from this intervention are presented in the form of ritual festivity of great poetic elegance and performative sublimity which, nonetheless, undermine both the moral authority of the colonizers and the spiritual security of the colonized. Finally, pressing historical circumstance in *The Bacchae of Euripides* is more indirectly indicated than in the other plays since this is after all an adapted play from classical European antiquity. It is indeed in the changes that Soyinka makes in the conflicts and characterization in his version of the Euripides play that we can see the pressure of historical context in the dramatic action of this play. For instance, Soyinka expands Euripides' chorus of non-Greek "Asian women" to include insurrectionary slaves whose leader is cast in the mold of the famous leaders of the black slave revolts in the African diaspora in the Americas. Moreover, in Soyinka's text, themes of empire and colony, of life-denying autocracy and the nature-based, life-affirming popular revolt that it engenders, assume far more explicit and urgent expression than they do in the Euripides original.

If these are Soyinka's "weightier plays" in terms of the historical or sociopolitical pertinence of the subject matter that they dramatize, they are no less notable in their dramaturgic distinctiveness. For in every one of these plays, the central conflict, even the entire compass of the dramatic action, is elaborately constructed around festive, ritual or carnivalesque performance modes; moreover, *The Road, Madmen and Specialists* and *The Bacchae of Euripides* also feature parodies and burlesques of the very performance modes that organize the particular play's central action and conflict. The deployment of this dramaturgic method is probably at its most formalistically extravagant in *A Dance of the Forests* and at its most controlled and most technically polished in *Death and the King's Horseman*. In the former play, the climactic scene – in which the unwelcome dead who return as revenant ghosts confront representatives of living generations – entails a stunning variety and clash of performance modes mobilized by the young playwright then at the beginning of his career as a dramatist. This dramaturgic boldness is also very much in evidence in *The Road* and *Madmen and Specialists*, even if these plays show greater artistic control than *A Dance of the Forests*. Ritual festivity is concentrated and reaches its climax in *The Road* in the flashback scene which reenacts the day of the accident during the drivers' festival when Murano, masked as an ancestral *egungun* spirit, was knocked down and presumed dead by Kotonu and Samson. But the entire dramatic action of the play is punctuated by songs, jests and plays-within-the-play performed by the ensemble of all the characters, occasionally including even Professor and Particulars Joe who are not part of the chorus of drivers, apprentices, passenger "touts" and layabouts that constitute a sort of ambiguous collective antagonist to Professor's protagonist role in the dramatic action of the play. As for *Madmen and Specialists*, no formal religious ritual or ceremony is deployed as an organizing apparatus for its dramatic action, but the play features elaborate parodies of both Christian liturgy and African ritual idioms in the games and antics of the mendicants and their mentor, the Old Man. And the play's central object of savage, ironic deflation is "As," a polyvalent dramatic conceit on fundamentalist or absolutist modes and systems of thought which, with their ancillary practices, work to normalize warfare, warmongering and gross abuses of power in the name of patriotism, honor or even religious duty and piety. It is as a deity, with its priesthood and apologists, that this conceit "As" is subjected to ferocious ironic debunking by the Old Man and his acolytes. This is the reason why, of all of Soyinka's plays, *Madmen and Specialists* is about the only drama in which the use of festive, carnivalesque performance modes has a completely unrelieved sardonic edge to it.

It has been necessary to demonstrate Soyinka's predilection, in this group of his most ambitious plays, for stretching generic boundaries, for mixing genres beyond their normative forms and conventions, because the critical and scholarly discussion of Soyinka's dramatic corpus is over-whelmingly dominated by a sort of neoclassicism which sees ritual – and idioms closely linked to it – as a sort of regulative dramaturgic paradigm in the playwright's major dramas, including all the plays discussed here. The underlying heuristic premise of the discussion of Soyinka's great-est plays in this chapter is that though it looms large in his armory of dramaturgic models, ritual is only one among a wide variety of per-formance modes appropriated by the playwright in his most ambitious plays. Moreover, it is significant that Soyinka constantly subjects ritual to what one scholar has called "comic inspection."[1] This has important implications for our discussion of Soyinka's most ambitious plays in this chapter.

In an important essay which attempts a summation of the common themes and forms linking all of Soyinka's plays, Brian Crow has described Soyinka's theatre as a "theatre of ritual vision."[2] Ritual undoubtedly plays a central role in Soyinka's major plays, and it is also a central element in his theories of drama and theatre. Consequently, there are literally scores of scholarly essays exploring ritual as theme and formal model in Soyinka's plays. Among the most notable of this body of schol-arly and critical exploration of ritual in Soyinka's drama and theatrical theory are chapters and extended sections in books by Oyin Ogunba, Stephan Larsen, Ketu Katrak, Derek Wright and Mary David, and es-says by Philip Brockbank, Brian Crow, Ato Quayson, Adebayo Williams and Isidore Okpewho.[3] In nearly all the books and essays written by these scholars and critics, there is a critical consensus that ritual – and all its as-sociated idioms and motifs – serves as an unambiguously vitalizing and enriching source for Soyinka's most original, most thought-provoking formal and thematic expressions. However, in spite of this consensus, Derek Wright has aptly observed that there is great unevenness in the critical and scholarly rigour of the essays dealing with the place of ritual in Soyinka's plays and theories.[4] Beyond this unevenness, two aspects of the Nigerian dramatist's interest in ritual, both in his plays and his theories, have been almost entirely left out of this extensive discussion, aspects that reveal far greater ambiguity in his appropriation of ritual than the scholarly and critical consensus would allow.

First, there is the fact that the rituals that Soyinka has generally incor-porated into his plays and that he has theorized about, are usually some of the most ancient, the most autochthonous rituals. In the light of this fact, though some of these rituals are still performed in traditional religious festivals today, they survive precariously under the combined weight of repressive Christian proselytization, the rise of secular, rational world-views, and the material forces of technology and economic production. From the perspective of the onslaught of these forces, cultic rituals are little more than archaisms without the dynamism they may have once had. In other words, the historic context of the ritual idioms that Soyinka deploys in his dramas corresponds remarkably to what Rene Girard in his seminal book, *Violence and the Sacred*, has called "the sacrificial crisis."[5] By this term Girard means the relentless and inevitable decline of the social and metaphysical sanctions which once gave sacrificial rituals their ethical legitimacy and psychological efficacy. As Girard blithely puts it: "If, as is often the case, we encounter the institution of sacrifice either in an advanced state of decay or reduced to relative insignificance, it is because it has already undergone a good deal of wear and tear (39)." It is part of Girard's ethnocentrism in this otherwise seminal work that for him, "the sacrificial crisis" has taken place only in the Western world, whereas a rigorous application of the logic of his insights should indicate that this "crisis" cannot but eventuate everywhere in the modern world. We will return later to the implications of this for Soyinka's most ambitious plays.

The second aspect of Soyinka's interest in ritual that has generally escaped the attention of students of his works seems like a direct obverse of the first aspect. This is the fact that in his writings as a theorist and critic, Soyinka has tended to approach other playwrights, writers and artists with the paradigm and values of what he calls the "ritual matrix." This practice has fostered a remarkably flexible and subtle deployment of the paradigm and has produced often compelling, highly idiosyncratic readings of diverse African and Western playwrights, directors and artists. Among Western dramatists in particular, this supple application by Soyinka of the paradigm of the "ritual matrix" has produced extraordinarily fresh readings of Aristophanes' *Lysistrata*, Shakespeare's *Anthony and Cleopatra*, Edward Albee's *Who's Afraid of Virginia Woolf*, Max Frisch's *Count Oederland* and Bertolt Brecht's *Baal*, and the work of the director Ariane Mnouchkine.[6] More generally, Soyinka's comments, through the symbolic prism of ritual, on such artists as Vassily Kandinsky, Francis Bacon and Peter Brook have provided a fresh approach to their works.[7] And among African dramatists and writers, he has, through this rubric of ritual and its alleged liberating values, produced notable if controversial readings of Duro Ladipo, J.P. Clark, Chinua Achebe and Femi Osofisan.[8]

It is a great challenge to reconcile these two aspects of Soyinka's theoretical and practical interest in ritual: the most autochthonous, pristine African ritual forms and idioms, side by side with a view of the "ritual matrix" as not only universal but inherently emancipatory and even revolutionary. Where most contemporary Western, and Western-influenced African and Asian interest in the interface between drama and ritual is deeply inflected with doubts and hesitations, Soyinka's approach to this interface is self-assured and clamant; and it is insistent that drama's renewal as a cultural medium able to respond to the great crises and contradictions of the present age lies in a recombining fusion with ritual. As we shall see, what gives this insistence compelling force is not an unambiguous recuperation of rituals and ritualism, but the fact that in his most successful plays and theoretical essays, Soyinka subjects ritual to what we may call "anti-ritual." Thus, if the Nigerian dramatist's theatre is indeed a "theatre of ritual vision," "ritual" in his dramas and theories comes with layers of formalistic and thematic reconfigurations which considerably interrogate the legitimacy and value of the pristine ritual traditions that Soyinka deploys in his plays, especially in his greatest dramatic creations.

Admittedly, the scholarly inflation of the significance of ritual in Soyinka's dramaturgy follows the lead provided by the playwright himself in his theoretical writings on drama and theatre. In all the essays on drama in *Myth, Literature and the African World* as well as a few in *Art, Dialogue and Outrage*, ritual is pervasively invoked as a revitalizing and revolutionizing source for contemporary drama and theatre. Particularly notable in this conception of ritual in Soyinka's theory of drama and performance is the complete phenomenological identity that he more or less establishes between ritual and revolution when he insists, in the essay "Drama and the Idioms of Liberation," on the "ritual nature of liberation itself (*ADO1*, 44)." From this perspective, Brian Crow is entirely justified in calling Soyinka's theatre a "theatre of ritual vision," just as Derek Wright in his book *Soyinka Revisited* has cause to devote two of his three chapters on Soyinka's dramatic corpus to ritual and its diverse expressions in his dramatic art. However, this is only a partial reading of Soyinka's theoretical writings. And as we have seen in the dramaturgic eclecticism that pervades Soyinka's major plays, it is a definitely skewed perspective on Soyinka's dramas themselves. Thus, as a theoretical framework for analyzing and interpreting Soyinka's most important plays, what I would call the "ritual problematic" in the analysis and evaluation of his achievements as a dramatist needs a review. Such a review will serve, in the present context, as background for an analysis of what is unique and significant in the plays discussed in this chapter.

With a hermeneutic neologism which tries to capture the eclectic, modular openness of dramatic form in some of Soyinka's tragic dramas, Philip Brockbank has identified formal and thematic patterns in Soyinka's dramas which he designates "tragic festival."[9] More expansively, Oyin Ogunba in the book, *Theatre in Africa*, makes a powerful case for adjudging "festivals" – as a composite performative paradigm – as perhaps the most fertile residual traditional model for modern African drama.[10] This is an extremely productive insight in opening up for our consideration the suggestion that the "festival complex," not ritual, is the fundamental underlying paradigm for dramatic form in both Soyinka's dramatic works and his theories of drama and theatre. The *modularity* of this "festival complex," both for containing and radically inverting and deconstructing all other performance modes and idioms, including ritual, is clearly and eloquently articulated in the following passage from one of Soyinka's most important – and largely ignored – theoretical essays on drama and theatre, "Theatre in African Traditional Cultures: Survival Patterns":

Festivals, compromising as they do, such variety of forms, from the most spectacular to the most secretive and emotionally charged, offer the most familiar hunting ground (for the roots of drama). What is more, they constitute in themselves *pure theatre* at its most prodigal and resourceful. In short, the persistent habit of dismissing festivals as belonging to a more "spontaneous" inartistic expression of communities demands reexamination. The level of organization involved, the integration of the sublime with the mundane, the endowment of the familiar with the properties of the unique . . . all indicate that it is to the heart of many African festivals that we should look for the most stirring expressions of man's instinct and need for drama at its most comprehensive and community-involving . . . What this implies is that instead of considering festivals from one point of view only – that of providing, in a primitive form, the ingredients of drama – we may even begin examining the opposite point of view: that contemporary drama, as we experience it today, is a contraction of drama, necessitated by the productive order of society in other directions. (*ADO2*, 138)

Can any one play, or even any corpus of plays of one playwright, successfully mobilize and exploit the attributes of the "festival complex" outlined in this passage? The inventory of features of this performative paradigm is daunting: "pure theatre at its most prodigal and resourceful," meeting "man's instinct for drama at its most comprehensive and community-involving"; integration of a "variety of forms, from the most spectacular to the most secret"; and a montage of modes bringing "the sublime with the mundane" and "the endowment of the familiar with the properties of the unique." In prefatory remarks that he appended to the publication of the English-language adaptation of Peter Weiss' celebrated play, *Marat-Sade*, which he had given a famous, critically successful production, Peter Brook mentions the fact that what some London critics hostile to the production of *Marat-Sade* had found dubious and unacceptable were the very things he found admirable in Weiss' play: fusion and clash of diverse forms and styles of performance – Brechtian, didactic, absurdist, total theatre, and Theatre of Cruelty.[11]

The hostility of the theatre critics that produced Brook's apologia for Weiss is a validation of Soyinka's contention in the quote from "Theatre in Traditional African Cultures" that "contemporary drama," as we experience it today, is a contraction of drama that is "necessitated by the productive order of society in other directions." But Soyinka and Brook seem to part company on the question of how to overcome that "contraction," or the resources available to the dramatist or director for its transcendence. Brook sees that transcendence as a rare occurrence, as indeed often fortuitous; by contrast, Soyinka sees it as repeatable, as indeed axiomatic, precisely because for him, unlike the Western playwright, the African dramatist has available vibrantly extant traditions of "festival theatre." And a consequence of this difference between Brook and Soyinka is that for Soyinka, the question of how to overcome the generic over-differentiation and "contraction" of drama is never one of mere technique or method, but is also one of socio-historical context. Specifically, in Soyinka's case, it is a matter of the "imperative of appropriate response" to the human and social crises and dilemmas of post-independence, postcolonial Africa and beyond these, the crises and malaise of the modern world.

These perspectives place the "ritual problematic" in Soyinka's greatest dramatic works in an expanded framework of form and subject matter, style and meaning, which drastically undercuts the inflation of the significance of ritual and its associated idioms to a controlling, regulative norm by many scholars of Soyinka's drama. Definitely, in each of the five plays discussed in this chapter, ritual is not only usually placed within a "festival complex" containing other performance modes, it is in fact quite often parodied, subverted or deconstructed by some of these other idioms. If this is the case, the central question for analysis and interpretation is how this pattern of simultaneous ritual affirmation and negation operates in each play, and the particular pressure of historic and sociopolitical circumstance which might be adjudged the instigating factor for the pattern that each play presents to us. Since these plays all belong in the same corpus, in the same career of a playwright responding to a volatile bloc of historical time, what follows is a comparative "symptomatic" reading of the five plays discussed in the chapter. Each of these plays, I shall argue, contains a dramatization, in form and content, of the "ritual problematic" as a homologous structure, a "symptom" of pervasive and deep existential, social and epistemological alienations and crises in post-colonial Africa in particular, and more generally, in the modern world. The dramaturgic distinctiveness of each play is thus a mark of what in Soyinka's career I have called the imperative of appropriate response. Thus, if we are searching for the most productive area of Soyinka's writings in which to explore the intersection of his political radicalism with his aesthetic avant-gardism, it is to this group of plays that we must turn.

The press release of the Swedish Academy which announced the award of the Nobel prize for literature for 1986 to Soyinka specifically chose *A Dance of the Forests* as one of the few works of the poet and playwright to highlight in the brief, two-page statement. It gave the following summation of the external features of the play: "A kind of African *Midsummer Night's Dream* with spirits, ghosts and gods. There is a distinct link here to indigenous ritual drama and to the Elizabethan drama."[12] This is an apt summary of *only* the external formal features of the play; in terms of the deep structures of plot and characterization, the resonance and allusions in this play are far less to *A Midsummer Night's Dream* than to *The Tempest*. Indeed, given the extensive borrowing in plot and characterization from the latter play, it is surprising that no critical commentary on *A Dance* and its "complexity" has looked to that Shakespeare play on fantasy and moral accountability, on guilt, remorse and expiation, for interpretive clues.

Like Prospero and Ariel in *The Tempest*, Forest Head and Aroni (a name that has phonetic echoes of Ariel) in *A Dance* lure some remorseless perpetrators of monstrous acts of criminality and venality to a reckoning in the heart of the forest. And, just as in *The Tempest*, the slow pace of the movement toward the settling of accounts results from the introduction of subplots and "distractions" which considerably complicate the main plot structure. In *The Tempest*, these complications arise from the conspiratorial "plots" of, on the one hand, the plebeian plotters, Caliban, Trinculo and Stephano, and, on the other hand, the aristocratic would-be regicides, Antonio and Sebastian. In Soyinka's play, the delayed-action structure of the plot results from the exertions of, again, two groups of plotters: the Old Man (Demoke's father) and Agboreko as they work to drive away the unwelcome dead and head off Demoke and his companions from Forest Head's design to have them be present as culprits at the ritual trial; and the ferocious antagonism of Eshuoro and Ogun which constantly thwarts and disrupts the proceedings at the "trial." Even the flashback scene to the court of Mata Kharibu recalls the inserted masque of Juno and Ceres in *The Tempest*: both enhance the magical, oneiric quality of each play's atmosphere as well as enlarge the spiritual and metaphoric compass of the themes of each play. Finally, beside the obvious and compelling parallelism of characters such as Forest Head, Aroni and Agboreko respectively with Prospero, Ariel and Gonzalo in *The Tempest*, Soyinka's play is also indebted to the Shakespeare play for the basic imaginative structure of the dramatic action, this being the use of an elaborate and extravagant fantasy to stage the day of reckoning for unrepentant perpetrators of serious crimes and misdemeanors.

For all its extensive borrowing from the plot of the Shakespeare play, *A Dance* is most decidedly not an imitative, derivative play. Indeed, considering the fact that Soyinka was a young playwright literally at the beginning of his career as a dramatist when he wrote and staged this play, it is remarkable the extent to which he was able to assimilate and creatively transform the powerful, daunting influence of a genius of the order of Shakespeare, and in one of his greatest dramatic creations too. Thus, the differences and departures from the dramatic structure and imaginative universe of *The Tempest* in Soyinka's play are just as startling as the similarities we have indicated above.

Unquestionably, the most crucial departure of *A Dance* from Shakespeare's play is the fact that the trial of the guilty party is made more central to the plot, and is given considerably more capacious "playing time" in action and dialogue than in *The Tempest*. And this, in turn, derives from the fact that this trial scene is patterned on the model afforded by the most powerful judicial-administrative cults in traditional African precolonial society, the type that Achebe brings to the narrative of *Things Fall Apart* in the tenth chapter of that novel.

Scholars of the institutional sources of spectacle in Elizabethan and Jacobean drama and theatre have pointed to the tradition of the elaborately staged public trials and, sometimes, royal pardons, of real and suspected plotters and adversaries by the monarchs of the period as a very probable source of the scene of Prospero's trial and pardon of his enemies in *The Tempest*. For *A Dance*, the model of the trial scene organized around masked and unmasked but costumed adjudicators can be glimpsed in the following dramatic exchange in the tenth chapter of *Things Fall Apart*. The exchange is based on the trial of the wife-beater, Uzowulu, by the *egwugwu*, a group of masqueraders representing ancestral spirits and acting on the occasion as the most powerful judicial institution in the land:

"I don't know why such a trifle should come before the *egwugwu*", said one elder to another. "Don't you know what kind of man Uzowulu is? He will not listen to any other decision", replied the other. As they spoke, two other groups of people had replaced the first before the *egwugwu* and a great land case began.[13]

In this quote, first the *egwugwu* try the trifling case of the unrepentant wife-beater, Uzowulu, and then proceed to the trial of "a great land case," just as in *A Dance*, the masked spirits summoned by Forest Head to "try" Demoke and the other humans are constantly distracted from this important task by the "trifling" quarrel of Eshuoro and Ogun. Consistent with his celebrated fictional method of using condensation and understatement to encompass vast socio-historical experiences and the institutional expressions through which they are mediated or negotiated, Achebe in this quote subsumes the middling case of Uzowulu to the "great land case," hopeful that his narrative art will easily secure the endorsement of the perceptive reader for his separation of "trifling" from serious matters in the cases that come before the *egwugwu* for adjudication. The extraordinarily dense and cryptic nature of the dramatization of the "ritual problematic" in *A Dance* is predicated on the fact that the ritual idioms that Soyinka appropriates for the climactic trial scene in the play derive their expressive and thematic intricacy and complexity from this same kind of judicial-adminstrative ritual, with however, nothing approaching the authority and legitimacy of its invocation in Achebe's novel which, after all, is set in the past, before the onset of the "sacrificial crisis." Nonetheless, Soyinka shows great originality in his conflation of both this pristine West African judicial-administrative ritual matrix and, in the persons of Forest Head and his servitor, Aroni, elements of the absolutist-monarchical paradigm of Prospero's trial of his enemies in *The Tempest*. The originality of this conflation of such disparate expressive idioms, as well as the signal weaknesses that derive from it and considerably compromise the artistic merits of the play, can only be established by a careful exegesis of plot, dramaturgy and symbolism in *A Dance*.

The surface plot of this complex play can be rapidly summarized. The humans are gathered for a festive celebration, "a gathering of the tribes," and they ask the deities and spirits of the sacred groves of the forest to send to the occasion illustrious ancestors as symbolic presences of the greatness and glory of the race. But the forest spirits, principally Forest Head, know better; they know of the past crimes and evils of individuals and groups in the community; they therefore plan to convert the euphoric supplication of the humans to its opposite: a cathartic, purgative confrontation by the gathered tribes with the truth of their past historical experience and reality. Thus, not illustrious ancestors but two restless dead are sent to the humans, accusers and gnawing spots in the buried collective conscience of the race (the dead man's name is "Mulieru" which literally means "He-who-is-enslaved" – he is a ghost returned to confirm the participation of black Africa in its darkest historical tragedy: the transatlantic slave trade). The humans in fury and evasion drive out these unwelcome guests; but the spirits of the forest are remorseless and they lure three of the most important personages among the humans, Demoke, Rola and Adenebi to an expiatory "dance" in the heart of the forest. These three representatives of the human community have recently repeated the cycle of moral corruption and murderous violence that they had each perpetrated in previous incarnations in a decadent and brutal kingdom of the past. In this ritual-judicial space in the heart of the forest, these humans are forced to confront both the restless dead and their other crimes and stupidities, which appear to them as objectified grotesqueries and phantoms. Day breaks in the forest and the three humans, chastened but still unsure and groping, return to the other humans.

This is the "conscious" storyline, the thematic surface of the play and it entails an exemplary action, an attempt at a cathartic exorcism of willful, defensive amnesia of collective guilt in the communal psyche of West Africa. There is, however, also buried in the deep structures of the play a "cultural unconscious" through which this "guilt" is homologously transformed into an underlying drama of ideological alienation in which thought, or the collective West African episteme, is tragically inadequate to the historical problems it is called to "solve." For this deeper structure, we have to pay rigorous attention to Soyinka's use of ritual idioms and symbolism – most of which, in this play, are at their most opaque in all of Soyinka's drama – to complicate and even call into question the literal, realistic plane of the dramatic action.

Critics have generally tended to further mystify the already complex texture of this play by stating that structurally, there are several levels of "being" represented in this play. One critic, Peter Nazareth, sees at least five orders or levels of "being" in the play: the community of living humans who are celebrating "the gathering of the tribes"; that of the

unwelcome dead who have returned to ask questions of the living; the
personages of history and the past whom we encounter in the flashback
to the Court of Mata Kharibu; the spirits and non-human beings of the
forest; and gods and deities like Ogun and Eshuoro.[14] This is too literal-
ist a reading of the symbolic intent of Soyinka's characterization in the
play. Beside, it is a reading that is also too heuristically idealist: "being"
is seen as an "essence," ahistorical, preexistent, trans-historical. If we,
however, choose to see "being" differently, that is, in its "materiality,"
its rootedness in actual processes within nature and society, we see that
in *A Dance*, structurally, there are only two levels of representation – the
spheres of humanity and divinity, or as spatially presented in the play,
the Forest and the Town. The action of the play is structured around this
polarity of human and divine, Forest and Village in ways that are decisive for a materialist interpretation of this extremely complex dramatic
work.

It is clear that the "divine," supernatural world of the deities and the
forest dominate the human world of the town. Not only does most of the
action take place in the forest, but the "forest" also symbolically stands
for nature and this makes the humans (including the Dead) supplicants
to it. This makes them beholden to the forest in many ways. This relationship, manifest everywhere in the play, is most clearly shown in the
following dialogue:

SECOND TRIPLET: (Stops suddenly. Goes to where Demoke, etc. stand huddled
   together. Sniffs them, turns to the Interpreter). But who are these?
FOREST HEAD: They are the lesser criminals, pursuing the destructive path of
   survival. Weak pitiable criminals, hiding their cowardice in sudden acts of
   bluster. And you obscenities . . . (Waves his hands towards the triplets, who
   shriek and dance in delight) you perversions are born when they acquire
   power over one another and their instincts are fulfilled a thousandfold, a
   hundred thousandfold. But wait, there is still the third triplet to come. You
   have as always decided your own fates. Today is no different from your
   lives. I merely sit and watch.

                                                          (*CP1*, 69)

Forest Head's last sentence in this dialogue is not to be understood in
its surface meaning, for *he* is responsible for this most decisive aspect
of the humans' affairs – their attempt at historical self-understanding.
He and his attending deity Aroni, the lame one, precipitate the humans'
act of cathartic self-renewal, for the humans merely demanded illustrious
ancestors. Indeed the godhead represented by Forest Head is presented as
absolute consciousness corresponding to the totalized Orisanla paradigm

discussed earlier in this study:

FOREST HEAD (more to himself): Trouble me no farther. The fooleries of beings whom I have fashioned closer to me weary and distress me. Yet I must persist, knowing that nothing is ever altered. My secret is my eternal burden – to pierce the encrustations of soul-deadening habit, and bare the mirror of original nakedness – knowing full well, it is all futility. Yet I must do this alone, and no more, since to intervene is to be guilty of contradiction, and yet to remain altogether unfelt is to make my long-rumored ineffectuality complete; hoping that when I have tortured awareness from their souls, that perhaps, only perhaps, in new beginnings . . . (*CP1*, 71)

It might well be objected that Forest Head and the beings of the forest are symbolic representations used by Soyinka to probe the complex nature of human motivations and, in the instance of Eshuoro and Ogun's rivalry mirrored in the parallel relationship between Demoke and Oremole, human compulsions toward, and propensities for destructiveness. No doubt this is part of the function of these beings in this play and this is a timeless device, folkloric and literary. But there is no question that Soyinka presents these representations as aspects of a living religious sensibility, hence as an ideological substratum with all the contradictions inherent in religious ideology. And chief of these contradictions is the antagonism which exists between the Forest and the Town, the supernatural beings and the humans, an antagonism which takes the form of mutual depredations between Forest and Town, and in which "injury" is traded for "injury":

MURETE: Oh. Oh. So you can count on them can you? You have been poisoning the minds of the ants.
ESHUORO: They were not difficult to win over. And they'll be present at our welcoming. Four hundred million of their dead will crush the humans in a load of guilt. Four hundred million callously smoked to death. Since when was the forest so weak that humans could smoke out the owners and sleep after?
MURETE: No one has complained much. We have claimed our own victims – for every tree that is felled or for every beast that is slaughtered, there is recompense, given or forced.

(*CP1*, 42)

Clearly, the ideological manifestation of the use of the forest and its denizens in this play lies in this, that it is no less than Nature objectified, anthropomorphized, peopled by its benefactions (Forest Head, Spirit of the Palm, Spirit of the Sun, Chorus of the Waters), its malevolence (Eshuoro, Spirit of Volcanoes, etc.), its capricious will (Ogun, Aroni) and its humor and spleen (Murete, Eshuoro's Jester). And it is necessary to emphasize that this anthropomorphized nature derives its sanction and operational value within an *animist* framework. This is what gives meaning to Eshuoro's gripe, his sense of "injury" at Demoke's carving on the live Araba tree, a sentiment otherwise incomprehensible:

ESHUORO: Am I his son or am I not? I have asked that he pass judgment for my limbs that were hacked off piece by piece. For my eyes that were gouged and my roots disrespectfully made naked to the world. For the desecration of my forest body (42)

This is the materialist basis of the major conflicts of this play: the forest as nature and humanity's struggle with nature, even as he wars with other men. Physical, external nature (the Forest) parallels and mirrors inner, subjective nature in man (the interior drama of the guilt feelings and compulsions of the human culprits). The ideological specificity of this representation lies in the fact that into this materialist base Soyinka infuses a fundamental animist tenet: external, cosmic nature encompasses and engulfs internal nature, and though there is a conflict between both, *the former is the ultimate measure of the latter.* Thus the "disrespect" man shows towards nature in his confident appropriation parallels man's violence towards his own kind. The specific shortcoming of previous criticism of this play in this regard is to focus entirely on the subjective drama and see the exterior antagonism only as incidental, even unintegrated detail.

The entirety of the central, emblematic scene of the play, the dance-trial, is a visual and symbolic representation of this decisive parallelism in the play's dramatic action, for just as the two restless dead, the triplets (the objectified corruptions of man), the half-child (human life aborted by human cruelties) and the ants (the millions of workers – "the masses" – ground underfoot in the "normal" run of production) all rise to condemn the humans, so do the spirits of natural phenomena and objects testify to the humans' depredatory war of exploitation of the resources of nature:

> Spirit of the Precious Stones:
> Still do I draw them down
> Into the pit that glitters, I
> Spirit of gold and diamonds
> Mine is the vain light courting death
> A-ah'. Blight this eye that threaded
> Rocks with light, earth with golden lodes
> Traitor to the guardian tribe, turn
> Turn to lead.
>
> (*CP1*, 65)

It is within this treatment of forest-nature, this validation of nature's integrity (earth, sea, wind, mountains, stone, trees and metals) against man's historic assault that Soyinka provides the specificity of the otherwise generalized canvas of the play. It is the validation of the animist wisdom of the mythic and ritual epistemologies of "tribal" West Africa against its historical experience: a precarious undertaking.[15] The humans depredate the forest-nature but the forest takes its toll, makes exactions. Moreover, Forest Head is supreme, meaning: the earth is old, nature subsists. To find, parallels to this absolute certainty of its own correctness by the pure, unsullied animist wisdom, one would have to move beyond the nineteenth-century Western romantic glorification of nature to the present profound doubts of the ecological movement of the West in the recognition that we will never subdue nature but will always remain part of it.[16] Still, this validation in the play proves illusory and precarious. Soyinka may be upholding Nature against History when Murete says:

I am not much concerned. But it seems to me that limb for limb, the forest has always proved victor (42).

But it is an affirmation which Soyinka achieves mostly by linguistic devices only, by rich imagery and poetic brilliance, and not by the use of antagonisms in the plot of the play. One instance of this can be seen when the "Chorus of Waters" warn:

> Chorus of the Waters:
> Let no man lave his feet
> In any stream, in any lake
> In rapids or in cataracts
> Let no woman think to bake
> Her cornmeal wrapped in leaves
> With water gathered of the rain
> He'll think his eye deceives
> Who treads the ripples where I run
> In shallows. These stones shall seem
> As kernels, his the presser's feet
> Standing in the rich, and red, and the
> cloying stream . . .
> Spirit of the Rivers:
> Then shall men say that I the Mother Have joined veins with the
>   Palm my Brother.
> Chorus of the Waters:
> Let the camel mend his leaking hump
> Let the squirrel guard the hollows in the stump.

> (*CP1*, 66)

For beside this mystic integrity of Nature, this wisdom of the ages, Soyinka also erects the remorseless exactions of historical experience, the ultimate of which is the example of the "economic laws" of the Slave Coast:

> FOREST HEAD: Hush! Mulieru, I knew you in the days of pillaging, in the days of sudden slaughter, and the parting of child and mother. I knew you in the days of grand destroying and you a part of the waste. Mulieru, you were one of those who journeyed in the market-ships of blood. You were sold Mulieru, for . . .
> QUESTIONER (who has been consulting his barks): . . . a flask of rum.
>
> (61–2)

And significantly, this historical negation not only mutilates humans and their relationships, but also worsts the forest-nature. The villagers attempt to drive off their unwelcome lead with petrol fumes from the belching exhaust of the hellish transport lorry, "Chimney of Ereko" and Agboreko of "the sealed lips" and cryptic knowledge, medium of animist wisdom, cautions:

> The Chimney of Ereko. Ah, Baba, will you never believe that you cannot get rid of ancestors with the little toys of children. (38)

No doubt Agboreko intends in this admonition a cautionary lesson that the sins and follies of the past, of the ancestors, cannot be wiped out by the inventions and "sophisticated" artifacts of the present civilization, but still the ancestors and the forest beings do retreat before the noxious petrol fumes. They are after all vulnerable, their domination of the humans not absolute. Indeed another aspect of their "vulnerability" is worthy of mention, for not only petrol fumes but the first shafts of sunlight send even Ogun and Eshuoro scampering away deeper into the dense, impenetrable heart of the forest:

> Noise of the beaters from a distance. Dawn is breaking. Ogun enters bearing Demoke, *eying the sky anxiously*. He is armed with a gun and cutlass. The sun creeps through; Ogun lays down Demoke, leaves his weapons beside him, flees. Eshuoro is still dancing as the foremost of the beaters break on the scene and then he flees after his Jester. It is now fully dawn. Agboreko and the Old Man enter, Murete, very drunk, dragging them on. The sound of the main body of beaters with the drummers continues in the distance (72) (My emphasis)

A Dance is not only an appreciation of the wisdom of animist thought in its full respect for the integral totalization of the nature *outside* and *inside* of man, it is also a criticism of it, a revelation of its historically determinate limits. It shows the dialectical self-dissolution of animist-mythical thought in history in the face of the relentless weight of new forms of consciousness: the shafts of sunlight dispel the spirits and gods because they are the fantasized creations of alienated consciousness, and the petrol fumes – a pollutant, mark – irritate the forest beings because the elements of a new mode of production rupture the ecological balance and the material base which subsume and validate the alienated animist consciousness.[17] Christopher Caudwell, in his brilliant but ignored monograph, *Studies and Further Studies in a Dying Culture*, has expressed the social and epistemological basis of this conjunctural crisis:

The religious distortion of consciousness is produced by the structure of the society in which it is generated. It is the outcome of an illusion, a flaw, an infection, in that society. Thus the criticism of religion is also a criticism of the society that produced it, and this does not mean a criticism of that society in the abstract but of its concrete reality, a criticism of all the social relations engendered by its level of economic production.[18]

In a way, *A Dance* shows the dialectic of artistic discipline and formalistic venturesomeness at its most fraught in Soyinka's major plays. Given the fact that the play was written and staged as part of Nigeria's independence celebrations, many critics have pondered the motivations which encouraged Soyinka to crowd, or even overload the plot and dramatic action of this play with a surfeit of incident and rather obscure metaphor and symbolism, especially in the climactic scene of the masque-dance in the forest. This is a play which, after all, is designed in its themes and conflicts to shock its expected middle-class audience out of amnesia about the past and out of euphoria about the present, these being the pervasive complacent spiritual and ideological attitudes of the elites of the then newly independent African countries. What could be more subversive of these attitudes than the play's central theme that the "nation-building" myths of a glorious past, of great, heroic ancestors, were dangerous obfuscations of both that past and a present deeply compromised by cruelty, cowardice and venality? But then, why shroud this theme in layers of "inscrutable" symbolism and metaphysics? This question leads us directly into the specific expressions of the "ritual problematic" in this play, especially as rendered in the climactic scene of the trial of the humans through a cultic ritual masque in the denouement of the play.

There are of course many extraordinarily insightful revelations of human character and motivation in this play. Among these are the revelation of a cowering insecurity beneath Mata Kharibu's blustering tyranny and Demoke's half-remorseful, half-unrepentant and boastful

"confession" of the psychological vulnerabilities and professional jeal-
ousies which prompted him to pluck his apprentice, Oremole, to his
death from his perch above his master at the crown of the Araba tree.
There are also passages of mature verse drama which gather genuine folk
and oracular wisdom into impeccably modern ideas about the perpetual
obstacles to social equality and environmental responsibility, obstacles often exacerbated by the march of "progress" itself. The testimony of the
phalanx of ants in the ritual masque scene is one of such instances of dramatic forcefulness and thematic depth fashioned out of the combination
of traditional Yoruba rhetoric associated with cultic, esoteric knowledge
and the symbolism of Western expressionist drama:

FOREST HEAD: If the hills are silent, who are these, if the sun is full and the
    winds are still whose hand is this that reaches from the grave?
ANT LEADER: We take our color from the loam and blindness hits them, and
    they tread us underfoot.
FOREST HEAD: Are you my sons?
ANT LEADER: We are the blazers of the trail; if you are Forest Father, we think
    we are your sons.
FOREST HEAD: But who are you?
ANT LEADER: We take our color from the fertile loam, our numbers from
    the hair-roots of the earth and terror blinds them. They know we are the
    children of earth. They break our skin upon the ground, fearful that we
    guard the wisdom of earth, our mother.
FOREST HEAD: Have you a grievance?
ANT LEADER: None Father, except great clods of earth pressed on our feet. The
    world is old but the rust of a million years has left the chains unloosened.
FOREST HEAD: Are you not free?
ANT LEADER: Freedom we have like the hunter on a precipice and the horns
    of a rhinoceros nuzzling his buttocks.
FOREST HEAD: Do you not walk? Talk, bear and suckle children by the gross?
ANT LEADER: Freedom indeed we have to choose our path to turn to the left
    or the right like the spider in the sand-pit and the great ball of eggs pressing
    on his back.
FOREST HEAD: But who are you?
    (The leader retreats, and another takes his place.)
ANT: I thought, staying this low, they would ignore me. I am the one that tried
    to be forgotten.
ANOTHER: I am the victim of the careless stride.
ANOTHER: I know the path was thin, a trickle in the marsh. Yet we mowed the
    roots, our bellies to the ground.
FOREST HEAD: Have you a Cause, or shall I preserve you like a riddle?
ANT LEADER: We are the ones remembered when nations build . . .
ANOTHER: . . . with tombstones.

ANOTHER: We are the dried leaves, impaled on one-eyed brooms.
ANOTHER: We are the headless bodies when the spade of progress delves.
ANOTHER: The ones that never looked up when the wind turned suddenly, erupting in our heads.
ANOTHER: Down the axis of the world, from the whirlwind to the frozen drifts, we are the ever legion of the world smitten, for – 'the good to come'.
ANT LEADER: Once my eyes were earthworms dragging in my tears.
ARONI (shouting): What is this? For what cursed future do you rise to speak?
ANT LEADER: Then the ring of scourges was complete and my hair rose on its tail like scorpions.

(*CP1*, 67–9)

This exchange between, on the one hand, the Ant Leader and his co-horts and, on the other hand, Forest Head and Aroni, is an almost perfect microcosm of the entire play in terms of the tension between, on the one hand, imaginative boldness and metaphoric richness and, on the other hand, lack of formal, technical mastery of materials threatening always to overwhelm the reader and the audience. The central idea in the exchange is an old, timeless theme of engaged literature: workers as ants trodden underfoot in the march of progress. The way in which Soyinka transforms this theme into one of the most resonant and lay-ered tropes in the ritual masque scene is worthy of review, as are the risks and slippages incurred in the process. First, the irruption of the ants into the scene is shrouded in mystery and enigma, for even Forest Head himself, the "father of secrets," does not immediately recognize them. Moreover, their ascension to centre stage within the scene is clothed in a myriad of metaphors that considerably enhance their associative link with too many forms, too many communities of exploitation, suffering and drudgery. They are said to be a collective "hand that reaches from the grave" (countless generations of the oppressed of past ages); they take their "color from the fertile loam," their "numbers from the hair roots of the earth" (peasants who live close to the land and base their supreme ethical values, their identity on the "soil"); they are the ones who try "to be forgotten" by "staying low" (anonymous toilers and drudges in their mass, "forgettable" existence); they are the ones remembered when nations "build with tombstones" (millions of war dead memorial-ized in the absurdity of cenotaphs erected in the name of the "unknown soldier"); and they are "the ever legion of the world smitten for the good to come" (the poor expropriated and disenfranchised by the promise of a better tomorrow which has been made to the countless generations of the ancestors of the present generation of the expropriated). The fact that these are just a few selected details from the dense overflow of ideas, tropes and symbols in the exchange between the ants and Forest Head and Aroni should give us an idea of just how much Soyinka puts into this play, and what difficulties this posed to him dramaturgically. The sprawling plot, the slow pace of the action, the questionable relevance of some subplots or plot fragments – the rivalry between Eshuoro and Ogun; and Murete, the tree imp's lassitude and drunken antics as the vehicle of mediation between the beings of the forest and the humans – seem less revealing of formalistic and stylistic boldness than inept artistic decisions made by a playwright just beginning his career and taking on a very big subject matter for a unique occasion.

These flaws are perhaps at their most confounding in the extreme overcrowding of the climactic ritual trial scene with too many incidents and too many metaphors and symbols of great obscurity. Considering the fact that this *is* the concluding moment of the trial scene in the play, it stands entirely to reason that the disruptive or diversionary games and contests indicated in the following stage directions for this scene would lead to a deadlocked verdict at the end of the ritual trial. And this has the effect of rendering the very legitimacy of the ritual itself profoundly ambiguous:

(The Half-Child continues slowly towards the Mother, Eshuoro imperiously offering his hand, furious as each step takes the child nearer her. Looks up sharply and finds Ogun on the other side of the woman, with hand similarly outstretched. Snaps his fingers suddenly at the Interpreter. A clap of drums, and the Interpreter begins another round of 'ampe' with the Third Triplet. The Woman's hand and the Half-Child's are just about to meet when this happens, and the child turns instantly, attracted by the game. The 'ampe' gradually increases tempo among the three Triplets. The Interpreter throws off his mask, reveals himself as Eshuoro's Jester. He draws the child into a game of 'ampe'. When the Half-Child is totally disarmed by the Jester, Eshuoro picks him up suddenly and throws him towards the Third Triplet who makes to catch him on the point of two knives as in the dance of the child acrobats. Rola screams, the child is tossed up by the Third Triplet who again goes through the same motion, the other two Triplets continuing the furious 'ampe' round him and yelling at the top of their voices. Demoke, Rola and Adenebi again cluster together. The Half-Child is now tossed back to Eshuoro, and suddenly Demoke dashes forward to intercept. Eshuoro laughs, pretends to throw the child back, Demoke dashes off only to find that he still retains the child. The Interpreter, Eshuoro and the Third Triplet all evading the knife-points at the last moment and catching the Half-Child in the crook of their elbows. They keep up this game for a brief period, with Demoke running between them, until Ogun appears behind the Interpreter, pulls him aside just as the child is thrown towards him, makes the catch himself passing it instantly to Demoke who has come running as before. All action stops again, including the first and second Triplets who have never ceased to 'ampe'. They all look at Demoke, who stands confused, not knowing what the next step should be. He decides eventually to restore the child to the Dead Woman, and attempts to do so. Eshuoro partially blocks his way and appeals to Forest Head. Ogun appeals against him.) (*CP1*, 70–1)

Most critics, following the suggestion of Eldred Jones in the first, full-length study of Soyinka's writings, have read the struggle of Eshuoro and Ogun for the Half-Child as a struggle for the life, the soul of the then newly independent nation of Nigeria and, beyond that, the "new nations" of Lucy Mair's famous monograph of the same title.[19] Since the Half-Child ends up with Demoke rather than Eshuoro, this has been read as a somewhat hopeful sign. This is an ingenious, if somewhat strained reading of the published script of the play, a reading which the performance script, the staged production, not only obscures, but actually considerably mystifies. Demoke and his companions leave the "dance in the forest" chastened, but they do so in the grip of an unshakable perplexity which has apparently extended to the scholarly commentary on the play. In *A Dance*, the destructive energies that must be ritually cleansed or purged are concentrated in Eshuoro and Ogun on the side of the deities, and in Demoke, Rola and Adenebi, on the side of the humans. The two deities are entirely unmoved by the catharsis of the trial scene, but the three human protagonists, especially Demoke, become less blind to the terrible destruction caused by the past and present acting out of their egotistical drives, desires or appetites. These are the dialogical faces of ritual negation and affirmation in Soyinka's dramatization of the "ritual problematic" in this play.

The Road and *Madmen and Specialists* have the distinction among Soyinka's most ambitious plays of locating ritual and festivity, as paradigms for dramatic form, among the "lower" social orders, ending up with rather startling expressions of the Bakhtinian carnival of the oppressed. Moreover, in both plays, these paradigms are mobilized and carefully manipulated by extremely eccentric and irreverent protagonists who, at one level, have made the cause of the oppressed their own. These are respectively Professor in *The Road* and the Old Man, perhaps the two most enigmatic and unforgettable characters in modern African drama. *The Road* and *Madmen and Specialists* are also the best examples in Soyinka's drama of "art theatre," of "cult plays" tailored to the aesthetic taste and sensibilities of a cultural elite which is institutionally transnational and cosmopolitan; paradoxically, however, both plays have strong roots in

Wole Soyinka

local Nigerian and African traditions and realities. Both plays also have all the hallmarks of modern, avant-garde drama: plotlessness, or radical non-linearity of plot; protagonists who defy any simple or coherent categorization in terms of who they are and what their motivations are; a dramaturgical method which foregrounds language and other means of expression as artistic means of production and representation whose yield in terms of aesthetic, political or ethical impact cannot be taken for granted. These qualities seem on the surface to mark these plays as dramas that deliberately eschew artistic constraints or even control. One critic has thus aptly called *The Road* a "play of poetry and atmosphere rather than action,"[20] and another critic has written of *Madmen and Specialists* as a play of "loose montage of performing stunts on the part of the mendicants, of abrupt changes or gradual slippages from events which are presented as the traditional dialogic interaction of established characters."[21] But this is only a partial aspect of these two plays which in fact, within the perspectives of the avant-garde, show a remarkable exercise of meticulous artistic discipline. Indeed, on the level of form and technique, these two plays mark a crucial line of departure from *A Dance* in terms of artistic decisions and choices imposed by a subject matter of great, disquieting import. For this reason, a comparison of similarities and resonances between the two plays is useful both for the light it casts on Soyinka's drama in general and for clarification of the peculiar strengths and achievements of each play.

The processes of social and technological change which *The Road* attempts to dramatize has been ably described by one critic in the following commentary in which the play is said to be marked by

its assimilation into specifically Nigerian terms of a universal phenomenon, brought by imperialism – petrol transport. In other words, it's about the real modern Nigeria: an enormous, inchoate territory whose ancient units of tribe and religion are being supplanted by the new patterns of technology – above all by the system of rough, weather-pitted roads along which thousands of ramshackle, picturesquely-named lorries speed goods and passengers hundreds of miles to market.[22]

Given the "inchoate," anarchic and profoundly dislocating nature of this vast social process which I have elsewhere described as urbanization without industrialization,[23] "plotlessness" would seem to be a sound artistic choice for the dramatic action of *The Road*. Similarly, *Madmen and Specialists*, in dealing with not only the Nigerian civil war but with all wars, with war psychosis as an analog for other irrationalities and barbarisms of (dis)organized social life, the play's departure from conventions of mimetic drama – linear plots supervened by the logic of probable, cause-and-effect development, intelligible dialogue between characters who dialogically act as interlocutors and respondents, all of these features operating within stable discursive regimes – is a deliberate artistic choice with its own non-mimetic logic. In effect, unlike the climactic scene of the ritual masque in *A Dance*, the many inscriptions of unassimilated detail and abrupt shifts in the dramatic action of the two plays under discussion here are carefully patterned, not on the conventional protocols of external plot structure but on the internal logic of related or contrastive motifs in *The Road*, and the free association of the phonetic and semantic resonances of words in *Madmen and Specialists*. For instance, death on the roads and the highways through horrific crashes, together with the diverse attitudes toward life and death which they engender provide a link with the myriad of seemingly disconnected motifs which undergird the "plotlessness" of *The Road*; they also provide a key to unraveling many seemingly esoteric, obscure inscriptions of action and thought in the play. Indeed, underlying the "plotlessness" of the play is a structural mythos which combines elements of a "crime mystery" with that of a "crime thriller": on the day of the drivers' festival which happened before the play proper begins, the funerary "egungun" masquerade was "killed" but the body "disappeared" and all the characters sense something fishy and untoward in this "disappearance." Particulars Joe, the corrupt policeman is in fact on the trail of Professor, the real "culprit"; at the end of the play, the body reappears in the "resurrection" planned by Professor; consequently, this "resurrection" and the terrified panic that it causes, leads to Professor's slaying at the hands of Say-Tokyo Kid, the most terrified and at the same time the least intimidated by Professor's reputed occult powers. Of course, there is no "crime" and the "disappearance" of the body is more apparent than real and it is precisely the totally imaginary nature of these motifs that enable Soyinka's treatment of this mythos of "crime mystery" and "thriller" to give death, the disappearance ("flesh dissolution") of bodies and the mystery of life, part romantic, part tragicomic expressions through powerfully realized characters in the grip of processes of historical change they barely understand.

This pattern also holds true for *Madmen and Specialists*, though in a somewhat more polarized fashion since the undergirding mythos here rests on the conflict between great, all-encompassing evil and forces and agents who act on behalf of a providential grace and munificence

(Iya Agba, Iya Mate, Si Bero and, ambiguously, the Old Man) and who have a keen, unromantic knowledge of evil and are thus not themselves averse to using evil to fight evil. It is the underlying polarity of this mythos which provides Soyinka with tight artistic control over the extreme radical discontinuities and disjunctures in the action of the play. The endless parodic improvisations of the four mendicants on just about every institution, every value propping up power, rank, duty and respectability are anchored in this underlying substructure of the duality of good and evil, the disease and its cure. Thus, *Madmen* shares many features with *The Road*; this comparative profile of the considerable dramaturgic and thematic similarities between these two radical and enigmatic dramatic parables on evil enables us to engage the enthralling textual and ideological inscriptions that the parable entails in each play.

"If they threaten me, I shall counter with a resurrection, capital R," says Professor in *The Road*. This is in reference to his epic battle with the Christian church and the congregation from which he has been expelled and in whose very frontage he has set up an oppositional redoubt in the form of his palm wine bar and "Aksident Store." But Professor's profane eccentricities extend beyond his parody of Christian ritual and liturgical motifs to embrace also traditional African matrices since in fact his threats of a counter "resurrection" rests on Murano, his deaf-mute servant who is none other than the masquerade who was knocked down and presumed dead on the day of the drivers' festival. The traditional metaphysical assumption being that Murano in cultic "egungun" masqueradery became transubstantiated into an ancestral spirit or a deity, this amounts to nothing less than Professor willfully holding "a god captive." In stark contrast and simmering conflict with this studied "irreverence" of Professor are the more conventionally "pious," reverential attitudes and beliefs of his subaltern confreres of drivers, apprentices and thugs: they hold Ogun in awe and reverence, just as they are enormously impressed by the poetry and drama of Sunday worship in the Christian church from which Professor has been expelled. It is this conflict which erupts at the end of the play leading to the slaying of Professor when he apparently makes good on his threat of a counter "resurrection" by finally allowing Murano to don his ritual "egungun" costume.

Oyin Ogunba's impressive work of uncovering the ethnographic background of the extensive cultic ritual materials deployed by Soyinka in *The Road* has been very helpful to students in tackling the "difficulty" of the play.[24] Nonetheless, there remains a tremendous challenge of uncovering "meaning" from the play's esoteric, though scintillating parodies of both Western and African religious rituals and their associated ideas of the sacred. But if "meaning" in this play is elusive and its articulations shrouded in esoteric discourses and symbols, nobody, reader or stage audience, could possibly miss what the play, phenomenologically, is *about*, what it powerfully evokes throughout its dramatic action: the carnage of human lives on the roads and highways of the coastal strip of West Africa. As we shall demonstrate later, Soyinka's achievement in this play is above all expressed in the manner in which he transforms this powerfully elegiac invocation of life and death on the roads into an allegory of larger and more complicated crises and dilemmas of technological and social change in modern-day West Africa.

Though *The Road* provides a more fully realized dramatization of a sublime conception of the evil that men do and must endure than any other Soyinka play, it presents us with a more formidable exegetical challenge. For there are no literal monstrously evil acts to be ritually exorcised in this play as in others like *A Dance* and *Madmen and Specialists*, and no autocratic rulers who unwittingly cause terrible havoc and suffering like Pilkings in *Death and the King's Horseman* and Pentheus in *The Bacchae of Euripides*. Moreover, the play's action contains perhaps the most zestful celebration of life and the struggle to survive in adverse, destructive conditions in all of modern African drama. Herein indeed lies the catch in the carnivalesque exuberance of the play: beneath the robust humor and the romance of the characters in this play lies the reality of life lived daily at the edge of inevitable disaster and ruin. The physical and verbal motifs which give the play this scale of representation of a world in which destructiveness *is* the medium in which everyone has his or her being are too many to enumerate. Apart from the many references to horrible road crashes involving mass slaughter of lorry drivers, their apprentices and their passengers, there is the enormously crucial fact that the huge void which exists where there should be a cohering or stable moral order is filled by the extremely bizarre personal moral codes of many characters of the play, all of these private codes revolving around the banality of meaningless, violent death or destruction. Three of these characters are worthy of brief scrutiny – Say-Tokyo Kid, Sergeant Burmah and, above everyone else, Professor.

Say-Tokyo Kid's personal and professional identity is perhaps the most colorful in the play because it is synthesized out of diverse models and sources African and foreign, traditional and modern. These include the veneration of Ogun, patron god of drivers and other workers in metalware; the heroes, values and discourses of American B grade movies; the subculture of marijuana smokers in the criminal underworld of petty felons and "hired guns" ("thugs"); and fierce professional pride in his job as a driver of timber-hauling lorries. The moral code by which he lives is compounded out of these diverse sources and models and is thus like a pastiche of half-digested ideas, but its rootedness in an underlying expectation of destruction is unmistakable and it shows through in his most memorable act of verbal self-presentation in the play:

THUG: Son of timber!
SAY T.: That's me kid. A guy is gorra have his principles. I'm a right guy. I mean you just look arrit this way. If you gonna be killed by a car, you don't wanna be killed by a Volkswagen. You wanra Limousine, a Ponriac or something like that. Well thas my principle. Suppose you was to come and find me in the ditch one day with one of them timber guys on ma back. Now ain't it gonna be a disgrace if the guy was some kinda cheap, wretched firewood full of ants and borers. So when I carry a guy of timber, its gorra be the biggest. One or two. If it's one, its gorra fill the whole lorry, no room even for the wedge. And high class timber kid. High class. Golden walnut. Obeche. Ironwood. Black Afara, Iroko, Ebony, Camwood. And the heartwood's gorra be sound. (Thumps his chest.) It's gorra have a solid beat like that. Like mahogany.
THUG: No dirty timber!
SAY T.: Timber is ma line. You show me the wood and I'll tell you what kinda insects gonna attack it, and I'll tell you how you take the skin off. And I'll tell you what kinda spirit is gonna be chasing you when you cut it down. If you ain't gorra strong head kid, you can't drive no guy of timber.
SAMSON: Just the same it doesn't much matter what you are carrying when it rolls over you.
SAY T.: You kidding? Just you speak for yourself man. And when that guy of timber gits real angry and plays me rough, I just don't wan no passenger piss running on ma head. You know, just last week I pass an accident on the road. There was a dead dame and you know what her pretty head was smeared with? Yam porrage. See what I mean? A swell dame is gonna die on the road just so the next passenger kin smear her head in yam porrage? No sirree. I ain't going with no one unless with ma own guy of timber.

$$(CP_1, 172\text{–}3)$$

Sergeant Burmah's personal moral code is even more vividly rendered since he is already dead when the action of the play begins and he is animated for our stultified regard by the impressive mimetic skills of Samson. Like Say-Tokyo Kid, Sergeant Burmah's identity revolves around his professional pride as a driver of oil tankers, but to this is added his open practice of cannibalizing every salable commodity from road crashes and their victims, even if these victims are acquaintances or professional colleagues. More importantly, the imputation by Soyinka of Sergeant Burmah's predatoriness on the dead to the fact of his being a shell-shocked, mentally-unhinged veteran of the Second World War enables the playwright to credibly and powerfully endow this character with a general "theory" of life that is at once utterly nihilistic and paradoxically life-affirming. This can be seen in the following scene in which, while Particulars Joe gives a running commentary on the charmed life of the late Sergeant Burma, Samson powerfully reanimates the dead man through mimetic ventriloquizing of his voice, mannerisms and embodied "philosophy":

PARTIC. JOE: We were made much of in those days. To have served in Burma was to have passed your London Matric. Sergeant Burma looked forward to retirement and his choice of business came as a matter of course . . . and Professor offered him the business corner of the drivers' haven . . . the Accident Corner.

SAMSON: Wetin enh? Wetin? You tink say myself I no go die some day? When person die, 'e done die and dat one done finish. I beg, if you see moto accident make you tell me. We sabbee good business . . . sell spare part and second-hand clothes. Wetin? You tink say I get dat kind sentimentation? Me wey I done see dead body so tey I no fit chop meat unless den cook am to nonsense? Go siddon my friend. Business na business. If you see accident make you tell me I go run go there before those useless men steal all the spare part finish.

PARTIC. JOE: Sergeant Burma looked forward to retiring and doing the spare part business full-time. But of course his brakes failed going down a hill . . . (*The group begins to dirge, softly as if singing to themselves. A short silence. Samson's face begins to show horror and he gasps as he realizes what he has been doing.*)

SAMSON (*tearing off the clothes*): God forgive me! Oh God, forgive me. Just see, I have been fooling around pretending to be a dead man. Oh God I was only playing I hope you realize. I was only playing.

PARTIC. JOE: Such a fire . . . such a fire . . . Nothing but black twigs left of the veteran of Burma campaign . . . I went to break the news to his wife. You know what she said?

SAMSON: No no, talk of something else I beg you.

PARTIC. JOE: She said, I always told him not to gather dead men's wallets. And she was coming here to set fire to the whole store.

PROFESSOR: Set fire to my store!

PARTIC. JOE: That's what I told her. Maybe the goods belong to your husband I said, but the idea, was Professor's.

PROFESSOR: A spiritual ownership – more important than the material.

SAMSON: I wish she'd burnt the whole place.

PARTIC.JOE: She wasn't going to burn his money though. Oh Sergeant Burma
    was a rich man. He searched the pockets before the police or the ambulance
    came. Looting was after all the custom in the front. You killed your enemy
    and you robbed him. He couldn't break the habit.
SAMSON: But this is not war.
PROFESSOR: Liar. Even these rags (waving a newspaper) understand its nature.
    Like a battlefield they always say. Like a battlefield.

                                                              (217–19)

Professor's sardonic comment in this passage that monstrously predatory
acts and behavior considered "normal" in war are no less valid in peace
time because life itself is essentially "like a battlefield" shows the link between his own enigmatic philosophy of life with the personal moral codes
of the likes of Say-Tokyo Kid and Sergeant Burma. But unlike those other
characters, Professor *is* a quester after "truth," after the mystery of life
and death, and this aspect of his personality has exercised considerable
fascination for many critics. His very first appearance in the action of
the play is laden with colorful enigma. He is described thus: "Professor
is a tall figure in Victorian outfit – tails, top hat, etc., all threadbare and
shiny at the lapels from much ironing. He carries four enormous bundles
of newspaper and a fifth of paper odds and ends impaled in a metal rod
stuck in a wooden rest. A chair stick hangs from one elbow, and the other
arm clutches a road-sign bearing a squiggle and the word 'BEND'" (CP1,
156–7). And Professor's first words match this appearance of enigmatic,
unnerving eccentricity with poetic flavor – he describes a road crash with
many deaths that he has just seen with phrases amounting to perhaps
the most memorable inscription of T.S. Eliot's concept of the "objective correlative" in Soyinka's plays: "Come then, I have a new wonder
to show you . . . a madness where a motor car throws itself against a
tree – Gbram! And showers of crystal flying on broken souls" (CP1, 158–
9). This dazzling use of language is sustained throughout the play and,
more specifically, is deployed to give Professor's interest – and trade – in
death its profoundly paradoxical combination of a tough-minded, unsentimental and predatory view of death as inseparable from life's central
material process of the production and circulation of commodities and
services, and an epic quest seeking to find the means with which to strip
death of its mastery over life as expressed above all in the processes of
putrefaction and "flesh dissolution." As he moves serially through exploration and then disavowals of, first, the liturgical rites and theological
beliefs of the Christian faith, second, traditional African ritual beliefs and
practices around institutions of spirit mediums and funerary cults, and

finally his own private esoteric system compounded out of cabalistic signs, numerology and necromancy, these two paradoxical aspects remain constant: a very materialistic, even opportunistic interest in the "spoils" of death on the roads and highways, and a radical spirituality which revolts against all the identity-forming institutions and practices of organized religion, indigenous and foreign, which impose fear and terror on men, especially the poor and the disenfranchised. This is why his closing, perorative "benefaction" at the moment of his death – significantly the last words in the play – entails a ferociously sardonic iteration of ritual and sacrificial motifs and beliefs, an iteration which impresses with its deep insights into mystic experience and phenomena, yet leaves absolutely no room for catharsis in its terrifyingly bleak vision of life's barren destructiveness (CP1, 228–9). Paradoxically however, while conventional ritual affirmation is subverted by the dramatic action of this play and the personal moral codes of characters like Say-Tokyo Kid, Sergeant Burma and Professor, there are unquestionable life-affirming, life-enhancing qualities in the imagined selves fashioned out of the pious and impious shards of ritual beliefs and practices of these and the other characters of this enigmatic play on the inchoate processes of social-cultural change in contemporary West Africa.

The grisly cannibal feast which stands at the centre of the subversion of sacrificial rituals in *Madmen and Specialists* is the brainchild of the play's protagonist, the Old Man; it is a very appropriate indicator of the scope of his towering, raging discontent with all traditional and conventional pieties, both in their religious expressions and in secular, "patriotic" formulations. Sickened to the soul by the mass slaughter that takes place in wars, especially wars justified in the name of "national integrity" or defense of a faith, this "madman" leaves for the war front, maneuvers himself into a position of some influence and successfully arranges to have all the war commanders unwittingly partake of a feast whose main course is the cooked flesh of the war dead. His utterly sardonic rationale: man is the only animal that kills wastefully, not for food; if we cannot end wars, we can at least end war's "wastefulness":

OLD MAN: Oh, their faces! That was a picture. All those faces round the table.
BERO: If they hadn't been too surprised they would have shot you on the spot.
OLD MAN: Your faces, gentlemen, your faces. You should see your faces. And your mouths are hanging open. You're drooling but I am not exactly sure why. Is there really much difference? All intelligent animals kill only for food, you know, and you are intelligent animals. Eat-eat-eat-eat-eat-Eat!
BERO (raises his arm): Stop it!

OLD MAN (turns and holds him with his eyes): Oh yes, you rushed out and
    vomited. You and the others. But afterwards you said I had done you a
    favour. Remember? (BERO slowly lowers his arm.) I'm glad you remember.
    Never admit you are a recidivist once you've tasted the favourite food of As.

(CP2, 254)

If the act of turning those who make wars into cannibals in order to
expose and decry the "wastefulness" of wars has a twisted humanistic
logic to it, the Old Man's exercise of his immensely subversive will in
this play consists precisely in expanding in all directions the tactic of
confronting logical systems which destroy human life and corrupt and
degrade both perpetrators and victims with their fundamentally illogical
foundations. For himself, the Old Man's weapon is his savagely deconstructive wit: the mere echoes of words and phrases, the mere phonemes
and syllables of ideas and concept-metaphors suffice for him to render
the verities and assurances of either spiritual solace or communicative
rationality that they proffer utterly meaningless. But over and beyond
his wit, or as an extension of it, the Old Man has also appropriated the
idioms of chants, recitations and rites of alms begging by the mendicants,
turning them on their head. This combination of his own deconstructive
wit with an inversion of the rites and locutions of alms begging that he
had appropriated from the mendicants is made with the intention of
confronting evil with platitudes which rationalize and justify it. This is
indeed acknowledged in the following scene by no less a person than
Dr. Bero, the specialist, the confounded target of the relentless assaults
of the Old Man and his disciples:

BERO (heatedly): It's not his charitable propensities I am concerned with. Fa-
    ther's assignment was to help the wounded readjust to the pieces and
    remnants of their bodies. Physically. Teach them to make baskets if they
    still had fingers. To use their mouths to ply needles if they had none, or use
    it to sing if their vocal cords had not been shot away. Teach them to amuse
    themselves, make something of themselves. Instead he began to teach them
    to think, think, THINK! Can you picture a more treacherous deed than
    to place a working mind in a mangled body?
SI BERO: Where is he?
BERO: Where? Here.
SI BERO: Here?
BERO (pointing to the MENDICANTS): There. When they open their mouths
    you can hear him. You! Come here! Tell her. Would you call yourself sane?
    The MENDICANTS *have approached,* AAFAA *in the lead.*
AAFAA: Certainly not, sir.
BERO: You got off lightly, Why?

AAFAA: I pleaded insanity.

BERO: Who made you insane?

AAFAA (by rote, raising his eyes to heaven): The Old Man, sir. He said things, he said things. My mind . . . I beg your pardon, sir, the thing I call my mind, well, was no longer there. He took advantage of me, sir, in that convalescent home. I was unconscious long stretches at a time. Whatever I saw when I came to was real. Whatever voice I heard was the truth. It was always him. Bending over my bed. I asked him, Who are you? He answered, The one and only truth . . .

CRIPPLE: Hear hear.

GOYI: Same here.

AAFAA: Always at me, he was, sir. I plead insanity.

CRIPPLE: Hear hear.

GOYI: Same here.

SI BERO What is this, Bero? Where is Father?

AAFAA: Within the cycle.

BLINDMAN: That's good. The cycle of As. Tell the Old Man that – he'll be pleased.

SI BERO: Where is he?

AAFAA: Where the cycle is complete there will As be found. As of the beginning, we praise thee.

SI BERO (shutting her ears): Oh God!

BERO (pointing to the MENDICANTS): Do you still want to see him?

AAFAA: As – Was – Is – Now.

SI BERO: Shut up, you loathsome toads!

(242–4)

There has been an extensive critical discussion of the meaning of "As," of its use as a concept-metaphor signifying both the surfeit and the ordinariness of evil in the order of things in nature and society.[25] This is due in large part to the extensive use by Soyinka in this play of irony of the species of the grotesque. And nowhere is this more evident than in the deployment of the conceit of "As." For, on the one hand, there is its very obvious and very explicit allusion to one of the most venerated mantras of grace and providential order in Christian liturgy – "As it was in the Beginning, Is Now and Ever Shall Be, World Without End." Simultaneously and contrastively, there is its assimilation to the cultic traditions of an imaginary, savage deity who feeds on human flesh, a deity who presides over bloodbaths and mangled human bodies. Thus, although "As" defies any simple, unambiguous exegetical analysis, it is not the case, as many of the play's critics have suggested that "As" finally defies comprehension. At any rate, it is also the case that "As" is elaborated performatively in the play with prismatic clarity, either in the mode of

verbal jousts and language games between linguistic duelists, or in the
spirit of a fervent evangelizing African nativist Christian worship in which
the sermonizing intensity of the Old Man, as an ironizing "evangelist" of
"As," is matched by the fervor of the response of his "congregationalist"
disciples, the four mendicants:

BLINDMAN: I hope I didn't do too badly.

OLD MAN (sighs, turns to face him): No. It was quite a good effort.

BLINDMAN: It was rather like old times.

OLD MAN: Very much like old times.

CRIPPLE: Hey, listen. The Old Man was pleased.

AAFAA: I should bloody well hope so. It was just like old times.

CRIPPLE: My feelings exactly. Just like old times.

GOYI: It . . . was . . . just . . . like old times.

AAFAA: *Yes. So why risk putting us here together?*

OLD MAN: *Because . . . we are together in As.* (He rises slowly.) As Is, and the System
is its mainstay though it wear a hundred masks and a thousand outward
forms. And because you are within the System, the cyst in the System that
irritates, the foul gurgle of the cistern, the expiring function of a faulty
cistern and are part of the material for reformulating the mind of a man
into the necessity of the moment's political As, the moment's scientific As,
metaphysic As, sociologic As, economic, recreative ethical As, you-cannot-
escape! There is but one constant in the life of the System and that constant
is AS. And what can you pit against the priesthood of that constant deity,
its gospellers, its enforcement agency. And even if you say unto them, do
I not know you, did I not know you in rompers, with leaky nose and
smutty face? Did I not know you thereafter, know you in the haunt of
cat-houses, did I not know you rifling the poor boxes in the local church,
did I not know you dissolving the night in fumes of human self-indulgence
simply, simply, simply did I not know you, do you not defecate, fornicate,
prevaricate when heaven and earth implore you to abdicate and are you
not prey to headaches, indigestion, colds, disc displacement, ingrowing toe-
nail, dysentery, malaria, flatfoot, corns and chilblains. Simply, simply, do I
not know you Man like me? Then shall they say unto you, I am chosen,
restored, redesignated and redestined and further further shall they say
unto you, you heresiarchs of the System arguing questioning, querying
weighing puzzling insisting rejecting upon you all shall we practise, without
passion -

MENDICANTS: Practise . . .

OLD MAN: With no ill-will . . .

MENDICANTS: Practise . . .

OLD MAN: With good conscience . . .

MENDICANTS: Practise . . .

OLD MAN: That the end shall . . .

MENDICANTS: Practise . . .

OLD MAN: Justify the meanness . . .
MENDICANTS: Practise . . .
OLD MAN: Without emotion . . .
MENDICANTS: Practise . . .
OLD MAN: Without human ties . . .
MENDICANTS: Practise . . .
OLD MAN: Without – no – Lest there be self-doubting . . .
MENDICANTS: Practise . . . As Was the Beginning, As Is, Now, As Ever Shall
    Be, World Without.

$$(271-2)$$

An entire monograph could be written on the nature of the spiritual and psychic intersubjectivity which binds the mendicants to the Old Man and aligns them to his frenzied "evangelization" against "As" and its "priesthood," "gospellers" and "enforcement agencies." The repeated refrain of "Practice" which is their "response" to the "call" constituted by the Old Man's litany of cynical abuses of power, would seem to indicate that they are absolutely controlled by the Old Man. But then we have seen them turn on their mentor in earlier moments of the play, even going as far as opportunistically betraying him to his arch-enemy, the Specialist. And the Old Man in turn not only generally condescends to the mendicants in ways that reinforce the inferiorized psychology that goes with their underdog status within a viciously hierarchical war and state machine, he in fact sees them as physically expendable in the cause of tearing away the masks from "As" and its orthodoxies of belief and practice. This is why, as this scene of ironic evangelization builds up to a crescendo, the Old Man, with help from other mendicants, attempts to cut the Cripple open on the Specialist's operating table in order to discover, as he puts it, "just what makes a heretic tick." That the other mendicants are willing to go along with the Old Man in this grotesque inversion of a sacrificial ritual obviously has something to do with the hysteria and collective self-hypnosis that often accompany religious fervor and ecstasy. But the Old Man's explanation is also apposite: "Because we are together in As." This is, finally, the bleakest insight of this profoundly pessimistic play: everyone is in the circle of As, there is ultimately no separation, as in Aristophanes' *The Clouds*, of "Right Logic" from "Wrong Logic"; all, perpetrators and victims, "specialists" and "madmen," can become the voluntary or unwitting victim of the ubiquitous scapegoating phenomenon when "As" is on the loose in a culture, a society, a historical epoch. The fact that it is indeed the Old Man himself and not the Cripple who is slain on Dr. Bero's operating table – an ersatz ritual altar – gives a pervasive but logical confirmation of the Old Man's deeply disturbing, sardonic insights.

There are of course important differences between *Death and the King's Horseman* and *The Bacchae of Euripides* in their dramatization of the "sacrificial crisis." And I do not mean by this the mere fact that Elesin Oba is a far more willing ritual "victim" than Pentheus. After all, Pentheus subliminally lusts for the emotional release available in the experience of ritual and he goes to his sacrificial fate like one going to taste the forbidden fruits of emotional ecstasy. The main difference between the two plays on this point lies in the far more important fact that even as Elesin readies himself for his ritual suicide, he mobilizes and orchestrates other festive idioms which will paradoxically subvert the ritual suicide and unintendedly work to keep him bound to this side of the passage between life and death, between the world of the living and that of the dead. By contrast, from first to last, Pentheus remains a novitiate ignorant of the sacrificial codes of his communicant role, even after he is dressed in drag in the vestments of female Bacchantes. We have to be as precise as possible on this issue. First, we are given some crucial details of Elesin's personality: "He is a man of enormous vitality, speaks, dances and sings with that infectious enjoyment of life which accompanies all his actions." (7) These details are important not only because they show Elesin's impeccable qualification for his ritual function as a willing scapegoat, but also because they reveal an excess which strains against that very ritual obligation for it is *not* a necessary part of his qualification for the role of ritual mediator between the world of the living and that of the departed to be simultaneously a *speaker*, *singer* and *dancer* of tales, if we may be allowed to signify on Albert Lord's famous monograph, *The Singer of Tales*.[26]

And what tales Elesin speaks, sings and dances! In all of contemporary African drama in English, there is probably no scene requiring from an actor the challenge of a simultaneity of acting, chanting and dancing as we have in Elesin's narration of the allegory of the Not-I bird in the first scene of the play. Soyinka's stage direction for the virtuosic performance expected of Elesin in this scene makes this point explicitly:

Elesin executes a brief, half-taunting dance. The drummer moves in and draws a rhythm out of his steps. Elesin dances towards the market place as he chants his story of the Not-I bird, his voice changing dexterously to mimic his characters. He performs like a born raconteur infecting his retinue with his humor and energy. (*DKH*, 9)

The specifications for the realization of Elesin's performance in this scene tacitly allude to the "contraction" in contemporary Western drama that Soyinka theorizes in the essay earlier discussed in this chapter, "Theatre in African Traditional Cultures." Western actors are not nowadays typically required to speak, chant, sing and dance their lines simultaneously, but there *was* a time in Western cultural and theatrical history when this was not the case. It certainly is the case with the traditions of acting in the great classical performance art of Asia like the Noh and the Kabuki. Soyinka's point, demonstrated both theoretically and practically, is that modern African theatre need not follow the evolutionary path of Western drama, away from the expansive roots of the theatre in festivals; furthermore, there is an insistence also that the modern theatre performer, African and non-African alike, has it within his or her natural endowment of body, voice, gesture and latent rhythms and energies to realize this simultaneous integration of skills which have come to be normatively separated and assigned to distinct, generically bounded arts of performance like dance, singing and acting.[27]

The actual content of the narrative danced, sung and mimetically acted by Elesin in this scene is an important parallel to its mode of presentation. The central linguistic and rhetorical construct in the scene, the "Not-I" cognomen given to the bird who comes visiting as Death's herald, is a term of elision from the much longer "It-is-not-I-who-saw-that-bird-of-ill-omen (Yoruba: "Kise-emi-lo-ri-eiye-irikuri-yen")." As the question is put to each character named in Elesin's narrative whether or not they had *seen* the bird, the terrified man or woman quickly invokes the longer phrase as a sort of mantra to ward off the "evil" of death – and takes to his or her heels. The "Not-I" bird thus takes its name from the universal human refusal to be reconciled to the inevitability of death. In his vividly animated tale, Elesin not only admits to seeing the bird, he also boasts of playing a willing and hospitable host to it, proudly asserting that for at least a season, the call of the Not-I bird will be heard neither by farm homesteaders or city dwellers.

This fabulous conceit of Elesin that he, and only he, is master of the universal fear of death, with all its hyperbolic frankness, is considerably beggared by the fanciful scale of another narrative that Elesin fashions at the end of this first scene of the play in order to consummate a sexual liaison with a nubile beauty on the very eve of his ritual suicide. By convention, a man in his position is allowed virtually any whim, any request, but since his wish must not be seen as that of a lecherous libertine, Elesin casts his request in the idiom institutionally reserved for the expression of the numinous, regenerative forces of nature. This is the only basis on which Iyaloja's hesitation, as the mother of the young man to whom the young girl is betrothed, is effectively overcome, and she can only acquiesce to Elesin's wish in the same fabulous idiom: "The voice I hear is already touched by the waiting fingers of our departed. I dare not refuse" (21). To a skeptical, agnostic consciousness, this is nothing less than a canard, a mere imposture opportunistically manipulating a symbolic order of discourse that transmutes gratuitous lust into life-enhancing regenerative powers, for in the logic of such skeptical rationalism, the question can be put: how is it certain that the bride will indeed conceive from this *one* sexual union, let alone bring the pregnancy to term, and give birth to a healthy, normal child? But this is precisely the point: such skepticism, in the context of the play's dramatization of the fragility of ritual and its sanctions and claims, is redundant. Ritual efficacy is not, *ab initio*, guaranteed; rather it is predicated on so many other factors beyond the control of the internal economy of the ritual act itself. One of these factors is indeed the precondition that the ritual act must not be interrupted or foreclosed before its completion. This is why we must take seriously Soyinka's insistence that the intervention of the Colonial District Officer is only a catalyst for the more decisive protagonist agency of Elesin's divided, conflicted will. The tragic flaw of the protagonist of this play is thus Elesin's willful misrecognition of his divided volition, willful because it is only by acting out and vibrantly playing the elaborate conceits of his mastery of death and his self-projection as an avatar of earth's regenerative powers that he is able to live the lie of being an absolutely willing ritual scapegoat. The lie of course catches up with him – and the ritual is aborted.

As we have remarked earlier, *Death and the King's Horseman* formalistically marks Soyinka at his most accomplished in terms of his exercise of tight artistic control over a daunting subject matter, while *The Bacchae of Euripides* shows the playwright returning to some of the lapses and excesses of *A Dance of the Forests*. Soyinka is at great pains in the prefatory note to *Death and the King's Horseman* to emphatically deny that the play is about the theme of culture clash, a theme which has fostered some of the worst, formulaic writings on fiction and drama in the postcolonial literatures of Africa and the developing world. As Adebayo Williams has demonstrated in an engrossing essay on the play, the task Soyinka sets himself is far more complex than this, which is to show how the undignified abomination of death by self-strangulation of Elesin that replaces the other "death" expected of him marks the cultural death of a whole people, an entire society.[28] This is not a transparent motif in the action of the play but it can be seen clearly if we contrast the rhapsodies of the Praise-Singer at the beginning and conclusion of the drama; in the former, he chants hymns to cultural continuity and sovereignty in the face of great historical calamities like slavery and colonialism and in the latter, he laments that the culture is "tumbling in the void of strangers." First, the paean to Elesin as a culture hero very early in the dramatic action of the play:

PRAISE-SINGER: Your name will be like the sweet berry a child places under his tongue to sweeten the passage of food. The world will never spit it out.

ELESIN: Come then, this market is my roost. When I come among the women I am a chicken with a hundred mothers. I become a monarch whose palace is built with tenderness and beauty.

PRAISE-SINGER: They love to spoil you but beware. The hands of women also weaken the unwary.

ELESIN: This night I'll lay my head upon their lap and go to sleep. This night I'll touch feet with their feet in a dance that is no longer of this earth. But the smell of their flesh, their sweat, the smell of indigo on their cloth, this is the last air I wish to breathe as I go to meet my great forebears.

PRAISE-SINGER: In their time the great wars came and went, the little wars came and went; the white slavers came and went, they took away the heart of our race, they bore away the mind and muscle of our race. The city fell and was rebuilt; the city fell and our people trudged through mountain and forest to find a new home but – Elesin Oba do you hear me?

ELESIN: I hear your voice Olohun-iyo.

PRAISE-SINGER: Our world was never wrenched from its true course.

(DKH, 9)

Then, the awesome excoriations which come closely on the heels of Elesin's aborted rite:

ELESIN: I cannot approach. Take off the cloth. I shall speak my message from heart to heart of silence.

IYALOJA (moves forward and removes the covering): Your courier Elesin, cast your eyes on the favoured companion of the King.

(Rolled up in the mat, his head and feet showing at either end, is the body of OLUNDE.)

There lies the honour of your household and of our race. Because he could not bear to let honour fly out of doors, he stopped it with his life. The son has proved the father, Elesin, and there is nothing left in your mouth to gnash but infant gums.

PRAISE-SINGER: Elesin, we placed the reins of the world in your hands yet you watched it plunge over the edge of the bitter precipice. You sat with folded arms while the evil strangers tilted the world from its course and crashed it beyond the edge of emptiness – you muttered, there is little that one man can do, you left us floundering in a blind future. Your heir has taken the burden on himself. What the end will be, we are not gods to tell. But this young shoot has poured its sap into the parent stalk, and we know this is not the way of life. Our world is tumbling in the void of strangers, Elesin.

                                                                        (82–3)

The skill with which Soyinka moves the action of the play from the first point of cultural pride and spiritual composure in the face of the ravages of slavery, colonization and internecine civil warfare to the end point of a deep sense of the loss of that previous state is expressed mostly in terms of carefully composed contrasts between scenes and, more crucially, *within* scenes. Between scenes, the striking contrasts are between *background* scenes dealing with the white colonizers and their world and the *fore-grounded* scenes dealing with the African community of the colonized: in nearly all instances, the latter scenes show much greater aesthetic investment on the part of the playwright in terms of characterization, dramatic action and, above all, language. And within scenes, Soyinka pays meticulous attention to expressive resources available for breathing vitality to a world-view characterized by its joy of life and calm acceptance of the stresses of existence and the fact of mortality, even as that world-view gradually unravels as the play moves forward to the shattering climactic denouement. In this play, we are a world away from the unwieldy overload of incident, metaphor and esoteric tropes of *A Dance*, but the profound interrogation of ritual and its idioms remains as consistent in the latter play as in Soyinka's first major, full-length play.

    The power of the modern dramatic parable, as compositely fashioned by some of the great dramatists of the twentieth century – Eugene O 'Neill, Bertolt Brecht, Jean Genet, Peter Weiss, Derek Walcott, John Arden, Brian Friel, Caryl Churchill and of course Soyinka himself – derives from the self-reflexive deployment of the idioms and techniques of performance and representation to explore and perhaps throw some light on the existential and social ramifications of the world-historical and structural contradictions of our age. To this extent, the most impressive achievement of *Death and the King's Horseman* is perhaps its extremely skillful deployment of the "ritual problematic" to make an original critique of both colonialism and the nationalist resistance to it at the level of their impact on the social and existential complacencies of the play's major characters. On this point, it is putting things rather mildly to say, in the critical idiom of conventional formal analysis, that none of these characters – Elesin Oba, Iyaloja, Olunde, Simon and Jane

Pilkings – remains unscathed at the end of the play, that is, at the end of the forcible prevention of the rite which would have secured Elesin Oba's ritual passage and at the end of the equally abortive reactivation of that ritual passage by Olunde's successful suicide. It is closer to the mark to see that by the operation of a stringent dialectic, Soyinka converts the futility of the forcible prevention of the rite to expose a conjunctural moment in the drama of imperialism and the resistances it generated, a moment which produces ramifications and consequences totally unanticipated by colonizer and colonized alike, a theme that has been brilliantly explored by Olakunle George in one of the most illuminating essays on this play.[29] Let us explore this point carefully.

On the part of the colonizers, nearly everything that Pilkings does and says undermines and negates the liberal humanist and rationalist values on the basis of which he acts to prevent the ritual suicide of Elesin. For in the course of the dramatic action of the play, we come to see that he is the representative of a social power that is nearly as feudal, nearly as shaped by expressive, ceremonial codes constructed around premodern patriachal-aristocratic values as the culture of the "subject race" over which he rules. Moreover, in word and deed, Pilkings does not place any real worth on the lives of those he presumes to teach respect for the worth of human life. Like the much-discussed hollow, self-serving "benevolence" of the reformist claims of the imperialist ban of the institution of "sati," widow-burning, in colonial India, Pilkings is motivated to intervene in Elesin Oba's suicide and thus "contain" the institutional matrix which sustains it because it stands beyond, and confounds, the spheres of his secular, political-administrative authority. Jane Pilkings is something of an incipient "border crosser" who sees and acts beyond the rigid boundaries of the world inhabited by her husband, the manichean world of incommensurable polarity of colonizers and colonized. But ultimately, she is the gendered, domesticated "helpmeet" of the colonialist patriarchy that pits Pilkings against Elesin Oba and against Olunde.

In the light of this reading of the essential conflicts of the play, Olunde is the ultimate nemesis of the authority and hegemony on which Pilkings can count for the stability and perpetuation of colonial rule. This is not only because his suicide literally ensures that Pilkings' efforts to prevent *one* death in fact leads to two deaths; more significant is the fact that Olunde's death completely undermines the brutal, reified dichotomization of the secular and the sacred, positivist, instrumental rationality and "mythical thought" and "irrationalism" that is the most serviceable

epistemic foundation of colonial authority. But by the same token,
Olunde is also the unhappy nemesis of his father's fond hopes for redemptive action from his son against Pilkings and the oppressive social
power that he represents, as is revealed in the following exchange between Pilkings and Elesin Oba in the play's denouement:

PILKINGS: Your son does not take so gloomy a view.
ELESIN: Are you dreaming now, white man? Were you not present at the re-
    union of shame? Did you not see when the world reversed itself and the
    father fell before his son, asking forgiveness?
PILKINGS: That was in the heat of the moment. I spoke to him and . . . if you
    want to know, he wishes he could cut out his tongue for uttering the words
    he did.
ELESIN: No. What he said must never be unsaid. The contempt of my own son
    rescued something of my shame at your hands. You have stopped me in
    my duty but I know now that I did give birth to a son. Once I mistrusted
    him for seeking the companionship of those my spirit knew as enemies of
    our race. Now I understand. One should seek to obtain the secrets of his
    enemies. He will avenge my shame, white one. His spirit will destroy you
    and yours.

                                                                    (69)

On one level, the dramatic irony at work here is utterly devastating to the
calculations of both Pilkings and Elesin, for offstage, Olunde in his bid
to reactivate the aborted rite, is already dead by the time this exchange is
taking place onstage. But it would be too simple to see the corrosiveness
of the dramatic irony mobilized here as appertaining equally to colonizer
and colonized. As we have noted earlier in this discussion, the subversion
of the epistemic foundations of colonial authority is the most articulate
signification of Olunde's suicide; and that undoes any interpretive move
to see an equivalence between the historic and ideological claims and
counter-claims of the colonizers and the colonized.

   In one of the most insightful essays on the place of ritual idioms and
paradigms in Soyinka's drama, an essay to which we have referred earlier
in this chapter, the late Philip Brockbank has urged a distinction between
the *primordial* and *literary* sources available to the contemporary dramatist
interested in exploring the possibilities inherent in the interface between
ritual and drama.[30] Unlike most contemporary Western playwrights, argues Brockbank in this essay, Shakespeare was responsive to both of these
sources of ritual because he recognized that complex, urban civilizations
are no less subject to the primordial psychic promptings which lie at the
root of ritual than earlier stages of culture and society. If this is true of

Shakespeare and the other Elizabethans, it is of course so much truer of the dramatists of classical European antiquity. Soyinka's adaptation of Euripides' *The Bacchae* is shaped by this factor of a differentiation of the sources of ritual and its idioms as between literary and non-literary, primordial matrices.

The very fact that *The Bacchae of Euripides* is an adapted play would seem to place the weight of relative priority on literary derivation rather than primordial matrices in Soyinka's text, especially with regard to the obstacles encountered in the observances of the rites of Dionysus and his Bacchic cult. Pentheus, like Pilkings in *Death and the King's Horseman*, wishes to stop what he considers "primitive," barbaric rites. This much Soyinka takes over from the Euripides text. It could also be argued that Teiresias' bitter "anti-ritual" protests as he is brutally whipped as a sub-stitute for the usual lower-class ritual scapegoat, is also a derivation from Euripides, albeit an indirect literary derivation since in Euripides' play, Teiresias merely enunciates, but does not make himself subject to the mortifications of ritual frenzy. But there are important changes made by Soyinka in his adaptation which are not of a literary derivation. One involves a significant change in the characterization of Dionysus, his protagonist being far less vengeful than the Dionysus of Euripides' play. The other change entails the transubstantiation of the blood dripping from the severed head of Pentheus into wine. Both of these changes are recognizable appropriations derived not from any antecedent literary influences, but from the ritual traditions associated with Ogun and his cults. The effect of this is to give the ritual sacrifice at the heart of the play, as extremely gruesome as it is, a more credible *necessitarian* logic than its dim, symbolic outlines in the text of the Euripides original. This is perhaps why this play marks the most convincing dramatization of Soyinka's theorization of ritual as a performative matrix for change and renewal. The final paragraph of Soyinka's Introduction to his adapta-tion of Euripides states this point with forcefulness and clarity; it stands as a sharp contrast with the densely elliptical and esoteric tropes and metaphors with which he formulates his theoretical apologia for ritual in "The Fourth Stage":

I see *The Bacchae*, finally, as a prodigious, barbaric banquet, an insightful man-ifestation of the universal need of man to match himself against Nature. The more than hinted at cannibalism corresponds to the periodic needs of humans to swill, gorge and copulate on a scale as huge as Nature's on her monstrous cycle of regeneration. The ritual, sublimated or expressive, is both social ther-apy and reaffirmation of group solidarity, a hankering back to the origins and formation of guilds and phratries. Man reaffirms his indebtedness to earth, dedicates himself to the demands of continuity and invokes the energies of productivity. Reabsorbed within the communal psyche he provokes the resources of Nature; he is in turn replenished for the cyclic drain in his fragile individual potency. (*TBE*, x–xi)

After the terrible sacrificial price exacted not only from Pentheus and his mother Agave, but from the whole house of Cadmus, a narrowly "sociologistic" and literal-minded critic might deem it absurd for Soyinka to wax lyrical in this passage about ritual: "both as therapy and affirmation of group solidarity, a hankering back to the origins and formation of guilds and phratries." But such critical response could be made only on the basis of ignoring the paradox of ritual. For it is true that, in its religious, cultural and institutional contexts, ritual also binds groups together for the enhancement of the values of cooperation, solidarity and renewal, even if this is a consequence of the death of the sacrificial "carrier" or scapegoat. This paradoxical face of ritual is extensively dramatized in *The Bacchae of Euripides*. Soyinka in fact goes out of his way to amplify *this* dimension of ritual beyond what there is of it in the Euripides text, as this exchange between Kadmos and Teiresias indicates:

TEIRESIAS: . . . only fools trifle with divinity. People will say, Aren't you ashamed? At your age, dancing, wreathing your head with ivy? Have you caught it? . . .

KADMOS: I am not ashamed. Damn them, did the god declare that only the young or women must dance? They mean to kill us off before our time.

TEIRESIAS: He has broken the barrier of age, the barrier of sex or slave and master. It is the will of Dionysus that no one be excluded from his worship.
(*TBE*, 26)

It is consistent with the paradox of ritual that until Pentheus' secretive and "impious" invasion of the rites of the Bacchantes, their frenzy and ecstasy had been expressed mostly in edenic, utopian forms. Thus, Soyinka's reading of Euripides' play as a "prodigious, barbaric banquet" which seeks to match nature's elemental force in both its terrifying forms and its benevolent, life-sustaining expressions is the closest we get in his dramas to an altogether positive resolution of the "ritual problematic."

That *The Bacchae of Euripides* repeats many of the lapses of *A Dance* is best conveyed by the fact that Soyinka's adaptation is much longer than the Euripides text, some of his expansion of scenes or subplots working to stall the action of the play needlessly. It is of course true that most of the changes made by Soyinka in his adaptation are intended to make the link between Dionysianism and social revolution more explicit and more compelling. But the very fact that these changes work to make the dramatic action diffuse and heavy-footed undercuts that intention. The most surprising of these changes is Soyinka's decision to insert two playlets which have little to do with the main plot of the play at the moment in Euripides' text when Pentheus is transformed from the autocratic, hawkish foe of the Dionysian rites to a covert voyeur after the ecstasies of the cult and its rites who allows himself to be dressed in drag so that he can secretly participate in the revels. In contrast to this, Soyinka's expansion of the chorus to include male and female slaves where Euripides' chorus comprised only non-Greek Asian women, though it contributes to the unwieldiness of the dramatic action, works more powerfully as theatre because of its infusion of some performance modes that Soyinka has mastered in the course of three decades of experimenting with diverse sources, styles and methods. The brief production note that Soyinka added to the published text of the play illustrates this point succinctly: "The Slaves and Bacchantes should be as mixed a cast as is possible, testifying to their varied origins. Solely because of the 'hollering' style suggested for the slave leader's solo in the play, it is recommended that this character be fully Negroid."

It is a great challenge that Soyinka takes on in his adaptation to make Euripides' pointed identification of Dionysianism as a non-Greek and mostly female cult encompass racial oppression and class exploitation. Hence his concern in the "Production Note" quoted above to make the category "Negroid" not a matter of racial essences but a mark of an expressive style born out of the dialectic of domination and struggle. In the play, the "hollering" of the mostly male slaves blends well and effectively with the women's keening, ululating cries of anguish and faith. The suggestion is that the terrifying powers of the god Dionysus – which derive from, and express elemental forces of nature – can merge with the cause of all oppressed people – women, slaves, workers. The terrible destruction of the ruler Pentheus and the undeserved psychic ravaging of his mother, Agave, constitute a sacrificial rite which might usher in restitution for the oppressed and renewal of the earth for all of its peoples. Among Soyinka's most ambitious plays, this drama is the most insistent on shifting the emphasis, in what we have identified as the paradox of ritual, away from the "negative" to the "positive" pole.

One of the most intriguing aspects of the dramas that we have explored in this chapter is the conflation of pessimism or even nihilism with extraordinary inventiveness and robustness of form, technique and language in the plays. The paradox of great theatrical and aesthetic resourcefulness serving as a vehicle of world-weary pessimism as inscribed in these particular plays is perhaps best understood in the light of the radically opposed views of the "sublime" as defined respectively by classical theorists of European antiquity and nineteenth-century German idealist aesthetic philosophy. For the former, the "sublime" happens when great, lofty thoughts and feelings find perfect expression in form, style and rhetoric. As Longinus put it, "sublimity is the echo of a great soul."[31] By this he meant that sublimity is achievable only by a rare order of artists who both have the capacity for great, lofty thoughts and feelings and are gifted with the powers of expression to give these rarefied thoughts and feelings perfect, unsurpassable formal expression:

There are, it may be said, five principal sources of elevated language . . . First and most important is the power of forming great conception . . . Secondly, there is vehement and inspired passion. These two components of the sublime are for the most part innate. Those which remain are partly the product of art. The due formation of figures deals with two sorts of figures, first those of thought and secondly those of expression. Next there is noble diction, which in turn comprises choice of words, and use of metaphors, and elaboration of language. The fifth cause of elevation – one which is the fitting conclusion of all that have preceded it – is dignified and elevated composition. (Dukore, 79)

This conception of the sublime as constituted by a correspondence between great feelings and thoughts and the rhetorical means of their expression that is so perfect as to approach the divine, is radically at odds with the theorizations of the sublime by Hegel and other nineteenth-century German idealist philosophers. For Hegel, the sublime indicates our experience of great, unassuageable feelings of inadequacy before that which in nature and life approaches the ineffable, the unbounded, the chaotic. Examples of these are: a violently tempestuous sea and natural disaster on a colossal scale. Indeed, what Longinus describes as the sublime approximates to what Hegel designates Beauty, which he then opposed to the Sublime. In this latter conception, especially as reimagined by many contemporary postmodernists, the "sublime" is the ultimate marker of the inexpressible, the unrepresentable, especially in the ways that it offers no satisfactory release, no catharsis for the powerfully agitated emotions it stirs up.[32]

Paul Gilroy's deployment of the notion of a "slave sublime" in his book, *The Black Atlantic*, derives from this Kantian-Hegelian notion of the sublime, without making the slightest nod to the classical uses of the term. Gilroy deploys this notion in order to write against what he calls "the fatal snare of sublimity" for enslaved or dominated groups. This is because for him, "certain modes of social remembrance in which protracted familiarity with ineffable, sublime terror may lead to the deployment of a political aesthetic" through which victims of a historical and social oppression on a monumental scale are "beatified" and consequently, their suffering yields, not tough-minded, epistemologically complex understanding of the self and the historical process, but a quietism that Gilroy calls "an alchemical moral magic." It is this danger which gives rise to Gilroy's clamant warning: "There are dangers to both Jews and blacks in accepting the historic and unsought association with sublimity."[33]

The plays discussed in this chapter attempt to have it both ways: the way of the classical theorists of antiquity and their conception of the sublime as the union of ideational high-mindedness with rhetorical and expressive perfection; and the way of the nineteenth-century German idealist-romantic identification of sublimity with extreme emotions aroused by the encounter with chaos, agitation and even terror. In general in these plays, the sublime of exquisitely crafted expression in the service of ideas and conceits of extraordinarily suggestive power is inextricable from the sublime of violent emotions and traumatic agitation. Perhaps the single exception to this pattern can be found only in those passages in *Death and the King's Horseman* where Elesin, in the opening scenes of the play, calmly and ecstatically embraces his destiny as one who must die to preserve and enhance the spiritual health of his people. In nearly all other instances of the sublime in this play – and in all the others discussed in this chapter – when language, rhetoric and non-verbal expressive idioms like music and dance combine and soar to heights of great aesthetic effect, that effect almost always entails both pleasure and harrowing disquiet. These are particularly pervasively evident in *The Road* and *Madmen*, but also deeply inflect the other plays as well. The ubiquity of this structure in Soyinka's greatest plays is perhaps due to the fact that while the "sublime" of ineffable terror and violence – as revealed in numbing acts of evil and corruption – impinges itself so powerfully on his ethical and political sensibilities, the "sublime" of words, language and rhetoric taken to their roots attempt a containment of the other matrix of terror-driven, psyche-numbing sublimity. In virtually all the plays discussed in this chapter, the dramatic action entails protagonists who engage in a decisive crossing of the line(s) of normality, "decency," respectability, prudence, complacency, or simple lack of imagination into areas of the forbidden so as to think the unthinkable or enact the incommensurable. They do this with the extremist logic of a resolve to do *anything* that it would take to set things aright, to make whole that which has been befouled or damaged by great, all-encompassing evil. And this nearly always entails nothing less than rending the entire fabric of social life or shaking the very foundations of the prevailing moral order, or indeed the underlying principle of the universe itself. In "The Fourth Stage," one of his few theoretical essays in which the notion of the sublime receives considerable, if indirect and elliptical elaboration, Soyinka describes the phenomenological and affective territory of the sublime as

the numinous territory of transition into which the artist obtains fleeting glimpses by ritual, sacrifice and a patient submission of rational awareness to the moment when fingers and voice relate the symbolic language of the cosmos (*ADO2*, 35)

Fortunately, the domains of experience and imagination explored as territories of the sublime in Soyinka's most ambitious plays that we have discussed in this chapter are more varied, more multifaceted and contradictory than the essentialist ritualism which this quote seeks to consecrate as the rarefied idiom of sublimity.

CHAPTER 5

The ambiguous freight of visionary mythopoesis: fictional and nonfictional prose works

What I do see is a new voice coming out of Africa, speaking in a worldwide language . . . The price a world language must be prepared to pay is submission to many different kinds of use. The African writer should aim to use English in a way that brings out his message best without altering the language to the extent that its value as a medium of international exchange will be lost.

> Chinua Achebe, "The African Writer and the English Language"

In narration he affects a disproportionate pomp of diction, and a wearisome train of circumlocution, and tells the incident imperfectly in many words, which might have been more plainly delivered in few. Narration in dramatic poetry is naturally tedious, as it is unanimated and inactive, and obstructs the progress of the action; it should therefore always be rapid, and enlivened by interruption. Shakespeare found it an incumbrance, and instead of lightening it by brevity, endeavoured to recommend it by dignity and splendour.

> Samuel Johnson, *Preface to the Plays of William Shakespeare*

Within the entire body of Soyinka's writings, the fictional and non-fictional prose works constitute the most uneven group of works. This poses a formidable challenge for scholars and critics. In this chapter, we explore the complex interplay between social vision and its artistic mediation in the seven works of fiction and nonfiction that constitute the complement of the Nigerian author's prose writings, minus the three volumes of collected critical and theoretical writings that we have earlier discussed in this study. These seven titles are: *The Interpreters* (1965), *The Man Died* (1972), *Season of Anomy* (1973), *Aké: The Years of Childhood* (1981), *Isara: A Voyage Around 'Essay'* (1989), *Ibadan: The 'Penkelemes' Years* (1994), and *The Open Sore of a Continent* (1995). Nothing affords a better discursive context for analyzing these works than a brief review of the controversies and paradoxes surrounding the reception of Soyinka's prose writings.

As much in his prose as in his poetry and drama, Soyinka's brilliance as a wordsmith in language is consistently in evidence and perhaps on display. This is a manifest and pervasive aspect of the texture of the seven works discussed in this chapter. But while many of these works have achieved considerable critical success and exerted significant intellectual influence as prose writings, it is equally true that Soyinka's use of language within the medium of prose has generated both high and equivocal praise and considerable hostility. This is largely on account of the fact that irrespective of the matter or substance at hand in these prose works, the use of language constantly draws attention to itself, becomes indeed a percept on its own terms. To many critics, this facet of Soyinka's prose, by itself, seems a willful infringement of one of the most widely accepted but generally unexamined regulative critical norms in African 'Europhone' writing in particular, and postcolonial literatures in general. This is the tacit understanding – reflected in perhaps its most influential articulation in the first epigraph to this chapter – that language should be used by African writers using English (or French, Portuguese or Spanish) as an effective medium or vehicle of expression which could, and perhaps should, be stretched and bent to accommodate African realities and sensibilities, but only to the extent that effectiveness of language as primarily a medium of communication is not compromised, that language usage does not draw attention to itself as *enoncé*, or to its very processes of enunciation.[1] Soyinka's prose style is an affront to this norm, especially given the fact that the visibility of his prose as *enoncé* is, with regard to matters of style, not that of the graceful, the compact, the lucidly and beautifully crafted (though many passages can be found in Soyinka's nonfiction prose writings which correspond to these styles). Thus, the adjectives and phrases which have been applied to Soyinka's prose style have been vociferous in their expression of either misgivings or serious reservations: "opaque," "convoluted," "harsh inscrutableness," "linguistic anomy." Some fundamental questions raised by this highly perceptible and demanding prose style in Soyinka's work in this genre have not been seriously addressed by students of his writings: is it permissible or even necessary for the African writer in English or French to use language not only or merely as a medium over which she or he need demonstrate just enough competence and creativity to embody a significant vision, but assertively and self-consciously as an idiom to stretch, bend, play with, draw attention to, and even willfully de-form? And given the fact that literary style in Yoruba drama and, especially, prose – one of whose classic texts Soyinka has in fact translated into English – normatively entails language usage as both medium of expression and an idiom with a materiality upon which the writer expends considerable playfulness and inventiveness, why should we not expect Soyinka to transfer these attitudes to his use of English?[2]

A charged, dramatic expression of this controversy is evident in the reception of Soyinka's fictional prose. His first novel, *The Interpreters*, was hailed as a distinctive, original contribution to modern African fiction. Critics praised its rich verbal texture, its complexity of narrative technique and unconventional mode of characterization, and its fresh and invigorating use of language. But the very terms of the critical praise for the novel negatively reinforced some of the prevailing theoretical and ideological confusions regarding the alleged non-African provenance of the novel and the presumed difficulties African novelists have in mastering the intricacies of the form, especially in its modernist, experimental mode. Thus, one critic, Charles Larson, on the basis of this single novel, hailed Soyinka, together with Ayi Kwei Armah, as a novelist whose work demonstrated a bright future for the novel in Africa. On the basis of this evaluation, Larson placed Soyinka and Armah at the apex of an evolutionary movement of the African novel away from narrative forms associated with realist modes toward modernist forms.[3]

Soyinka's second novel, *Season of Anomy* confounded such expectations, both because it is, so far, the only other novel "proper" that Soyinka has written, and, more importantly, because compared with *The Interpreters*, this novel was a huge disappointment, so much so that for many critics, it seriously undermined the Nigerian dramatist's stature as a novelist.[4] The adverse critical response it generated was strong enough to elicit the following self-critical qualifications from Soyinka himself about his attitude to the novel as a literary genre, as an idiom for his sensibilities as a writer-activist:

I'm not really a keen novelist. And I don't consider myself a novelist. The first novel happened purely by accident. In fact I used to refer to it purely as a 'happening'. I used to write short stories, by the way, which was ok. But the novel for me is a strange territory – it still is – and I turned to it at that particular time because it was not possible for me to function in the theatre. Then, again, *Season of Anomy* was written at a period when it was (also) not possible for me to function in the theatre. So I don't consider myself a novelist. And the novel form for me is not a very congenial form.[5]

It would be difficult to get a more frank admission of the limits imposed by generic imperatives on his otherwise unquestionably impressive artistic versatility than this statement by Soyinka on his aversions toward the novel as a literary form. But beyond this awareness of limits is the related issue of working with and through limits. This factor may explain why, following the critical debacle of *Season of Anomy*, Soyinka has increasingly turned to other prose forms like fictionalized biography and the autobiographical memoir to engage closely related aesthetic and moral challenges and dilemmas that he had engaged in his dramas, poetry and novels. The fact that two of these nonfiction works, *Aké* and *Isara*, have won huge critical acclaim on the scale of the successes of his most accomplished works of drama and poetry would seem to indicate that the place of prose in the Nigerian author's literary corpus ought to be far more carefully explored than the term "novel," with its tangled African vocation and its more general problematic status in contemporary world literature – a form whose "death" is perennially bruited and withdrawn – would allow.

In this chapter then, the discussion of Soyinka's prose works will not be bound by formal, generic distinctions between fiction and nonfiction, between the novel and its presumed "impure," ancillary offshoots. For it is manifestly clear in these prose works that Soyinka himself not only refuses to be bound by such distinctions, he in fact transgresses them extensively. For more than either poetry or drama, it is in his prose works that Soyinka executes such a level of self-quotation and intertextual transfers between fictional and nonfictional works that this pattern in itself assumes the status of a central heuristic issue for analysis and interpretation. If, with the possible exception of his agit-prop dramatic sketches – his "shotgun" pieces as he calls them – prose provides Soyinka a greater latitude than either poetry or drama for bringing closer his writing and his activism, his private self and his public persona, it is because prose is the medium on which, intriguingly, he has placed his greatest faith in the efficacy of his project of self-constitution and self-presentation as a visionary artist and a radical public intellectual.

Writing in *Myth, Literature and the African World* on the achievement of Duro Ladipo's classic Yoruba-language tragedy, *Oba Koso*, Soyinka attributes the acclaim that the play received from audiences of varied linguistic communities all over the world to the fact that the play "straddles the modernist gulf between symbol and expository action and dialogue with the essence of poetry" (MLAW, 55). It is a commonplace of modern critical theory that a chasm typically exists between, on the one hand, symbol, metaphor and sign and, on the other other hand, exposition through a strong, linear narrative structure. But Duro Ladipo's great play, *Oba Koso*, is most definitely not a "modernist" work and while it does have a richness of symbolism and allusiveness to the universe of Yoruba mythic and esoteric lore, it is not strong in "expository action and dialogue." Thus, what Ladipo's play shares with modernism is a richness of figural, symbolic and allusive language acting as an eloquent replacement for the realist reliance on expository modes of expression. This leads us to the probability that this comment on Ladipo's play is a sort of metacommentary on Soyinka's own writings, in the present case his prose writings, with their strong affinities with modernist techniques and idioms. For in varying degrees, these works eschew realist conventions of narration and characterization, substituting these with a strong aesthetic investment in sheer linguistic exuberance and, more pointedly, widely ramifying metaphors and tropes. In other words, in these prose works of Soyinka, it is language pressed into service and used repeatedly to create an elaborate mythopoesis that serves to bridge the chasm between, on the one hand, symbol, metaphor and ritual archetype, and on the other hand, "exposition." Stated differently, these works, as a crucial dimension of their composite aesthetic and ideational identity, are freighted with a vast architecture of mythopoesis to a degree somewhat "excessive" of the scale deemed appropriate in realist works but otherwise normative in modernist and avant-garde writing. This excess of mythopoeic symbol and archetype achieved by the sheer force of linguistic exuberance is perhaps the most general, unifying pattern among the extremely varied works which make up the corpus of Soyinka's prose writings.

The foregoing observations provide an indispensable background for the analysis and interpretation of the seven works of fictional and nonfictional prose in this chapter. It will be argued that more than works of poetry and drama, our author's prose works show certain consistencies or patterns of formal design and ethical and ideological investments. We have already indicated one such pattern, at a level of considerable generality, this being the great pressure that an often over-elaborate mythopoesis places on Soyinka's *prose* works, a pressure characteristically much more productively engaged in the dramas and the poetry. There are two other patterns which are more concrete and more constitutive of the collective ideological and aesthetic identity of Soyinka's prose works which ought to be noted here. One is the foregrounding in each narrative of lone or plural protagonists whose identities and fates are explicitly and intimately bound up with their coming to an acute consciousness of a monstrously dehumanizing and alienating social environment and accepting the challenge that this poses of asserting and expanding a humane, life-affirming ethic. This pattern corresponds to what I shall call the "heroic mythos" in Soyinka's prose works, a mythos almost wholly absent in his dramas and found, in the entire body of his poetic writings, only in the long dramatic poem "Idanre" and *Ogun Abibiman*. The other pattern that is worthy of note in Soyinka's prose works is the ubiquity and pervasiveness of intertextual transfers between these works, whether fictional or nonfictional. Against the background of these underlying or "unifying" patterns, it is useful to explore the distinctiveness and particularity, aesthetic and moral-ideological, of each of these works considered singly or in clusters.

Perhaps more than any other full-length work of Soyinka, *The Interpreters* is the work of a youthful writer writing about self and milieu with the mixture of exultant panache and playful levity in the use of language that most young, gifted writers display at the start of their careers. The "drink lobes" of Biodun Sagoe, one of the eponymous "interpreters" of the novel's title, has entered the lore of Anglophone African critical discourse as one of the literature's most bracingly ludic conceits. This conceit comes from the very first sentence of the novel – "metal on concrete jars my drink lobes" – which itself has become one of the most widely discussed opening sentences in the modern African novel, second in fame perhaps only to the first sentence of Ken Saro-Wiwa's *Sozaboy*.[6] Decoded from its hermetic provenance in the in-group jokes and witticisms of the "interpreters," the sentence means, prosaically, "the sound of the cars on the asphalt surfaces of the city streets is irksome to me, to my efforts to drink up like a man." Thus, with all its playful levity, the conceit is actually emblematic of the novel's imaginative universe since much of the "present tense" action of *Interpreters*, as distinct from action set in the past, actually takes place in bars and nightclubs. Readers in the know about the social "watering holes" frequented by the circle of writers, artists and intellectuals that Soyinka was closely associated with at the time of the writing of the novel cannot miss the tremendous resonance of legends of the socializing rituals of the then newly emergent national literati in this conceit of the metaphoric, non-physiological organ of "drink lobes." The novel is indeed top heavy with such self-referential tropes and conceits, from more general symbols and metaphors like Kola's painting of the entirety of the Yoruba mythological pantheon and Sagoe's nonsense philosophy of "voidancy," to the minutiae of tropes which help to individualize each of the "interpreters": Egbo's propensity for spiritualizing his sexual liaisons; Sekoni's stutter and "cobbles"; Sagoe's recourse to fantasy, daytime nightmares and absurdist language games to negotiate his monumental listlessness; and Bandele's sensitive, compassionate tac-iturnity. Each of these collective protagonists is compositely drawn and also functions as a technical device, but many Nigerian readers of the novel whose formative cultural experience goes back to the period cov-ered in the narrative have long played a sort of "show and tell" which identifies each "interpreter" with the famous artists and writers of the Mbari group, with Soyinka himself – as more or less Egbo – featuring prominently in the speculations.

The Interpreters is thus also very much a novel of place, of a specific milieu. Concretely, and like the extended portraits of cities like Paris and Dublin in canonical works of Western modernist fiction, Soyinka's first work of fiction is a novel of Lagos and, to a lesser extent, of Ibadan, the city and the university, in the early 1960s. Not only are well-known suburbs, streets and thoroughfares of Lagos named and evoked in a manner that Soyinka would later reprise in writing of the city of his birth, Abeokuta, in *Aké*, his autobiographical memoir, but *The Interpreters* also alludes to famous or notorious events and personalities of the pe-riod. These include the infamous "Aladura" prelate who pronounced himself the reincarnation of Christ, Odumosu, "Jesus of Oyingbo"; the notorious Preventive Detention Act of the Balewa regime and its rabid anti-communism; the emergent subculture of university students, with its jejune, women-hating, scandal-mongering yellow journalism; and the rise of "national" daily newspapers tied to bitterly fractious elite political and business groups. There is also the narrator's love-hate attitude to Lagos: the filth and squalor of the cityscapes, as well as the casual bru-talities of the city's populace are registered with a scatological piquancy only a few steps behind the scale of Ayi Kwei Armah's depiction of Accra and its environs in *The Beautyful Ones Are Not Yet Born*. At the same time, the novel also celebrates the vitality and vibrancy of the city's street culture and night life.

As a novel that is evocative of a particular place and time, *The Inter-preters* is remarkable in the way that it eschews an event-driven plot and an expository narrative technique. The most dramatic event that hap-pens in the "recent" temporal sequence of the narrative is the death of Noah at the unwitting hands of his would-be homosexual seducer, Joe Golder. This is somewhat paralleled in the "past" temporal sequence of the narrative by the death by drowning of the parents of Egbo, per-haps the most prominent of the "interpreters." Sekoni's death in a road crash, and the several emotional and psychic responses it provokes in the other protagonists of the novel, is of course equally dramatic and tragic, but it is given far less narrative space than the death of Noah. Apart from these deaths, no earth-shaking event happens in the novel and we see no monstrous acts of duplicity or atrocity, as in *The Man Died*, *Season of Anomy*, *Ibadan* and, to a much lesser extent, *Isara*. Moreover, in its manner of telling which constantly shifts between past and present and "outer" and "inner" in the lives of the novel's protagonists – with the links thinly supplied by the echoes, traces and resonance of words and phrases spoken, thought or remembered – the novel makes little concession to culturally and ideologically conditioned expectations of readers for narrative continuity, causality and coherence. However, for all its relative "thinness" of action and event, and its radical disruption of linearity and continuity, *The Interpreters* is remarkable in being a novel that is highly evocative of "real" time, place and people. This particular point compels us to explore carefully the maturity of artistic vision and nuanced, progressive social criticism that mark this very youthful work.

Very early in the novel, Egbo contemplates the difficult choice he faces between, on the one hand, accepting the throne of a small fishing community that comes to him from the line of descent established by his maternal grandfather and, on the other hand, his civil service job as a top bureaucrat in the foreign office of his newly independent nation. The former option binds him to the past, to ancestral heritage and indigenous cultural matrices, while the latter, potentially at least, opens out to the wider world and the external relations of the emergent nation. Egbo ultimately sticks to his bureaucrat's job, but according to the narrator in a phrase which evokes the tragic fate of his parents, this choice is "like a choice of drowning," for Egbo "knew and despised the (new) age which sought to mutilate his beginnings." In other words, Egbo sees clearly that he works to prop up the power structure and moral order of an age that is gradually and inexorably mutilating what was good and wholesome in the world of his ancestral heritage. The question then is, if not much happens in the novel by way of truly heinous, evil events and acts, how can the narrator of this novel give credible force to such portentous, devastating negative commentary on this new age of black elites replacing the departing white colonizers?

One answer to this question lies in the fact that though the novel does not have great earth-shattering events, it does contain memorable pro-files of aspects of the moral order of the new black pseudo-bourgeois elite, with riveting passages on specific and general aspects of the social malaise such as miasmic corruption in the ranks of the political and

bureaucratic elite, hypocrisy and mediocrity among middle-class professionals and technocrats, naked social climbing and casual callousness in
the entire gamut of groups and classes within the populace. These profiles provoke varied attitudes in the "interpreters" ranging from cynical
scorn (Sagoe) and willful aloofness and self-absorption (Egbo) to acts of
great sensitivity, compassion and faith (Bandele). The sly invitation to
the reader in the differentiations between these profiles of the protagonists' own responses to the social and moral morass surrounding them
is to make his or her own choice of whichever evil is less egregious in
the vast canvas of decadence and sterility exposed by the narrator of the
novel. At the end of the narrative, it is the mixture of moral hypocrisy
and casual callousness in the Oguazors and Lumoyes of the national
pseudo-bourgeoisie – especially toward the plight of the young and the
female of this "new" nation – which seems ranked by the narrator as the
worst or deadliest of the social evils depicted so graphically in the novel,
since this is what provokes from Bandele – the most equable, the most
compassionate among the "interpreters" – the terrible imprecation: "I
hope you all live to bury your daughters" (251). This is a malediction
which in the imaginative scheme of the novel metonymically stands as
a terrible judgment on the whole tottering moral and spiritual edifice of
the new age.

In more concrete and all-embracing terms, the weight of such generalized profiles of dystopia and decadence is constructed on the narrator's
graphic if fragmentary account of the slow and inexorable entrenchment
of mediocrity at the highest levels of commercial, bureaucratic and political decision-making institutions of the new nation-state. This receives
perhaps its most telling and unforgettable depiction in the harrowing fate
of Sekoni, a gifted engineer who returns home from professional studies
abroad fired by dreams of engineering inventiveness which, he hopes,
will combine with the efforts of like-minded compatriots to transform the
physical environment of the country and better the lives of the people.
With great naiveté and the faith of the eternal optimist, he overcomes the
intense frustration of his confinement to a pen-pushing desk job by his
bureaucratic bosses and even his transfer to a rural backwater where it is
hoped that the flame of his idealism would be doused by the arid realities
of his posting. But Sekoni is undaunted and he builds an electric power
station out of scrap materials with an aim to bring electrification to his
new rural community. In a final *coup de grace*, his unrelenting bosses back
at the capital ensure the power station is not commissioned and put to
use by spreading a false and destructive rumor that the plant will explode

and destroy the village if any attempt is made to test its workability. Told in this dry paraphrase, this seems a conventional allegory of the morbid fear of genius by mediocrity, but Soyinka's *manner* of telling the story is anything but schematic.

On a deeper level, the weight of the narrator's portentous negative indictment of the new post-independence age is validated by Soyinka's meticulous and imaginative attentiveness to the impact of the moral order of the new elite on the inner, psychic lives of the "interpreters" and other finely drawn characters like Monica Faseyi, Joe Golder and Lazarus, the "aladura" prophet who claims, like his Biblical namesake, to have risen from the dead. Among the "interpreters," Sekoni experiences great, traumatic suffering and after going through a period of nervous breakdown, emerges from that region of ineffable anguish and disorientation with immense artistic power and spiritual grace. Joe Golder, the near white African-American homosexual consumed by an intense, race-driven self-hatred and sexual frustration, cannot possibly find fulfillment, even solace, in *this* debilitating human milieu. Monica Faseyi, alone among the expatriates and foreigners in this novel, is totally free of either the reactionary bigotry of colonial whites like Pinkshore and the unresolved racial complexes of condescension and over-effusive "love" of blacks like Peter, the German journalist slumming it through black Africa; Monica suffers a lot from her marriage to Ayo Faseyi, an insufferable prude and ingratiating social climber, but she retains a remarkable control over her inner psychic life. The claim of the albino "prophet" Lazarus to have risen from the dead is of course unverifiable, but as Bandele remarks of him, whether or not his claim is true, he seems to be a person who has undergone a searing, traumatic experience. Like all the "aladura" prophets in Soyinka's works, the taint of charlatanism hangs heavy around his person, but his ministry of redemption and rehabilitation of the social dregs of a fallen, degraded world strikes a deep chord of responsiveness in Kola, the artist. Indeed, Lazarus' cry of anguish at the failure of his attempted conversion of Noah, the petty thief, carries a powerful resonance with the diverse struggles of the "interpreters" to find a transformative meaning in the surrounding sea of shallowness, cynicism and predatoriness:

'What is truly important to me is that I know the arithmetic of religion. The murderer is your future martyr, he is your most willing martyr. Few fools know that.'

'Tell me, how did you convert Noah?' Kola was only half-attentive, and the albino's reaction shattered his concentration.

He was nearly shouting. 'Convert! I converted nothing. What you wrestle with, what you fight and defeat, that is true conversion. To change the nature of a real thief in a week, did you ever hear of that! I persisted only because it was the time of floods and this is the time for our Revivalist Services. We needed Noah. My true disciples are the thieves, the rejected of society. One of the apostles is a forger who has spent five years in prison. Another was the only member who escaped arrest when his gang was caught after a bank robbery. Urgent though my need was, I could not break this rule. I had to find a sinner!

'Any murderers?' Kola asked.

'One. He matcheted his wife in a village near Ughelli.'

Some minutes later, recovering his calm, he said, 'I must try to see that Noah does not return to the gutter.' (*TI*, 229–30)

Lazarus is perhaps the first in a long line of prophets or visionaries in Soyinka's works whose religious or secular "ministry" is with the downtrodden, the lumpen, unemployed underclass of criminals as well as déclassé outcasts from "polite" society. This is a line that includes Professor in *The Road*, the Old Man in *Madmen and Specialists*, Maren, Soyinka's own assumed moniker in his autobiographical memoir, *Ibadan*, and Dionysus in *The Bacchae of Euripides*. Of all the individual incarnations of this prototype, Lazarus seems the most genuine and unambiguous in his solicitude for the "fallen" and the disenfranchised that he brings under his tutelage.

Except for Sekoni, the "interpreters" as a whole do not, singly and collectively, experience truly degrading, brutalizing suffering, but their anguish, their great zest for life, together with their imperfections and alienation, occupy the narrative foreground of the novel. For in general, theirs is the terrible burden of "knowledge", of seeing all and having to bear witness and render an account to themselves. This is indeed why they bear the collective designation indicated in the title of the novel. As they live through, observe and talk about the encompassing rot which has so swiftly overtaken their "new" nation, they are forced to delve deep into a scrutiny of motives, causes and effects, of theirs' and others' actions, behavior and attitudes. It is a stroke of artistic genius that Soyinka makes one of them, Kola, the painter and art teacher, press the others into service as models for the deities and spirits of the Yoruba mythological pantheon that he is painting for an upcoming exhibition. For the "interpreters" are models whose virtues and graces fall far below the transcendental scale of moral perfection of divine idealities, even if, in accordance with the paradoxical truths of the Yoruba pantheon, the gods themselves, as etched in narratological profiles in the novel in general and specifically in Kola's painting, are flawed and "incomplete" essences who must themselves constantly seek completion by periodically reuniting with the human community. This subtle critique, given in some of the novel's most evocative passages, has the effect of "earthing" the often overwrought inscriptions and discourses of archetypes, essences and idealities in this novel in a way that is almost unparalleled in Soyinka's prose works.

The Man Died and *Season of Anomy* are the two prose works in Soyinka's tetralogy on the Nigerian civil war. The other two titles in this quartet are the volume of poems collected in *A Shuttle in the Crypt* and *Madmen and Specialists*, the great allegorical drama discussed in the previous chapter. These works constitute a tetralogy both in the ordinary sense of four titles sharing common themes and deriving from a common event or experience and in the older classical sense in which the dramatic poets of ancient Athens performed four consecutive plays in the *City Dionysia*, the four plays comprising three tragedies and a "satyr play." The "satyr play," a farcical, ribald drama lacking in the artistic polish and thematic gravities of the three tragedies, was intended to ironize and deflate the high-minded seriousness of the other three plays. Given the extensive use of burlesque and parody in *Madmen and Specialists*, it would at a first approximation seem that this is the "satyr play" in Soyinka's civil war tetralogy; but this is inaccurate since *Madmen and Specialist* is an utterly serious play that is meticulously crafted and that achieves a consummate synthesis of radical social vision and avant-garde aesthetic form. The true "satyr play" in this tetralogy is *Season of Anomy* which is without question Soyinka's greatest artistic flop, the cause of the reversal of critical opinion of Soyinka's stature as a novelist after the impressive success of *The Interpreters*. Since *The Man Died* derives from the same personal experience and historical event as *Season of Anomy*, it is useful to discuss both works comparatively and intertextually in order to account for the ferocious power and poignancy of the one and the spectacular artistic failure of the other.

In the very brief prefatory note to *The Man Died* titled "the unacknowledged," Soyinka writes poignantly about the severely limited scope of reading and writing he was allowed by his jailers during his twenty-seven month incarceration during the Nigerian civil war. There is nothing gratuitous about his bitter observations in this prefatory note, his main intention being to demonstrate how and why his captors were particularly meticulous in preventing books that were sent to him from ever reaching him, and how the writing he was thus able to do was made possible by the unusual writing tablets provided by the few books that did somehow manage to reach him. "Books and all forms of writing have always been objects of terror to those who suppress the truth," he writes in this prefatory note. And of the writing which he managed to do, against all the obstacles erected by his vigilant captors, Soyinka makes the following assertions which throw a useful light on the genesis of both *The Man Died* itself and quite possibly *Season of Anomy*:

> Between the lines of Paul Radin's *Primitive Religion* and my own *Idanre* are scribbled fragments of plays, poems, a novel and portions of the prison notes which make up this book. Six other volumes have been similarly defaced with my writing. For fear of providing a clue which would lead to a reconstruction of the circumstances and the certain persecution of probably innocent officers, I cannot even provide titles of these books, much less indicate at which periods of my imprisonment they were smuggled in to me one by one. After the indescribably exquisite pleasure of reading, I proceeded to cover spaces between the lines with my own writing. (*TMD*, 8)

Beyond giving the bare but crucial information regarding the genesis, in prison, of not only *The Man Died* itself, but also nearly all the writings which later collectively became Soyinka's civil war tetralogy, this passage provides vital interpretive clues to the special place of his civil war writings in Soyinka's literary corpus, and quite possibly in the trajectory of his entire post-incarceration output. For in a way far more portentous than its literal connotation in this passage, Soyinka's civil war writing constitutes writing "between the lines" of his previous and future works. Bearing in mind what this phrase literally and metaphorically connotes, it is not fanciful to suggest that it is precisely with these texts on, and generated by, the civil war that Soyinka as author begins a mediated but extensive intrusion into his own works. In other words, it is with these texts written "between the lines" of his pre-incarceration writings and the works which come after his civil war tetralogy that the literary and ideological construction of a persona, in all its guises and articulations, begins to occur in nearly all of our author's post-war writings, some subliminally, others quite obtrusively. *The Man Died* and *Season of Anomy* are the first harvests of this development in Soyinka's writing and between them they show the extremes of the artistic and ideological effects and consequences of this pattern.

The particular dimension which the first person narrative voice and point of view takes in *The Man Died* is probably without any comparison in modern African literature in its completely unselfconscious and unembarrassed assertion of the indissociable identity of the author/narrator

with the cause of Truth, Justice and Humanity. Where else in modern
African literature would one find both the tenor and the substance of the
following assertions in the section of *The Man Died* appropriately titled
"A letter to Compatriots":

> I recognized . . . that I moved long ago beyond compromise, that this book is
> *now*, and that only such things should be left out which might imperil those on
> whom true revolution within the country depends. My judgment alone must
> serve in such matters, *and my experience which, it strikes me more and more, is unique
> among the fifty million people of my country* (1314) (My emphasis)

The stance articulated in this passage may be read as the expression
of an extreme self-absorption caused by Soyinka's long incarceration in
solitary confinement. Or it can be read as a radical insistence that individual moral autonomy expressed by privileging personal perceptions and
intuitions in a period of war-induced dictatorship matters profoundly
and should unapologetically be asserted and defended. A third possible
reading of course is that these two interpretations intersect. But whatever one makes of it, the vital fact remains that Soyinka did not adopt
this stance on the uniqueness of his experience and intuitions in a fit
of absent-mindedness, and that in adopting it he was placing himself,
and the writings born of that stance, at great risk. Definitely, from the
number of highly placed political and military figures named and ferociously savaged in the book, we know what personal risks the book
entailed for its author. The ban which was for a time placed on the sale
of the book in Nigeria, and the long period of estrangement between
Soyinka and erstwhile friends and confreres in the community of the
country's literary intelligentsia are also a dimension of the personal risks
provoked by the uncompromising moral and spiritual authority claimed
by the author-protagonist as the ambiguous and bitter harvest of his
unique experiences among his countrymen and women.[7] The artistic,
ideological and ethical risks in the particular tenor of the radical stance
of the author-narrator in this work calls for careful analysis.

The very title of the prison memoir, *The Man Died*, enormously com-
plicates Soyinka's uncompromising privileging of his individual moral
vision in the book. For we know that the incarcerated writer survived. An
unfortunate broadcast journalist, Segun Sowemimo, whose death from
medical complications arising from a brutal beating ordered by a military governor in General Gowon's regime, supplied the title for the book.
What Sowemimo's death has to do with Soyinka's incarceration, or with
the thousands murdered in the genocidal slaughter of Igbo residents of
Northern Nigeria in May and September 1966, or with the million killed

in the war itself, lends "death" a special resonance in the book as appertaining to both mass slaughter of innocents through allegedly organized
atrocities and the death of the spirit apparently intended by the imposition of tyrannical rule on the nation. This is what gives Soyinka's assertion
of the exceptionalism of his moral vision and political testament in this
book, in spite of the unquestionably self-absorbed and self-inflated terms
in which it is often expressed, convincing social validity. In this vision, the
author-protagonist's own incarceration and attempted physical liquida-
tion while in detention is linked with other great and small acts of abuse
and corruption of power to metonymically depict a "season of anomy"
on a grand scale. The list is depressingly long: the brutal beating of the
journalist, Segun Sowemimo and many instances of the public flogging
of members of the civilian population by a sadistic soldiery documented
in the appendices to the book; the continued abduction, detention and
more slayings of individuals and groups of Igbos by military fanatics even
as the war to bring them back into the country was being prosecuted; the
flippant and callous indifference to the horrors of the war and its human
toll revealed in the declaration by the federal authorities that the immi-
nent fall of the Biafran capital in mid-1969 was going to be "a special
wedding present" to General Gowon; and the use of the apparatus and
protocols of office by the military rulers to cower the mass of ordinary
citizens into a submissive, docile and cynically apathetic populace so as
to consolidate a tyrannical military dictatorship. These events and trends
are told in diverse narratives which are deliberately kept unintegrated in
the narrative scheme of the book. Nonetheless, from their juxtaposition –
helped by the many digressions comprising the author-protagonist's
editorial comments on events long after the time of their actual occurrence – a single powerful testament does emerge, at least in the view
of the author-narrator-protagonist, as the core ideological and moral
vision of *The Man Died*.

This testament entails an indictment of the victors of the war as "power
profiteers" who used the *de facto* legitimation afforded by victory in war
and the ideological serviceableness of the claim of having kept the nation from fragmenting to entrench and consolidate dictatorship which
inaugurated flagrant and pervasive human rights violations and abuses.
Before *The Man Died* was published and instantly took the nation by
storm, there *were* protests and demonstrations against these abuses and
violations; and there were militant actions against economic and social
injustices. Moreover, these took place before and during the war when
there was a state of emergency in force abrogating democratic rights
and freedoms and suspending the legal and judicial instruments for their

protection.[8] It was indeed at the height of this civil war-induced state of emergency that the famous Agbekoya revolts broke out in many parts of rural western Nigeria, ultimately culminating in a march on Ibadan, the regional capital, where some police stations were stormed and raided for weapons and the main prison at Agodi was "liberated." But while these tumultuous events which provide a context for Soyinka's accounts of his unique experiences are significantly left out of the narrative, it must be acknowledged that as to the precise question of linking the civil war "victors" to the beginnings of a brutal military dictatorship in Nigeria, Soyinka in *The Man Died* was virtually alone in warning the nation – in particular the community of militants and progressive intellectuals – of this development and its dire portents. It was not necessary, not inevitable, Soyinka argues, that in order to win the war and keep the nation together a dictatorship had to be imposed on the country. And even if one accepted this rationalization, why, Soyinka further asks, did the repressiveness, the wanton violation of civil liberties continue and deepen after the end of the war? The heinous incident which supplied the title of the book as well as all the other incidents of power arrogance and sadistic acts of military potentates documented in the Appendix to the book, all of these happened, after all, well *after* the cessation of hostilities. And perhaps the most important political and ideological question posed by this testament: what happens to a people on whom a dictatorship is imposed and justified in the name of patriotism, and as a blackmail based on the specter of the breakup of the nation and a descent into chaos?

To give maximum moral and ideological force to his answer to this question as well as place this "local" Nigerian sociopolitical tragedy in a wider historical context, Soyinka makes a far-ranging comparison of his nation in the aftermath of the civil war to other places and other times throughout the world when tyranny in the form of partial or complete police states are gradually imposed on a populace, quoting many writers and thinkers on the imperative of political and spiritual resistance based on uncompromising ethical absolutes. One of the most eloquent of these is the Greek writer, George Mangakis, who is quoted by Soyinka for his warning on one of the worst things that happen when dictatorship is imposed on a people, this being a particular form of failure and its consequences. This is the failure to

acquire an extraordinary historic acuity of vision and see with total clarity that humiliated nations are inevitably led either to a lethal decadence, a moral and spiritual withering, or to a passion for revenge which results in bloodshed and upheavals. (*TMD*, 19)

Except for the fact that a second civil war has not taken place in Nigeria and the "passion for revenge which results in bloodshed and upheavals" has not taken the extremely savage and bizarre expressions that have taken dreadful political and human tolls in other African countries like Liberia, Somalia, Sierra Leone, Rwanda, Burundi and the Democratic Republic of the Congo, every single one of these dire warnings spelled graphically in the text of *The Man Died* have been played out in Nigeria in the three decades since the book was published. This makes this work a great human and political document, one of the notable antifascist writings of the second half of the twentieth century. Indeed, but for certain moral and ideological lapses in the book's powerful and eloquent exposure of the equivocations and complacencies of an entire citizenry which make dictatorship possible, the quality of the antifascist testament of *The Man Died* would have placed the book in the ranks of the greatest political testaments against authoritarianism of the century like Arthur Koestler's *Darkness at Noon*, Aleksander Solzhenitsyn's *The Gulag Archipelago*, George Orwell's *Animal Farm*, C.L.R. James' *Mariners, Renegades and Castaways* and Vaclav Havel's *The Power of the Powerless*. It is no accident that these are all prose works, for prose has incontestable advantages over other literary forms in the testamentary mode of writing to which these works belong precisely because the ethical burdens and generic conventions of the idiom of prose compel maximum use of the classical prose "virtues" of clarity, elegance, and eloquence, just as it enables astute appropriations of the most economical and expressive features of the genres of drama and poetry.

The best literary and moral aspects of the narrative of *The Man Died* are traceable to the strengths of this testamentary writing. In the best expressions of this tradition of writing, without condescension toward one's compatriots, sustained narrative focus on deeply personal experience of privation and suffering merge with a powerful, unsentimental and selfless solicitude for the general wrongs done to defenseless or dispossessed victims of terror. The sections of this prison memoir which record Soyinka's encounter with other prisoners and his identification with their condition are unequaled in his prose writings for their clarity and evocativeness. Particularly affecting are the sections on the treatment of the detained Igbo prisoners, on his observations on the peculiar world of condemned prisoners on death row, and the pathos of the inmates of the lunatic wing of the prison. In these mini-narratives, the prose style assumes a haunting, almost sacramental gracefulness, which is not the same thing as idealizing or aestheticizing suffering in order to dull the outrage that the perpetration of suffering on the weak and defenseless should cause. This is particularly true of the many passages of what can be more appropriately called the "mindscapes" of Soyinka's reveries and visionary projections in solitary confinement, most of which occur in the third of the three main sections of the book, "Kaduna '69." One of the most affecting of these "mindscapes" is the following passage which expresses the incarcerated writer's selfless assimilation of his individual fate to the fates of all the victims of organized, dictatorial terror:

Tenth day of fast. By day a speck of dust on sunbeam. By night a slow shuttle in the cosmos. Night . . . A clear night, and the moon pouring into my cell. I thought, a shroud? I have returned again and again to this night of greatest weakness and lassitude, to the hours of lying still on the stark clear-headed acceptance of the thought that said: it is painless. The body weakens and breath slows to a stop. Gone was the fear that a life-urge might make me retreat at this moment. I held no direct thought of death, only of probable end of a course of action. I felt the weakness in the joints of my bones and within the bone itself. A dry tongue that rasped loosely in the mouth. I felt a great repose in me, an enervating peace of the world and the universe within me, a peace that "passeth all understanding." I wrote . . .

> I anoint my flesh
> Thought is hallowed in the lean
> Oil of solitude
> I call you forth, all upon
> Terraces of light. Let the dark withdraw
>
> I anoint my voice
> And let it sound hereafter
> Or dissolve upon its lonely passage
> In your void. Voices new
> Shall rouse the echoes when
> Evil shall again arise.
>
> I anoint my heart
> Within its flame I lay
> Spent ashes of your hate –
> Let evil die.
>
> (*TMD*, 252–3)

Certainly, *The Man Died* has the distinction – an equivocal distinction which, we can be sure, Soyinka would have never wished for this book – of being one of the earliest and perhaps the most powerful in a long line of prison writings of writer-activists in postcolonial African literature of which another great exemplar is Ngugi wa Thiong'o's *Detained: A Writer's Prison Diary*.[9] It is important to state this fact because there are serious ethical, ideological and aesthetic lapses in the book and these have tended to rather unduly condition critical commentaries on the work. Of these commentaries, the responses of persons who have felt personally attacked, or felt that the political communities and interests which they represent are portrayed unfairly in the book have been, understandably, vitriolic and lacking in balanced, dispassionate judgment, much like the most flawed aspects of the book itself.[10] More importantly, it is these flaws which have conditioned the commentaries of many critics and scholars who have not indeed failed to respond to the more positive, the more moving and edifying aspects of the work.[11] Of this group of scholars, the final, summative judgment of Derek Wright on the book is characteristic:

. . . the outstanding value of *The Man Died* is as a human and personal, not a political document. It is a brave and brilliant testament to the resilience of the human mind in extremity, thrown back entirely upon itself and its own inner resources in its bid to survive. It remains however, one man's vision. (Wright, 138)

These commentaries – of Soyinka's political adversaries acting on their sense of savage and unfair treatment in *The Man Died*, and of critics whose responses are overdetermined by the disturbing mix in the work of idealism and mean-spirited vengefulness – highlight, more than any work of Soyinka, the politics of location in both the creative process and its complement, the act of interpretation. By this is meant the fact that when confronted by a work of such fractured and "schizophrenic" effects as this prison memoir of our author, the situatedness of both the creative and the critical acts in a particular place and time, a particular socio-economic class, a particular irreducible existential condition, normatively a "hidden" factor, becomes explicit or even obtrusive. A brief elaboration on this issue in the way that it massively determines the use of language in *The Man Died* will serve to conclude our discussion of this work.

In narrating how a change of circumstance in his status as *one* detainee among other prison inmates in Lagos to complete solitary detention when he was moved to Kaduna was registered by bodily sensations,

Soyinka remarkably privileges language and words as is shown in the
following passage:

> I recognize, and welcome the beginning of a withdrawal process, an accentuation
> of the imposed isolation by an instinctive self-isolation. I find first of all that my
> body rejects all objects, a process which did not take place during my four
> months in Lagos. My body adjusted to its surrounding, picked up a rhythm of
> the prison, accepted its pulse, sounds, the touch and feel of food. It reacted only
> against things which would normally disgust me: filth and bad smells, treachery
> between prisoners, callousness among the warders. I slipped into prison life as
> one dives into a stream, an unnatural element but one to which the body does
> adjust. The reverse has happened here. I reject everything, make no contact.
> One object after another is rejected by my skin. Lying down, even this involves
> no contact. Walking, I do not feel I touch the ground. The process accelerates
> towards total completion. Reality is killed and buried with memories of the past.
> Words play a part of it, hypnotizing the mind and de-sensitizing the body. For
> instance, as the last gate was opened I found I had set up an aimless cycle of
> words. Over and over it repeated itself, over and over until my conscious mind at
> long last took note of this incantation. A quotation from a long-forgotten book?
> Or simply the creative mind's originality-at-all-costs variant of that familiar
> theme: Abandon hope all who enter here? No matter, it goes thus and in an
> accent of bell chimes: In time of evil come I to this place of evil brought by evil
> hands and who knows but I may come to evil in this evil place . . . Then it begins
> over again. (*TMD*, 128–9)

The way that language operates in the experience narrated in this passage to hone the psychic reserves of the author-detainee is emblematic of
the over-investment in this book in the fundamentally constitutive role of
language in all areas of experience. In this particular example, words and
language encode and supplement subliminal and presumably precogni-
tive bodily processes, consolidating at deep psychic levels the author-
protagonist's survival in "that time and place of evil." At one level, this
all-encompassing investment in the efficacy of words and language in
The Man Died is the product of the cynical and deliberate deprivation of
the author-detainee of books and materials with which to write. Indeed,
Soyinka's battle to contest this deprivation and to fashion quite ingenious
stratagems to overcome the effects apparently desired by his captors is a
major theme of the second part of the book. I would, however, suggest
that the all-encompassing investment in language in the book cuts deeper
than this and affects the construction of the underlying moral-ideological
scheme of the narrative – the very source of some of the text's most serious
lapses. In other words, at this level we encounter a dialectical structure
of affirmation and negation, of high-minded idealism and extraordinary

expressions of spitefulness and vengefulness in the author-detainee's investment in the power of words and language. One of the most egregious expressions of the pole of negativity in this dialectic is the extensive use by the author-protagonist of hyperbolic metaphor and imagery to dehumanize or bestialize many of his captors without providing any details whatsoever to show action or behavior on the part of those so targeted to convince the reader that the application of the hyperbolic metaphor to them is warranted. Similar to this is the author-protagonist's tactic of comparing some of his captors with notorious figures culled from atrocity legends of the Nazi death camps, again without indicating acts or deeds of a scale of brutality to sustain the associations mobilized by these analogies. In other words, language and words are excessively proffered and just as exceedingly withheld according to a moral scheme whose instantiations are so insubstantial that one is left with the conclusion that these language acts are justified only because for the author-protagonist, language and words often suffice as values unto themselves. A somewhat lesser expression of this pattern, but one nonetheless frustrating for even the most positive and generous readers of this work, is the author's withholding of information on the scope, nature and location of actions and initiatives proffered, through extraordinarily eloquent uses of language, as countervailing moral and ideological forces to the bestialized and anathematized despots who ordered Soyinka's incarceration, plunged the nation to war and then used the war to consolidate both organized and random acts of state terror.[12]

Perhaps the most troubling of these flaws, one which again is consummated by unquestionably dazzling feats of language use, is the scale to which the author-protagonist actually permits himself to pour scorn on the very human community of his nation-state which is the object of his solicitude in his efforts to expose and oppose dictatorial terror and sustain hopes of renewal. No matter how expansively one wishes to read the following passage, this is what comes through clearly and unambiguously:

But the words hammer strident opposition to the waves of negations that engulf me, to the mob hatred that I distinctly hear even in this barred wilderness. It nerves me to mutter – Brainwashed, gullible fools, many-headed multitudes, why should your voices in ignorance affect my peace? But they do. I cannot deny it. (*TMD*, 90)

It must of course be admitted that the textual context for this passage is the honest expression by Soyinka in this work of the shifting moods that he experienced in the psychic and spiritual extremity of solitary detention in prison. That being said, it must be acknowledged that when linked to other expressions in this book detailing the uniqueness of the author-protagonist's experiences and perceptions "among the fifty million" of his countrymen and women, these words assume the Coriolanus-type *hauteur* of the highly placed and highly gifted citizen who is superciliously insistent on his superiority as a political being endowed with superhuman qualities. The following passage is only one of many others of this expression in the book:

> If *he* could break and break so abjectly then anyone can break. This army is a force that can break anyone. And will. (*TMD*, 79) (Emphasis in the text)

In the opinions of some critics, such flaws are not mere lapses but are constitutive, and they considerably compromise, if not effectively neutralize the value of *The Man Died* as a searing moral indictment of dictatorship.[13] But this, in the opinion of this writer, is a misreading which ignores the fact that for nearly every expression of self-absorption and self-inflation in this work, there is an articulate and compelling act of self-questioning and self-transcendence. This misreading also ignores the fact that any critical engagement of this work which is sufficiently self-aware of its own situatedness cannot but locate the ambiguities and fractures in *The Man Died* in the recognition that it is not unusual for a powerful antifascist document such as *The Man Died* to come from the kind of self-divided egalitarian-elitist consciousness that the author-protagonist of this work so pervasively embodies in this particular book and in Soyinka's second novel, *Season of Anomy*. This is indeed an appropriate note on which to move to our discussion of this work.

The flaws that we have identified in parts of *The Man Died* which somewhat compromise, but do not significantly diminish the aesthetic and moral force of that book are magnified a hundredfold in *Season of Anomy*. Since, as we have seen, this novel has its gestative origins in Soyinka's incarceration, all the bile and vengeful anger contained and transfigured by the humanity and grace of many parts of *The Man Died* seem to have found uninhibited release and little artistic mediation in *Season of Anomy*. For at the most general level, language, or more precisely, prose as a vehicle of valuable moral and spiritual insights, consistently overreaches itself in this novel in the manner in which narration, description or even dialogue is inflated far beyond the incidents or events they relate to, or the information available to the reader. And at an even more basic, elementary level, the plot – and the shifts and transitions which propel it – is often so implausible that any reader without knowledge or information about the infamous events and personalities in the Nigerian crises of 1964–66 would be hard put to grasp, let alone make sense of what exactly is going on at presumably crucial moments in the narrative. This flaw is so pervasive, so stark in *Season* that the only plausible explanation for its occurrence in a work by a writer of Soyinka's stature is the likelihood that the Nigerian author overrates his or *any* writer's capacity to make highly wrought, evocative prose breathe vitality or even conviction to the flimsiest and most implausible narrative imaginable, even if that narrative is located within the framework of the pre-novelistic conventions of the allegory as a mode of narration.[14] Apparently, as indicated by the second epigraph to this chapter – comments by Samuel Johnson on Shakespeare's excesses with language – this flaw is particularly "congenital" to the very qualities which make for greatness in writers whose love of their medium of expression is compounded of excess.

There is sufficient critical commentary on *Season of Anomy* now to enable readers of the novel to grasp the main outlines of its deployment of the myth of Orpheus and Eurydice to tell an allegorical narrative of good and evil in the terrible social and political turmoil in the western and northern regions of Nigeria in 1965 and 1966 which ultimately led to the civil war. Of these commentaries, Dan Izevbaye's detailed exegesis of correspondences with the Orpheus-Eurydice myth is especially insightful.[15] Ofeyi and Iriyise, hero and heroine of the novel, are given names easily identifiable with Orpheus and Eurydice. Consistent with the Orpheus-Eurydice myth, the captive abductee in *Season of Anomy* is Iriyise, substituting for Soyinka's embodiment of that archetype in himself in *The Man Died*. Indeed, in *Season*, Iriyise is being held in a place called Kuntua, a substitute name for Kaduna where Soyinka was held for most of the period of his detention and where most of the accounts of the long solitary phase of his incarceration in *The Man Died* are located. One of the most bitter political criticisms made in that book of Soyinka's prison experience is the continuum that the imprisoned writer perceives between the repressive, degrading regimen of prison life and the fascist system choking life outside the prison in crisis-ridden, war-torn Nigeria. The quest of Ofeyi for Iriyise's freedom in *Season of Anomy* provides Soyinka, as author, the means to bear witness to the scope of the evil which that fascist system consolidated as the basis of its grip on power and which it apparently succeeded in reproducing in the beleaguered, traumatized populace. Thus, anyone who has read the acts and scenes of mindless, callous mass murder, bestiality and cynicism of the rulers and the ruled in

Yambo Ouloguem's *Bound to Violence* will find parallels in *Season of Anomy*. But unlike the former where the narrator successfully adopts, or affects, a completely amoral indifference to the monstrously evil acts narrated or described, the narrator of *Season of Anomy* identifies closely and intimately with Ofeyi as he wanders through the landscapes of human carnage and moral nullity in search of his Iriyise. The problem is not so much the sheer fact of the total identification of narrator with protagonist in the novel, although this nearly always proves problematic, as the fact that in proposing Ofeyi as a protagonist who is not a mere wandering witness to the "season of anomy" in his homeland, but a promethean revolutionary seeking to mobilize all the dormant regenerative energies of society, there is very little in information about character and events supplied by the narrator to lend plausibility to the unfolding narrative as it increasingly casts Ofeyi in a superlative promethean stature.

It is difficult to tell which artistic solecism is more costly to the narrative of *Season of Anomy*, the hollowness and implausibility of Ofeyi and Iriyise as symbols of revolutionary renewal in the revisionary version of the Orphic myth deployed in this novel, or its corollary, the great strain between symbol and referent in the depiction of the Cartel's bosses, Zaki Amuri, Batoki and Chief Biga as symbols of incarnate evil. This latter point applies as well to the depiction of "Cross-River" – the physical terrain and the people – as a natural habitat of the monstrous evils which Ofeyi, the Dentist and the new herald men of Aiyero must defeat if the land is to be regenerated. It might help to clarify the argument being advanced here if we look more closely at, on the one hand, Ofeyi and Iriyise as symbols of regenerative will and revolutionary consciousness and on the other hand, Zaki Amuri, Batoki and the Cross-River terrain as symbols of an incarnate, unregenerate evil.

Ofeyi and Iriyise work in the sales promotions division of a corporation which has a monopoly of cocoa products, he as songwriter and creative publicist and she as singer, dancer and performer of the songs and skits that Ofeyi creates. They are in reality underground revolutionaries working against the corporation's monopolistic greed and exploitativeness, their subversiveness indeed extending to the internal workings of the Cartel, the shadowy ruling oligarchic alliance in the country which controls the cocoa corporation, Ofeyi and Iriysie's employers. On the evidence given by the narrator, their "subversiveness," like that of Daodu and Segi in *Kongi's Harvest*, is almost puerile and certainly unconvincing. This evidence comes mostly in the form of samples of Ofeyi's "subversive" lyrics (*SOA*, 32, 35, 74), none of which remotely comes close to the lyrical eloquence and lacerating satire of Soyinka's own "Unlimited Liability Company" and "Etiko Revo Wetin," the ballads he composed and recorded as a long-playing record album in 1983. And when Ofeyi and Iriyise visit Aiyero, a socialist commune in the riverine delta (based on the historic communalistic Aiyetoro village in the Ikale-Ilaje division of Ondo state), the offer to Ofeyi of succession to the leadership of the community as "Custodian of the Grain" upon the expected demise of the present incumbent, as well as the adoption of Iriyise to a venerated position among the commune's women's groups, is simply and inexplicably made, without the slightest information given by the narrator as to what it is in Ofeyi and Iriyise that makes a tried and tested idealistic community adopt them into the highest leadership positions of their society. The pattern of discursive iteration, through densely poetic and myth-encrusted prose, of these two characters as symbols embodying the associations encoded in their names runs throughout the entire narrative, thereby implying that this pattern suffices to secure their credibility as acting protagonists. One of the most astounding instances of the pattern occurs when, in their Cross-River search for Iriyise, Ofeyi and Zaccheus, his companion and a reluctant activist, having just had their presence registered as witnesses to the mass slaughter of a neighborhood of "aliens" in Cross-River by a mob of the locals aided by the police, then go directly to demand of that same complicitous police force that a raid be made on the house where Iriyise is allegedly being held in order to free her. The strain on plausibility and artistic control in this narrative sequence is taken beyond breaking point when we then learn that the house in question is owned by Zaki Amuri, head of the Cartel, the brain behind the mob killings and orchestrator of the complicity of the police and security forces in the killings Ofeyi and Zaccheus had just witnessed! (*SOA*, 197–201)

The symbolization of Zaki Amuri, Batoki and Chief Biga, the unholy triumvirate of the Cartel, as incarnate evil takes similar patterns as that of Ofeyi and Iriyise as archetypes of the regenerative forces of nature, although it involves a different method. For where Ofeyi and Iriyise are invested with their symbolic essences not so much through action and behavior but by evocative prose descriptions, the figures making up the Cartel are presented in acts and behavior unambiguously and one-sidedly evil. The scenes of Zaki Amuri and Batoki's depravity and venality are very graphically rendered – and they are mostly pure melodrama. Since, as we shall demonstrate later, some of these same scenes are reprised in Soyinka's nonfictional memoir, *Ibadan*, this presents a special problem in Soyinka's prose works. Within the allegorical framework of narrative in *Season of Anomy*, these melodramatic scenes depicting actual historical figures as embodiments of great, monstrous evil represent the lowest possible point of artistic and intellectual yield. And this is without ignoring the fact that the moral scheme of the sub-genre of allegory traditionally has a binary, dichotomizing pattern of essential Good confronting essential Evil since this pertains to the pre-novelistic forms of allegory.

Between the first three of Soyinka's prose works, *The Interpreters*, *The Man Died*, and *Season of Anomy*, and the subsequent three, *Aké*, *Isara* and *Ibadan*, there is a hiatus of about a decade in the publication dates. As we have remarked earlier, with the publication of *Season of Anomy*, the last title in the first three prose works, it seemed that Soyinka had come to a dead end, as far as writing novels was concerned. This fact somewhat helps to explain the hiatus in the publication history of the two sets of his prose works. There is of course the added factor that the years between the publication of these two sets of prose writings were years when Soyinka was at his most active in the theatre, his preferred medium of expression. Finally, it is important to note that if it is probably the case that a writer of Soyinka's profound and sustained curiosity about the sources and nature of his talents and sensibilities as an artist would sooner or later have written *Aké*, the work of childhood memoir, *Isara* and *Ibadan*, as Soyinka asserts in the prefatory note to *Ibadan*, are "happenings" which were provoked by social and political crises demanding the writer-activist's artistic responses in the form of the biographical or autobiographical memoir.

Aké, *Isara* and *Ibadan*, as memoirs, share many things in common, although at a first approximation the difference of authorial intent and achieved aesthetic effects between the three works seem to outweigh the similarities. I would urge, however, that underlying the mass of differences between the three texts is the fact that the narrative in each work is organized around the idea of a powerful subliminal psychic *tropism* that drives individuals and social groups towards emotional and spiritual fulfillment and its many modalities – community, wholeness, love and grace.

Aké, as a memoir of Soyinka's childhood years is not a conventional *Bildungsroman*, a coming of age narrative; it is not a story of growing up through an embittering loss of innocence or of a traumatic shedding of illusions through very painful experience. The most sorrowful event in the narrative is the death of a sibling at exactly her first birthday anniversary. What *Aké* is about is the process of individuation of the future author from the earliest years of very dim, unformed consciousness of a distinct selfhood to the emergence of a remarkably strong sense of his own uniqueness against the backdrop of family, hometown, nation and the world. The very well deserved critical success of the book derives from the memorable, richly textured and convincing manner in which this process of a unique individuation is narrated. One of the means by which this is achieved is the author's gift of near total recall and the imagistic manner of rendering recollection and memory of the earliest experiences, though the accuracy of some of his recollections in this memoir has been challenged by a leading feminist critic and scholar, Molara Ogundipe.[16] For instance, in one of these powerful renditions of recollected memory, at about the age of two, the legends of Ajai Crowther's historic tenure in the Aké bishopric literally come alive as an apparition of the famous cleric steps out of his framed picture making the terrified boy flee in fear. In another mesmerizing narrative sequence, Bukola, a playmate of the author deemed to be a "spirit child" shares a meal and holds an animated, lively conversation with her companions from the spirit world in a locked room in which she is the only living human being.

Perhaps the single most effective narrative technique used in *Aké* – a technique first used in *The Interpreters* but almost entirely absent in *Season of Anomy* – is that of an effective, powerful animation of a large cast of characters and personalities as a human backdrop to the individuation process of the young protagonist of the narrative. Given the fact that this technique is at the core of the novelist's art, its effective use in *Aké*, *Isara* and *Ibadan*, in a descending order of execution, lends force to our contention that there is a blurring of generic boundaries between the novel proper and other ancillary sub-genres in Soyinka's prose works.

It is remarkable that as a childhood memoir, the large cast of characters animated in *Aké* as a human backdrop to the protagonist's evolving sensibilities is made up largely of adult figures. At the centre of these figures are of course the portraits of the author's parents, "Essay" and "Wild Christian," the former presented more extensively and intricately than the latter, but both collectively profiled as surely one of the most well-matched monogamous marital couples in modern African literature.[17] This profile is all the more surprising given the fact that "Essay" and "Wild Christian" are presented as the very quintessence of basic contrasts in temperament and sensibility: "Essay" is the essence of order, composure and unflappable self-possession, while "Wild Christian," as

the appellation suggests and as revealed in the riot of disorder in her bedroom and the profligate jumble of commodities and objects in her market
stalls, embodies flamboyant disorganization and barely contained chaos.
There is a slight hint in the author-protagonist's structuring of these contrasts in the sensibilities of his parents, that this may be the foundation
of the mature artists' embrace of duality and contradiction as the very
source of art in general and the Ogun muse in particular, the "wildness"
of the mother corresponding to the fiery aspect of Ogun's temper and
"Essay's" passion for order and organization corresponding to the god's
more deliberative, recreative traits, especially since in *Isara*, Soditan, the
cognomen that "Essay" assumes in that work, embodies many of Ogun's
questing and creative attributes.

   The complement of other adult figures who populate the growing
protagonist's consciousness is a large amalgam of social and moral types
who are, in every instance, brilliantly presented in their individualities
or even eccentricities. This large cast includes "Daodu" and "Beere"
(the Revd. And Mrs. Ransome-Kuti) who together compositely embody
the ethic of uncompromising personal and national self-reliance and
civic-mindedness; "Mayself," the sponger who ultimately wears out the
immense hospitality of the author's parents; the author's grandfather,
one of the last in a vanishing breed of hardy Yoruba yeomanry; and the
lunatic pair of husband and wife, Sorowanke and Yokolu, whose place
in the imaginative universe of the memoir lends credence to Foucault's
claims in *Madness and Civilization* that before it became medicalized, in-
stitutionalized and confined, "madness" had a voice, a logic of its own
which was not merely "unreason," not merely the incommensurable
"Other" of Reason, but was one of the accepted modalities of social
being.[18]

   One of the most astonishing features of the narrative of *Aké* is the relative absence, compared with the preponderance of profiles of adult
figures, of powerfully rendered portraits of members of the author-
protagonist's own peer group. In all, only about three children or playmates of the young Soyinka are given any tangible, individualized presence in this memoir of childhood. These are Bukola, the "emere" child,
Osiki, a primary school playmate and Iku, the quintessential intransi-
gent *flanneur* that we encounter in the briefly narrated episode of the
author's secondary schooldays at the Abeokuta Grammar School. It
must be said however, that what *Aké* lacks in numbers regarding the
presence of age mates of the protagonist it makes up for in the intensity and resonance of the author's re-creation of these three figures from

his childhood. The first American edition of *Aké* had on the cover of the dust jacket a powerful imagist drawing of a child in flight from an undeclared source of terror: this was apparently derived from the episode in the narrative which tells of Osiki in whom Soyinka as a child first discovered the reality of speed as an independent phenomenal entity. This comes from an episode that narrates how, in misjudging his weight on a seesaw platform, the hapless Osiki catapulted the narrator-protagonist high into the air and in the resultant crash unintentionally inflicted a deep gash in Soyinka's temple. Finding himself pursued for retribution, Osiki takes to his heels. But what starts as a halfhearted pursuit soon becomes pure wonder as Soyinka is halted in his tracks, totally rapt in his discovery of this thing that is motion – in the wondrous dimension of speed. Iku's brief appearance in the narrative takes a different form from the phenomenal appearance of Osiki's natural gift for running to the auhor-narrator, but is no less memorable. For Iku it is who, to the young Soyinka's great fascination, dares to take the illogicalities of the adult world to their absurd limits. The matter has to do with Daodu, the school principal's absolutist liberal rationalism which holds that any schoolboy who can make a convincing and impeccably rational case for his defense will be exculpated of guilt for any infraction, no matter how palpable the circumstantial evidence of guilt. Iku raids the school principal's own poultry for one of its prize kestrels which he and his accomplices consume, but he brazenly but "convincingly" argues his way out of punishment for the misdemeanor on the grounds of a "phlogiston" theory of "total and instantaneous combustion" which, according to Iku "consumed" the rooster, he and his mates merely completing what a small fire during a scientific experiment began.

Why are there such few members of Soyinka's own peer group in this childhood memoir spanning the age of two years to eleven? There is no evidence whatsoever that the author was a child who totally kept to himself and had no playmates, even though a central motif in this memoir is the protagonist's tendency towards inwardness and radical individual autonomy. Indeed, the relative absence of other children in the book applies equally to the author's siblings. For even the two siblings among a complement of six, who we are told in the prefatory "Dedication" inhabited the memory span of the contents of *Aké*, are not given as much narrative space as Bukola, Osiki and Iku and definitely far less than the adult characters. This point is made, it must be quickly stated, not to point out an artistic flaw; rather, the point assumes significance only in relation to what appears to be the underlying premise of the author's focus on the world of adults in this memoir of his childhood. For I think it is fair to say that this comes from the adult author's retrospective realization that for the growing, evolving consciousness of a deeply observant and sensitive child who is preternaturally prone to following his own perceptions and intuitions wherever, and as far as they may lead him, the "reality principle" is that constituted by the world of adults. Or, more precisely, *worlds*.

Within the first three pages of *Aké*, we are introduced to the three composite "worlds" which will vie for his imaginative, spiritual and moral allegiance: the world of Africanized, middle-class Christianity; the "pagan" world of Yoruba rites, festivals, beliefs and practices which stands as a powerful redoubt to colonial and Christian incursions; and a spirit world of supernatural beings who are invisible but are nonetheless felt as active presences, this being generally symbolic of the eternal world of the imagination and the spirit. Indeed, these three "worlds" are encountered within the space of the second and third paragraphs of the first chapter of the memoir and in a profile written in a narrative voice which tries to mirror the consciousness of the two-year-old child, a child highly receptive to the ideas and sensibilities contained in each of these three "worlds":

On a misty day, the steep rise toward Itoko would join the sky. If God did not actually live there, there was little doubt that he descended first on its crest, then took his one gigantic stride over those babbling markets – which dared to sell on Sundays – into St. Peter's Church, afterwards visiting the parsonage for tea with the Canon. There was the small consolation that, in spite of the temptation to arrive on horseback, he never stopped first at the Chief's who was known to be a pagan; certainly the Chief was never seen at a church service except at the anniversaries of the Alake's coronation. Instead God strode straight into St. Peter's for morning service, paused briefly at the afternoon service, but reserved his most formal, exotic presence for the evening service which, in his honour, was always held in the English tongue. The organ took on a dark, smoky sonority at evening service, and there was no doubt that the organ was adapting its normal sounds to accompany God's own sepulchral responses, with its timbre of the *egúngún*, to those prayers that were offered to him.

Only the Canon's residence could have housed the weekly Guest. For one thing, it was the only storey-building in the parsonage square and stolid as the Canon himself, riddled with black wooden-framed windows. Bishops Court was also a storey-building but only pupils lived in it, so it was not a house. From the upper floor of the Canon's home one *almost* looked the top of Itókò straight in its pagan eye. It stood at the highest lived-in point of the parsonage, just missing overlooking the gate. Its back was turned to the world of spirits and ghommids who inhabited the thick woods and chased home children who had wandered too deeply in them for firewood, mushrooms and snails. The Canon's square white building was a bulwark against the menace and the siege of the wood spirits. Its rear wall demarcated their territory, stopped them from taking liberties with the world of humans. (*Aké*, 1–2)

One reason why *Aké* is the unqualified critical success it is derives from the fact that the growing protagonist never comes to feel that these "worlds" are riven by incommensurable conflicts, that he has to take a stand for one against the others. His parents are of course uncompromising in the cause of Christianity, High Church Anglican variety, but the growing Soyinka is powerfully drawn in as yet inexplicable ways to the world of Yoruba rituals and festivals, as witnessed by the gratified, moving poetic prose that he devotes to his account of his grandfather's ritual dedication of his grandson to the gods of his people. Far more subliminally, the author-protagonist is drawn most especially to the third "world" of spiritual idealities and essences which in fact embraces both conflicting worlds of Christianity and Yoruba myths, rituals and festivals – and more. *Aké*, the text, derives from this harmonious, unsutured acceptance of those worlds of spirit and imagination.

All is not of course harmonious integration of disparate spiritual traditions and imaginative universes, or absence of social antagonisms in *Aké*. Nothing reveals this more than the fact that the last four chapters of the book (*Aké*, 177–222) are almost entirely given to an account of the historic Egba women's revolt against both the local "native authority" centralized in the person of the Alaké and the colonial British administration. Much of this section is narrated in the racy, dramatic prose of an action or adventure narrative as the young Soyinka, now about eleven years old, acts as an enthusiastic courier between spheres of action of the embattled women and their patron, "Daodu" himself, the legendary nationalist fighter and educational and social reformer. But it is an "adventure" narrative in external form only, for the overeager, young courier is attentive to, and prescient about the issues involved in the struggle, and he weaves this awareness into his presentation of the protagonists and antagonists in the struggle: the Alaké, some of his "Ogboni" chiefs, and British colonial administrators and political officers on the one hand, and on the other hand, "Beere," Daodu's wife, Funmilayo Ransome-Kuti, "Wild Christian," the author's mother, and the other leaders of the women's struggles.

In an ascending order of centrality in the plot structure of each work, social antagonisms – and the social movements and energies to which they give rise – occupy the foreground of the narrative in *Isara* and *Ibadan*, in a sublimated and artfully ludic mode in the former and in a literal, pervasive though fragmentary form in the latter. While in *Aké* and *Isara* the narrativization of social struggles and movements is mediated by techniques which distance the author-narrator – who is at any rate not a participant in the experiences recounted in these texts – from the events narrated, in *Ibadan* the entire narrative seems to be driven by the author-protagonist's excessive self-regard as the pivot around which diverse insurrectionary activities and currents revolve.

One key aspect of the overdetermining importance of the world of adults in the formation of the young Soyinka's sensibility and conscious-ness in *Aké* is the fascination exercised on his imagination by the pas-sionate debates and arguments of his father and his friends on just about every topic under the sun, but principally on the rapidly changing times in which they lived. In his "Author's Note" to *Isara*, Soyinka ascribes the impulse to write this loving and respectful memoir of his father and his generation to his discovery of a tin box belonging to his late fa-ther and the consequent "eavesdropping" on the contents of the box – "letters, old journals with marked pages and annotations, notebook jot-tings, tax and other levy receipts, minutes of meetings and school reports, program notes of special events and so on (*Isara*, v)." These "found" items of a rather special heirloom can only be considered complemen-tary to Soyinka's own direct experience of the passionate disputations of his father and his circle of friends and colleagues, an experience amply recorded in *Aké*. And perhaps the one truly new item in the contents of the tin-box heirloom is the correspondence between the author's fa-ther and an American "pen pal," Wade Cudeback, resident of an exotic sounding place-name in the United States – Ashtabula. What the cache of correspondence between the two adds to what Soyinka already knew about his father and his cohorts is brilliantly encoded in the presenta-tion of Ashtabula as a point on the mental and imaginative horizon of Yode Soditan and his circle of friends that is a polar opposite to their internal, indigenous reference point, their hometown, Isara. However, by a narratological sleight of hand, Soyinka brings these two polar op-posites of inside and outside, the home and the world, the local and the foreign within the compass of mutually constituted locations in a com-mon earth such that when Wade Cudeback finally shows up in person in Isara at the end of the narrative, Soditan can say to him: "Welcome to

Ashtabula!" This is why *Isara*, the memoir, is Soyinka's most densely structured, and ingeniously textured prose work, for neither *Aké* nor *Ibadan* has
an "Ashtabula" as a social imaginary which powerfully encodes perspectives that might enable breaking free of narrow, bounded and constrain-
ing horizons for the elites of colonized (and neocolonial) spaces. And
indeed, it requires a careful labor of textual exegesis to track the complexity which Soyinka infuses into his depiction of this Isara-Ashtabula
continuum.

Very early in the narrative of *Isara* we are allowed a glimpse into the
thoughts which the name "Ashtabula" has provoked in Yode Soditan,
the fictionalized name of the author's father:

It had taken quite a while before the schoolteacher brought himself to accept
the word as yet another place-name. Like Isara. Or Kaura Namoda. That had
made him pause. What would the natives of Ashtabula think of that one? Or
Olomitutu? How did it sound in their ears? Even so, as a name for white people –
Ashtabula? This hand from beyond the seas had stretched the bounds of place-
naming beyond easy acceptance. What spirits had presided over the naming
ceremonies of such a place? A settlement was no different from a child, you
recognized its essence in the name. That was the problem – there was nothing
remotely European about the name Ashtabula! Or were Americans now far
removed from white stock and breeding? (*Isara*, 6)

The silent disquisition on naming and identity in this passage is not the
familiar one in contemporary critical theory on the vital link between
hegemonic consolidation of power and its almost limitless capacity to
entrench itself through the capacity to "own" things and control relationships by acts of naming;[19] rather, Yode's thoughts here belong to an
older Yoruba tradition embedded in Ifa divinatory lore which sees naming things, people and relationships "correctly" and "appropriately" as
flexibly linked to essence and fate.[20] It is this premise which leads Yode to
conjecture that Ashtabula could *not* possibly be a white American place-
name, unless of course white Americans had totally cut themselves off
from their natal stock in the "old countries" in Europe. But then that other
conception of naming and identity in contemporary cultural criticism
which hinges on power and domination is very much part of the deliberately ludic ensemble of tropes on naming that feature so extensively
in *Isara*. This particular conception actually structures the tensions and
antagonisms in the following passage from the fifth chapter of the work,
titled "Homecoming" where "home" stands for many things: Isara, the
natal village; locally produced goods and services in competition with

foreign, imported products; the educational and social policies of the
nationalist and reform movements in colonial West Africa:

First to call was the widow, Mrs. Esan, taking the fight to Akinyode for leaving
Morola behind. She had traveled from Saki with bales of *eleto etu* cloth and, with
great pride, samples of the Saki variant of the imported velvet *petùje*, whose influx
on the market had threatened the local weave from Iseyin and Saki. A former
trainee teacher under Soditan, she had imbibed some of his resentment at the
claims of this cloth, which the Lagosians had named, with such disloyalty, "the
cloth which eclipses *etù*." *Etù*, that noble cloth whose warp and weft spun the
very fabric of history of the Yoruba! Isolated in the Women's Training College
to which she had been posted, she thought often of this outrage wrought against
the local product by the insensitive elite of Lagos. It was bad enough that this
so-called *petùje* should command outrageous prices yet be so much sought-after
but to lord it, in addition, by the sheer power of naming, over a passive product
of undisputed worth – this was augmented thievery, aided and abetted by the
shameless children of the house! She was in charge of home crafts at the training
school, and aided by the weavers of Saki and Iseyin, she set up her looms in
the school, unraveled the velvet impostor along patterns borrowed from the
disparaged *etù*, then filled in the cotton yarns, based on the original color motifs.
The result was lighter, more porous, and therefore more suited to the climate.
She named it *èye etù* (151)

The little allegorical narrative in this passage must not go unexamined.
"Etu" is one of the brands of highly valued woven cloths, noted especially
for its rich texture. "Èye etù" ("glory of etù") which the intrepid Mrs.
Esan fashions as a counter to "petùje" ("the cloth which eclipses etu") is
made by unraveling color motifs from the "velvet foreign impostor" and
overlaying these with patterns borrowed from the traditional "etu" itself,
but with cotton yarns which make the entirely new product, "eye etu,"
"lighter, more porous and more suited to the climate." In other words, it is
an entirely new homemade product which is fashioned in response to the
claims of superiority of the imported foreign product. This means that,
parallel to the efficacies enabled by naming things through marshaling
the resources of language, there is a materiality, a referent in the world of
objects and relationships to which linguistic acts of naming relates. This
is radically different from the conception of the links between language
and identity in Yode's ruminations on Ashtabula as a place name, a
conception in which the potency of words and utterances inheres in the
order of nature itself and the secret, occult correspondences between the
essence of things and their names. *Isara* is a remarkable text in the way
it deploys these two radically different conceptions, not as the antithesis
of each other, but in both playful and utterly serious juxtapositions, the

valence of playfulness and seriousness depending on the person, the occasion, the challenge faced.

This factor surely lies behind the considerable difference in the profiles of "Essay" in *Aké* and Yode Soditan in *Isara*, even though these are profiles of the same person, the author's father. The latter profile is far more rounded since it belongs to a text that is, after all, a memoir of Yode Soditan and his generation. But even so, what makes the *Isara* profile more intriguing is the considerable amplification of the flashes of wit, great sense of humor, the vulnerabilities and unfulfilled professional and emotional yearnings of the author's father that we only dimly perceive in *Aké*. The "Essay" of that work is, within the constraints imposed by home, profession and familial obligations, supremely in control of everything, indeed cannot brook loss of control over environment and circumstance, as the incident of "Lemo" ("graft it back") involving the hapless teacher who helps himself to a flower stalk from Essay's garden, demonstrates. By contrast, Yode Soditan in *Isara* is in a much vaster "garden" where such control is impossible, for this is a "garden" linking the natal village to the colonized national territory and the wider world of the British empire and its European competitors. As with V.S. Naipaul's *A House for Mr. Biswas*, *Isara* is the tribute of a famous son to a gifted father who did not have, could not have had, the opportunities available to his son and his son's generation.

It would not be an exaggeration to say that the entire narrative of *Isara*, as multifaceted as it is, turns on the exchange of letters between Yode Soditan and Wade Cudeback. Or more precisely, on the use of this correspondence – and the diverse tropes it provides – for powerful narrativizations of the continuities and discontinuities between the home and the world, indigenous and foreign. For prior to the inception of this correspondence with his American pen-pal, Yode had traveled out of the natal village and had become part of the "Ex-Iles," a vanguard of educators of the next generation. But Cudeback's letters take the process significantly further by instigating a radical awareness of the severely limited nature of the education purveyed in Yode's alma mater, St. Simeons and, more generally, the values and premises of British colonial education of the "natives" in the Nigerian protectorate. This awareness is precipitated by Yode's realization that in his replies to Cudeback's letters, he could barely match the latter's wealth of details regarding local history and places and sites of cultural significance precisely because, though an educated, gifted man, nothing in Yode's formal education had prepared him for acquiring such knowledge. The passage which

expresses this radical shift in Yode's sense of the conflicting epistemic
bases of individual and social selfhood is a crucial passage:

So where were the trails, the spots, the landmarks? Where could he take his senior
pupils – assuming he could persuade the mission to such a bold extension of
the history classroom? And yet why not? It was the kind of excursion that was
endorsed in principle by *The Nigerian Teacher* – so where could he take even a
handful of pupils on such an exercise? Then set them down to write the story
of their passage among the ghosts of their own history. He would pick out the
best essay and send it off to Wade Cudeback – yes, here is something in return
for your Magnetic Mountains and Reversing Falls and the marathon runner
Paul Revere. The thought depressed him: Where did the seminarian tutors of
St. Simeon's ever take him? Yet in his youth had he not often traversed those
grounds, those battle-contested grounds of Yoruba kingdoms? From Isarà to
Ilesa, at least four times a year – twice only as he grew older and became inured
to a prolonged exile – passing through Saki, Iseyin, and the ancient city of
Oyo, walking, cycling, entombed in a dust-filled rickety transport. Through the
years of training, were the seminarians ever taught to look? Had his youth truly
vanished through so much history without even knowing that one had to *look*!
(*Isara*, 12)

In the light of the musings of Yode Soditan in this passage, what
Cudeback's letters precipitated in Yode's consciousness is nothing akin
to the classic paradigm of knowledge acquisition encoded in Plato's myth
of the cave – coming out of the darkness of ignorance and illusion into
the sudden blinding light of truth and reality. Rather, Cudeback's letters,
symbolized in the meta-trope of "Ashtabula," divides Yode's consciousness of self, place and history into "unseeing" and "seeing" phases where
"seeing" signifies openness to all sources of knowledge. The emphasis
in this, it should be noted, is on the word all, for as a Westernized,
Christianized native *evolué*, Yode would normally be expected to follow the prevailing tendency to disparage local, indigenous sources of
knowledge. But as the passage indicates, his "seeing" phase entails re-
valorization of local sources of knowledge not in isolation, but in a dy-
namic, comparative relationship with foreign sources of knowledge. This
is why there is a much narrower gap in *Isara* between Yode and his father
Josiah, on the matter of Christianity versus "paganism" than in *Aké*. This
is also why Soyinka is somewhat inaccurate in declaring in his "Author's
Note" to *Isara* that Yode and his generation embarked on "an intense
quest for a place in the new order, and one of a far more soul-searching
dimension than the generation they spawned would later undertake (vi)."
On the evidence of what we actually encounter in *Isara* Yode and the
"Ex-Iles" are definitely more self-sacrificing than his son's generation of

the professional and literary elites of the post-independent nation-state
of Nigeria, but the soul-searching of the "interpreters" in the novel of
that title, and of Maren, the protagonist of Soyinka's autobiographical
memoir, *Ibadan,* is far more intense and psychically wrenching than what
we see of Yode and the "Ex-Iles" in *Isara.*

Isara is thus replete with inscriptions of diverse but related mini-
narratives and tropes of new modes of "seeing" which do not, *a priori,* exclude *any* source of knowledge. Some of these tropes and mini-narratives
are indescribably funny and intriguing, like the one involving the invocation of the "Spirit of Layeni" by Sipe Efuape, the most irrepressibly
venturesome of the "Ex-Iles." Even when, as in the following passage
where, in a consultation of the occult powers of the dead, the medium
happens to communicate in barely literate English, Efuape keeps his
options open:

*Invocation of Spirit of Layeni. On the Questions of the Proposed Mystic Services by T. S.
Onayemi*
Questions presented to the medium:

1. Is it wholly profitable if this (Name of Business) is done and should there be
   no course of shortening one's life?
2. What of sacrifice of commission to be duly offered every month?
3. Is there any rule which can cause any ineffect on its part?
4. What do you aware of the ingredient whether they are strong enough to be
   compounded or not?

Sipe could not resist an indulgent smile. It proved something – he was not
quite certain what – but a large proportion of successful businessmen was either
illiterate or semiliterate. He turned to the second sheet of paper, which contained
the answers to the first. It was headed:

Paper II. *Reply or Rejoinder of the Spirit to Questions as Numbered in Paper I.*

What a punctilious civil servant this Onayemi would have made! Obviously
wasted in the private sector, but no doubt he kept good books in his business.
Sipe already knew the answers by heart but went through them again:

Question 1. No least course to regret the experiment.
Question 2. Inconstancy of this will issue serious fruits. (*Isara,* 72–3)

The humor of this passage is nothing if not a veritable example of the
pervasive catachresis of the hybrid culture of colonized social and cultural spaces: both supplicant and spirit medium, in the light of changed
conditions in the colony, communicate not in Yoruba but in English,
in bad, risibly ungrammatical English; moreover, the written exchange

between them is presented to a highly literate middle class entrepreneur as inducement to also consult the occult powers of the illiterate spirit medium; our literate entrepreneur must thus decide whether he will be dissuaded by the bad grammar or be persuaded by the high recommendation of the spirit medium's powers of prophecy and divination, powers presumably not in any way compromised by infractions against the grammatical structures of the English language!

On a far more serious and controversial note, this openness to all sources of knowledge including the esoteric and the occult, entangle the narrative of *Isara* in very problematic textualizations of the fusion of, on the one hand, new ways of "seeing" introduced by colonialism and its contradictions with, on the other hand, old ways of "seeing" recuperable from precolonial sources. This attempted fusion is played out in diverse domains and levels like religion, herbal lore and medicine, business and the professions, and most dramatic of all, the institution of traditional precolonial governance embodied in such organs and institutions as the "oshugbo," the "ogboni" and the throne of the "Odemo." Deliberately, Soyinka as author, and through the mediation of Yode and his cohorts as protagonists, adopts a cultural nationalist stance in the conflicts and antagonisms between indigenous and foreign sources of knowledge, this being an open-ended nationalism that admits of a distant horizon signified in "Ashtabula," but then relocates that horizon at "home" in Isara. This nuanced, enlightened and multicultural nationalism is however subjected to occultation in the case of the struggle for succession to the throne of Isara.

This struggle is given considerable narrative space and is narrated in the most enthralling and dramatic sequences in *Isara*. And like the narration of the struggle of the Egba women in *Aké*, it ends the larger narrative of the entire memoir. The reader's sympathies are nudged in a not too subtle fashion in the direction of the camp of Akinsanya's candidacy, the radical trade unionist who is expected to bring to the traditionalism of the institution of kingship the progressive and enlightened consciousness he has garnered from his work and activities in Lagos. But the opposing camp of reactionary traditionalists and opportunists is backed by Agunrin Odubona, the most venerated warrior-hero of Isara's past struggles against local and British incursions into the Isara heartland, a fierce opponent of anything foreign, Western and new. Given his venerable status, it is recognized that if he speaks on behalf of the opposing camp at the palaver convened to adjudicate between the competing claimants, all is lost. Thus, Jagun, the next most venerated custodian of

Isara customs and traditions, decides that Agunrin Odubona "must be called home" and he goes into "osugbo," the "place where he cannot be reached," to accomplish this task. And in a demonstration of that conception of language which holds that a secret, inscrutable potency inheres in words and the act of naming, Agunrin Odubona dies at the very moment when his intervention at the palaver is about to take place and would have effected a reversal in the fortunes of the progressive, enlightened camp: he has indeed been "called home" by Jagun from the innermost recesses of the "heart of divination." Given the considerable narrative space that Soyinka gives to this concluding sequence in the narrative of *Isara*, some issues of authorial purpose and achieved effect in this sequence need to be addressed.

On one level, the problematic concluding narrative sequence of *Isara* means nothing more than a mimetic, realist inclusion of an important detail in the struggle for ascension to a traditional institution whose core values, even in a modern setting, include as much of ritual, occult beliefs and practices as they are also cognizant of rational awareness of, and pragmatic accommodation to changing times and conditions. At this level, Soyinka as author is being faithful to the mimetic demands of the representation of the event by showing accurately the two levels of the struggle as the Isara citizenry saw it and talked about it: a struggle between two shamans for the soul of a community still steeped in the values of shamanism, and the struggle of the community's new elites, one camp adamantly "traditionalist" and the other forward-looking and "progressive." But at a more problematic level, mimetic realism translates to epistemological obscurantism because in the very manner of his telling of the "calling home" of Agunrin Odubona, Soyinka seems to imply that the occult, inscrutable powers of "oshugbo" not only constituted "the heart of knowledge" and ethics in the traditional precolonial order (clearly a highly problematic postulate), in the changing, conjunctural space of colonizing modernity it also remains a decisive force for negotiating the dilemmas and contradictions of the new social order.

Isara is one of the very rare instances of a synthesis of simplicity and complexity in Soyinka's prose works. In its depiction of the acute sense of generational encounters with self and tradition under the pressure of dislocating historical change, it paves the way for the much bleaker and unsettling narrative of *Ibadan*, Soyinka's sequel to *Aké*. Nothing reveals the prefiguring of the acute dilemmas and crises of consciousness of the protagonist of *Ibadan* by the protagonist of the earlier text, *Isara*, more than the sober, realistic but grim summation of Yode Soditan, the author's father, of the daunting task that he and his generation face in their success in installing one of their number, "Saaki," the fiery trade unionist and nationalist on the throne of Isara. In the Agunrin Odubona episode, Soyinka, as author-narrator, goes out of his way to dwell on the intervention of the occult forces of "osugbo" in securing the victory of "Saaki." By contrast, the following passage recording Yode's thoughts on the herculean task they face in transforming Isara while retaining its best values and traditions, constitutes a dialogical and tonic commentary on the occultation of the social contract purveyed in Soyinka's idealization of his narration of the Agunrin-Jagun metaphysical conflict:

Akinyode Soditan turned his attention to Saaki's ramrod figure on the horse, yes, this was indeed homecoming. But would he truly "return to sender"? The tasks were daunting. Beneath the finery that surrounded them, the teacher was only too aware of bodies eaten by yaws, a fate that seemed to overtake an unfair proportion of Isara inhabitants. The children's close-cropped heads did not all glisten in the sun; tracks of ringworm ran circles throughout stubs of hair. The mobile clinic which serviced Isara and other towns in Remo district was infrequent. Sometimes, an expectant mother would deliver her baby on the roadside, having set off too late to reach the maternity clinic at Ode. Within that crowd, Akinyode's eyes caught sight of a goitre round a woman's neck, the size of a pawpaw; he knew the woman. The Ex-Ilés had once gathered funds to send her for an operation in Sagamu but she would have none of it. If anyone was going to cut her up, let it be done, she said, within Isara. Dysentery took the lives of far too many infants, even before they were weaned. It was a symbolic reminder, the clinic that had closed down for lack of staff. It was a good thing that Sipe had turned it into the headquarters from which Saaki would make his bid for the crown. There was no running water; not one faucet had ever been installed in Isara. The streets, swept abnormally clean for this day, were often like the interiors of far too many homes which remembered the feel of brooms only at the approach of Goriola. . . . Ah, yes, Saaki's shoulders might look straight enough; Akinyode saw them already bowed under the load of expectations. "Am I that heavy in your hands?" he had exclaimed with touching gratitude. It is Isara, Saaki, which alas, will weigh heavy in your hands. Must. And you dare expect no gratitude, only more demands, more expectations, and miracles, yes, nothing short of miracles. But no gratitude. That emotion, Akinyode felt often, did not exist in Isara dialect. (*Isara*, 258–9)

From one particular perspective – the perspective of a rigorous critique of the mystification of the forces, knowledges and energies which conserve or transform history and tradition – this long, sober and compassionate analysis of the enormously debilitating social malaise of village or small town communal life in colonial Africa should have no place in the narrative of *Isara*. If this is shifted around, the question arises: with this kind of acute consciousness of the determinate causes of rural poverty and underdevelopment in colonial Nigeria in the time of his father's generation, why does Soyinka give so much space and weight to the occult in the Agunrin-Jagun mystical narrative? Soyinka's answer to this would be that one knowledge matrix, one "explanation" does not exclude the other. Moreover, this question could only be put by readers or critics unfamiliar with, or unsympathetic to the productive aporias and antinomies of Soyinka's best works of drama, fictional and nonfictional prose and poetry which I have elsewhere explored extensively.[21]

If *Isara* is a work imbued with an acute sense of the complex interplay between the "home" and the "world," literally and metaphorically, *Ibadan* is an exile's book. It was written during the period of Soyinka's exile, between 1994 and 1998, from Sani Abacha's Nigeria. Of the author's many enforced exiles, there is no question that this was the most onerous, the most dislocating. As the whole world knows, Abacha relentlessly hounded Soyinka and other exiles who constituted a very effective external opposition to his regime, by placing a price on the head of Soyinka and some other exiles like Chief Anthony Enahoro and General Alani Akinrinade, and by having these men and others charged *in absentia* with the crime of treason, a charge carrying capital punishment. *Ibadan*, we are informed, began to take shape in the mind of the author at the uncertain beginning of this particularly onerous of Soyinka's many exiles:

I had long given up the President-Elect as a stubborn, irredeemable disciple of the philosophy of nonviolence and, early that morning, had been in a totally different kind of gathering. This also involved other fugitives from the mailed fists of the Nigerian military, including the ex-soldier who was introduced as having been involved in the attempted *putsch* of 22 April 1990 against Babangida. At the Swiss Cottage get-together, however I was struck by the contrast between the moods of the two gatherings—both resolute and committed, yes, but one upbeat while the other was somber. At the end of the earlier meeting, I knew I was about to set off on a long journey, had no idea how long it would be, or how it would end, but I found that I had come yet again to an acceptance of a less pacific principle of response as being justifiable in the course of terminating the *penkelemes* of Babangida's eight-year military despotism. I suppose that it is at such moments that one tends to look back on one's existence, and begin to accept the necessity of setting something down. Certainly, I began to think seriously of hoarding some exile time for the project. (*Ibadan*, xii–xiii)

This passage gives a very concrete, particular and different valence to the well-known enforced or voluntary exocentricity of the genre of "exile" writing because it speaks of the violence of the "penkelemes" of Nigeria's political pathologies. The word is a corruption of "peculiar mess" and was coined by the popular supporters of the demagogic, charismatic and populist politician, Adegoke Adelabu who had used the phrase "peculiar mess" in the regional assembly to characterize the violent and volatile fight-to-the-finish, take-no-prisoners political culture of the country's postcolonial rulers. As deployed in the quote, the word signifies the national political space as one that more or less makes exile as much an interior, spiritual condition as it is an experience of external, physical removal from the national homeland. This is why tropes of "home" and "homecoming" in *Ibadan* assume a considerably more alienating and dystopian expression than in *Isara* – or indeed any other work of Soyinka.

Written and published in the early 1990s but spanning the years 1946 to 1965, *Ibadan* is nonetheless hardly a work of recollection, as far as the sections dealing with the Nigerian political "penkelemes" are concerned. As Soyinka says in the book's Foreword: *"plus ça change?"* (xiv) Every single crisis from independence in 1960 to the 1990s repeats, in ever-widening and intensifying forms, that national political malaise of "penkelemes." *Ibadan*, on the author's own testimony, is meant to be a setting down by Soyinka of the facts and realities of this Nigerian "peculiar mess" in order to redeem the amnesia which, in his despairing view, the condition of "penkelemes" breeds in his compatriots.

The manner in which Soyinka sets about this task in *Ibadan* makes the book extremely fraught and controversial in the way in which it weaves a seamless, mutually reinforcing narrative between the "plot" of his own political coming of age story and that of the larger story of the coming into being and gradual unraveling of his new nation. And because much of this conflation of personal biography and national *telos* are in fact quarried from many of Soyinka's fictional and nonfictional works dealing with Nigeria's post-independence crisis, *Ibadan* reads far less like a work of recollection than one of, as the post-structuralists put it, "repetition and revision" of old and new texts. Indeed, *Ibadan* can be validly seen as deriving each of its two conflated subplots – the *Bildungsroman* of the coming of age of the protagonist hero; and the national mock-epic of rebirth after colonial bondage followed speedily by slow death throes – respectively from *Aké* and *Isara*. *Aké* had set the terms of the unique individuation which would shape the personality and identity of the adult artist as a visionary "okunrin ogun" (man of conflicts, of volatile controversies) while *Isara* had problematized the social coordinates of self in the expanding circles of family and kin, natal hometown together with the congeries of nation, continent, "race" and the world. Thus, the conflation in *Ibadan* of the subplot of an epic hero's life with the subplot of a national telos that is anything but heroic will, alas, give this work an undue, simplifying weight in future studies of the complex relationship between Soyinka's writings and his tumultuous career as a public intellectual.

The coming of age and growing into young adulthood subplot does not begin with the motif of the promethean hero. Indeed, it takes a while for the young, pint-sized boy who arrives at Government College, Ibadan, from Aké, Abeokuta, to assert himself decisively as a "top dog" among the usual hardened pack of bullies and tyrannical seniors. Like Stephen Dedalus in James Joyce's *Portrait of the Artist*, the first impressions and feelings away from home of Maren – the moniker which Soyinka assumes in this memoir – take shape around a sense of freedom to pursue promptings of spirit and imagination and the usual boyhood predilections for mischief. Except that the lighthearted nature of the narrative in the secondary school sections of the work also contain intimations of the writer-intellectual whose fate it would be to serve as the bell-weather for his country's diverse seasons of "penkelemes." As the following passage makes clear, it was in secondary school at Ibadan that an inkling of this special destiny began to take shape in Maren's consciousness:

Then the iconic names of nationalism – Azikiwe, Imoudu, Herbert Macaulay, Mbonu Ojike, Tony Enahoro – all came alive in Government College, Ibadan, bolder than the boulders of Apataganga. It was from Apata that he had played truant and traveled to Mushin in Lagos to listen to Imoudu's fiery oratory after the massacre of Iva Valley miners, and later to watch Hubert Ogunde's musical drama on the events, *Bread and Bullets*, and be no longer surprised that the colonial Government would ban the play and imprison Hubert Ogunde for his daring. And then, of course, his own bloodying in numerous petty battles with bullies and the trivial and not-so-trivial causes, but all passionate, of life-and-death magnitude on a secondary school scale: from the very first entry through those gates he had guessed that the place would mark him for life. There was something about Ibadan itself, a definite feeling, both restraining and exciting, that he had taken away with him after his final year in school, a year earlier than more than half the class, since he was one of those not selected to participate in the post School Certificate year, newly introduced.

This feeling was that it would not be Lagos, where he had first earned a living and which might therefore claim to have turned him into an adult; and that it would not be Abeokuta where, after all, he had been born; nor Isara, his second home and birthplace of his truculent grandfather; nor indeed any place that he had yet to visit, but Ibadan itself, with its rusted arteries, its ancient warrens and passions and intrigues, that would confirm what he had begun to be apprehensive about, in himself. Others might give it different names, but he was inclined to see it as having a preternatural affinity to a lightning rod. (*Ibadan*, 16–17)

The suggestion in this passage that if Maren does not seek trouble – or "penkelemes" – trouble will seek him out must be distinguished from the outsize promethean heroism that later in the narrative dominates Maren's role as the protagonist of this memoir. For by a deft weaving of compelling details of character, coincidence and portents, Soyinka convincingly presents Maren as the prototype of "okunrin ogun," the quintessential human magnet for conflict and dissension. This is continuous with, but quite distinct from Maren's other qualities that are captured in the series of prescient nicknames which his godmother had given him in his boyhood days at Aké: "okunrin jeje" ("gentle, peaceable man") and "Otolorin" ("the one who walks apart/alone"). Significantly, the adult Maren accepts these names and their encoded attributes, but tells his friend Komi upon his arrival from his five-year sojourn in Britain: "I can (now) get down to the business of re-naming myself (*Ibadan*, 21)."

This business of fashioning the self through acts and embodied attitudes which are precipitated by the pressures and crises of the newly independent nation gives *Ibadan* its defining narrative texture, positively but also problematically. The most positive, most affecting and especially informative for students of Soyinka's writings are the renderings of self-constitution relating to Maren's brand of idealistic, radical artistic and cultural activities. Accounts of the contexts in which the series of sketches grouped under the title *Before the Blackout* were staged, of the circumstances which made *Dance of the Forests* an unwelcome item in the official program of the independence celebrations (67–68), of the incredible gathering of talent, energy and idealism in the theatre companies "Nineteen Sixty Masks" and "Orisun Theatre," these provide the only unambiguously positive and fulfilling spiritual "home" for Maren in the entire narrative. This much is indeed implicitly admitted by Maren himself in his rueful observations on the composition and work of those two theatre companies:

If no one else missed the Nineteen Sixty Masks after it gradually dissolved in the seventies and gave way to Orisun Theatre, the *suya* vendors of Sagamu surely did, for Orisun Theatre, tighter, younger and less experienced than the Masks but full-time, more flexible and more (politically) adventurous, was to stay in one place, Ibadan, basing most of its activities on the Mbari Arts Club, right in the teeming heart of Gbagi market and the surrounding streets that were only an extension of the market.

It was exhilarating, and it did mean for him the long-dreamt-of homecoming – what more could a theatre-obsessed mind desire? The ingredients were all present – a creative reunion, experimentation and innovation. The creative energy around him appeared inexhaustible; not even the already evident profligacy of the politicians could deplete *that* – it was mercifully beyond their reach. The complexity and physical demands of *A Dance* extracted from the participants resources that most admitted they had never suspected in themselves, being long accustomed to a standard fare of J.B. Priestly, Galsworthy or Sheridan, the occasional Bernard Shaw, the operettas of Gilbert and Sullivan, and the genteel volunteerism of amateur productions . . .

Patrick Ozieh, a petroleum engineer; Olga Adeniyi-Jones, of a long-indigenised 'expatriate' line, and an accomplished contralto; Ralph Opara, Yemi Lijadu, Segun Olusola, all broadcasters; Funmi Asekun, of ample proportions, who soon abandoned stage appearances but continued to effectively 'mother' the company; Francesca Pereira, of an old Brazilian stock, a mellifluous soprano . . . Giaus Anoka, a schoolteacher, as was Dapo Adelugba . . . Then the fledglings, Tunji Oyelana, Femi Fatoba, Sola Rhodes, Yewande Akinbo, Segun Sofowote, Femi Euba, Wale Ogunyemi, Jimi Solanke and others who would form the core of the new Orisun Theatre, less the ones that got away, the parents barring the gates against their wards . . .

No matter, Orisun Theatre continued to draw nourishment from the teats of the Nineteen-Sixty Masks, whose individual and collective pedigrees and backgrounds were every bit as prominent as the claims of the 'colonial aristocrats', as variegated as those of the nation itself, the company's internal fusion and generous bond of fellowship seemed to reflect the nation's ambitions to weld together such apparent incompatibles. Alas, in that regard, there was no question about which had the greater success. (*Ibadan*, 68–70)

Given the crucial fact that "homecoming," or more precisely, the impossibility of a fulfilling, creative and transformative "homecoming," structures the entire narrative of *Ibadan*, this passage which almost rapturously celebrates "bond of fellowship" within the membership of the Nineteen-Sixty Masks and Orisun Theatre stands in stark contrast to the innumerable passages which recount the actions and experiences of the groups or formations in which Maren sought a sort of political-spiritual homecoming. Moreover, while Soyinka in the quote gives vivid, individualizing touches to his reminiscence of members of both theatre groups, almost without exception, the members of the bands and circles of Maren's followers and supporters are not named, or they are shadowy in relation to the very visible prometheanism of Maren. This pattern of course has its own poignancy: the struggle of Maren to achieve moral and spiritual autonomy from the death-of-the-spirit encroachments of family and kin is nothing if not exemplary, especially in a neocolonial setting where these encroachments have distinct compulsions toward petty-bourgeois conformism about them. The resistance to these compulsions pose a large ethical dilemma for the radical artist: how might a gifted, visionary writer and intellectual remain true to his or her vision and impulses, goals and objectives, if he or she cannot create an autonomous space which cannot, must not be breached by the often well-intentioned but philistine, domesticating importunations of the extended family, and how might that autonomous space be created without exerting great, emotional turmoil in the lives of individual members of one's family networks? What Maren tells his flabbergasted parents at one of several confrontations with family and kin that are narrated in the book shows the scope of the spiritual homelessness which would later serve to accentuate and distort Maren's prometheanism: "the university is more secure than the throne of Isara" (86). Later on, of course, Maren would be stripped of this illusion that the university system in Nigeria could be a free zone uncontaminated by the social contradictions of the academic elites of the new nation-state and could be a "home," a redoubt against the forces of reaction and divisiveness.

This process of profound disillusionment intensifies as first University College, Ibadan, then the University of Ife, to be followed by the University of Lagos, succumbed to the corrosive forces of chauvinistic ethnic politics, opportunism and moral and intellectual cowardice. One moment of Maren's disillusionment on this point is expressed in his ruminations after writing a letter withdrawing permission from the Ibadan University Press to publish a collection of his plays. The letter was written in protest against the capitulation of the university, administration and main academic body inclusive, to the retrograde forces then beginning to gradually entrench themselves in state and society in the new nation. This was apparently consummated through a strategy of wiping out opposition in the country at large by first eroding the autonomy of the universities and thereby eliminating the refuge available to the campus-based radicals and dissidents. Writing this letter brought a clarity of vision to Maren, but the relief which he felt was, ironically, an intensification of his feelings of spiritual homelessness:

It was all over, and he was glad. He had no constituency home to go to but one could be found, could be built up from nothing, or built around, only this time with no expectations, no baggage of ideals to attempt to impose on such a waystop – which was what it would ever be, no matter how much of a destination it gave the illusion of being. He felt consoled that it had happened so early, before he put down roots in an arbitrary choice of home. Two years had passed since he stepped onto the tarmac at Ikeja Airport, the end of a five-year absence. His Land Rover had taken him through at least two-thirds of the country, probing its ritual tissues for a contemporary theatre vision, or perhaps a mere statement of being. Despite it all, he was left with the strange sensation of being poised on the nation's airspace all over again, floating in a cloud of the uncertain and unknowable, wondering yet again what homecoming promised or would bring. (196–7)

In the closing chapters of *Ibadan*, Soyinka provides an account of how Nigeria lurched from one crisis to another between 1962 and 1965. This account, in the main, is a version of the "official script" of the making and unmaking of Nigeria held by most of the country's progressives and radicals, especially the Southern-based formations and individuals. This "script" holds that the political and administrative arrangements put in place by the departing British to ensure the hegemony of the most conservative political forces in the country – the ruling, neotraditional, neofeudal elites of the North as unchallengeable senior partners in a coalition with pseudo-bourgeois forces in the other regions of the country – began to unravel in these years, causing a desperate backlash comprising the use of the judiciary for repression and of the police and security forces for intimidation and terror. Furthermore, the "script" reads Nigeria's mid-1960s "penkelemes" as an expression of the fact that effective opposition to the fascist backlash resided in the uneasy and always tenuous alliance of the spontaneous militancy of the rural and urban poor, random and periodic work-stoppages and strikes precipitated by progressive elements within the trade union movement, disruption of the legislative process by the rump of the progressive, social-democratic opposition parties, and protests, rallies and demonstrations organized by the academic champions of popular causes.

Soyinka's version of this same turbulent history and politics, as presented in the closing chapters of *Ibadan*, differs significantly from this "script." In Soyinka's version, after the sellout of many leaders of the labor movement which led to the collapse of the General Strike of 1964, and after the imprisonment of Chief Awolowo and other prominent leaders of the Action Group in the treason trials of that year, no effective opposition emerged to a naked, vicious fascist consolidation of the reactionary alliance of the Northern and Western regional governments, except perhaps in the East whose regional government was still controlled by one of the populist, bourgeois-democratic opposition parties, the NCNC. Soyinka's version is vigorously insistent on this point: many of the academic "radicals" were textbook revolutionaries, and the opposition parties outside the East were in disarray, and at any rate had no credible response whatsoever to the state terrorism being unleashed on the country. Into this void steps Maren, relying mostly on rehabilitated lumpen and criminal elements and a few academic radicals who coalesced around the ideological and ethical centre provided by Maren's exemplary heroism. The last four chapters of *Ibadan* show Maren picking up the pieces of the dispersed, fragmented opposition forces and giving the consolidated fascist leadership and their agents the fight of their lives, sometimes using their own tactics of intimidation and terror through thugs, and more refined underground conspiratorial, vanguardist tactics. This last, Maren claims, he uses to foment the famous rural and urban mass revolts of 1964 and 1965 known as "Weti e" ("Douse him with petrol and set him aflame!"). This grandiloquent claim that he, Maren, was the sole planner and formentor of the popular uprisings in western Nigeria in 1964 and 1965 runs counter to the mainstream view of most Nigerian progressives that those revolts were spontaneous irruptions of popular anger and resentment that were never effectively organized into any strategic shape until the emergence of the Agbekoya uprisings during the Nigerian civil war.

Incontestably, many of the incidental and circumstantial facts on which Soyinka bases this account of the Nigerian crisis of the mid-1960s will be challenged, and perhaps refuted by other future accounts of this period of Nigerian history. Indeed, this Soyinkan version is somewhat undermined by the fact that *Ibadan* contains a myriad of minor errors of fact, chronology and detail, all of which could easily have been corrected by assiduous editorial work on the manuscript before publication.[22] These minor errors apart, there are more substantial questions of authorial taste and judgment provoked by this account of his heroic role in the Nigerian "penkelemes" of the mid-1960s, an account which indeed marks the denouement of the extraordinarily moving, eloquent and problematic memoir, *Ibadan*.

It is significant that each of Soyinka's three books of biographical and autobiographical memoir, *Aké*, *Isara* and *Ibadan*, ends with a long concluding section which, in racy, dramatic and action-filled narrative, tells of a sociopolitical struggle against the entrenched forces of reaction, corruption or terror. In *Aké*, this is the famous Egba Women's Revolts of 1947; in *Isara*, it is the struggle for succession to the throne of Isara, a struggle which pits progressive, modernizing elites against reactionary traditionalists; in *Ibadan*, as we have seen, it is the struggle of one man, Maren, supported only by a small band of friends, colleagues and

followers, against the consolidated forces of rapine, lawlessness and terror that gradually and relentlessly made a bid for absolute power in the
Western and Northern regions and in the central government before the
interventions of the two military coups of 1966. Because Soyinka, as author of *Ibadan*, is unable to distance himself from Maren, the protagonist
of the narrative who, after all, is none other than his Doppelganger, the
artistic control which he is able to exert on the materials in the concluding sections of *Aké* and *Isara* is almost completely absent in *Ibadan*. On this
point, it is indeed instructive to compare the middle sections of the narrative of this memoir with that concluding section which tells of Maren's
herculean battles against the nascent fascism of elements of the Nigerian
post-independence political class. In the former, in episodes drawn from
his high school days at the famous Government College, Ibadan, Soyinka
writes convincingly and movingly of the fear, confusion and also exhil-
aration of standing up to bullies and taking a stand on controversial
issues in religion, science and ethics which often went against the grain
of the arid, philistine conformism of his peers. By contrast, some of the
escapades narrated in the concluding sections of *Ibadan* which highlight
the promethean heroism of Maren are either unbelievably melodramatic
or plainly lacking in credibility, taste or good judgment. Perhaps the most
flawed of these is the incident at Cairo airport where, as we are told in
a mini-narrative that reads very much like an episode in the screenplay
of a Bruce Lee film, Soyinka in a bizarre physical combat singly floored
and incapacitated four of eight men armed with heavy wooden cudgels.
(308–12) No less wondrous is the episode which tells of the invasion of
Soyinka's home by a gang of thugs and minions of the ruling political
party of S.L. Akintola, Premier of the Western region. This incident is
told with great relish; it narrates how Maren, Soyinka's doppelganger
in this memoir, fooled this gang into thinking that he had the firepower
to match theirs, the murderous invaders fleeing in terrified, cowardly
disarray. The narrative, already creakily melodramatic, becomes over-
strained when the narrator actually tells of conversations between the
terrified men and the man who sent them on their mission, all expressing
their awe at the demonic power of their would-be victim-turned attacker,
these being things Maren simply could not have been privy to (*Ibadan*,
230–9).

These flaws in *Ibadan* stand in high relief against the fact that there is
much in this memoir to match the best writings of Soyinka himself and
of the genre of autobiographical memoirs. There are indeed many sections which consolidate the claim of *Ibadan* to being considered a lasting

contribution to the genre of modern African and English-language autobiographical memoir. Particularly notable in this regard are sections which, in fragmentary and discontinuous vignettes, detail the single-mindedness with which Maren seeks to retain his own unique spiritual and moral selfhood and protect its intuitions and insights while at the same time remaining deeply and irrevocably responsive to diverse life-enhancing and affirming values and projects. These include the work of creation with other writers, artists and performers; genuine solicitude for the disenfranchised; and permanent engagement of causes promoting nation-weal and the unity and progress of the African continent.

If *Ibadan*, with its achievements and serious flaws, shows the formidable challenge of writing about the self where that self is both a vital participant in, and a compelling witness to great sociopolitical upheavals, *The Open Sore of a Continent: A Personal Narrative of the Nigerian Crisis* shows Soyinka rising brilliantly to this challenge of writing the self while writing history. The Soyinka that we encounter in this book speaks as much in his own idiosyncratic and inimitable voice as he does in the exteriorized voices of his fictionalized surrogates or doubles in the other memoirs. This is because *Open Sore* is a passionate affirmation of popular energies and a celebration of elemental bodily and cultural solidarities as bulwarks against those reifying abstractions of the modern African nation-state like "territorial integrity" and "national sovereignty" which are used by tyrants and oligarchs to justify and rationalize their misrule, their iron-fisted grip on power.

Open Sore is an extended meditation, in three essays and a postscript, on the "birth" and "death" agonies of the Nigerian nation in its transfixion throughout most of the 1980s and 1990s as a vast military camp under the regimes of Generals Buhari, Babangida and Abacha. Beyond these regimes, the book's purview extends to the corrupt police state created by the civilian government of Shehu Shagari (1979–83). In Soyinka's reckoning, at the centre of this historic perspective on military and civilian autocracy in Nigeria are two particularly portentous events. These are the "pacification" of Ogoniland in the Niger delta by units of the Nigerian army, together with the execution of Ken Saro-Wiwa and the other eight Ogoni environmental activists on November 10, 1995, and the annulment of the results of the presidential elections of June 12, 1993.[23] These two events take on significance for Soyinka because to him, they showed in the clearest manner possible, the destruction unto nullity of all the most hopeful auguries and portents of egalitarian, humane and multicultural "nation-being," all in the name of abstractions like "federal

character," and "indivisible national unity." Given Soyinka's predilection
for the metaphysics of the ineffable and the nuomenal, it comes as a surprise to find that all the "auguries" and "portents" whose nullification is
mourned in this book are rooted in the concrete solidary movement of
the mass of ordinary Nigerians acting across the real and manufactured
divisions which had always kept them apart and therefore susceptible to
manipulation by political opportunists and nation-wreckers. This is why
in its most moving passages, *Open Sore* celebrates the author's apparently
newfound faith that it is the will of the Nigerian people and not that of
Ogunnian prometheans that will sound the death knell of military and
civilian despotism. This perspective even shows through in Soyinka's
lyricization of the "heroic" virtues of patience and discipline displayed
by the Nigerian people – not generally credited with these virtues! – in
their response to the stratagems deployed by the Babangida regime to
prevent the elections of June 1993 from taking place, or to make sure
that if the elections did take place, it would be so hopelessly botched
by deliberately organized confusion and mayhem that its cancellation
would be unquestionable. Thus, while it is true that *Open Sore*, in characteristic Soyinkan penchant for mystical experiences and phenomena,
also celebrates, often with great poetic license, imponderable "auguries"
of nature, accident and circumstance in the defeat of Babangida's efforts
to render the June 12, 1993 elections a non-event, it is really the intervention of a popular electoral will across the length and breadth of Nigeria
that the writer credits with his sense of the "birth" of the nation on that
date. Except that in much of its contents, this book is not about a *birth*,
but an aborted delivery leading to a stillborn entity.

Open Sore is a deeply affirming and challenging book in many ways.
This point needs to be strongly emphasized because the final, closing
vision of the book is a despairing one, since its core thesis about the
nation-building project that is Nigeria is that all the crises prior to June
1993 should be seen as either "birth pains" or "death throes." The most
debatable aspects of *Open Sore* derive from its rhetorical, metaphorical
extemporizations on the motifs and images of death and mortality which
provide some of the book's most memorable passages and insights: the
death of compatriots like Tai Solarin, Ken Saro-Wiwa and the other
Ogoni activists, the hundreds slaughtered in Lagos in the protests against
the annulment of the June 12 electoral mandate, and the "death" of
the passionate aspirations of the Nigerian people for a better life, for
recognition of their sense of innate dignity and self-worth against the
negations of naked, brutish power. All these literal and psychological

"deaths" presage, for Soyinka, the "death" of the nation since, nations are made of people, not abstractions. But Soyinka does overextend the metaphor of birth and death with respect to June 12, 1993. In sacralizing this date as the unique, originary moment of the "birthing" of Nigeria, Soyinka is of course exercising a writer's prerogative, much as he had done with the figure of the Half-Child as a symbol of the newly independent nation in his first major play, *A Dance of the Forests*, significantly his contribution to the Independence celebrations in 1960. But the poetic playwright is in great tension with the theorist of radical democratic politics here, for except in sutured, symbolic narrativizations of the life and demise of imagined nations, no one single, liminal and "auspicious" event or moment can serve as the birth or even conception, either of a truly democratic polis, or of the nation itself. This observation needs to be understood in all its complexity: the elections of June 12, 1993 were the freest and most democratic elections ever held in Nigeria, even if those elections were conducted under the aegis of a military dictatorship which did everything possible to prevent free and fair elections and, ultimately annulled the elections on the fateful day of June 22, 1993. Thus, there are concrete political and strategic considerations for regarding June 12, 1993 as a watershed in Nigeria's political evolution and these are open to principled debate and discussion. Soyinka in the book does in fact extensively engage some of these factors, but primarily within an over-poeticized discourse which sacralizes June 12, 1993 and this tends to move the event outside and beyond such discussion and debate.

To say this is to give acknowledgment to two underlying features of Soyinka's political prose which make his observations and reflections on the projects of nation-building and democratization in Africa and the developing world in this particular book one of the most important interventions in recent debates on postnationalism and civil society in postcolonial societies of the developing world. One of these defining features of Soyinka's political prose is the brilliant use that he makes of anecdotal, unwritten, unofficial "scripts" and discourses. As he says himself at the beginning of the second essay in the book, "The Spoils of Power: the Buhari-Shagari Casebook," it is necessary "to provide pertinent space for the anecdotal material of history, far too often neglected (61)." Arguably, some of the best written and the most moving passages in the book are the sharp, memorable vignettes of the outsize villains, opportunists, and cynical power-mongers on the one hand, and on the other hand, the selfless altruists and patriots. What is involved here is perhaps Soyinka's impressive acuity of vision in his attentiveness to the role of paradox, chance and contingency in human affairs, especially given the fact that these typically find little space in "scientific" and even journalistic expostulations on politics and the political. The second and far more contentious feature of Soyinka's political writing, is his all-encompassing investment in the decisive role of subjective, voluntaristic forces in history, and arising from this, his over-valorization of will and volition in the confrontation of human subjects with political and social calamities of the magnitude imposed, at one level of macro-political structures, on Nigeria and much of the African continent by the run of military and civilian despots who have dominated political governance in the entire post-independence period. The specific expressions and consequences of this privileging of voluntarism by Soyinka in writing the self and writing the nation and the continent into history are taken up for further discussion in the concluding chapter of this study.

CHAPTER 6

Poetry, versification and the fractured burdens of commitment

The roots of Soyinka's English are uncompromisingly Anglo-Saxon rather than Hellenic or Latinate because they represent for him the closest approximation to the primal roots of Yoruba cultic diction. But the virtue of 'originality' lies not merely in its freshness or quaintness but indeed in its vitality, in its ability to evoke in the mind a memory of the dynamism of original Yoruba. For Soyinka, particularly in those poems in which legend, tradition and ancestral custom constitute the internal structure of his poetry, is in fact a translator. That is to say that to anyone who even vaguely understands the tonalities of the Yoruba language . . . the structure and fertile ambiance of Soyinka's English derives, in fact, more from the Yoruba than from the English.

Stanley Macebuh, "Poetics and the Mythic Imagination"

More than three decades after the publication of Soyinka's first volume of poetry, *Idanre and Other Poems*, the preface poem to that volume now appears as a reflexive metacommentary that is radically at variance with generally held critical opinions on the contents of the volume itself and, more generally, on Soyinka's reputation as a poet. A quatrain without end-rhymes, the wistful etherialism of this preface poem suggests a beguilingly harmonious, even trouble-free pact between the poet and his muse, and between the poet and his audience that virtually no critic now associates with Soyinka's writings, least of all his poetry. The poem is short enough to be quoted in its entirety:

> Such webs as these we build our dreams upon
> To quiver lightly and to fly
> The sun comes down in stately visit
> The spider feeds him pearls (*IOP*, 8)

The "webs" of the first line obviously and unambiguously – a very rare occurrence in Soyinka's poetry – refers to the poems we shall encounter in the volume, the "spider" of the last line standing for the poet who has spun these webs. The third line of the poem, which tells of the sun coming down in "stately visit" to the poet, suggests the shamanistic power of poetry to move even the world of nature and the elements; thus, the image seems to be in accordance with the strong orphic strain of much of Soyinka's poetry. However, the suggestion of a beatific visitation of the Muse is at odds with the tumultuous, bloody passage rites and the contradictoriness that the title poem of the volume, "Idanre," give to Soyinka's muse, Ogun. As we have learned from Soyinka and his critics over the decades, this Yoruba god of war and lyric poetry, of destruction and creation, is not a Muse who comes to his favored devotees in the quiescent majesty of an untroubled royal visitation. Even far more incongruous to what we have come to associate with Soyinka's poetry in the decades since the publication of *Idanre and Other Poems* is the conceit in the second line of this preface poem which speaks both of the poetic act and its end product as means with which "to quiver lightly and to fly." Many of the poems in the sections titled "of birth and death" and "for women" are poems of tenderness and whimsy, but they do not evince the tremulousness evoked by the "lightly quivering" imagery, just as the thundering stanzas of "Idanre," the title poem, are anything but ethereal. Indeed, the passage rites which literally and symbolically organize the poems in the volume receive their distinctive texture from brooding, strife-torn myths, from landscapes of grief, decay and alienation, and from tortured quests for wholeness and regeneration.

In thus presenting us with a Soyinka we do not now easily recognize, this preface poem in *Idanre* in effect shows that the critical act is often wise only belatedly, prescient only when time and accumulated commentaries enable a wide-angled view of the forest of the total poetic corpus containing individual "trees" of single poems or clusters of poems. For if the particular poetic "tree" which this preface poem represents does not look anything like the "forest" of vintage Soyinka poetry, this is neither a cause for regret – "why aren't most of his poems this accessible and coherent" – nor for gratified and uncritical celebration – "who would have thought, from this annunciation of the preface poem to his first volume of poems, that he would go on to write poems which would attempt nothing short of the exploration of the self-encounter of a whole nation and an entire continent in the modern world, at both the most private levels and the most public contexts?" Rather, what this preface poem in Soyinka's first published volume of poetry nudges us towards is a preparedness, in a fresh critical review and evaluation of the Nigerian writer's corpus of poetry, to encounter many poems which read nothing like the Soyinka we have come to expect from the accumulated critical commentary of more than three decades.

In the light of this critical orthodoxy on Soyinka's poetry, taking a measure of his merits and stature as a poet often depends on which side the critic or interpreter stands in a critical line which has been drawn in the sand on the question of the alleged forbidding obscurity, complexity or inaccessibility of much of the long and short pieces in his five volumes of poetry. Behind the formalism of this strong divide in the critical reception of Soyinka's poetry is the apparent consensus on the presumed burden of the modern African poet to both her African roots and her audience. For the underlying premise of this consensus is the view that "complexity" or "obscurity" constitutes a form of cultural deracination, a divorce from the nourishing wellsprings of traditional oral poetry and from the often asserted public vocation of poetry in Africa and the developing world.[1] It is perhaps on account of this factor that though he has not particularly cared to refute the charge of the "obscurity" or "complexity" of his poetry, a spirited disavowal of the charge of divorce from oral, communal roots and from a public vocation is a theme that recurs in nearly all of the three or four essays of Soyinka dealing exclusively or substantially with poetry and the search for a vital poetics in modern African writing.[2] We find this refutation in a forceful articulation in Soyinka's careful delineation of the features and qualities of traditional African poetry in the following passage from his essay, "Neo-Tarzanism: the Poetics of Pseudo-Tradition":

Traditional African poetry is not merely those verses which, being easiest to translate, have found their way into anthologies and school texts; it is not merely those lyrics, which, because they are favorites at Festivals of the Arts haunted by ethnologists with tape recorders, supply the readiest source-material for up-rooted academics; nor is it restricted solely to the praise of yams and gods, invocations of blessings and evocations of the pristine. Traditional poetry is all of this; it is however also to be found in the very technique of riddles, in the pharmacology of healers, in the utterance of the possessed medium, in the enigmas of diviners, in the liturgy of divine and cultic mysteries . . . in the unique temper of world comprehension that permeates language for the truly immersed – from the Ifa priest to the haggler in the market, inspired perhaps by economic frustration! (*ADO2*, 293)

The ringing assertion in this apologia that poetry transcends the generic boundaries of versification, that it finds habitation and expression in diverse specialized and non-specialized media and contexts was calculated to startle most of Soyinka's academic critics who, on the question of his merits as a poet, have tirelessly inveighed against what they consider the overspecialized nature of his poetry, and consequently, against the alleged inaccessibility of many poems in the five published volumes beside the popular and endlessly anthologized pieces like "Telephone Conversation" and "Abiku." This assertion by Soyinka of the non-specialized, protean nature of traditional African poetry in particular and all poetry in general, flies in the face of the fact that, with one or two notable exceptions, neither the defenders nor the accusers in the charge of "obscurity" and "inaccessibility" in Soyinka's poetry have ever brought into their critical purview the pervasive presence of poetry, metrical and non-metrical, in both the dramatic and prose works of the Nigerian author.[3]

The five volumes of Soyinka's formal poetry that are discussed in this chapter singly and collectively participate in a dialectical articulation between the elegantly conventional and the bracingly experimental in the exploration of serious and pressing issues specific to the negations and contradictions of postcolonial Africa but of vital pertinence to the more general expressions of what many contemporary thinkers have called the malaise of modernity.[4] These works are *Idanre and Other Poems* (1967), *A Shuttle in the Crypt* (1972), *Ogun Abibiman* (1976), *Mandela's Earth* (1988) and *Outsiders* (1999). The main burden of the discussion of these works in this chapter is a shift of attention in the critical discourse on Soyinka's poetry away from the polarized debate on "complexity" and "obscurity," considered as independent, abstract and determining vectors. This shift is enabled by an intertextual comparison of the poetry *in* Soyinka's dramatic works with the poetry *of* his formal verse writings. I shall in effect base my readings of Soyinka's poetry on a central, organizing thesis. This is the thesis that a stand for or against "complexity" or "obscurity" should not be the ultimate or overdetermining factor in taking a measure of Soyinka's significance as a poet since, in much of his dramatic poetry and formal verse, we are often taken beyond "obscurity" as complex, evanescent experiences and modes of being and thought are given formal poetic expression of considerable lyrical force and memorable articulation. If this is the case, we are forced to look elsewhere for a point of departure in our assessment of the nature and scope of our author's poetic output. This point of departure I would locate in the dialectical tension between "poetry" and "versification" in Soyinka's writings in this genre. "Poetry" here implies a more inclusive, less generically bounded category, whereas "versification" pertains to matters of technical craftsmanship and highly differentiated techniques and idioms requiring an appropriate degree of technical expertise, learnedness and specialism. Stated differently, the distinction being urged here is perhaps captured in the contention that if all good or great poets are perforce obliged to be good or great versifiers, not all good or great versifiers make good poets. Applied to the subject of our present discussion, the line of departure established by this dialectic of "poetry" and "versification" indicates that while Soyinka is both a poet and a versifier, the great controversies generated by his volumes of poetry have tended mostly to focus on issues and problems of versification, of technique and diction to the extent that they allegedly impede or confound readers' efforts at sympathetic engagement with our author's exhilarating and challenging poetry. To adequately account for the workings of this dialectic in our evaluation of Soyinka's merits as a poet, it is necessary, I repeat, to move mostly within, but also beyond the confines of the volumes of his formal verse. Thus, what follows is a juxtaposition of discussion of the poems collected in the five volumes of collected poetry with critical forays into the pervasive inscriptions of poetic utterance, design and vision in some of Soyinka's dramas. In practical terms, the focus in the discussion in the rest of this chapter will be primarily on Soyinka's first two volumes of poems, *Idanre* and *Shuttle* and the fifth and last volume, *Outsiders*. This is because these first two volumes between them contain the bulk of Soyinka's published poetry. The third and fourth volumes, *Ogun Abibiman*, *Mandela's Earth*, comprise poems which are based for the most part on realities and events in southern Africa. *Ogun Abibiman* and *Mandela's Earth* contain poems which in effect reprise, in other human and social spaces, the themes and not a little of the technical and stylistic armory of the poetry of the first two volumes.

The impressive work of scholarly reconstruction of the gestative origins of the poems collected in *Idanre and Other Poems* that Robert Fraser executes in his seminal study, *West African Poetry: A Critical History* is as good as any point from which to start a reappraisal of this first volume of Soyinka's published poetry. Two important facts carefully uncovered by Fraser are particularly apposite here. One is the fact that the ordering of the seven sequences of poems in the volume does not correspond to a chronological pattern since the last poem in the volume, the title poem "Idanre," was in fact written before many of the poems which sequentially precede it in the collection. Second, Fraser highlights the broad biographical connection of the young Soyinka's personal life and burgeoning artistic career with many of the poems in this first collection of his poetry. Thus, according to this meticulous scholar-critic, as Soyinka wrote these early poems – and the dramas and essays of his early career – he was going through the normal business of living at that stage of life – roughing it out in Paris as a student on the edge of pecuniary insolvency, getting into and out of a first marriage, having children, returning home to Nigeria and, most important of all, attempting to achieve a breakthrough in the fusion of his aesthetic ideas with a morality of art which could adequately respond to the powerful, conflicting "nation-building" currents of integration and fragmentation in his newly independent country. Many of the poems in the volume thus grew out of, and in some respects poetically transpose facets of the familial, social and aesthetic experiences of Soyinka at that stage of his career. Most important of all, Fraser remarks on how the gestative pains of the title poem, "Idanre," are particularly notable, if only because they have largely been ignored by most of Soyinka's critics:

The title poem . . . poured forth in one day as the result of a transforming spiritual awakening, a coming together of many strands, early in 1965. Though later publicly recited in London, it was in no sense a commissioned piece, but rather the culmination of a process of fusion binding together particles in the poet's mental make-up which had, as his manuscript note to the typescript implies, until that time obstinately refused to cohere. (Fraser, 233)

We can see from this vital information why Soyinka would interrupt the chronological sequence of the poems in the volume and place "Idanre" at the apex of his first collection of poems since it represented a defining moment not only for his poetry but for all his writing. And in this respect, it is significant that Soyinka excludes from the published prefatory remarks to "Idanre" the manuscript note on which Fraser bases his superb work of constructive biographical criticism of the poem. Here is that manuscript note; it reads nothing like the published prefatory remarks to "Idanre" which generally present the poem as having crystallized in the poet's mind as more or less fully formed:

For a long time I could not accept why Ogun, the Creator God, should also be the agency of death. Interpretation of his domain, the road, proved particularly depressing and symbolically vexed especially inasmuch as the road is so obviously part of this same cyclic order. I know nothing more futile, more monotonous or boring than a circle.[5]

The metaphysics of the inextricable and necessary duality of birth and death, creation and destruction broached succinctly in this note was to take at least half a decade before it blossomed into a generally coherent and all-encompassing philosophy of life and art in Soyinka's later theoretical writings like the essay, "The Fourth Stage" and some of the pieces collected in *Myth, Literature and the African World*. The great spiritual and epistemological awakening implied here is the recognition, at last, that the monotony and repetitiousness inherent in the figure of the cycle – as in the image of the tail-devouring serpent – as a symbol of history and human existence subsists within a larger cosmic order which involves the duality of decay and renewal, destruction and creation. This awakening of the young poet-philosopher takes the form, in the poems collected in this first volume of his poetry, of an extremely tenuous and contradiction-ridden "coherence." And if this is true of the title poem, it is even truer of the "unity" between the seven sections making up the entire volume.

Thus, the challenge to the critic who comes to the poems in *Idanre* more than thirty years after their publication, is neither to succumb, as some critics have done, to the notion that a mythographic unity and coherence is given to the entire volume by the title poem, nor to dismiss outright the fact that many "mythemes" loosely and suggestively connect many poems in the volume, from poems expressing deeply felt private perceptions, intuitions and emotions to poems of open spaces, public events, communal experiences and collective memory. Examples of poems in the former category are "Luo Plains," "A Cry in the Night," "A First Deathday," and "To My First White Hairs," while the latter category is exemplified by poems like the much anthologized "Abiku," "Season," "Night" and the six poems in the penultimate section of the volume, "October '66." Indeed, it is instructive in this regard to compare "A First Deathday" which is a very private poem about the recollected death of the poet's sibling, Folashade, in infancy (told briefly but movingly in *Aké*) with "Abiku," a poem on a figure in Yoruba cosmology and one of the most successful and widely acclaimed poems of Soyinka. Beyond this, it is also instructive to see how "mythemes" which are only fragmentarily explored in these two poems are vastly amplified in *The Road* to give hints that there is in Soyinka's corpus some kind of intertextual poetic discourse between these diverse texts of verse and drama.

The two poems "A First Deathday" and "Abiku" derive from totally different emotional matrices, yet they both register and celebrate will as a phenomenon linked to mystical, transcendent and sometimes malevolent forces of the cosmos. "Grief has long receded," the much older, adult poet tells us in the fourth line of "A First Deathday," but the bereavement experienced in childhood lingers and is very subtly registered in the way the poet chooses to celebrate the dead sibling's memory by investing the "precision" of her demise on the first anniversary of her birth – "almost to the hour" – with a preternaturally superior will for one so young. The complexly formulated homage allows the poet to shift startlingly in the last two lines of the poem from the third-person voice narrating the experience of the poem to the persona of the dead sibling, boastful of her superior will, calling Time itself, the great confounder and thief of will, to bear witness to her "victory":

> She was not one more veil, dark across
> The Secret; Folashade ran bridal to the Spouse
> Wise to fore-planning – bear witness, Time
> To my young will, in this last breath of mockery.
>
> (*IOP*, 26)

The cynical pose implied in the "mockery" of the last line is compromised by a cluster of associated images subtly hinting at a deep sentiment of residual grief – the resonance between "veil" of the first line and "bridal" in the second line as a form of elegiac parody of conventional associations of the bridal veil; this, in conjunction with the substitution of Death for the "Spouse" the dead sibling was never to have suggests the collapse of the poet's own composure as the narrating persona of the poem. This compromised taunting pose of the poet's departed sibling becomes in "Abiku" a savagely mocking boastfulness that is tinged with a sadistic, gleeful malevolence at work in the cosmic order. "Abiku" is thus the more powerful, haunting poem because whereas the lyric mode in "A First Deathday" shifts to the dramatic mode only in the last two lines of that poem, the two modes interpenetrate throughout the whole of the powerful mythopoem that is "Abiku" in the same manner in which we encounter the fusion of these two modes – the lyric and the dramatic – in the most powerful passages of Soyinka's dramatic verse in plays like *A Dance of the Forests* and *Death and the King's Horseman*. The specific appropriation and deployment of the dramatic mode in "Abiku" is that of the interior monologue, albeit shouted across the footlights of the monster child's imaginings to a faceless, generalized audience of bereaved, forlorn motherhood in the darkened theatre of human existence:

> Night, and abiku sucks the oil
> From lamps. Mothers! I'll be the
> Suppliant snake coiled on the doorstep.
> Yours the killing cry.
>
> (30)

The gratuitous but also willful, deliberate evil suggested in snuffing light from the enveloping darkness of night before the serpentine strike is, in another context, appropriated by Soyinka to represent the "abiku" motif as essence of willful, gratuitous sadism and terror.[6] Thus, in "Abiku" we are far from the elegeiac, self-divided "mockery" of the long departed sibling in "A First Deathday." The two poems are nonetheless linked by the "mytheme" of passage rites which, though they "go wrong" by taking the form of "unnatural" aberrations, are still part of the great metaphysical cycle of birth and death, creation and destruction, transience and eternity. This way of interpreting isolated but tropologically linked poems of Soyinka is bolstered by the remarkable fact that these same mythemes are given far more technically polished and thematically powerful poetic expressions in the dramatic action of *The Road*. If we remember that this play was written and first staged at about the same time that many of the poems in *Idanre* were written, it does matter for our consideration of Soyinka as a poet to read the poetry in *The Road* intertextually with the formal verse in *Idanre*. Certainly, one of the most compelling poetic sequences in the play in this regard is Professor's harrowing, mocking prose-poem at the moment just before his death, a peroration which constitutes the last, eschatologically bleak words of the play:

Be even like the road itself. Flatten your bellies with the hunger of an unpropitious day, power your hands with the knowledge of death. In the heat of the afternoon when the sheen raises false forests and a watered haven, let the event first unravel before your eyes. Or in the dust, when ghost lorries pass you by and your shouts your tears fall on deaf panels and the dust swallows them. Dip in the same basin as the man that makes his last journey and stir with one finger, wobbling reflections of two hands, two hands, but one face only. Breathe like the road. Be the road. Coil your self in dreams, lay flat in treachery and deceit and at the moment of a trusting step, rear your head and strike the traveler in his confidence, swallow him whole or break him on the earth. Spread a broad sheet for death with the length and the time of the sun between you until the one face multiplies and the one shadow is cast by all the doomed. Breathe like the road, be even like the road itself... (*CP1*, 228–9)

The imperative, apodictic tone through which this passage commands acceptance of, or identification with Professor's vision of the road's, or life's, barren destructiveness tremendously amplifies the mocking, supercilious malevolence of "A First Deathday" and "Abiku." But here, in the context of the denouement of a play which both ritualizes and mourns the fear and terror of death with exuberance, wit and humor, Professor's "abiku" pose is far more suggestively ambiguous, far more open to aporetic, contradictory readings than anything we find in either poem. In the present context, I offer two mutually opposed readings. First, at one level, the projection of the banality and impersonality of death on the road in this passage is underscored by Professor with an unmitigated, even misanthropic despair whose intention seems to be to undermine the search for, and faith in hopeful portents that (all) travelers – in actual, literal travels and metaphorically in the journey of life – start out with and struggle to retain in the course of an actual journey or the symbolic travel of existence. This reading is authorized by attentiveness to the way in which Soyinka in the passage catachrestically conflates divinatory and predatory metaphors which, in the poems in *Idanre* are kept apart: "Dip in the same bowl as the man that makes his last journey and stir with one finger, wobbling reflections of two hands" (an image drawn from the practice of consulting an Ifa priest before setting out on an important journey) and "Coil yourself in dreams, lay flat in treachery and deceit and at the moment of a trusting step, rear your head and strike the traveler in his confidence" (an image of a serpent's fatal strike at an unwary farmer or hunter in the bush). But another contradictory reading of the passage is possible, one in which there is a subtle message of stubborn, ironic hope in Professor's bleak, nihilistic conceits: if the road, as literal highway for commerce and travel and as metaphor for the journey through life, is destructively treacherous, to "breathe like the road," to "be even like the road itself" is to live without illusions, to become equal to the destructiveness of the road. The first reading entails a sympathetic projection into the ritual and sacrificial "mythemes" embedded in that conflation of divinatory and predatory metaphors which we have identified, while the second reading in fact entails a scrupulous separation and demythologization of precisely these same metaphors. What is important about this is the fact that such conflicting inscriptions find in Soyinka's plays embodiment in memorable, riveting characters in ways that are generically foreclosed to the isolated poem in his volumes of poetry. Thus, what seems intractable or confounding in one genre (formal verse) is almost effortlessly consummated in another genre (drama).

Apart from "Abiku," "A First Death-day" and the title poem "Idanre" itself, the only other poems in this first volume of Soyinka's poetry volume which can be adjudged to have a heavy freight of mythologization about them are the first two poems in the volume, "Dawn" and "Death in the Dawn," together with "Easter." Definitely, there is nothing remotely esoteric and mythologizing about the eight incredibly whimsical, almost

Négritudinous poems in the fourth section of the volume titled "for women." And this point applies as well to the six "political" poems of the sixth section, "October '66." This observation generally holds true for the "mood" poems of the fifth section, "grey seasons," if exception is made for an indication of vegetative myths in the imagery of the third poem of the section, "Season." Indeed in love poems like "Psalm" and "Her Joy is Wild," in place of the tantalizingly enigmatic mythic fragments which make even a short, revisionary sonnet like "Dawn" the despair of anti-mythologizing exegetes, what we have is a cluster of rather conventional sexual imagery of a kind only very infrequently seen in Soyinka's poetry and drama. An apt example of this is the following scrambled group of couplets from "Psalm" which casts what appears to be a sexual union of two lovers not only in conventionalized imagery but also in an artificial rhyming scheme that ends in an apparently unintended bathos in the quatrain concluding the seven couplets making up the main body of the poem:

> Swaddlings of my gratitude
> Stir within your plenitude
> Moist the quickening consciousness
> Sealed in warm mis-shapennness . . .
>
> Sealed in earth your sanctuary
> Yields to light, and a mystery
>
> Of pulses and the stranger life
> Comes to harvest and release
>
> The germ of life exegesis
> Inspiration of your genesis (*IOP*, 34)

It must in fairness be acknowledged that these rather awkward lines come from a poem which probably was part of the corpus of recitations and songs that Soyinka performed in his very first "outing" as a fledgling dramatist, poet and actor on the stage of the Royal Court Theatre. But if the other "recitations" and "songs" in the cycle of "for women" are not as awkward in their metrical and rhyming schemes and as sentimental and conventional in their imagery as "Psalm," neither do they show Soyinka at his best as a lyric poet. That distinction falls to poems in which the confidence and wonder in his own ardent intuitions and original insights find arresting, memorable expression either in entirely new and fresh imagery, or in the poet's inspired reworking of conventional imagery and rhetorical tropes from traditional Yoruba ritual chants, beliefs, practices and sayings. Even the deceptively simple "Koko Oloro" is illustrative of this point:

> Dolorous Knot
> Plead for me
> Farm or hill
> Plead for me
> Stream and wind
> Take my voice
> Home or road
> Plead for me
> On this shoot,
> I bind your leaves
> Stalk and bud
> Berries three
> On the threshold
> Cast my voice
> Knot of bitters
> Plead for me (*IOP*, 23)

No great exegetical enigmas are posed by this adaptation of a traditional children's propitiation chant, but still there is an engrossing interest in the title "Koko Oloro," rendered in the first line of the poem as "dolorous knot" and in the fifteenth line as "knot of bitters." Lines nine and ten give an intratextual gloss on the word "knot": "On this shoot, I/Bind your leaves." Connectively, lines eleven and twelve speak of "Stalk and bud/Berries three," which must be the "bitters" or "dolorous" predicating the "knot" created by the "bound leaves" of lines nine and ten. The child who performs this simple ritual act, accompanying it with the words of the chant, is being schooled in a lesson in life's paradoxes: knotty, embittering privations may hold the key to negotiating the confounding perplexities and defeats of existence and lead to a tractable progress through life's tragicomic journey. The spare, compact and sinewy lines of the poem, combined with the metaphoric suggestiveness of a child ritually binding the leaves of an organic, growing shoot to create the "knot of bitters," together with the incantatory effect of the repetition of the refrain "plead for me" four times (with its variants of "take my voice" and "cast my voice"), create a haunting lyric poem on faith and hope pregnant with a burden of the knowledge of pain and "dolor."

To forestall a charge that this "simple" poetic reprise of a children's propitiation song has been "over-read," let us address the contextual pertinence of this reading to an assessment of the scope and nature of Soyinka's performance as a lyric poet in this volume. Pain, grief, loss and more grandiosely, violence, terror and alienation, are the subjects of many of the poems in the volume, not as abstractions but as either experiences conveyed with skintight intimacy or with projective identification with others in lone, single experiences or general communal calamities. The justly celebrated and widely discussed "Death in the Dawn" records the poet's encounter with the road crash death of an unknown fellow traveler in an elegy which is deeply affecting in the way in which the poem delicately captures the hopeful portents felt by all dawn travelers only to end in a gruesome death and its chastening dramatization of the futility of those portents. "A Cry in the Night" is wrenching in its evocation of the unabating grief of a mother burying her stillborn child in the vast loneliness of the night in which her bereavement seems hers and hers alone in an empty universe; but her grief is actually shared by the unperceived poet, whose silent but deep sympathetic acknowledgment of her bereavement gives meaning to the event by memorializing it. The poems in the cycle "October '66," the most "public" pieces in the volume, are affecting because the diverse experiences of fear, terror, hate and creeping derangement of social cohesion and decency which they record as Nigeria moved ever closer to a fratricidal civil war, are rendered with the best effects of lyric poetry: intensely personal and deeply felt emotion, concrete and arresting images, startling anchoring of abstract, general ideas in fresh, vivid and memorable use of language.

Poetry, including especially lyric poetry, can contain such extremely contradictory intuitions and emotions because in its sheer delight in language and its semantic, phonetic and ideational resources, it often goes to the roots of words and based on this, it has the capacity to hermiticize within a single episode or passage tropes, metaphors and sentiments from diverse and conflicting domains of life and experience. Lyric poetry of this type pervades Soyinka's dramas, most notably *A Dance*, *The Road*, *Madmen* and *The Bacchae of Euripides*. Moreover, in the generically more capacious framework of his great dramatic parables, techniques and idioms of the lyric which in Soyinka's formal verse seem to stand in truncated and splendid isolation weld into arresting clusters and configurations of powerful emotions and intuitions which encompass disparate, or even conflicting aspects and domains of life. The following short scene from Part Two of *Madmen* is as good as any from these plays in illustrating this point:

Old Man (His voice has risen to a frenzy.)

Practise, Practise, Practise ... on the cyst in the system ...
(Bero is checked in his stride by the voice. He now hesitates between the distractions.)
... you cyst, you cyst, you splint in the arrow of arrogance, the dog in dogma, tick of a heretic, the tick in politics, the mock of democracy the mar of marxism, a tic of the fanatic, the boo in buddhism, the ham in Mohammed, the dash in the criss-cross of Christ, a dot on the I of ego, An ass in the mass, the ash in ashram, a boot in kibbutz, the pee of priesthood, the peepee of perfect priesthood, oh how dare you raise your hindquarters you dog of dogma and cast the scent of your existence on the lamppost of Destiny you HOLE IN THE ZERO of NOTHING! (*CP2*, 275)

In this passage, the "divine frenzy" of the Old Man achieves a powerful imaginative intelligibility in the manner in which a deconstructive assault on the ideational bases of an "ecumenical" social cannibalism through which humanity preys upon itself is achieved by taking concepts, words, and slogans from a bewildering array of cultures, religions, secular creeds and spiritual dispositions apart to reveal the complicity of language in this social cannibalism. The scene, physical action and linguistic articulation combined, is paralleled in post-Second World War world drama only by Samuel Beckett and a few of the Absurdists in its assault on all ethical, religious, rationalist and discursive foundations of liberal humanism. At work here is Soyinka's reliance in his dramas on poetic inspiration and utterance to seemingly effortlessly achieve the sort of hermetic total-ization of widely divergent areas of life, history and experience that is rather rare in his poetry precisely because of generic constraints.

Idanre and Other Poems – together with *Outsiders*, Soyinka's fifth volume of poetry – is distinguished by the fact that, unlike *A Shuttle in the Crypt*, and perhaps even *Ogun Abibiman* and *Mandela's Earth*, it places at the core of its organizing central vision a distinction between hurt, pain, terror and alienation which are unabating, senseless and without relief or redemption, and those which, being tragic or ironic consequences of social and cosmic checks and balances between contradictory reali-ties and forces, are either preventable or capable of remediation. This dualistic vision on the whole finds adequate, often startling expression in Soyinka's lyric poetry, give or take the occasional quirks of willfully opaque and confounding poetic diction and syntactical aporias which do not seem to derive from any perceptible deconstructive logic, as in poems like "Dawn," "The Hunchback of Dugbe," "Luo Plains" and "Easter." In the longer epic and narrative title poem, this dualistic vision finds a much tougher formal impediment to its artistic realization, but ultimately, it achieves a remarkable breakthrough in the mobilization of language, form and vision to bring within its imaginative universe startling ideas and views about history and existence which, at that stage of Soyinka's career, were still rather inchoate.

In approaching the title poem of the volume, "Idanre" as a complex poem which poses tremendous methodological problems of analysis and interpretation for the critic or scholar, certain unhelpful formulations of these problems must first be dispelled. Derek Wright, for instance, accurately advances the view that the poem aggrandizingly attempts to do too many things. However, this unquestionable assessment leads Wright to make the following patently inaccurate and unproductive remarks on the history of the critical reception of the poem: "What all these elements amount to, practically, is as hard to say now as when the poem was published, and the preface and notes are more distracting than illuminating (158)." For a statement which comes from a book published in 1993, Wright unaccountably misrepresents the interpretive challenges posed by the poem by projecting a nonexistent critical *cul de sac* in the scholarly reception of the poem. At the very least, Robert Fraser in *West African Poetry*, published in 1986, had in his discussion of "Idanre" sorted out the confusions in the first set of critical responses to the poem, in the process identifying a credible imaginative and symbolic centre linking the diverse thematic strands of the poem: the poet's first impassioned glimmerings of a possible rupture in metaphoric and epistemological constructions of the repetitive cycles of creation and destruction, decay and renewal – of Being and existence, and in nature and history. However, in his level-headed and inspired commentary on the poem, Fraser does not undertake an assessment of how, and with what effect, Soyinka gives form and shape to the deeply *personal* spiritual and imaginative "awakening" that the vision communicated in the poem represents for him. On this point, the following observations from Soyinka's prefatory note to the poem is particularly apposite:

Idanre was born of two separate halves of the same experience. The first was a visit to the rockhills of that name, a god-suffused grazing of primal giants and mastodons, petrified through some strange history, suckled by mists and clouds. Three years later and some two hundred miles away, a rainstorm rived apart the intervening years and space, leaving a sediment of disquiet which linked me to lingering, unresolved sensations of my first climb up Idanre. I abandoned my work – it was middle of the night – and walked. *Idanre* is the record of that walk through wet woods on the outskirts of Molete, a pilgrimage to Idanre in company of presences such as dilate the head and erase known worlds. (*IOP*, 57)

The question that arises from this note by Soyinka himself on the origins of the poem is: why does he need the symbolic framework of that walk in the night in the woods of Molete on the outskirts of Ibadan to poetically narrate and celebrate the central creation myths, the central aetiological legends of the Yoruba people – which is what, in its substantive contents, "Idanre" is about? The question is particularly pertinent given the fact that not only does Soyinka propose that night walk as a "pilgrimage" which recalls and reenacts an earlier "pilgrimage" to the "god-suffused" rockhills of Idanre, he indeed speaks in that same prefatory note of both "pilgrimages" – to Idanre and through the woods of Molete – as involving not just himself but "in company of presences such as dilate the head and erase known worlds." Thus, the answer to the question of how requisite the elaborate symbolic framework is for Soyinka's expressed purposes in writing this poem, surely, is that the poetic recreation of the central myths and legends of the Yoruba people comes out of what must have been a profoundly mystical or spiritual experience on those "pilgrimages." Presumably, these myths and legends came powerfully and imaginatively alive for the poet on those "pilgrimages" and effected an awakening, a turning point in his artistic consciousness. The challenge to the critic or interpreter of the poem therefore lies in clearing a careful interpretive space between the Scylla of literalism – "who or what exactly are those "presences" that accompanied the poet on those lone pilgrimages? – and the Charybdis of complete surrender to Soyinka's penchant for over-valorizing occult, esoteric experiences and phenomena. In the meantime of course, there is also the more practical question of the formidable obstacles to comprehension posed by the multiplicity of nonlinear and fragmentary narratives embedded in the poem. Additionally, sympathetic identification with the protagonists of the drama of the myths and legends explored and celebrated in the poem is often blocked by ellipsis of technique and diction neither of which makes any concession to readers used to the classical virtues of narrative linearity, plot-driven action, clearly motivated or probable transitions between episodes or "sections," and a linguistic currency of simple, common vocabulary.

"Idanre" is thus perhaps best approached not from the aesthetic and philosophical premises which undergird traditional epic or heroic poetic and prose narratives like *Beowulf* or *Sundiata*, but from those which subtend the elaborately allusive and internally self-divided modernist "epics" like *The Wasteland* or *The Cantos*. Definitely, the first two of the seven sections of the poem respectively titled "deluge" and "and after," are resolutely unmindful of narrative continuity, or of even clear markers or distinctions between the personae and avatars who show up in these sections. With the rather fragmentary gloss that Soyinka himself provides to these and other sections of the poem, with the accumulated exegeses on the poem, and with some effort, the assiduous reader comes to a sense of what events and which myths are being celebrated in these two opening sections of the poem. Thus, "deluge" tells of the beginning of time, of the emergence of culture – especially *agri*-culture – and the neolithic revolution to the inception of the Iron Age, with Ogun and Sango being the central protagonists. The second section, "and after," cinematically "fast forwards" to succeeding epochs and at the same time "rewinds" again to earlier epochs. Particularly worthy of note in this section is the poet's considerable fixation on the paradoxically tragic cost of the march of civilization, especially as reflected in the carnage wrought on the roads (and highways) built to advance progress:

                                              And we
        Have honeycombed beneath his hills, worked ores and paid
        With wrecks of last year's suppers, paved his roads
        With shells, milestones of breathless bones –
        Ogun is a demanding god (*IOP*, 64)

Also worthy of note in these two non-mimetic, non-diegetic sections of "Idanre" is the fact that they seem patterned on the traditional form of the "ijuba," the panegyric prologue of Yoruba chants, songs and theatre. The "ijuba" typically combines a poet's, singer's or performer's self-presentation with terse, sometimes cryptic foreshadowing of the main themes of the song, chant or performance to be presented.[7] It is a matter of surprise that these two opening sections are followed by two sections, "pilgrimage" and "the beginning" which are more or less shaped by conventions of narrative continuity. Consequently, of all the sections of the poem, these two contain rounded stories which can be easily apprehended, even by the average reader. Perhaps this is because these are the sections that deal with the specific myths and legends of Ogun in his more heroically creative, life-enhancing and selfless incarnations. The third section, "pilgrimage," the shortest section of the poem, is also perhaps the most conventionally diegetic in the way in which, having briefly narrated how the original godhead which contained all the deities in the pantheon was smashed into fragments and how Ogun recombined in himself the most diverse aspects of the shattered totality, the poem moves, not as might be expected to exultation, but to "grieving" by Ogun and his protégé, the poet, for that forever lost unified and totalized essence. Section four, "the beginning," logically moves to complete the story begun in the immediately preceding section: with the advantage of being the avatar who contains the largest and most heterogeneous stock of attributes of the fragmented supreme godhead, Ogun succeeds where the other deities fail in the next great task of creation and existence – unification of the gods with mankind, or recombining of divine essence with human existence. This Ogun achieves by forging the implements with which to clear the immense primeval thickets which separated the abode of the gods from mankind. This is perhaps why this particular section contains the longest profusion of the "oriki" or praise poems of Ogun. Except of course that the section ends with a foreshadowing of the great lapse that is to come when the humans, against his protestations, make Ogun their warrior-king and the god, in a subsequent moment of inebriation, perpetrates a mass slaughter of both the enemy and his own people.

Of the three remaining sections of the poem, section five, "the battle," is the longest and the most varied in stanzaic form. This is explained perhaps by the fact the "battle" announced in the section title, though narrated almost entirely as an external event, is not so much about a battle between two armies as it is an account of a sustained slaughter of his own men by Ogun, who had first wiped out the enemy forces. Since this external shell of the story lacks a dramatic agon, Soyinka, it seems, has to vary the stanzaic forms deployed in the section, matching this with a scale of diction calculated to infuse drama and tragic grandeur to a narration that essentially lacks a propulsive motion. As we have seen in the first two sections of the poem, rhetoric, diction and cadence are already pitched at a self-consciously grandiloquent scale. In this section, Soyinka pushes this scale even higher and attempts to sustain this effort for a much longer stretch than in any other section of the poem – in fact over the course of 36 stanzas of no less than 179 lines. The strain shows everywhere and thus the creaking, enforced assonance formed by the conjoining and repetition of "incarnate" with "in carnage" in the

following quote is fairly representative of the unintended poetic solecisms
of this section:

> There are air-beams unfelt by human breath
> Unseen by sight, intangible. Whose throat
> Draws breath in a god's preserve
> Breathes the heart of fire
>
> Murderer, stay your iron hand
> Your men lie slain – Cannibal!
>
> Ay, ring summons on the deafened god
> His fingers sow red earth. His being incarnate
> Bathes in carnage, anoints godhead
> In carnage.
>
> *(IOP,* 76)

If there is a moral to the repetition of the word "carnage" in this passage,
it is surely that the follies and foibles of humankind assume colossal
dimensions when yoked to transcendent idealities encoded in the deities,
idealities which, after all, are none other than the projections of our own
natural propensities, of drives and passions rooted deep in our natures.
The Aristotelian moment of *anagnorisis*, of recognition of this insight by
the poet-witness of the "carnage" is one of the few instances in this section
when the strain of fustian rhetoric gives way to an almost quiescent
antistrophe:

> Light filled me then, intruder though
> I watched a god's excorsis; clearly
> The blasphemy of my humanity rose accusatory
> In my ears, and understanding came
> Of a fatal condemnation . . .
>
> Life, the two-cowrie change of the dealer
> In trinkets lay about him in broken threads
> Oh the squirrel ran up an iroko tree
> And the hunter's chase
> Was ended (79–80)

The deliberate, almost quiescent bathos of the lines of the second stanza
is intended as a contrast to the soaring language of lines which express the
tragic grandeur of moments like Ogun's triumph where the other deities
had failed to effect reunion with mankind. Consequently, the humility
that the chastened god experiences after the carnage leads to the true
moment of *anagnorisis*, of recognition, in the entire poem – the moment
in the sixth section when the poet comes to an awareness that the break

from the repetitive cycle of destruction lies, after all, not with Ogun's
dare against original chaos but with the defining act of that primal rebel,
Atunda:

> You who have borne the first separation, bide you
> Severed still; he who guards the Creative Flint
> Walks, purged spirit, contemptuous of womb-yearnings
> He shall teach us to ignite our several kilns
> And glory in each bronzed emergence
>
> All hail Saint Atunda, First revolutionary
> Grand iconoclast at genesis – and the rest in logic
> Zeus, Osiris, Jahweh, Christ in trifoliate
> Pact with creation, and the wisdom of Orunmila, Ifa
> Divining eyes, multiform
>
> Evolution of the self-devouring snake to spatials
> New in symbol, banked loop of the 'Mobius Strip'
> And interlock of re-creative rings, one surface
> Yet full comb of angles, uni-plane, yet sensuous with
> Complexities of mind and motion.
>
> (82–3)

The scrambled, disjunctive ordering of these lines reflects the incredible diversity of the sources that went into the conception of this poem,
as well as the great ideational ecumenism of its achieved artistic vision.
The synthesizing allusion to figures from the religious myths of Egyptian
and Greek antiquity, Judaism and Christianity is meant to extend the
ramifications of the "multiform," "divining eyes" of the Yoruba oracular deity Ifa/Orunmila. Yet the poem is paradoxically deeply rooted in
specifically Yoruba creation myths, Yoruba aetiological legends of the
emergence of historic social and cultural forms, especially of agriculture
from pre-sedentary, migratory social formations; it cryptically narrates
the coming of the iron age to West Africa, and the rise and fall of cults
associated with specific deities and their associated social power. Part
of the achievement of this poem is to have teased out of these creation
myths and migration legends of the Yoruba people universally general-
izable spiritual and psychological aspirations and values. Of the latter,
the most important are the perpetual yearnings for union between the
human and the divine, matter and spirit, and the dialectical interpene-
tration of the partial and the whole, the fragment and the totality. This
is inherent in the myths narrated in the poem of Ogun's forging of the
implements with which to clear vast primal growths so the gods could be
reunited with mankind; in this we see the scrupulous anachronism of the

aetiological fiction of the coming of the iron age to Yorubaland reaching back and forward to universal myths of gods who become incarnate and of humankind aspiring to transcendent, divine essence. Correspondingly, the theme of the partial in the whole, the fragment in the totality inheres in the Atunda myth which is nothing if not a symbolization of violence as a necessary, perhaps inevitable dimension of identity formation.

If Soyinka in this poem does not quite manage to successfully work through the antinomies and paradoxes of the diverse traditions which informed this very inclusive and open-ended vision of the phenomenon of humanity and its complex and contradictory yearnings, it is necessary to bear in mind that this is, after all, a relatively early work in his corpus. Indeed, it is perhaps best to see the poem as prolegomenon to, and wellspring of ideas, tropes and plot fragments for other artistically more successful and intellectually more mature works in Soyinka's corpus. Even more pointedly, "Idanre" can be validly seen as clearing ground and preparatory exercise for the superb, startling fusion of lyric, dramatic and narrative poetic modes in the plays of Soyinka's mature dramaturgy like *The Road, Death and the King's Horseman* and *The Bacchae of Euripides*. And by a reverse interpretive logic, the ease with which these modes are fused in these plays affords a rereading of "Idanre" which is not unduly intimidated by the disjunctures and tensions between these modes in the tumultuous sweep of that poem's thundering stanzas and lines.

There is far less to speculate about the gestative origins of *A Shuttle in the Crypt*, Soyinka's second volume of collected poems, than the enigma of the origins of "Idanre" in that phantasmic night walk in the woods of Molete in Ibadan. Soyinka informs us in the Preface to the volume: "Except for two or three poems in the section 'Poems of bread and earth,' this volume consists of poems written in gaol in spite of the deprivation of reading and writing material in nearly two years of solitary confinement (vii)." Since, in the opinion of this writer, this is Soyinka's most accomplished collection of poetry, he obviously turned the extreme privation of incarceration in solitary confinement to extraordinary creative expression. This fact is central to any consideration of the nature and scale of the achievement of the poems collected in this volume, especially those gathered in its two central sections, "Phases of Peril" and "Climes of Silence."

The cultural myth of the spiritual quester who goes into seclusion in the wilderness of a desert or a jungle and returns with a heightened, deeper sense of the nature of evil and the resources needed to confront it is a major aspect of the quest motif in Soyinka's works, including works written and published before *A Shuttle in the Crypt*. Indeed, in *The Road*, the play's protagonist, Professor, specifically expresses a yearning to spend a part of his years of retirement in prison, and in solitary confinement too. It would of course be fatuous to read into this peculiar aspiration of Professor Soyinka's prophetic intimation of his own future incarceration. But on a more heuristic and imaginative plane, the idea of a protagonist representing a visionary artistic or intellectual figure who goes into a period of seclusion to hone his spiritual and psychic powers had been expressed in Soyinka's writings before *A Shuttle*. The clearest example of this inscription is Isola in *Camwood on the Leaves*, but we also see it in more fragmentary and oblique forms in Eman in *The Strong Breed* and Egbo in *The Interpreters*. Its specific linkage to a spell in prison by Professor in *The Road* partakes of the dark, ironic and tragicomic atmosphere which pervades the dramatic action of that play, but it also contains a serious undertone which, linked to similar inscriptions in other works of Soyinka, amounts to a profound artistic interest in the travails of voluntary or coerced sequestration from the human community as a liminal space in which to sharpen the powers of intuition and projection of the visionary artist and intellectual. This is why, despite the extreme isolation and irreplaceably unique experience of his detention in solitary confinement, Soyinka writes of the experience in his Preface to *A Shuttle*: "the landscape of the poems is not uncommon; physical details differ, but finally the landscape of the loss of human contact is the same (viii)."

These observations help to provide a clarifying context for what, surely, is the most startling aspect of many of the poems in this volume. This is the juxtaposition of experiences and moods of great, excruciating negativity with consistently exquisite and polished formal expression. Most of the poems in this volume, given the context in which they were written, plumb deeply into the innermost recesses of the poet's fears, anxieties, reveries, waking nightmares and the very infrequent moments of grace and solace in solitary confinement. *Moreover, many of the poems were first written even as the poet actually lived these experiences.* It is thus a matter of great literary interest that these same poems are some of the most formally polished and even meticulously crafted in Soyinka's poetry. Indeed, so few are the poems giving rise to the old, accustomed accusations of "obscurity" and "incoherence" in this volume that where they are encountered, they have a definite source which cannot easily be identified for similar poetic gaffes in Soyinka's other volumes of poetry. For always in this particular volume, the source of "obscurity" or "incoherence" seems to lie in the fact that the regress into the innermost recesses of a psyche under stress – a psyche on the brink of dissolution – is so deep that it defies and confounds "containment" by the externalities of formal versification.

The six poems in the opening section of the volume, "Phases of Peril," are exceptional in Soyinka's poetry in two respects. In the first place, they openly and frankly express the poet's vulnerabilities in a "confessional" mode very rare in his writings. At the same time, however, these poems effectively use techniques of ingenious modulation of lyric voice and barely noticeable but carefully structured ellipsis to deploy a plethora of images, metaphors and symbols that sculpt the incommensurable acts and processes of evil responsible for both the poet's "perils" and those of past, present and future victims of oppression and dehumanization. For instance, "O Roots!," the first poem in the volume, comprises no less than thirty-seven almost perfectly sculpted couplets with a scheme of loose, but generally interrelated rhymes, half-rhymes and assonances. For the first thirty-one of these couplets, the poem deploys the metaphor of "roots" as an elaborate poetic conceit seeking to "earth" the poet's imagination and spirit in every conceivable landscape of good and evil and of grace and spite, the suggestion being that these are indeed warring tendencies in the mind and psyche of the poet in his solitary cell. Moreover, the voice which takes the poet and the reader through these dialogical locutions of spirit and psyche is effectively cast in the register of a long, sustained prayerful apostrophe. One such group of couplets at the beginning of the poem sets the tone and the logic of metaphoric discourse for the rest of the poem:

> Feet of pilgrims pause by charted pools
> Balm seeking. Dipped, their thirsty bowls
>
> Raise bubbles of corruption, sludge
> Of evil, graves unlaid to tears to dirge
>
> Roots, I pray you lead away from streams
> Of tainted seepage lest I, of these crimes
>
> Partake, from fouled communion earth
> In ashes scattered from a common hearth (*Shuttle*, 1)

The opening image in the fourth stanza of a parched, wandering pilgrim in some barren landscape who comes upon a "charted pool" which is expected to provide "balm" for his or her thirst obviously alludes to phantasmic projections by the fevered mind of the incarcerated poet. The emotional and spiritual condition of the prisoner-poet is more concretely evoked in the following image in which the "wandering pilgrims" draw foul or poisoned water – imaged here as "bubbles of corruption, sludge/Of evil, graves unlaid to tears or dirge." This then leads to the desperate prayer of the sixth and seventh couplets, a prayer whose transcendent accents have been prepared by the scale of corruption and evil imaged in the two preceding couplets wherein "graves unlaid to tears or dirge" distinctly recall the massacre of Igbos in northern Nigeria in 1966 which was a major catalyst in the slide to the country's civil war in 1967. It is indeed this careful anchoring of transcendent ruminations and imaginings in collective and personal experience which makes *A Shuttle* more than a volume of protest poetry. There is in some of the groupings of couplets in this particular poem, a tendency to push the scale of the identification of the poet's wandering mind with, on the one hand, elemental regenerative processes of nature, and on the other, the degradation of organic life and processes, to levels of abstraction unsupported by the immediate, or surrounding, cluster of metaphors and images. But it is also the case in nearly every instance that the alert critic or reader who has maintained a sustained grasp of the shifting plethora of images in the progression of the poem can find echoes, associations and resonances which connect what, on the surface, appears to be floating abstractions. One example of this pattern is the one we encounter in the sixteenth to the twentieth couplets:

> Roots, be the network of my large
> Design, hold to your secret charge
>
> All bedrock architecture raised to heal
> Desert cries, desert lacerations; seal
>
> In barks of age, test on battering-rams
> Of your granite caps O breaker of dams
>
> Pestle in earth mortar, ringer of chimes
> In rock funnels, render mine Time's
>
> Chaplets, and stress to your eternal season
> These inward plinths I raise against unreason.
>
> (*Shuttle*, 2–3)

Without referring back to the "shuttle" as the master trope of stratagems and projections which both ensured the poet's survival from the mind-destroying threat of solitary confinement for nearly two years and enabled him to be creatively productive in spite of the prohibitions of his incarceration, it would be impossible to keep track of the connection between image or symbol and the transcendent values referenced in this sequence of couplets. The series of metaphors and images which substitute for "roots" in the eighteenth and nineteenth couplets – "breakers of dams," "battering-rams" made of "granite caps" and "ringer of chimes" – become more and more grandiose such that by the twentieth couplet they are merged with "Time's chaplets" making them coincident with eternity itself ("stress to your eternal seasons"). Soyinka's gloss, in the Preface to *A Shuttle*, on the master trope of "shuttle" helps provide an imaginative context for such radical juxtapositions in this and other poems in the volume:

"The shuttle is a unique species of the caged animal, a restless bolt of energy, a trapped weaver-bird yet charged in repose with unspoken forms and designs. In motion or at rest it is a secretive seed, shrine, kernel, phallus and well of creative mysteries." (vii)

With the possible exception of "Conversation at night with a cock-roach" which immediately follows it, "Roots" comes closest in the entire volume to a full poetic mobilization of all the suggestive associations and resonances of this master trope of the "shuttle." But even so, the flight into unanchored transcendent projections that we see in the sixteenth to twentieth couplets are infrequent in the poem. And it ought to be noted that the very strict metrical ordering of the poem imposes external constraints that have a redounding effect on the internal economy of the poem's metaphorical armature. Indeed the last six couplets of the poem function somewhat like an antistrophe to the preceding thirty-one couplets which thus form the "strophe," the main line of poetic discourse. To the peripatetic and grandiose movement of that "strophe," the sub-dued "recessional" tone of the last six couplets shows the poet despairing that he may not physically and spiritually survive the conditions of his incarceration and, stopping just short of a fatal death-wish, tries to come to terms gracefully with that possibility:

> . . . The prow
> Is pointed to a pull of undertows
>
> A grey plunge in pools of silence, peace
> Of bygone voyagers, to the close transforming pass.
>
> Cleansed, they await, the seeker come
> To a drought of centers, to slipholds on the climb
>
> And heart may yield to strange upwelling thrusts
> Promising from far to slake immortal thirsts (4)

"Conversations at night with a cockroach" is a long poem of eighteen stanzas which combines lyric, dramatic and narrative poetic modes. In external form, the poem is structured by a conventional strope-antistrophe dialogical interchange wherein the poet (the voice in the strophe) speaks the stanzas which recall the idealistic, utopian attempts of his generation to forge a just, cohesive social order out of the diverse, plural communities making up his newly independent nation, and the intruder cockroach in his prison cell speaks the stanzas recalling the forces which not only thwarted those efforts but are now consolidating and expanding their reign of terror and mediocrity (antistrophe). Typical of this pattern is the following exchange between one long stanzaic "strophe" and two short refrains of "antistrophe" from the opening section of the poem:

> (Strophe)
> In that year's crucible we sought
> To force impurities in nationweal
> Belly-up, heat-drawn by fires
> Of truth. In that year's crucible
> We sought to cleanse the faulted lodes
> To raise new dwellings pillared on crags
> Washed by mountain streams; to reach
> Hands around Kaura hills, beyond
> Obudu ranges, to dance on rockhills
> Through Idanre. We sought to speak
> Each to each in accents of trust
> Dispersing ancient mists in clean breezes
> To clear the path of lowland barriers
> Forge new realities, free our earth
> Of distorting shadows cast by old
> And modern necromancers. No more
> Rose cry and purpose, no more the fences
> Of deceit, no more perpetuity
> Of ancient wrongs
>
> (Antistrophe)
> But we were wise to portents, tuned
> As tinsel vanes to the dread approach
> Of the visitation. And while the rumble yet
> Was far, we closed, we spread tentacles.
> We knew the tread and heard
> The gathering heartbeat of the cyclone heart
> And quick our hands to forge coalitions new
> Of tried corruptions, East to West, North to South.

Survival was insured in policies to embrace
The degree of wavering weather vanes.
Our sirens poised inked talons on the open
Cheques, their songs inflamed each hidden longing . . . (6–7)

It is an educated but safe guess to suggest that the twice-repeated phrase, "in that year's crucible" of the first four lines of the "strophe" is an allusion to the popular political rebellions in western Nigeria leading up to the military coup of January 1966, two events which Soyinka, with due reservations about their internal contradictions, has defended and celebrated in his writings, notably in *The Man Died* and *Ibadan*. Indeed, the whole section making up what we've called the "strophe" is the closest we get to a baldly partisan and explicitly political expression by Soyinka in any of the poems in *A Shuttle*. In this regard, while the "antistrophe" inscribed in the two shorter stanzas may also be said to be partisan, this is a partisanship which the poet finds reprehensible, which he in fact casts in a strongly ironic light. For the partisanship here is on behalf of the alliance of the conservative regional governments of the West and the North, especially in the way that both tone and imagery in the stanzas recall the contempt that top members of the NNDP government of S.L. Akintola, the premier of the western region, openly expressed toward the populace on which they had imposed their tyrannical misrule. Finally, since both "strophe" and "antistrophe" deploy related images of a looming political explosion – "force impurities . . . belly-up, heat-drawn by fires of truth"; "while the rumble yet was far"; "the gathering heartbeat of the cyclone" – it is very likely that the allusions here are to the coup and the countercoup of January and July 1966 respectively. Thus, like Christopher Okigbo's "Path of Thunder," "Conversations at Night" is a poem which allegorizes the fateful events that took place between 1964 and 1966 in Nigeria in unambiguous poetic accents. And again as in Okigbo's last group of poems, "Conversations at Night" demonstrates that eschewal of obscure diction and radically disjunct syntax does not lead to the sacrifice of a complex vision of the sociopolitical crises engaged by the poet. All the same, Soyinka is never one to stick to an uncomplicated structure, and so in the course of the poem he finesses the agon between the poet and his unwelcome interlocutor by transforming the cockroach, on account of its habits of foraging and scavenging in sewers and other sites of putrefaction, into a sort of grotesque, vulpine witness to the atrocities and massacres which took place in northern Nigeria in May and September of 1966. This transforms the cockroach into an accuser who can shift moral responsibility for the carnage to the poet as a representative citizen of a nation in which the unremitting surfeit of violence and atrocities encompasses everyone, perpetrator and victim, the rulers and the ruled, the reformers and the destroyers:

> Peace. The spillage dried with time
> We nibbled blood where it had caked
> You lit the fires, you, and saw
> Your dawn of dawning yield
> To our noon of darkness
> Half-way up your grove of union
> We watched you stumble – mere men
> Lose footing on the peaks of deities
> The torch was quenched, the void
> Of darkness rang with madness
> Each his own priest, quick, easy
> The act of sacrifice. We know to wait
> We nibble blood before it cakes.
>
> (*Shuttle*, 9)

For readers who actually lived through this period of Nigerian political history, "Conversations at Night" could be an extremely uncomfortable, extremely bracing poem to read. This, presumably, is precisely the "purpose" of the poem: an evocation of a time of evil and mass atrocities so graphic, so stark, so strangely familiar that it quickly leads the reader to seek somewhat dubious relief in linking these Nigerian perpetrations with massacres and atrocities in other places and other times – episodes from the Holocaust, the killing fields of Cambodia, of Rwanda and Burundi and of Kosovo, episodes of unspeakable barbarities where the perpetrators also strove to ensure that knowledge or memory of their crimes will vanish with the extermination of their victims:

> . . . Death came
> In the color of foul thoughts and whispers
> Fouled intentions, color of calculations
> A contrivance to erase the red and black
> Of debt and credit, gangrene to discolor
> Records for future reckoning, bile to blur
> Precision of the mind to past exploitation
> A scheming for intestate legacies
> Conversions, appropriations, a mine
> Of gold-filling in the teeth of death
> A color blindness to red standards
> Which tomorrow shall uphold against
> The horrors of today (12)

"Conversations at Night" ought to become a poem of conscientization hung on the moral soul of progressive humanity; it is especially powerful in evoking vivid and harrowing forms of atrocities and massacres visited on "stranger populations" by their host community or by zealots of "master race" ideologies, often with the connivance of collaborators who are themselves powerless. Against the background of such stanzas, the poem's concluding lines express the same bitter and dystopian irony as the extended conceit of "As" in *Madmen and Specialists*:

> All was well. All was even
> As it was in the beginning (13)

Not all the poems in this first section of *A Shuttle*, "Phases of Peril," are of this nihilistic or bitterly ironic expression, the title of the section notwithstanding. Indeed, the very next poem after "Conversations at Night," "A Cobweb's Touch in the Dark," builds upon the suggestion in that title that even the sheerest gossamer contact with another object in the poet's cell other than the cockroach of the preceding poem enables the incarcerated poet to make projections which access the spiritual grace available in the ordinary objects and phenomena of nature – wind, trees, leaves. These evoke more humane, healing times and invisible, benevolent presences. In such moods, it is too tempting for Soyinka not to access and re-inscribe one of his favorite tropes of metaphysical solace – the spiritual munificence of ancestral guardians:

> A skin
> Whose hairs are brushed by winds that shade
> Spaces where dead memories are laid
>
> A thread
> Lays its moment on the flesh, a rime
> Of things gone by, a brush of time
>
> It slips
> Against the dark, radial and ebb-
> line to the heart of the ancestral web.
>
> (14)

Other poems which build upon and expand on these rare moments of grace and hope in a volume of poems containing Soyinka's bleakest poetic vision are "I Anoint My Flesh," the last poem of the first section of the volume, and "Seed," the last poem of the sequence "Chimes of

Silence," the volume's longest and central section. Typical of the fusion
of spare, austere formal technique with high moral purpose in these two
poems are the following two stanzas, each from "I Anoint Myself" and
"Seed" respectively:

> I anoint my heart
> Within its flame I lay
> Spent ashes of your hate –
> Let evil die. (19)

> I speak in the voice of gentle rain
> In whispers of growth
> In sleight of light
> I speak in aged hairs of wind
> Midwife to cloud
> And sheaves on threshing-floor (56)

The four "archetypes" of the section which bears that title, Joseph,
Hamlet, Gulliver and Ulysses, are figures from Western canonical religious and secular texts, respectively the Bible, Shakespeare's *Hamlet*,
Jonathan Swift's *Gulliver's Travels*, and James Joyce's *Ulysses*. Not surprisingly, these are the most academic, the most bookishly allusive poems
in *A Shuttle*. In fact the whole tenor of "Gulliver," its diction and style,
distinctly and elaborately echo British Augustan poetry, specifically of
the mock-epic mode. And concerning "Ulysses" Soyinka adds a significant explanatory gloss: "Notes from here to my Joyce class (*Shuttle*,
27)." The "here" is of course his solitary detention cell, the "Joyce class"
metonymically standing for the reader-addressees of the poem. Thus, the
four poems in this section of *A Shuttle* are constructed with the assumption
that the reader will recognize the allusions to the poem's textual sources.
In this regard "Joseph" and "Hamlet" make much fewer demands of
"learnedness" on the reader than do "Gulliver" and "Ulysses," the latter being especially recondite and forbidding in the manner in which
it appropriates the tropes of the legend of Ulysses to narrate the angst
of an enervated quester, of a voyager who has come to a quiescent but
troubled senescence. If this portrait seems to refer to the poet himself,
it ought to be added that it does so only in the register of a cautionary parable: the incarcerated poet hopes that this will not be his fate.
"Hamlet" and "Gulliver" are perhaps the most successful of the
"Archetype" poems in this regard, even though there is in "Gulliver"
a slight touch of what we have identified in this study as the Coriolanus
complex. In these two poems, Soyinka appropriates the central legends of

these two figures from Western literature to make ironic, self-deprecating comments on idealists and visionaries who would set a world out of joint aright, Hamlet with his will to action paralyzed by endless questioning of motives and ends, and Gulliver with his outsize intellect and sensibility held in thrall in a land of spiritual and ethical midgets. The final stanza of "Gulliver" perhaps best expresses this ironic contemplation of his incarceration that Soyinka makes in this section of *A Shuttle* by appropriating moral and ideological values associated with these archetypal figures from Western canonical texts. The stanza alludes to the trial of Gulliver by the Lilliputians in Swift's classic text. In the light – or darkness – of the sentence pronounced on Gulliver, his "crime" is generalized beyond any personal action or motives to a universal value dreaded by all tyrants and hegemons – acuity of critical intelligence and moral insight:

> The fault is not in ill-will but in seeing ill
> The drab-horse labors best with blinkers
> We pardon him to lose his sight to a cure
> Of heated needles, that proven cure for all
> Abnormalities of view – foresight, insight
> Second sight and all solecisms of seeing –
> Called vision!
>
> (*Shuttle*, 26)

All five poems in "Prisonnettes" have about them two mutually self-cancelling features which justify the ironic diminutive coined from the word "prison" in the section's title: on the one hand, a rigid, unvarying stanzaic pattern in which, without exception, each poem is made up of five-line stanzas, the fifth line of each stanza being the only line with ten or eleven syllables, each of the remaining four lines comprising between two to six syllables; and on the other hand, uniformly sardonic sentiments and attitudes uncontainable, it seems, by the extreme formalism of the stanzaic pattern. Thus, while the overall effect of these "prisonnettes" is not unlike that of the "shotgun" sketches and revues of Soyinka's agit-prop drama – roughhewn, hard-hitting and wickedly satiric and parodic social criticism – the formalism of the metrical pattern acts to considerably defamiliarize the protest embodied by this group of poems. This general profile works least in "Anymistic Spells" where obscurity of allusions make the "cursifying" articulations either opaque or gratuitous; it works best in a poem like "Background and Friezes" and "Future Plans" where the objects or events targeted are easily recognizable. In "Anymistic

Spells," the target is Yakubu Gowon, head of the civil-war military regime in power in Lagos during Soyinka's incarceration; in "Future Plans" the event (or phenomenon) referred to is the bizarre pattern of international alliances formed either in support of, or against secession during the civil war. In general then, the "Prisonnettes" poems show Soyinka using his tried and tested weapons of protest and resistance – satire, parody, invective – without the mediation of his complex mythopoesis, but with a discreet technical formalism which skillfully exploits the confinement imposed by his detention. The last two stanzas of "Future Plans" are particularly illustrative of the resulting nuanced protest of this poetic pastiche:

> Projects in view:
> Mao Tse Tung in league
> With Chiang Kai. Nkrumah
> Makes a secret
> Pact with Verwood, sworn by Hastings Banda
>
> Proven: Arafat
> In flagrante cum
> Golda Meier. Castro drunk
> With Richard Nixon
> Contraceptions stacked beneath the papal bunk . . .
> *and more to come* (75)

The complement of proselytizing, left-identified poems gathered in the section "Poems of Bread and Earth" is the most uneven of the five sections of *A Shuttle*. Nearly all of the poems exploit the dialectical tension between the literal and symbolic connotations of the two keywords of the section's title, "bread" and "earth." In addition to these two key tropes, some of the poems in the section, like "Ever-Ready Bank Accounts" and "Apres La Guerre" exploit replacement metaphors for "bread" and "earth," often in the form of an extended wordplay. In the former poem, this doesn't work quite effectively because much of the metaphoric wordplay used to express the pathos of poverty and exploitation seems strained and precious. Conversely, the same technique works trenchantly in "Relief," Soyinka first deftly building up a contrast between life-sustaining and life-negating dependence on bread as an all-embracing trope for physical sustenance, and then going on to deploy this contrast in an uproarious send-up of the notoriety of the extravagance of the banqueting at Yakubu Gowon's wedding during the dark days of the Nigerian civil war. From this perspective of exploiting the tension between the literal or factual and the metaphoric and symbolic, perhaps the most successful poem in this section is "Ujamaa" which turns out to be only deceptively simple and uncomplicated in its vigorous celebration of labor. Dedicated to Julius Nyerere, the poem is a condensed poetic meditation on the Marxian labor theory of value, its specific variation on this theme making, not workers' labor but "earth," or the "land," with its "natural" munificence, the ultimate measure of value ("Earth replete/Seeks no homage from the toil of earth"). This sets the stage for the poem's frontal attack on two historic modes of labor exploitation: the tributes extracted by feudal and bourgeois relations of production and that extracted by the deformations of bureaucratic, repressive socialist collectivization. There seems to be a slight racialization of Nyerere's "African socialism" in the sixth line of this poem of thirteen lines, but read in the context of the poem's gritty humanism, "African socialism" in "Ujamaa" is continuous with the ethical and spiritual universalism that Soyinka celebrates in this and other poems in the volume:

> Your black earth hands unchain
> Hope from death messengers, from
> In-bred dogmanoids that prove
> Grimmer than the Grim Reaper, insatiate
> Predators on humanity, their fodder
> Sweet is leaven, bread, Ujamaa
> Bread of the earth, by the earth
> For the earth. Earth is all people (80)

In the general Preface to *A Shuttle in the Crypt*, Soyinka writes that the section "Chimes of Silence" is "central to the entire experience" of writing poetry under the peculiar and unique conditions of his prison confinement. It is thus no wonder that having said this of the section in the general Preface, Soyinka would also append a special section preface to the cycle of poems in "Chimes of Silence." Perhaps more than any other prefatory gloss on his own plays, poetry and nonfictional prose works, this preface to the central section of *A Shuttle* is the most illuminating. For not only does it provide helpful contextual notes to the allusions to very private experiences in the poems of the cycle, it also enables the reader to link many of these allusions to other writings of Soyinka, most especially the writings on the Nigerian civil war. This factor has a lot to do with the fact that the "Chimes of Silence" cycle is probably the most successful sequence of poems in Soyinka's five volumes of poetry.

It is from this preface, for instance, that we get a sense of the extreme desolation of the psychobiographical condition behind the arresting oxymoron in the section title contained in the conjoining of the word "chimes" with its semantic inversion, "silence." Apparently in order to increase the psychological ennui of Soyinka's solitary confinement, his jailers at a certain stage in his imprisonment virtually sealed off all the holes or breaches in the walls of his prison cell, thus literally transforming the cell into the "crypt" of the title of the entire volume, *A Shuttle in the Crypt.* This act of attempted psychological strangulation apparently worked in the way that it transformed the "crypt" of the poet's cell into a harrowing echo chamber in which *all* sounds were magnified a thousand fold. ("When it thunders, my skull is the anvil of the gods") As Soyinka remarks in that same preface: "Sounds. Sounds acquire a fourth dimension in a living crypt. A definition which, as in the case of thunder, becomes physically unbearable. In the case of the awaited but unheard, psychically punishing (32)."

The three most successful poems of the section are "Bearings," "Procession," and "Seed." They all derive their power from a dialectical inversion of the psychic negations of life in the "crypt," accomplished through the incarcerated poet's astonishing but highly disciplined acts of imaginative and verbal extemporization of the unceasing and pervasive experience of adversity. For instance in "Bearings," the very act of *naming* other topographic sites of the prison complex which Soyinka cannot see but from which sounds of various kinds invade his "crypt" yields the arresting tropological titles of the five poems in the cycle "Bearings." These are "Wailing Wall," "Wall of Mists," "Amber Wall," "Purgatory" and "Vault Centre." "Wailing Wall" is so named because the poet once heard from a wing of the prison complex the sustained wailing of a prison inmate who was apparently in his death throes, the wailing lasting all day from dawn to dusk when the man finally died. This particular incident must have left a lasting emotional impact on Soyinka because he has alluded to it in powerful, recurrent terms in other works like *The Man Died* and *From Zia with Love.* In "Wailing Wall," the experience of being an unwilling witness to this long, unrelieved cry of human anguish from within the echo chamber of his "crypt" draws from the poet a powerfully parodic juxtaposition of liturgical symbols normatively associated with hope, faith and grace with images of scavenging birds of prey like vultures and crows; the effect, given the primary allusion of the poem to the hapless wailing, dying inmate, is a grimly sardonic vision of the

overturning of the sustaining positive values of faith and grace preached
by all religious creeds:

> Vulture presides in tattered surplice
> In schism for collection plates, with –
> Crow in white collar, legs
> Of toothpick death plunged
> Deep in a salvaged morsel. Choirmaster
> When a hymn is called he conducts,
> Baton-breaking their massed discordance
> Invocation to the broken Word
> On broken voices
>
> Air-tramp, black verger
> Descend on dry prayers
> To altars of evil
> And a charity of victims (*Shuttle*, 34)

In "Walls of Mists" there is an even more dense and scathing marshaling
of metaphors and tropes of unregenerate evil, precisely because this
is the "wall" from which the poet daily hears prayers and hymns from
female prison inmates. Concerning this wall, Soyinka writes in the section
Preface: "From beyond the Wall of Mists the perverse piety of women,
that inhuman patience to which they were born, drifts across to lash
the anguish from the Wall of Purgatory (33)." The "Wall of Purgatory"
alludes to the torture and flagellation wing of the prison; its juxtaposition
with the "Wall of Mists" from which comes the prayers and hymns of the
female inmates needs no comment. But it is also the case that from the
"Wall of Mists" also comes to the poet the shrill laughter and keening cries
of deranged female inmates. Thus, the daily round of prayers ("vespers")
of the religious sorority becomes for the "encrypted" poet, the "Witches
Sabbath" of the second stanza of the poem, a transmogrification worthy
of the most oneiric metamorphoses in Ovid or Dante:

> Witches' Sabbath what you hold
> Vermilion lizards on sun orgies
> Monster beetles in wall ulcers, broiled
> In steam of mildew drying
> Mists of metamorphosis
> Men to swine, strength to blows
> Grace to lizard prances, honor
> To sweetmeats on the tongue of vileness (35–6)

Indeed, Dante is subtly invoked in "Purgatory," the fourth poem in the
"Bearings" cycle. The allusion of this poem, as we have observed, is to

the prison chamber for the physical and mental torture of prisoners. In the following lines from the poem, this is envisioned by Soyinka in the graphic terms of a Dantesque vision of a humanity stripped of all redeeming values, of even the most ordinary and equable decencies:

> For here the mad commingle with the damned.
> Epileptics, seers and visionaries
> Addicts of unknown addictions, soulmates
> To the vegetable soul, and grey
> Companions to the ghosts of landmarks
> Trudging the lifelong road to a dread
> Judicial sentence.
>
> (38-9)

Not all the poems in "Bearings" are driven by this sardonic view of social life seen from the viewpoint of the most ill-used individuals and social groups. "Vault Centre," which brings the topography of "Bearings" to the very core of the poet's psychic lacerations in the "crypt," contains moving projections of the imagination of the incarcerated poet-artificer into the soaring flights of the birds he can see from the *only* open space directly accessible to him – the bits of skyline visible from slits in the decrepit ceiling of his cell. It is this same cramped skyline which enables the poet to get a glimpse of a young boy atop a mango tree reaching out for the fruit at the topmost branch of the tree. And it is this sight which elicits from Soyinka in "Amber Wall" perhaps the only completely unambiguously optimistic poem in the "Bearings" cycle. There is remarkable economy and elegance in this poem in its narration of this experience of contact by the confined poet with another human being in the very act of garnering the beneficence of nature:

> His hands upon the loftiest branches
> Halted on the prize, eyes in wonderlust
> Questioned this mystery of man's isolation
>
> Fantasies richer than burning mangoes
> Flickered through his royal mind, an open
> Noon above the door that closed
>
> I would you may discover, mid-morning
> To the man's estate, with lesser pain
> The wall of gain within the outer loss
>
> Your flutes at evening, your seed-awakening
> Dances fill the night with growth; I hear
> The sun's sad chorus to your starlit songs (37)

If it seems serendipitous that the third and fourth of Soyinka's five volumes of poetry, *Ogun Abibiman* and *Mandela's Earth*, are primarily based on Africa's own "deep South" and its tragic history, it ought to be remembered that the erstwhile South African apartheid regime, with its "master race" ideology, its institutions of state racism, and its universally condemned laws, policies and practices, had always obsessed Soyinka as a writer and activist. As a fledgling playwright, he wrote and tried to stage a play on apartheid, *The Invention*, but the effort was aborted because Soyinka himself realized that try as much as he would, he could not write about South Africa authentically and credibly because he lacked the intimacy, the human and existential immersion in the actualities of life under the apartheid regime. Thereafter, he shifted his searing indictment of apartheid to the more pliable genre of the essay, producing powerful and eloquent critical vignettes of the South African racist nightmare in such diverse pieces as "The Writer in the Modern African State," parts of *Myth, Literature and the African World*, his Nobel acceptance speech, "This Past Must Address Its Present" and "Climates of Art." It therefore seems that these two particular volumes of Soyinka's poems return to the challenge that had bucked him in *The Invention*, this time not in the medium of drama, but through sub-genres of poetry like the hybridized mix of the lyric, the epic and the neotraditional Yoruba *ijala* chant. *Mandela's Earth* of course contains a lot else beside the poems on South Africa; indeed of all the volumes of Soyinka's poetry, this is the least organized around a cluster of associated themes.

The group of poems which give *Ogun Abibiman* its title is not only the opening section of the volume, it is also the longest. Additionally, in some of the pieces in this volume we see a new, higher level of political poetry than in any previous effort by Soyinka in that sub-genre. By 1976 when the collection was published, Frantz Fanon's prophetic prediction that race as a powerful mobilizing political ideology would become less and less effective than it had been in the heyday of anti-colonialism throughout Africa, that indeed it would become more and more cut off from the realities and dilemmas of postcolonial Africa, had been extensively confirmed nearly everywhere on the continent.[8] Race did remain a powerful ideological and discursive marker in Southern Africa, but even there the realities of "independent" Africa to the north did substantially redound on debates within the liberation movements in southern Africa by giving class an increasingly decisive pertinence which had been nearly invisible in the anticolonial struggles of the pre- and post Second World War periods. In literature, especially in poetry, the heady and pervasive racialization that decisively shaped Négritude and to a lesser extent marked protest poetry in Anglophone Africa had become a spent force by 1976 when *Ogun Abibiman* burst on the literary scene with the force of a thunderstorm, with its reprise of race as a fount of political community, its insistence on historic redress of ancient and modern wrongs against black people, and its project of articulating the deepest promptings of the collective psyche of a continent. The gloss that Soyinka provides on the word *Abibiman* is explicit on these points:

Abibiman: The Black nation; the Land of the Black Peoples; the Black World; that which pertains to, the matter, the affair of Black peoples. (*OA*, 23)

In its conception, *Ogun Abibiman* may have been going against the grain of cultural politics and ideological discourses when it was published, but by seizing on a specific event which did cause ripples throughout Africa, it gave substance and compelling force to its immersion in racial myths of heroic, redemptive action by messianic "race men" like the two protagonists of the poem, Ogun and Shaka. This event was the declaration by the late Samora Machel, then president of the nation-state of Mozambique, that from that year 1976, the people of his nation were placing themselves in readiness for war against the illegal white supremacist regime in Rhodesia and the bastion of state racism further south. Moreover, *Ogun Abibiman* sought and found emotive, symbolic force for racial mobilization by exposing the deeply racialist, deeply ethnocentric universalism of the supporters and backers of apartheid in the West.

   A poem of course works or fails not primarily on account of the circumstances of its conception and composition, but on the basis of its achieved effect or impact. All the same, Soyinka seems to have taken care to bring auspicious political and cultural events to bear on his apparent objective in writing this poem, this being the ideological mobilization of an entire continent to give apartheid the fight of its life. One of these events is of course the poem's origin in Samora Machel's historic declaration. Other auspicious material quarried by Soyinka in the poem is the tradition of the racial ethnopoetics of Négritude in its classical period in the 1940s and 50s.[9] The mobilization of these two events works to enhance the desired impact of *Ogun Abibiman*. Perhaps the most striking expression of this is in the heightened aural and performative idiom and tone that the poem appropriates from Négritude poetry of the 1940s and from Yoruba *ijala* poetry. Thus, though on one level *Ogun Abibiman* is highly literary, it is a poem very much intended to be spoken aloud and performed. It very

consciously builds on the axiomatics of chanted, performed oral poetry
in its extensive use of a single image, idea or theme repeated in rising and
falling rhythms in alternation. This is why, in terms of pure narrativity,
there is little movement in the entire 3 sections, 52 stanzas and 483 lines
of the poem. In place of a movement between unfolding historic episodes
in the confrontation of black Africa with apartheid and its legacies, what
we encounter in the poem is basically a prolonged, detailed exploration
of two moments: the present time of readying and honing the collective
will of the continent for the final battle with apartheid, a present time
very much like Walter Benjamin's famous notion of "messianic time";[10] a
retrospective time of the last great stand of the southern African peoples
against the white invaders under the rallying banner of the amaZulu
and their monarch, Shaka. For the former, Soyinka returns to "Idanre"
as a sort of prolegomenon to re-animate Ogun, but this time both the
external profile of the god's attributes and the plunge into the deity's
inner psychic states are expressed in much clearer, much sharper lyric
and narrative poetry:

> Pleas are ended in the Court of Rights. Hope
> Has fled the Cape miscalled – Good Hope
> We speak no more of mind or grace denied
> Armed in secret knowledge as of old.
> In time of race, no beauty slights the duicker's
> in time of strength, the elephant stands alone
> In time of hunt, the lion's grace is holy
> In time of flight, the egret mocks the envious
> In time of strife, none vies with Him
> Of seven paths, Ogun, who to right a wrong
> Emptied reservoirs of blood in heaven
> Yet raged with thirst – I read
> His savage beauty on black brows
> In depths of molten bronze aflame
> Beyond their eyes' fixated distances –
> And tremble!
>
> (*OA*, 6–7)

The last twelve lines of this concluding stanza of "Induction," the first
section of *Ogun Abibiman*, are direct borrowings, appropriately worked
over for a new context, from traditional *ijala* chants in praise of Ogun.
Incidentally, the same lines are repeated as the penultimate stanza of
the entire poem (*OA*, 22). The repetition and variations on the con-
stative phrase, "In time of," all complemented by imagery from the
world of nature, is the kind of discreet folkloricism deftly deployed in

this poem to conflate myth and history and to merge willed pastoralism with tragic catharsis in order to create the fetching lyricism of the first section of *Ogun Abibiman*. This folkloricism is even more pronounced in the following section, "Retrospect for Marchers: Shaka!" And not only in the refrain which runs throughout the entire section, a refrain entirely expressed in untranslated Yoruba words, the Yoruba cadences approximating the harshly metallic and ecstatic rhythms of the music of *bata* drums. Far more profound than a tapping into oral poetic matrices in this section is Soyinka's recourse to a mode of poetic discourse which is alien to the metropolitan, "British" traditions of English poetic discourse – the use of self-addressed *oriki* or praise poems which reorder cosmic balances and reciprocities between mankind and the gods, between the human and the divine. This kind of *oriki* pervades Shaka's long dramatic monologue in this second section, but it is particularly evident in the following lines which both express the great hubris of Shaka and give it a self-transcending communitarian ethic:

> If man cannot, what god dare claim perfection?
> The gods that show remorse lay claim to man's
> Forgiveness – a founder king shall dare no less.
> My nightmare, living, was the sun's collapse
> When man surrenders judgment over
> God or man. Shaka was *all* men. Would,
> To the best of amaZulu, Shaka were also a man,
> A leader yes, next to the imperfect god –
> Would I be Shaka if I asked less? . . . What I did
> Was Shaka, but Shaka was not always I.
> Beset by demons of blood, Shaka reaped
> Harvest of manhood when time wavered
> Uncertainly and mind was transposed in
> Another place. Yet Shaka, king and general
> Fought battles, invented rare techniques, created
> Order from chaos, colored the sights of men
> In self-transcending visions, sought
> Man's renewal in the fount of knowledge.
> From shards of tribe and bandit mores, Shaka
> Raised the city of men in commonweal.
> This last, this Shaka I, crave release
> From masks, from cracked mirrors in the socket of skulls.
>
> (*OA*, 14–15)

That Soyinka is very much aware that in lines such as these he could be said to be rationalizing the megalomania and bloody excesses of the historical Shaka is shown, if not adequately in the poem itself, in the commentary that he enters on the Zulu monarch in his glossary to the poem:

Shaka: King of the amaZulu, easily Africa's most renowned nation builder. A military and socio-organizational genius, he suffered from what, from this distance, we can only surmise as manic depression. It resulted in the decimation of his own people, a history which reminds one of a similar lapse in Ogun's own leadership of men (*OA*, 23)

But it is not clear, *in the poem*, that Soyinka escapes from a charge he once leveled at the Négritude poets in his essay, "And After the Narcissist?." This is the charge of confusing the "totemic poet" with the "poet's totem." By this he meant that in speaking for, or on behalf of a whole people or "race," the poet often confuses his own subjectivity, his own selfhood for the collective racial selfhood touted by the Négritude poets. In *Ogun Abibiman*, the cast of protagonists, of speaking voices is exactly three: Ogun, Shaka and the poet-chronicler-celebrant. Consequently the "racial burden," such as it is, falls on the mirror-images of one another projected by these three protagonists. It is normally a tall representational and epistemological order for *one man* to represent the collective will of a "race" or a continent without the sacrifice, ultimately, of ideological progressivism and philosophical consistency. Of the instances in *Ogun Abibiman* when the flaws that result from this problem are starkly revealed, none is more astounding than the following lines wherein Shaka's self-examination for the causes of his defeat from within (his own generals and rival chieftains) and from without (the white invaders) is expressed in imagery and tropes that reduce the complexity of history and the multiplicity of causes to a rather conservative phallocratism:

> The task must gain completion, our fount
> Of being cleansed from termites' spittle –
> In this alone I seek my own completion.
> Shall I be plain? The blade driven
> True to paths of treachery – my trusting back –
> This gangrene seeps, not through Shaka's heart
> But in his loins. The sere bequest yet haunts
> Descendants of the amaZulu, empty husks
> Worm-hollowed in place of bursting germ.
> The purifying path lies in this knowledge –
> The termites that would eat the kingdom
> First build their nest
> In the loin-cloth of the king (13)

If read somewhat expansively and "sympathetically," what these lines amount to is the suggestion that apartheid, with its destructive hatred of Black people and its legacy of supremacist arrogance, has not met its match because there have not been *men* like Shaka, or stated somewhat differently, because of the loss of the collective manhood of the race. But read with critical rigor, the lines imply a baffling, even trivializing neo-Négritudist symbolization of the will to resistance, the will to emancipation of a whole continent by male sexual or generative prowess.

Ogun Abibiman, in its totality, transcends such astonishing flaws in its racial discourse. Skillfully weaving history, myth and powerful vignettes of the cynical pragmatism of modern-day "Great Powers" diplomacy with bitter but gritty exposure of the compromises and betrayals of neo-colonial African regimes, the poem constitutes a remarkable attempt at reinventing heroic poetry for a continent in the grip of profound self-doubts and in the wake of a stolidly unheroic, postmodern age with little appetite for the *grands récits* of traditional heroic poetry.

That the central section of *Mandela's Earth* lends its title to the entire collection is no surprise because, of the four sections making up the volume, it is the only one organized around a central figure – Nelson Mandela – and a consuming desire to meet and subvert the extreme racial provocation of apartheid on a scale of imagination, intellect and will equal to the racial mindset of the ideologues and theorists of apartheid and their Western backers. In this respect, it is remarkable that the five poems in this section can be said to take off where the inflated diction and rhetoric of *Ogun Abibiman* inevitably succumb to the laws of gravity – as far as using the figure of one promethean hero to stand for the will and destiny of a continent is concerned.

The *tone* of address in the poems of the "Mandela's Earth" cycle is no less reverential in their run of celebrative apostrophes to the courage, integrity and will of Nelson Mandela than the tone which consummates the idealization of Ogun and Shaka in *Ogun Abibiman*. But tone – and mood and diction – in the "Mandela's Earth" cycle of poems is deeply inflected by a corrosive, deflationary wit that is totally absent in *Ogun Abibiman*. And this wit pits the moral and spiritual stature of Nelson Mandela, imprisoned for more than a quarter of a century, against the absurd, paranoiac logic of his apartheid captors:

> Your patience grows inhuman, Mandela.
> Do you grow food? Do you make friends
> Of mice and lizards? Measure the growth of grass
> For time's unhurried pace?

Are you now the crossword puzzle expert?
Chess? Ah, no! Subversion lurks among
Chess pieces. Structured clash of black and white,
Equal ranged and paced? An equal board? No!
Not on Robben Island.

(*ME*, 4)

These lines come from the first poem of the volume, "Your Logic
Frightens Me, Mandela." The careful, astute student of Soyinka's writings may detect in the lines echoes of the praise singer, Olohun Iyo's
praise chants to Elesin Oba in *Death and the King's Horseman*, especially in
the manner in which the apostrophes to the heroism of the protagonist
takes the form of repeated rhetorical questions whose imagery derives
from a threatened or fallen pastoral lifeworld. ("Do you grow food? Do
you make friends with mice and lizards? Measure the growth of grass/For
time's unhurried pace?"). This feeling is enhanced by the fact that in this
and the other poems of the section, the poet as interlocutor and rhap-
sodist nearly always speaks in the accents of a "griot," a bard of the racial
"tribe." But if this is true, it is no less true that unlike Olohun Iyo in *Death
and the King's Horseman*, the bard who celebrates Mandela in these poems
is a modernist, ironizing "griot" whose locutions come from an acute
consciousness of a continent, a world which has been "wrenched from
its grooves." This is why in "Your Logic Frightens Me, Mandela," we see
a reversal of the restorative ethic of protagonist heroism which powers
the plot of *Death and the King's Horseman*. For in that play, the loss of nerve
or will of the hero wrenches the metaphysical order of the world from
its course; in this poem, the heroic protagonist is completely self-present
in his will and volition and only this portends restorative bounty to a
"will-voided" racial community which parasitically feeds on the will of
the protagonist hero:

Your bounty threatens me, Mandela, that taut
Drumskin of your heart on which our millions
Dance. I fear we latch, fat leeches
On your veins. Our daily imprecisions
Dull keen edges of your will.
Compromises deplete your acts's repletion –
Feeding will-voided stomachs of a continent,
What will be left of you, Mandela?

(*ME*, 5)

Since nearly all the poems in this section of *Mandela's Earth* are sharply
focused on events, personalities and institutions in South Africa of the

post-Soweto period, this construction of Mandela in the mold of the Coriolanus complex may be excused as an expression of the poet's despair at the ebb of revolutionary currents of the 1980s. This retreat from the revolutionary momentum of the encirclement of apartheid in the immediate post-Soweto period saw the embrace, covertly and overtly, of "Dialogue" and "constructive engagement" with the apartheid regime by some influential African governments; in effect South African politics became very much an active internal dimension of the politics of the African nation-states to the north. And this is why in nearly all the other poems in this section, Soyinka no longer writes of southern Africa from the seemingly unbreachable distance that had produced the stillbirth of *The Invention.* With the additional factor of the internationalization of the struggle against apartheid and the special intimacy afforded by the revolutions in the media and the communications industry, Soyinka's perspectives in these poems achieve a convincing imaginative immersion into the storm centre of the South African liberation struggle which he had not hitherto been able to achieve in his previous literary efforts, including *Ogun Abibiman.* At any rate, these poems teach a lesson about political poetry that is rare in Soyinka's previous volumes of poems: ideology, ethical principle or life-affirming values, though crucial, cannot substitute for finely observed rendition of the human reality affirmed or protested. "Funeral Sermon, Soweto" is perhaps the most successful in this regard and to say this is also to insist that the mode of reception appropriate for such political poetry is not one which looks for instant or clamorous effects, but one which makes great demands on the reader's concentration and imaginative sympathy. For as it gradually builds up a vast profile of diverse funerary rites and obsequies for the wealthy, the powerful and the hegemons of different times and places, the poem subtly and gradually gives a new and startling edge to the politicization of funerals in that period of post-Soweto South Africa. The irony deployed is palpable and extensive but it is unforced. As deeply moving as it is, it also subtly calls for renewed opposition to apartheid even in the ironically capitulationist accents that the funeral homily was forced to adopt because those funerals had to be "allowed" by the bureaucrats and law-keepers of the apartheid Reich:

> We wish to bury our dead. Let all take note,
> Our dead were none of the eternal hoarders –
> Does the buyer of nothing seek after-sales service?
> Not as prophetic intuitions, or sly
> Subversive chant do we invoke these ancient

Ghosts, but as that ritual homily
Time-honored in the office of loss
Not seeking martyrdom, the midnight knock,
Desecration of our altars, vestments,
Not counting ninety-day detention laws,
The state seal on the voice of man – and God . . .

We wish only to bury our dead. Shorn
Of all but name, our indelible origin,
For indeed our pride once boasted empires,
Kings and nation-builders. Too soon
The brace of conquest circumscribed our being
Yet found us rooted in that unyielding
Will to life bequeathed from birth, we
Sought no transferred deed of earthly holdings
Slaves do not possess their kind. Nor do
The truly free.

                                        (*ME*, 18–19)

It would be almost trivializing to offer a paraphrase of these lines of such crystalline clarity. Nonetheless, it is necessary to draw attention to how the persona who speaks these lines discharges the burden of memorializing the victims of apartheid through a superbly modulated anger which assails the arrogance of supremacist power with the rhetoric of a naturalistic conception of justice in which the dispossession of the enslaved is the very mark of the unfreedom of the enslaver. This is why revolutionary, ethical principle in this poem traverses vast temporal and spatial units of history and ranges across the experiences of diverse peoples and races, but not such that it overwhelms the harrowing immediacy of the political funerals of post-Soweto South Africa.

It is perhaps appropriate to end our discussion of the poems in the "South Africa" cycle in *Mandela's Earth* with a brief account of how the contrasting techniques deployed in two poems, "Like Rudolf Hess, the man Said!" and "'No!' He Said" work in different ways to achieve this impressive integration of totalizing revolutionary principle with sharply observed profiles of the horrendous actualities of apartheid. In the former poem, we are in the world of Soyinka's excessive love of punning and the use of deflationary wordplay in order to tease maximum satire and humanistic protest out of the *reductio ad absurdum* of the infamous statement made by the then foreign minister of South Africa, Pik Botha, that the apartheid regime was holding Nelson Mandela captive in the same way that the Allied Powers were holding the Nazi war criminal, Rudolf Hess. As is well-known, the apartheid regime had historic and ideological links

with the Nazis.¹¹ But since by itself punning is not high on the totem
pole of poetic metaphorization, Soyinka makes a recourse to linking
wordplay in this poem to a truly Swiftian fixation on the deranged logic
of the comparison of Nelson Mandela to Nazi war criminals. This yields
a ballooning, spiraling send-up of Mr. Botha's statement by transforming
Mandela to the evil genius behind all the atrocities, all the "crimes against
humanity" (U.N. Declaration against apartheid, 1973) of not only the
Nazis but also of the apartheid regime itself:

> Got you! Trust the Israelis.
> I bet they flushed him out, raced him down
> From Auschwitz to Durban, and Robben Island.
> Mandela? Mandel . . . Mendel . . . Mengel . . . Mengele!
> It's he! Nazi superman in sneaky blackface! . . . (6)
> Cute Mandgela, sought everywhere,
> Cooly ensconced on Robben Island.
> I saw your hand in Biko's death, that perfect
> Medical scenario, tailormade for you.
> And hundreds more of young Icarus syndrome-
> Flying suspects, self-propelled
> From fifty-story floors
> To land on pavements labeled – WHITES ONLY!
> You question them only in white preserves –
> How would a high-rise building fit in shanty-town? (8)

If these lines push the illogicality of the ideological discourses of the
apartheid regime to their grotesque limits, the allegorization of the phantasmic aspects of the apartheid imagination exceeds those limits in the
poem, "'No!' He Said." This poem celebrates the legendary steadfast-
ness of Mandela in the face of the use of every ruse and stratagem to
make him renounce the struggle against the apartheid regime and cut a
personal deal with both that regime's power brokers and the foreign Cold
War geopolitical pragmatists who, to the end, sustained the apartheid
regime by the specious logic of global "Realpolitick." In the elaborate
allegory outlined in this poem, Mandela is bearded in his solitary cell
on Robben Island by tempters in a modern-day version of a medieval
mystery cycle. This produces in this poem one of the most accomplished
pieces in all of Soyinka's poetry of the sub-genre of narrative poetry. And
this is hardly surprising because in this poem, there are several speaking
voices and the juxtaposition of these voices entails the fusion of the lyric,
dramatic and narrative modes at a consummate level rare in Soyinka's
formal verse but often almost effortlessly achieved in the poetry of his

dramatic verse dialogues in plays like *The Lion and the Jewel, Death and the King's Horseman* and *The Bacchae of Euripides*. In this respect, it is significant that the whole poem is structured by a tacit distribution of the stanzas and lines of the poem between three "speakers": the first two of the ten stanzas of the poem, as well as the concluding two-line stanza, are spoken by the poet-narrator; the longest section comprising the seven middle stanzas of the poem are spoken by the "Tempters" who have come to Mandela's cell to break him; the ninth or penultimate stanza is spoken by Mandela himself. The only deviation from this basic stanzaic pattern is that every single stanza in the poem ends with the refrain of the poem's title, "no, he said." This pattern affords Soyinka a tremendous scope for indicting all who collaborated with the monstrous evil of apartheid, by complacency as much as active connivance. Beyond this, the poem executes a devastating dismantling of the logics of old and new forms of racist discourses and supremacist social imaginaries very rare in contemporary poetry. Nowhere is this more eloquently articulated than in the sixth, seventh and eighth stanzas, the core of the Tempters' gauntlet to Mandela:

> The axis of the world has shifted. Even the polar star
> Loses its fixity, nudged by man-made planets.
> The universe has shrunk. History reechoes as
> We plant new space flags of a master race.
> You are the afterburn of our crudest launch.
> The stars disown you, but – no, he said.
>
> Your tongue is swollen, a mute keel
> Upended on the seabed of forgotten time.
> The present breeds new tasks, same taskmasters.
> On that star planet of our galaxy, code-named Bantustan,
> They sieve rare diamonds from moon dust. In the choice reserves
> Venerably pastured, you . . . but – no, he said.
>
> That ancient largess on the mountaintop
> Shrinks before our gift's munificence, an offer even
> Christ, second-come, could not refuse. Be ebony mascot
> On the flagship of our space fleet, still
> Through every turbulence, spectator of our Brave New World
> Come, Ancient Mariner, but – no, he said.

> (*ME*, 22–3)

Mandela as an "ebony mascot" on the flagship of a space fleet probing the "Milky Way" is an image which seems to confer a seal of nobility on Black suffering, just as it also subtly suggests a readiness to accept a discreet *melaninization* of the presumed "whiteness" of the achievements of modern civilization in commerce, science and space exploration. In this manner, the racial confrontations specific to apartheid are in these lines absorbed into the abstract non-racialism of some postmodern discourses of race and identity. This abstract non-racialism entails a putative sublation of the crude "master race" discourses of the nineteenth-century "prehistory" of modern racism: from the discourses of racial hierarchies and "manifest destinies" to the discourse of a world without "races," even as entire peoples continue to be viewed and treated as inferior, incommensurable and threatening others.[12] For in the manner of all sublations, what is "crude" or, in the present case, what is embodied as a literal, epidermal datum, is not totally expelled or even transcended, it is merely transformed into an idealized, aestheticized version of the "lower" term. Thus, even as the Tempters in these lines pressure Mandela in his prison cell with an offer "even/Christ, second-come, could not refuse," they let out that the "star planet" at the end of their intergalactic probe is "code-named" – "Bantustan." The superbly modulated irony of these metaphors and images around the exemplary figure of Mandela mark the remarkable ideological distance between the rendering of racial identity in relation to global peace and justice in *Mandela's Earth* and the masculinist essentialism of the collective will to emancipation of Black people that we uncovered in our reading of *Ogun Abibiman*.

Outsiders, the fifth and most recently published volume of Soyinka's poetry is, in many respects, compositely a worthy sequel to the best of the poems in *Mandela's Earth*. Though the volume was published in January 1999, all the seven poems in it appear to have been written between 1994 and 1998, the years of Soyinka's most recent encounter with involuntary exile during the inglorious reign of the dictator, Sani Abacha. As we have observed in the first chapter of this study, those years saw Soyinka in a commanding role in the external opposition to the Abacha regime; as a consequence of this, Soyinka and eleven other leaders of that external opposition were charged with treason in March 1997. Previous to this farcical attempt to make dedication to freedom and justice treasonous, the Abacha regime had in November 1995 hanged Ken Saro-Wiwa, the world-famous writer and environmental activist, together with eight other Ogoni activists. Five of the seven poems in *Outsiders* have these events as their informing background, seen in the broader context of the human factor in a homeland under a tyranny so brutal, so corrupt and mediocre that it seemed like an occupying foreign power without any program for its subject population beyond plunder and repression. These are the first four poems in the volume, "Ah, Demosthenes!," "The Children of this Land," "Pens for Hire," and "Hours Lost, Hour Stolen" and the seventh and final poem of the volume, "Calling Josef Brodsky for Ken Saro-Wiwa." In this last poem, Soyinka celebrates the late fellow Nobel laureate, Brodsky, as an embodiment of something Nadine Gordimer has described as "the madness of the brave."[13] By this Gordimer meant the quality of total disregard of the perils to the self in those who oppose forms of political power which lack any respect for human life. In Gordimer's view, this "mad" bravery is something at the core of the existence of such women and men which makes them uncontainable by tyranny, no matter how extreme it is. In this poem, Soyinka says of Brodsky that he carried this "thing" at the core of his existence everywhere and became a symbol for his homeland, "in and out of pro patria." From this I would argue that even though there are dozens of poems on Nigeria in its "seasons of anomy" and collective peril in Soyinka's previous volumes of poetry before *Outsiders*, this most recent volume contains his quintessential "pro patria" poetry, his poems of *civitas*, the classical conception of patriotism as a virtue indissociable from honor, justice and service to the collective good. And this extends even to the other two poems in the volume, "Business Lunch – the Bag Lady" and "Exit," both of which, ostensibly, are not on subjects or issues pertaining to Nigeria under the Abacha dictatorship. Indeed, these two poems are the only poems in the volume written with a light, playful or mock-serious tone. But precisely because each of these two poems celebrates aspects of life that the poet who penned the other five poems in the volume wishes almost desperately to preserve, aspects he has in fact celebrated in some of his other works as part of the lasting human and cultural legacy of his society, these two poems partake of the "pro patria" vintage of the other five poems of loss, dispossession and desolation in the "homeland." For this reason, I shall approach the five "civitas" poems through these two poems of "home away from home." Before doing this, it is perhaps important to stress here that because this volume probably shows Soyinka at his most accessible, at his most "unobscure" and "undifficult," those students of his poetry who have bemoaned the mix of opacity and lyricism, of syntactical untidiness and startling eloquence in his poetry over the last four decades will welcome the clarity and easeful intelligibility of virtually all the poems in this volume. But this is perhaps something of a ruse, for even when he is this accessible and intelligible, Soyinka remains a poet of great, nearly unparaphraseable density and *gravitas*.

"Exit," the shortest poem in *Outsiders*, is dedicated to the late French President, François Mitterand. This is not, however, an ordinary dedication since the poem is in fact about Mitterand's last few hours of life, about the deeply moving way in which, realizing that the end was near, he made his peace with this world, joked about dying – "I do not mind the face of death, but find/Not being around distasteful" – and came to a "negotiated settlement" with his physician which enabled the regimen of "time-delaying pills" keeping him alive to be stopped so that he could die – "quit" as the poem expresses it – with dignity. We are not too far in this poem, it seems, from the spiritual universe of the values celebrated in the parable of the "Not-I Bird" in the first scene of *Death and the King's Horseman*. And more appropriate to the "pro patria" context of the "civitas" poems in *Outsiders*, there is the point that the world, our world, does contain powerful rulers who not only know when to "quit," but more importantly how to "quit" so that life is renewed and reaffirmed even by their exit.

The dedication in "Business Lunch – the Bag Lady" is to the late Femi Johnson, a close personal friend of the poet whose passion for life, especially his unalloyed sybaritic delight in the best food and wine in the company of friends with whom to enjoy them is captured in parts of *Ibadan – the 'Penkelemes' Years*. In this poem, the "bag lady" of the title of the poem who looks and acts every bit the human and social archetype of the confirmed vagrant, wanders into a high-class restaurant where upper echelon business executives dine only with others of their kind. She then proceeds to order choice dishes which she consumes with meticulous and rather noisy zeal, totally oblivious of the incongruity of her person in that space. The poet who narrates this startling encounter with total rapture is equally responsive to the two effects which the hedonistic "bag lady" produces on all who are present at the "happening": the tacit but eloquent deflation of class pretensions in the "bag lady's" total lack of self-consciousness in a place where all eyes and ears wished her anywhere else but there; the exemplary, almost sacramental quality of this vagrant woman's enjoyment of her repast. On one level, this poem celebrates social "border-crossing" in the most unexpected of places, but ultimately, it is a lyrically funny celebration of a rare moment when the joy of life triumphs over the constrictions of social distinctions.

Outsiders has a very insightful introduction written by Rudolph P. Byrd, a professor of English at Emory University where Soyinka held one of the prestigious Woodruff professorships when this volume was published. In this introduction, Byrd observes that "for a writer in exile, the only home is language and the genres of literature in which the exigencies of exile assume significance (vii)." This is a very helpful commentary inasmuch as we conceive of the "home" afforded the writer-in-exile by language and the genres of literature to be conditioned by the exigencies inherent in the uses of language and the motility of the genres and idioms of literary expression themselves. This point is in fact thematized repeatedly in the first three of the five "pro patria" poems, "Ah, Demosthenes!," "The Children of this Land," and "Pens for Hire." In "Ah, Demosthenes!," Soyinka summons the example of the third-century Athenian patriot and orator who defended the cause of democracy in his homeland against the encroachments of tyranny and ultimately imbibed poison rather than live under autocracy. At its surface level, the poem proffers extended variation on a part solemn, part gleeful iteration of the vocation of all the Demosthenes of the past and the present, the vocation to be a nettlesome irritant to the peace and security of tyrants. But at a deeper level, there is great bitterness in the poem, and it is directed not so much at the tyrants and dictators as at the complacencies of the ruled and, especially, the world. This is all the more unacceptable to the poet who dedicates himself to the vocation of Demosthenes because the complacencies of the world at large to the rule and proliferation of tyrants are often enacted through and by inadequacies and infelicities of language. This "betrayal" by and with language and words is what draws the ringing threats of intransigence of gargantuan proportions from the poet in the following lines:

> I'll thrust all fingers down the throat
> Demosthenes
> To raise a spout of bile to drown the world.
> It's petrified, Demosthenes, mere forms
> Usurp the hearts we knew, mere rasps.
> This stuttering does not become the world,
> This tongue of millions fugitive from truth –
> I'll thrust all fingers down the throat.
>
> (5)

These lines of the fifth stanza of a poem of six stanzas build on the skillful use of apostrophe and repetition in the previous stanzas both to mobilize and to renew every means available to the poet of delivering verbal toxins and other forms of "majele," poison, which will be fatal to the rule of tyrants in the poet's own country and continent. But here, in these particular lines, the passion is directed at the conscience of an indifferent world, a world of "millions fugitive from truth," a world where "mere forms usurp the hearts" of otherwise decent people, turning their feeble protests against tyranny "out there" in Africa "mere rasps." That Soyinka can in this and other poems in this volume turn the towering anger of his despair at the human cost of the brutal misrule of tyrants in Africa on the world of "outsiders" (the title of the volume) is both because our world is so interconnected now that "outsiders" and "insiders" are co-implicated in the state of things everywhere in the world, and equally important, because Soyinka is totally unsparing on the culpability, the responsibility of the "insiders" of his homeland and continent for the desolation caused by the long, seemingly interminable misrule of the tyrants.

"The Children of this Land" and "Pens for Hire" are nearly unbearable for the power of their evocation of this desolation in Abacha's Nigeria and much of contemporary Africa. In the introduction to the volume, Rudolph Byrd writes of "majesties of language" in this volume; perhaps nowhere else in the volume are these more evident than in these two poems. "The Children of this Land" attempts a reckoning of the scope of loss and dispossession that are the bequest of the young of a country whose great historical misfortune it is to fall prey to marauding rulers who come in an unending succession of one brutal and mediocre tyrant after another. Part elegy for loss on this monumental scale and part righteous excoriation for those whose complacencies and lack of acuity have made ruination and desolation of such proportions possible, "The Children of this Land" is ultimately a cautionary, prophetic national allegory. This particular dimension of the poem assumes its most graphic and chastening expression in the fourth of the five stanzas of the poem:

> These are the offspring of the dispossessed,
> The hope and land deprived. Contempt replaces
> Filial bonds. The children of this land
> Are always in holed crafts, all tortoise skin
> And scales – the callous of their afterbirth.
> Their hands are clawed for rooting, their tongues
> Propagate new social codes, and laws.
> A new race will supersede the present –
> Where love is banished stranger, lonely
> Wanderer in forests prowled by lust
> On feral pads of power,
> Where love is a hidden, ancient ruin, crushed
> By memory, in this present
> Robbed of presence (5–6)

"Poems for Hire" shows that perhaps the terrifying advance phalanx of the "new race (which) will supersede the present" is already here and ensconced in the most unlikely of places – in the ranks of writers and journalists and those who deal in the currency of language and the word. For the "hired pens" of this poem are those who take up the cause of murderous tyrants and dictators and proceed to distort facts and truths and fabricate lies and falsehoods, especially against the defenders of freedom and the foes of their patrons. Of these there were many both surprising and unsurprising figures in Abacha's Nigeria.[14] In the logic of this poem, the targeting of opponents of tyrannical regimes and their symbolic assassination through words and language prepares the way for and justifies the literal assassinations, the bloodbaths which keep tyrants in power. More concretely, the immediate context for the poem is the massive propaganda apparatus which the Abacha regime set up between 1996 and 1998 which entailed an expenditure of hundreds of millions of dollars to "buy" willing spokespersons at home and abroad in this period when the regime faced almost total international censure and opprobrium largely as a consequence of the hanging of Ken Saro-Wiwa in November 1995. The list is long of respected or influential journalists, American congressmen and women, and publicists who became apologists for the regime of terror in Nigeria.[15] For good measure this poem contains a fierce excoriation of such "hired pens," but in the final analysis the measure of the poem is etched not in the condemnation of those who chose to speak flattery and blandishments to power, who became complicit with illegitimate and dehumanizing power; rather, it is the revelatory power of the poem that stands as its real achievement as it startles the reader into a territory of ineffable human and social wreckage hidden behind the lies and equivocations concocted by the "pens for hire":

> Some, we have come to know. They served
> And were served in turn. Some believed,
> And others cashed their souls in make-belief.
> But both are immunised against the testament
> Of eyes, and ears, the stench and guilt of power
> And anomy of reddening rain, of plagues of locusts
> Deaths of firstborns, seven lean years and
> Yet again the eighth and sequent round –
> Of death and dearth.
>
>   (7–8)

There couldn't be two more dissimilar poems than "Hours Lost, Hours Stolen" and "Calling Josef Brodsky for Ken Saro-Wiwa," the fourth and seventh poems respectively in the collection and the last two poems for review in this discussion. With the possible exception of the first poem of the volume, the poems in *Outsiders* are not combative poems in the manner in which one has come to expect much of Soyinka's political poems to be combative over the course of his previous four volumes of poetry. Stated differently, the poems in this volume are remarkable in the ways in which indignation and ridicule, or conversely, the passion for freedom and justice are modulated by strategies and effects of an elaborate, perhaps deliberate artfulness of rhetoric, tone and imagery. "Hours Lost, Hours Stolen" is probably the most successful poem in this volume in this particular respect, though "The Children of the Land" and "Calling Josef Brodsky for Ken Saro-Wiwa" are close enough to the consummate power of "Hours Lost, Hours Stolen." In this particular poem, there are extraordinarily eloquent expressions of intimate, private dimensions of the condition of enforced exile from a homeland from which the poet is alienated not only because of the tyrants in power but also on account of the effects of tyrannical misrule on present and future generations. These private, intimate moments of the desperate exigencies of exile are not rendered in a confessional, sentimental mode; but even so, *sentiment*, not sentimentality, pervades the poem. This is sentiment of an ancient, almost religious kind and it is based on the notion of debts and responsibilities owed to the land, the earth which "spawned" all of us. In the scale of such values, large public matters of national community and of belonging and "smaller" issues of private deprivations and vexations in the condition of enforced exile assume interconnections only because the poet has the skill of craftsmanship and precision to evoke landscapes in which public and private, personal deprivations and collective traumas are powerfully fused:

> The jackals only seem at bay, or in retreat.
> A new pack is regrouping just beyond the brush.
> The cackle is familiar, no remorse. They know
> The trees against whose bark their hindlegs
> Were last raised – they home in on their odours.
> Daylight will flush them out, not chase them home
> The future they may reject, and memories deny them
> But now, they kill us slowly, from shrine to township
> They kill us slowly on farmstead, in ivory towers
> And factories. They kill our children in their cribs.
>
> (9–10)

The strange and haunting mixture of rage and sobriety, of anger and equanimity in these lines is almost unprecedented in Soyinka's poetry up to the publication of this most recent of his five volumes of poetry. I think this is probably due to a powerful impulse: simply to register, and to bear witness to the scale of loss and suffering and trauma in his homeland and continent at the present time.

"Calling Josef Brodsky for Ken Saro-Wiwa" is, in its twelve stanzas of iii lines, the longest poem in the volume. It is a powerfully moving funeral dirge linking the deaths (and lives) of the Russian poet with the Nigerian novelist and environmental activist. Much of this long poem is constructed in the form of a bantering address to the departed Brodsky, beseeching him to keep the hanged Nigerian activist's restless soul company as they both make the crossing to the great beyond. This is of course an appropriation of a motif and an idiom of traditional African funeral dirges which, in the ritual act of invoking a smooth transition of the departed to the after-life is really about the life of the dead on *this* side of existence and nonexistence, together with the legacies left for the living by the departed. This is why for most of the poem we are treated to a skillful interweaving of the "crimes" and "sins" of both Josef Brodsky and Saro-Wiwa against the autocratic rulers in power in their respective homelands, one spending a large part of his adult life in almost permanent exile in the arid wastes of Siberia and the other in the dungeons of a kleptocratic military regime. Common to both men is, in the opinion of the poet, a tendency to infuriate the regimes in power in their native lands and their judicial and administrative hirelings with their cantankerous disrespect of power, their "refusenik" resolution not to dignify the usurpation of legality and respectability of regimes scornful of natural justice and respect for human life with observance of the protocols of the dutiful, obedient citizen. It would of course be misleading to give the impression that the dominant mood or tone of this poem is that of muted sarcasm and irony since, indeed, as the poem moves to its overwhelming last stanza, *gravitas* predominates as the tone of lines and stanzas shaped by an acute repugnance for the violence of totalitarian regimes of the left and the right. "I never really knew you," Soyinka says to the shade of Brodsky, "but I cling to yours (death) because I own a closer death, a death that dared elude/Prophetic sight." (22) Indeed, the last four stanzas of this poem are imbued with a deep sense of the great violence of the hanging of Saro-Wiwa and the other eight Ogoni activists. This is why in the address of the last stanza to Brodsky, we can hear the distinct tones of a desperate impulse to assuage the extreme brutality of that death in the following lines in which Soyinka beseeches Brodsky to seek out Saro-Wiwa and his other hanged compatriots and render them service that would assuage the great terror of their deaths at the hand of the tyrants in power in their homeland:

> Death that takes brutally breeds restless souls
> You'll find him in a throng of nine, seeking landmarks.
> His soul's violation, the weight of a task unfinished
> May rob him of bearing yonder. Take his hand,
> Lead him, be led by him.

(22)

When the important exceptions have been acknowledged, Soyinka in his poetry shows the same openness to an extraordinarily wide range of forms, idioms and models that is the aesthetic and ideological motive driving his dramas, especially the most ambitious plays that we explored in the fourth chapter of this study. That said, it is also true that in his verse he has shown a proclivity for an over-literariness and a formalism which are rare in his drama. However, on the other hand, there is always at work in Soyinka's poetry and verse a highly focused and unwavering commitment to the defense and expansion of humane values against their erosion by the culture of impunity and repression in much of post-independence Africa. The matter is further complicated by the fact that this dialectic of an often highly wrought, over-literary and resolutely non-populist poetic idiom and diction in the service of a tenacious and consistent advocacy of humane values is played out on many levels in his poetry. Often, the mode of expression shifts back and forth between comic, satiric and tragic forms while the themes and subject matter traverse spaces encompassing deeply private intuitions and expansively communal promptings, local Nigerian and West African realities and cosmopolitan currents of modern global civilization. Moreover, these diverse poetic landscapes and idioms engage projects frankly announced as appertaining specifically to "race-retrieval" in the "Black world" and projects indubitably internationalist and universalistic. In this capacious poetic corpus, Soyinka, as we have seen, can be fiercely partisan in his political identifications and, side by side with this, he is on occasion unapologetically mystical or metaphysical in some of his visionary projections. These intricacies of his poetry and his activism indicate that if for now and for a long time to come there can be no final word, no definitive summation of his impact and legacy, we can at least review the nature, sources and stress points of his considerable influence in contemporary African literature and the Anglophone writings of the world. In the final chapter of this study, we now turn to this topic.

CHAPTER 7

"Things fall together": Wole Soyinka in his Own Write

> The Will of man is placed beyond surrender. Without the know-
> ing of Divinity by man, can Deity survive? Oh hesitant one,
> Man's conceiving is fathomless; his community will rise beyond
> the present reaches of the mind. Orisa reveals destiny as SELF-
> DESTINATION
>
> > Wole Soyinka, "The Credo of Being and Nothingness"

> The very vocabulary of chaos – disintegration, fragmentation,
> dislocation – implies a breaking away or a breaking apart. But the
> defining thing of the Modernist mode is not so much that things fall
> *apart* but that they fall *together*.
>
> > James McFarlane, "The Mind of Modernism"

In his important book, *Forms of Attention*, the English scholar and critic, Frank Kermode, has suggested that the fate of literature, the survival of literature, depends ultimately on the degree to which it continues to be talked about.[1] Consistent with the title of the book, Kermode also makes the qualification that a lot depends, not just on literature continuing to get talked about, but also on *how* it is talked about, on the "forms of attention" that individual authors and entire literary traditions receive. The works and career of Soyinka amply demonstrate that it is also of significance *who* talks about literature or the corpus of a particular author with regard to its sources, impact and legacy.

At least a decade before either of them received the Nobel prize for literature, Derek Walcott made a comment on the stature of Wole Soyinka as a writer which gives a fair, though indirect indication of one important "form of attention" that Soyinka has received from his own contemporaries. The comment was made in the context of an interview with Walcott on the relative differences between influence by a member of one's own generation and influence by great authors of the past. I do not think Walcott has ever made the kind of comment that he makes on

Soyinka about any other living or dead contemporary writer – except perhaps Borges and St. John Perse – in the following quote from the interview:

(G): What about Soyinka as a master?

(W): I'm not saying that there aren't emerging black writers who could not be great, that there are not masterpieces among the emerging literature. I consider *The Road* a masterpiece. But the man is a contemporary of mine; we have gone through the same evolution in terms of writing in countries where, previously, there had not been a large body of recorded literature. So this masterpiece, any masterpiece created by a contemporary is his. There is no one among my contemporaries who I wish to apprentice myself to.[2]

At its most apparent level, the disavowal by Walcott in this quote of any influence by Soyinka and more generally any "intra-generational" influences from his own contemporaries is unremarkable, for it is a very rare occurrence in literary history for writers of the same generation to admit to tutelage within and among cohorts. What makes Walcott's observations in the quote remarkable is the fact that a writer of his stature found it necessary to disavow tutelage to Soyinka, much as he admired the Nigerian author's writings. This, I would argue, indirectly reveals an aspect of Soyinka's impact on his own society and his own times that is often overlooked by most students of his writings. This is the fact that among postcolonial African writers, Soyinka is probably the closest approximation there is to what could be described as "the writers' writer," the writer in whose corpus "writing" stands out clearly in its own right, as a percept, a value which exercises tremendous, if heterodox fascination for other writers. This dimension of the impact of Soyinka's writings reveals the significance, of how and *by whom* his works have been talked about by his contemporaries. For among all groups of commentators on Soyinka's writings, it is among other writers that there has been the most enthusiastic praise for Soyinka's writings as *writing* and thus the weakest link in the chain of resistance to the alleged "complexity" and "difficulty" of his works. Among the many major contemporary African and non-African writers who, with due caveats and the usual qualifications, have given eloquent testimony to the power of Soyinka's writings are Chinua Achebe, Nadine Gordimer, Wilson Harris, Walcott himself in another context entirely different from the quote above, John Arden, Femi Osofisan, Niyi Osundare and Caryl Philips.[3]

There is an aspect of this "writerly" form of attention on the writings of Soyinka which is more indirect, more subliminal and therefore perhaps even more significant than direct commentary or praise. This is the incidence of perceptible echoes of Soyinka's writings, or of Soyinka as a literary figure, in the works of other living authors. Perhaps the most obvious examples of this pattern in contemporary writing are to be found in Francis Imbuga's *Betrayal in the City* and Gloria Naylor's *Linden Hills*, each respectively from the canons of contemporary Anglophone African and African American literatures. In the Kenyan dramatist's 1977 play, the youthful rebels of a burgeoning social movement dedicated to ending the neocolonial tyranny and corruption in their country name and invoke the example of Soyinka and his works as one of the intellectual and spiritual sources of their inspiration. In an almost identical pattern in Gloria Naylor's 1985 novel, Willie, a fledgling poet, the more conscientious and sensitive of the two protagonists of the novel, invokes Soyinka as one of a body of living and dead poets who are his mentors in a list which includes names like Keats, Whitman and Baraka. Soyinka himself has written about the indirect, "ghostly" influence that writers exercise on one another across generations, cultures and literary traditions.[4] It is a safe guess that in time, patient, careful scholarship will uncover the significant direct and indirect influence that Soyinka has exercised on writers of his own emergent postcolonial African writing and on writers elsewhere in world literature in the English language of the last quarter of the twentieth century and beyond. Meanwhile, one can venture a tentative but secure opinion on some of the most likely candidates: Femi Osofisan, Bode Sowande, Niyi Osundare, Ben Okri and the late Dambudzo Marechera.[5]

And yet in spite of this "writerly" dimension of Soyinka's influence and appeal – or rather because of it, because he takes all levels and forms of writing seriously – there is an "Everyman's" Soyinka that has wide, popular appeal but nonetheless entails as much wit and sophistication as can be found in his most ambitious and complex works. For if it is the case that two particular poems of Soyinka, "Abiku" and "Telephone Conversation," are perhaps the two most widely and consistently anthologized and popular poems in modern African poetry, it is also true that these are poems crafted with considerable skill and eloquence of expression. This point is equally true of the dramatic sketches in the famous "Before the Blackout" series which Soyinka himself designated "shotgun" pieces. By this he meant that they were topical, extemporized pieces devised to meet specific demands of protest and social criticism and nothing more. From all accounts, these were as memorable and effective as artistic expressions as they were wildly and wickedly funny barbs directed at corrupt, demagogic politicians of the 1960s in Nigeria. And going farther afield in the Soyinka corpus, plays like *The Trials of Brother Jero*, *Jero's Metamorphosis*, *The Lion and the Jewel* and *The Swamp Dwellers* which have all become favorite dramas of amateur theatre groups on the African continent, all evince considerable dramaturgic skill. The conclusion is thus inescapable that Soyinka's observance of the demands of craft and technique in writing is so consistent that he probably could not write down to the popular masses even if he tried to do so. Indeed, in the essay "Drama and the Idioms of Liberation," there is an extensive and cogently argued theorization of the pitfalls of condescension toward the popular masses in much of the work of middle class writers who consciously and overzealously set out to write for and to the masses.[6]

In an essay on Soyinka that raises some of these issues, Nadine Gordimer has made a point similar to this same cautionary observation of Soyinka, but more generally with regard to the relationship between modern African writers and their relatively newly constituted teeming readerships on the continent:

Soyinka is a sophisticate whose making free use of the tricks and techniques of European literatures are seen by some as a contradiction. I have heard him criticized by black writers for being too difficult to be read by ordinary black people; you must understand, there is an uneasy conflict among us, in Africa, between the genuine and determined desire to extend the mind-opening pleasures of literature to millions who have had to regard these as the privilege of an elite, and the sure knowledge that you stunt and stultify that literature, to the millions' eventual deprivation, if you ask writers to limit complexity of thought, reduce vocabulary, trim codes of reference to some accessible common denominator of comprehension.[7]

In another context, I have demonstrated that the racialization of the problem by Gordimer in this quote is only one side of the story.[8] For it is also the case, as I hope to have shown in parts of this study, that quite a number of Euro-American scholars and critics have also expressed impatience and frustration with Soyinka's complexity as a writer, either because, consciously or unconsciously, they have come to expect only "simplicity" from an African writer, or because on the basis of a rearguard hostility to modernist and postmodernist avant-gardism, they simply expect and demand "simplicity" and "coherence" from *any* writer, Euro-American, African or Asian.

It is my hope in this study to have demonstrated that the issue of "complexity" and "obscurity" in Soyinka's writings is not the overdetermining or regulative problem that it has been made out to be in four decades of Soyinka criticism. Rather, as in any other major writer's work, it is a "problem" that applies to specific works of Soyinka and is differentially distributed within the different genres of his corpus. More concretely, it has been the purpose of this study to demonstrate that the greatest stress point in Soyinka's writings is paradoxically the very source of his strengths as a writer, this being his tremendous investment in the power of language, specifically the power of metaphor, symbol, myth, archetype and other figures to make words and language hard to hold down to function and referent as conceived by literal, positivist and intentionalist usages. It is my hope to have demonstrated that where(ever) Soyinka falters aesthetically and ideationally, it is almost always the case that this is the result of his overconfident faith in the power of language to withhold or reveal at will. This, I have argued, is a result of a probably overconfident faith in the power of his superior gifts and talents, unmindful of readerly resistances to, and mistrust of language, especially language that is often performatively dazzling. As a stress point, this is compounded by the fact that the medium is English, *Anglophone* English which for Soyinka and the mass of his readers in Africa and the developing world is a language of colonial derivation: to so unapologetically and even exuberantly inhabit, and be inhabited by this historically "compromised" medium goes against some of the deepest though largely unspoken orthodoxies of postcolonial critical discourse.

From the perspectives of the progressive formations of this postcolonial critical discourse, perhaps the ultimate challenge of Soyinka's works and career lies in the fact that the metanarratives that imaginatively and discursively legitimated the great liberation movements of the twentieth century do not feature in his works in their conventional and familiar configurations. These movements include the anti-colonial revolutions which pitched colonies and "postcolonies" against empires and metropolitan centres of global power; the class struggles of working people and the poor for better conditions of life and work; the struggles for gender equality in the home, in the workplace and for the control of bodies and reproductive rights. And overarching all the struggles waged by these movements is the struggle for self-representation as the existential and expressive roots of human freedom. It is a remarkable feature of Soyinka's writings that unlike what we encounter in the works of fellow African writers like Chinua Achebe, Ousmane Sembene, Ngugi wa Thiong'o, Ama Ata Aidoo and the late Mariama Ba, the metanarratives that legitimated the struggles of these social movements – to which Soyinka has undoubted deep ideological allegiances – appear in his writings as fragments, and almost always in ironic de-formations. The best examples of this structure in Soyinka's works are *A Dance of the Forests*, *Kongi's Harvests*, *The Road*, *Madmen and Specialists*, *The Interpreters* and *From Zia with Love*. Indeed, where Soyinka, like most of these other African writers, has tried to write positively and unambiguously about narratives of emancipation and disalienation – as in *Season of Anomy* and parts of *The Man Died*, *Ibadan: the 'Penkelemes' Years* and *Ogun Abibiman* – the results, as we have shown in this study, have usually been the worst aesthetic flaws and ideological solecisms in Soyinka's corpus. One cause of this, it was suggested, is the distorting, simplifying over-intrusion of heroic doubles and surrogates of the self in these works, but the main reason is unquestionably the paradoxical fact that for all his passionate pursuit of progressive, democratic causes, Soyinka writes best about the need for radical transformative changes in Africa and the global order when he writes with ferocious, searing irony. In this matter, Soyinka is in the company of a younger generational cohort of postcolonial writers like Salman Rushdie, J.M. Coetzee and the late Dambudzo Marechera, writers who consistently submit the metanarratives of the emancipa-tion of colonized societies and subaltern groups to a severe and skeptical inspection which is sometimes ludic and funny but also often grimly sardonic and even nihilistic. What separates Soyinka from writers like Rushdie, Coetzee and Marechera is his unshaken retention, into the beginning of the fifth decade of his literary career, of the idealistic and romantic rebelliousness of his youth.

This last point, which is crucial for an appreciation of the inextrica-ble mix of ambiguity and "freedom" in Soyinka's writings, is superbly illustrated by a parable which is chanted in the first scene of *Death and the King's Horseman*. This pertains to the Praise-Singer's chanted ode to Elesin Oba's munificence on the day that the god of wealth came on a visit to his homestead dressed in the rags of poverty. With intuition, with insight and with grace Elesin Oba welcomes and fetes the disguised deity and thereby becomes a beneficiary of the largess of the god, a largess that in the course of the dramatic action of the play he dissipates – with tragic consequences. This parable is remarkably analogous to the aes-thetics and poetics of Soyinka's transmutation of his passionate political activism into the superbly ironic inscriptions of his major literary works in the fact that it is nearly always in the figure of the *pharmakon* – the disease which is also the harbinger of health, the poison which is also the cure – that the striving for freedom finds expression in Soyinka's writings. Extending the ramifications of this parable further, it could be argued that the god of revolution chose to make a habitation in Soyinka's writings, not in the familiar mask of the righteous judge and executioner of the unjust, the exploiters and the despots, but in the confounding and contradictory doubleness of prophet and charlatan, altruist and misanthrope, victim and perpetrator, creator and destroyer. Ogun, Soyinka's acknowledged Muse, Professor in *The Road*, Demoke in *A Dance of the Forests*, the Old Man in *Madmen and Specialists*, Elesin Oba in *Death and the King's Horseman* and the composite group of the protagonists of Soyinka's first novel, *The Interpreters*, all of these characters and nearly all the major protagonist figures in Soyinka's writings, as in the great dramatic parables of Bertolt Brecht, bear the marks or the traces of this ambiguous, aporetic doubleness in relation to the striving for human emancipation. I hope that enough has been said in this study to indicate that this pattern reflects, on Soyinka's part, neither a reactionary recoil from all talk of revolution that is a decisive feature of the ideological temper of the present historical period, nor a convergence with the postmodernists' radical skepticism concerning the place of reason in revolution and its agents and forces.

One "form of attention" which has been influential in the reception of Soyinka's works is that of professional critics, especially with regard to the institutionalization of the academic study of Anglophone writings of the developing world in the second half of the twentieth century. Perhaps the most succinct scholarly statement on the achievement of Soyinka's works to date is that contained in the very short, one-paragraph "Introduction" to the book, *Research on Wole Soyinka*, edited by James Gibbs and Bernth Lindfors and published in 1993. The brevity of this "Introduction" makes it possible for it to be quoted in its entirety:

Most of the articles in this volume were originally published in *Research in African Literatures*, the exceptions being a few essays of our own covering topics or materials that others have not yet studied. Our intention has been to provide a reasonably broad introduction to the works of Soyinka and to the varieties of critical methodologies represented, ranging from those concerned with verbal texture (linguistic, structural and textual approaches) to those focusing on cultural context (historical, mythological and comparative studies). One will also find plenty of metacriticism – critics quarreling with one another about fine points of interpretation or surveying a wide range of response to a particular text or issue. Soyinka's complex, nuanced art affords an inexhaustible source of stimulation to sensitive readers, so it is not surprising that there are so many different readings of his works. We do not expect that the essays collected here will bring an end to such controversies; rather, we would hope that they will prompt rigorous new research leading to fresh appraisals of the achievements of one of Africa's most abundantly gifted writers. Although more has been published on Soyinka than any other Anglophone African writer, much more needs to be written before we will be able to comprehend and measure the expansive dimensions of his creativity. This book is meant merely as an appetizer for the feast of commentary to come. (ix)

The emphasis in this comment on the need to be attentive to complexity, nuance and diversity in approaching Soyinka's writings is one that is routinely encountered in Soyinka criticism, from commentary on the earliest works like *A Dance of the Forests* and *The Interpreters* to critical reception of one of his most recent published works, *The Burden of Memory, the Muse of Forgiveness*. On the basis of the consistency of this view in the reception of Soyinka's works in the last four decades, it is probably safe to say that we are still too close to these works and to their author to be able to make any definitive assessments of each work and of the entire corpus. In this respect, the last sentence of this quote is an apt commentary on any book or monograph on Soyinka's writings and career that takes on the daunting challenge of taking stock of the Nigerian author's entire *oeuvre*.

Inevitably, this last point leads to one of the most important, but so far largely unresolved issues of textual exegesis and socio-historical explanation in Soyinka criticism to date. This pertains to the great theoretical and practical investment of Soyinka's writings and career, taken as a whole, in being *representative* of the capacity of the heritage of imagination and spirit in Africa to respond adequately and even powerfully to the challenges and dilemmas of modernity as African peoples and societies have experienced them through colonial capitalism and the ravages of neocolonial marginalization in the global order of "late," transnational capitalism. In inscriptions interpreted in this study as homologies of the self and the social, Soyinka has in nearly all his major works approached these challenges and dilemmas through the imaginative prism of what he deems inextricable dualities in nature and human existence in general, but with particular regard to the phenomenon of violence: destruction and creation, reactionary terror and restorative, cleansing bloodletting. There is a metaphysical dimension to this conception of violence and Soyinka's theoretical essays and imaginative writings are topheavy with images and tropes from nature and from what he calls "nuomenal forces" to shore up this metaphysics. But there is a pragmatic, even revolutionary sociology involved as well, for Soyinka has never abandoned his consuming need to expose and debunk the reactionary, self-serving terror and violence of corrupt, tyrannical despots, even if he has steadfastly refused to romanticize and idealize the counter-hegemonic violence of his great protagonist characters and their followers. This is indeed why these protagonist characters of Soyinka's most ambitious works are men of violence who carry within themselves part of the evil which they oppose and try to confront by violently jolting complacencies of custom and thought in their societies.

At the bottom of Soyinka's artistic sensibilities and political activism is a profound and unflinching preoccupation with the place of violence in human affairs and also in the processes of nature, making the sum of his views and attitudes on this subject seeming like a compendium of Georges Sorel, Frantz Fanon, the anarcho-syndicalists and Rene Girard on violence.[9] His aesthetic philosophy, as formulated in a recondite and densely symbolic essay like "The Fourth Stage" or essays of great clarity and eloquence like "The Writer in a Modern African State" and "Climates of Art" is one founded on the *generativity* and the contradictoriness of violence. Violence in this conception is both productive and destructive, both potentially reactionary and revolutionary, depending on matters of circumstance, interests and will. If anything gives coherence to the extraordinary range of our author's activist involvements and interventions in the political life of his country in the last four decades, it is this utter preparedness not to flinch from the seeming central place of violence in human affairs, either in consolidating the reign of terror and repression in Africa and other regions of the world or, conversely in mobilizing effective opposition to the violence of the rulers as sedimented in the instruments of force and coercion.

In the dominant strains of Soyinka criticism, the Nigerian author's metaphysics and pragmatics of violence and evil have been more or less accepted on their own terms and based on this, much has been written that is useful for the light that it sheds on the sources of the symbolic and imaginative richness of Soyinka's most important works of fiction, drama and poetry. But reading the protagonists of Soyinka's most ambitious works as "Ogunnian" heroes who bear the marks of the god's duality and contradictoriness has been too perfunctory, too formulaic an exercise in Soyinka criticism. There is ample textual evidence in Soyinka's major works, as this study has tried to show, that the Nigerian author himself is not untroubled by the cultural time-warp inherent in resuscitating warrior-heroes and their myths and legends as paradigms for the personality of the artist, especially a *revolutionary* artist, in the world of the crisis-ridden African postcolony. But this textual evidence has largely been ignored for the easy purchase on textual commentary afforded by Soyinka's unqualified theoretical endorsement of the "Ogunnian" archetype as paradigm of the artist in modern Africa in his most important metacritical essays.

If the radical or revolutionary potential of Soyinka's mythopoesis is to be taken seriously, at least two qualifications about this mythopoeic aesthetic has to be carefully engaged. First, it has to be admitted that the "Ogunnian" archetype is at best a codification of radical subjectivity as essentially *patrician*, and as we elaborated in Chapter 2 of this study, as also *patriarchal*. This does not automatically negate the radical or revolutionary potential in the archetype, it merely indicates the extremely limited nature of that potential – limits of class inflections and a highly gendered world-view indicating a "revolution" from the top down, from a vanguard of *male* patricians of spirit and will to the world of the degraded, disenfranchised masses. Second and associatively, there is an overvalorization of will in this archetype since all the "Ogunnian" protagonists of Soyinka's works are patterned on a divinity who is an embodiment of Will as the primal instrument of self-fashioning and self-destination. In the rigor and richness of artistic representation in some of Soyinka's most ambitious and successful works like *The Road* and *Madmen and Specialists*, Will is not presented as an independent, voluntaristic category standing beyond and outside the limits and constraints of history, culture and the material forces of social reproduction. To express this concretely, in these works the force of volition or agency of a protagonist like Professor or the Old Man is "contained" by supra-individual structures – of language, "mind" or relations of production – which are experienced as the absent or invisible causes of effects which can neither be adequately understood nor controlled by even these Ogunnian heroic protagonists. But this is not the case in Soyinka's theoretical reflections in essays like "The Fourth Stage" and "The Climates of Art" where "will" is admittedly presented as paradoxical and contradictory, but only in the terms of its own primal self-constitution.[10]

Conjecturally, this last point seems to provide some explanation for the great tension between, on the one hand, Soyinka's tremendous aesthetic resourcefulness, his artistic avant-gardism and, on the other hand, his political and ideological radicalism. At the most elementary level, Soyinka's works and career present us with a rather neat, congruent division of his artistic labors, as far as their political ramifications are concerned, between those works which are addressed to specific issues and contexts and are for this reason, direct and generally unambiguous and works which are far more complex and presumably engage contradictions and crises deeper and more endemic than immediate realities and surface symptoms. The best examples of the first category of works in Soyinka's corpus are perhaps the so-called "shotgun" agit-prop dramatic skits of the "Before the Blackout" series and the "Rice Unlimited" series with the "Guerrilla Unit" of the University of Ife Theatre during the years of the Shagari civilian misrule. Others are plays like *Opera Wonyosi*, and *The Beatification of An Area Boy* and quite a number of poems in all five of Soyinka's volumes of poetry. In the second category of works are the great dramas discussed in the fourth chapter of this study and virtually all of the fictional and nonfictional prose works, with the possible exception of *The Man Died* and *Season of Anomy*.

The great tension, the great conundrum in the interface between Soyinka's aesthetic and political radicalism lies in the fact that while he is supremely impatient for change, supremely direct and unambiguous about what needs to be done in the "direct-action" texts, he is equally supremely ambiguous, to the point sometimes of nihilism, in his most ambitious works, works which address the prospects of long-term changes in consciousness, in individual morality and in social relationships. Might this conundrum be explained by the unexamined overvalorization and reification of "will" in Soyinka's theories? For it could be argued that in the first category of texts identified above, "will" expresses itself directly and efficiently in the immediacies of protest and direct-action intervention; in the second category where there is rigorous fidelity to the demands of complex and sophisticated artistic representation, the reification of "will" as an independent, preexistent value does not prevent it from meeting its limits in determinate institutional and socioeconomic structures; consequently, sticking to the overvalorization of "will" in such imaginative contexts cannot but produce pessimism and nihilism, even where paradox and contradiction are admitted as valences of "will."

Earlier in this chapter, we encountered a quotation from a book on research projections on Soyinka's works which place unqualified emphasis on diversity, complexity and sheer range in the Soyinka corpus. I would like to end this concluding chapter with a brief illustration of one expression of this fundamental aspect of Soyinka's career as a writer and public intellectual. This particular expression has a direct pertinence to future critical and scholarly work on the Nigerian author because it in fact deals with Soyinka as a theorist and critic. The expression is perceptible only if we make a juxtaposition of his critical writings from all the three phases of his critical thought that we identified in the second chapter of this study. This juxtaposition allows us to see that the full complement of Soyinka's critical prose embraces positions usually deemed incompatible or mutually self-canceling in currently fashionable theories of postcolonial discourse and cultural studies. Some of these positions are:

Nativism: the search for origins and the call for a return to foundational sources; the valorization of essences and continuities in the construction of cultural tradition; the assertion of normative, traditional values and world-views; the recuperation of primordial, autochthonous oral, preliterate matrices of artistic and cultural forms as a reaction to the homogenizing cultural effects of capitalist globalization;

Orphism: artistic expression and utterance as vehicles of prophetic revelation, occult or paranormal experiences and mystical intuitions;

Resistance and Oppositionality: the recourse to the insurgent carnivalesque counter-discourses of non-canonical, popular, unofficial, marginal and transgressive cultural forms, styles, idioms and practices;

Cosmopolitanism: the encouragement and celebration of hybrid, syncretist, "crossover" and transcultural affinities and influences across all kinds of boundaries – racial, national, geopolitical and ideological.

A careful exploration of all the three phases of Soyinka's critical thought, such as we attempted in the second chapter of this study, would show that in the body of his critical prose, it is only in his essays of the 1980s and 1990s that Soyinka was able to inhabit simultaneously all of these positions without seriously undermining the radical humanism of his works and career. How remarkable then that in his imaginative writings, especially in the most ambitious and successful works of drama and poetry, Soyinka had all along powerfully and resonantly inhabited all of these positions. There is considerable tension in simultaneously locating oneself in these conflicting views and positions, but Soyinka's fecundity and complexity as a writer-activist are powerfully enabling means of negotiating this tension productively. Indeed, it is perhaps best to understand the matter of inhabiting these postions and views – nativism, orphism, resistance and oppositionality, and cosmopolitanism – not as abstract identitarian positions, but as chronotopes and lifeworlds of the pre-capitalist, capitalist and late-capitalist epochs. In the densely symbolic, archetypal idiom of Soyinka's most "difficult" and important theoretical essays, these positions are formulated as the metaphysically coexistent and coeval "worlds" of the ancestors and the past, of living generations and the present, and of unborn generations and the future. Soyinka criticism has in the main read this formulation as appertaining only to the world of Yoruba cosmology, or at best and by extension, the "African world," the "Black world." It is time to go with Soyinka's most ambitious and challenging works like *A Dance of the Forests, The Road, Madmen and Specialists, Death and the King's Horseman, A Shuttle in the Crypt, The Bacchae of Euripides, Isara,* and *Outsiders* and read them complexly and comparatively as appertaining both to Africa and the developing world and the whole of humanity. This radical hermeneutic act can be helped if we secularize and historicize the significations of these "worlds": the ancestors, living generations and unborn denizens of the world are co-extensive in the ways that the defeats, victories, energies and capacities of the precolonial and colonial pasts are still residually with us in the postcolonial present and future, just as "structures of feeling" of the epochs of precapitalism and capitalism still haunt the present of late capitalism, with important intimations and portents for our future post-capitalist world.

Notes

I. 'REPRESENTATIVE' AND UNREPRESENTABLE MODALITIES OF THE
SELF: THE GNOSTIC, WORLDLY AND RADICAL HUMANISM OF
WOLE SOYINKA

1 Bernth Lindfors, "The Early Writings of Wole Soyinka" in James Gibbs (ed.), *Critical Perspectives on Wole Soyinka*, London: Heinemann and Washington, DC: Three Continents Press, 1980, 19–44.

2 In *The Interpreters*, the motif of the mock-serious joke is built into an elaborate scatological satire and social commentary in the journalist Biodun Sagoe's philosophy of "voidancy"; in *The Road*, nearly all the songs and jokes of the denizens of the motor-parks and the highways are ribald and subversive of authority, respectability or piety.

3 See Soyinka's review of J.P. Clark's *America, Their America*, "A Maverick in America," *Ibadan*, 22 (June), 1966, 59–61. For Clark's angry response see his "Letter to the Editor," *Ibadan*, 23 (October), 1966, 55.

4 Penelope Gilliat, "A Nigerian Original" in James Gibbs (ed.), *Critical Perspectives on Wole Soyinka*, Washington, DC: Three Continents Press, 1981, 106–8.

5 The sixteen countries were the Cameroon, Central African Republic, Chad, Congo Republic, Dahomey (now Benin), Gabon, Mauritania, Cote D'Voire, Malagasy, Mali, Niger, Nigeria, Senegal, Somalia, Togo and Upper Volta (now Burkina Fasso).

6 Political independence from colonial rule came to different parts of Africa and the developing world in waves and cycles. In Africa, Liberia was never colonized and except for Mussolini's brief incursion into Ethiopia, that country was also uncolonized. Egypt became independent in 1923, thirty-four years before Ghana, whereas independence did not come to the Portuguese colonies until the 1970s and to Zimbabwe in 1980.

7 For a comprehensive but highly problematic profile of the African postcolony, see Achille Mbembe, *On the Postcolony*, Berkeley: University of California Press, 2001.

8 These aspects of his early career and development are extensively explored by Soyinka himself in *Ibadan: the 'Penkelemes' Years*.

9 For substantial discussions of these cultural and literary currents, see Kofi Awoonor, *The Breast of the Earth: A Survey of the History, Culture and Literature*

of Africa South of the Sahara, Garden City, NY: Anchor Press, 1975; Claude Wauthier, *The Literature and Thought of Modern Africa*, (translated by Shirley Kay) Washington, DC: Three Continents Press, 1979 and Robert July, *An African Voice: the Role of the Humanities in African Independence*, Durham, NC: Duke University Press, 1987.

10 For the excitement generated by the emergence of this body of writings, see the early issues of the journals, *Black Orpheus* and *Transition*.

11 For a book-length study of this aspect of modern Nigerian literature, see James Booth, *Writers and Politics in Nigeria*, London: Hodder and Stoughton, 1981.

12 For two critical studies of some of the writers in this group, see Chris Dunton, *Make Man Talk True: Nigerian Drama in English Since 1970*, London and New York: Hans Zell Publishers, 1992 and Ahmed Yerima and Ayo Akinwale, eds., *Theatre and Democracy in Nigeria*, Ibadan, Nigeria: Kraft Books, 2002. For a vigorously polemical criticism of the aesthetic and ideological maturity of the fiction of some writers in this group, see Adewale Maja-Pearce, *A Mask Dancing: Nigerian Novelists of the Eighties*, London and New York: Hans Zell Publishers, 1992.

13 For two representative and influential texts of the Nigerian radical intelligentsia, see Yusufu Bala Usman, *For the Liberation of Nigeria*, London: New Beacon Books, 1979 and Edwin Madunagu, *Nigeria: the Economy and the People*, London: New Beacon Books, 1983.

14 The judge who tried Wole Soyinka in this famous case, Justice Kayode Eso, has written very extensively on the trial in his memoir, *The Mystery Gunman: History, Politics, Power-Play, Justice*, Ibadan: Spectrum Books, 1996, Chapters 8–18, 185–243.

15 The "Third Force" initiative is very critically discussed by Kole Omotoso in his book, *Achebe or Soyinka: A Study in Contrasts*, Hans Zell Publishers, 1996, Chapter 7, "Minority Voices and the Nigerian Civil War."

16 Transcriptions of the lyrics of both sides of the album are published in the appendix to Toyin Falola and Julius Ihonvbere, *The Rise and the Fall of Nigeria's Second Republic, 1978–84*, London: Zed Press Books, 1985.

17 In his book, *Wole Soyinka*, James Gibbs erroneously remarks that Soyinka never joined any political party. As a matter of fact, Soyinka did briefly join the People's Redemption Party and at a time was that party's Deputy Director of Research, a position whose responsibilities he however never found the time to meet.

18 This was a parastatal created to supplement the work of the regular national police in reducing the horrific scale of the carnage on the Nigerian highways caused by a combination of many factors – totally unsafe and reckless driving habits; extremely high numbers of vehicles that are not minimally roadworthy on the roads; the corruption and lack of professionalism of the motor traffic constabulary. Despite the many bureaucratic obstacles placed in its path, this organization did very laudable work on the country's highways before intrigues and machinations of various kinds rendered it ineffectual by the mid-1990s.

19 In "Press Release from the Swedish Academy," *Black American Literature Forum*, vol. 22, no. 3 (Fall 1988), 425.

20 The most caustic of the negative reviews of the staging of the play as part of the Independence celebrations was Peter Pan's (Enahoro) revealingly titled notice, "*A Dance of the Forests*: Wole Soyinka has Overdone It This Time" in *Daily Times* (Lagos), (7 October 1960), p. 5. For other reviews at the time, see Ulli Beier, "Review of *Dance of the Forests*," *Black Orpheus* 8, 1960, 57–8, and Una Cockshott, "*A Dance of the Forests*," *Ibadan*, 10 (November 1960), 30–2.

21 On this point, Gibbs has written the following observations based on the first stage performance of the play that he watched: "In 1978, Derek Bullock directed the play with boys from Government College, Kaduna, and it was performed at the University of Ibadan. The production was not perfect: the set did not fit the Arts Theatre stage, the music and dance elements had not been adequately worked out and the cast was uneven. However, Funso Alabi as Samson and Bullock as Professor were outstandingly good and the play made a tremendous impact. The audience was held throughout; responsive laughter greeted humor which, in reading the text, I had thought was rather labored . . . The lesson to draw from this is that it is necessary to stand back from Soyinka's words in order to appreciate the stage images he creates and the patterns into which his plays fall." In James Gibbs, *Wole Soyinka*, New York: Grove Press, 1986, 85–6.

22 See Femi Osofisan's moving tribute to Soyinka's influence on himself and a whole generation of Nigerian playwrights and actors, "Wole Soyinka and a Living Dramatist: A Playwright's Encounter with Soyinka's Drama," in Adele Maja-Pearce (ed.), *Wole Soyinka: An Appraisal*, Heinemann, 1994, 43–60.

23 For informative and moving testimonies on their work with Soyinka, see the contributions of some of these collaborators and followers of Soyinka to the book of tributes to the author, *Before Our Very Eyes*, ed. Dapo Adelugba, Ibadan, Nigeria: Spectrum Books, 1987.

24 Michael Etherton, *The Development of African Drama*, London: Hutchinson University Library for Africa, 1982, Chapter 1, "Traditional Performance in Contemporary Society," 28–61; and Karen Barber, *I Could Speak Until Tomorrow: "Oriki," Women and the Past in a Yoruba Town*, Washington, DC: Smithsonian Institution Press, 1991, especially Chapter 6, "The 'Oriki' of Big Men," 183–247. Etherton and Barber both discuss the complex and fascinating ways in which "big men" appropriate important Yoruba expressive and performative forms and idioms to enhance their self-esteem and social standing. The following observations by Etherton is fairly indicative of this point: "Ogunde's theatre company is Hubert Ogunde. His theatre is a Yoruba theatre, performed in Yoruba which embraces wit and poetry. The fans come to see and hear him; and to an outsider it appears that no member of his cast can steal the focus of the audience from him. This is the essence, it seems, of the most successful of the travelling theatres: the creation of a 'personality,' a unique person through whom Yoruba of all walks

of life can find a central image of the contemporary world." (49) While the observations made here about Hubert Ogunde and *his* company are generally accurate, the generalization of these observations into an "essence" of the travelling theatre in general is highly debatable. And with regard to Soyinka and his "circle," we have, as I hope to have shown, a far more complex, more dialogical pattern than the profiles drawn by Barber and Etherton.

25 Remarkably, Soyinka has pointedly left out "Telephone Conversation," his most widely anthologized poem, from all of the five volumes of his published poetry.

26 I have discussed this issue extensively in my Introduction to *Perspectives on Wole Soyinka: Freedom and Complexity*, Biodun Jeyifo (ed.), Jackson, Mississippi: University Press of Mississippi, 2001.

27 For a powerful defense of Soyinka against the charges of "difficulty" and "obscurity" see Stanley Macebuh, "Poetics and the Mythic Imagination," in James Gibbs (ed.), *Critical Perspectives on Wole Soyinka*, 200–12.

28 This is exactly the form in which Bernth Lindfors allegedly phrased his objections to the radical, experimental form of Soyinka's drama at a conference, as recounted by Annemarie Heywood in her "The Fox's Dance: the Staging of Soyinka's Plays." *Critical Perspectives on Wole Soyinka*, 130–8. For a full-blown expression of Lindfors' scathing critique of Soyinka on this issue, see his article, "Wole Soyinka, When Are You Coming Home?," *Yale French Studies* 53 (1976), 197–210.

29 Needless to say, I am far less interested in self-fashioning as a mode of astheticization of the self than in the tensions between textual, psychoanalytic and materialist theories of subject-formation. See note 38 below.

30 In Introduction to Gibbs, *Critical Perspectives on Wole Soyinka*, 3.

31 Abiola Irele, "The Season of a Mind: Wole Soyinka and the Nigerian Crisis," in his book of essays, *The African Experience in Literature and Ideology*," London: HEB, 1981; Eldred Jones, *The Writings of Wole Soyinka*, London: Heinemann, 1973; Gerald Moore, *Wole Soyinka*, London: Evans, 1971.

32 Ngugi wa Thiong'o, *Decolonizing the Mind: the Politics of Language in African Literature*, London: James Currey, 1986.

33 I have explored these contradictions and their impact on the study of African literatures in "The Order of Things: Arrested Decolonization and Critical Theory," *Research in African Literatures*, 21 (1990).

34 Aristotle, "The Poetics," in Bernard F. Dukore (ed.), *Dramatic Theory and Criticism: Greeks to Grotowski*, New York: Holt, Rinehart and Winston, 1974, 38–9.

35 Pierre Macherey, *A Theory of Literary Production* (translated by Geoffrey Wall), London, Boston: Routledge and Kegan Paul, 1978.

36 As reported and quoted in the *New York Times*, October 17, 1986.

37 Frantz Fanon, *The Wretched of the Earth*, New York: Grove Press, 1963, especially the chapter "The Pitfalls of National Consciousness," 119–63; Amilcar Cabral, *Unity and Struggle*, London: Heinemann Educational Books, 1980.

38 Ashis Nandy's under-appreciated book is easily one of the best on the subject of the sources and contexts of subject-formation and self-invention under colonialism. In this respect, Nandy's book is to be compared with another seminal book on the subject of self-invention, Stephen Greenblatt's *Renaissance Self-fashioning: From More to Shakespeare*, University of Chicago Press, 1980. Greenblatt's book shows the institutional and discursive constraints on what appeared to be autonomous acts of self-fashioning of towering writers and intellectuals of the European renaissance; Nandy also explores these material and discursive constraints, but he emphasizes the important fact that in colonized spaces, "self-fashioning" was as much collective projects as they were focused or poignant acts of canonical figures. See Nandy, *The Intimate Enemy: Loss and Recovery of the Self Under Colonialism*, Delhi: Oxford University Press, 1983.

39 A corruption of the phrase "peculiar mess," the word occurs in the title of Soyinka's third book of autobiographical memoir, *Ibadan: the 'Penkelemes' Years*. It was coined by the popular supporters of a populist Ibadan politician, Adegoke Adelabu, who had used the phrase "peculiar mess" in the Western regional assembly to describe the volatile, scorched-earth political culture of the first decade of independence.

40 Initially, Soyinka was surreptitiously and wickedly called "Kongi" behind his back by many of his students and admirers in Nigeria. Kongi is, of course, the dictator in his play, *Kongi's Harvest*. Once Soyinka himself played the title role in the film version of the play in 1970, this lent effective consecration, so it seems, to "Kongi" as Soyinka's most widely used moniker.

41 For two interesting books on the subject of madness, misanthropy and sociopathy in the personalities of enormously creative people, see Albert Rothenberg, *Creativity and Madness*, Baltimore: The Johns Hopkins Press, 1990 and Hendrik M. Ruitenbeck (ed.), *The Creative Imagination: Psychoanalysis and the Genius of Inspiration*, Chicago: Quadrangle Books, 1965.

42 Ulli Beier (ed.), *Orisa Liberates the Mind: Wole Soyinka in Conversation with Ulli Beier*, Bayreuth, Germany: Iwalewa, 1992, 11–12.

43 See Biodun Jeyifo, "What Is the Will of Ogun?" in Yemi Ogunbiyi (ed.), *Perspectives on Nigerian Literature: 1700 to the Present*, Lagos: Guardian Books, 1988, 169–85.

44 Isidore Okpewho, *Myth in Africa*, New York: Cambridge University Press, 1983, 257.

45 Martin Heidegger, *On the Way to Language*, New York: Harper and Row, 1971, 5.

46 J.L. Austin, *How To Do Things with Words*, Cambridge, MA: Harvard University Press, 1962.

47 For one of the most extensive and provocative theoretical elaborations on the poststructuralist concept of articulation, see the third chapter of Ernesto Laclau and Chantal Mouffe, *Hegemony and Socialist Strategy: Towards a Radical Democratic Politics*, London: Verso, 1985.

48 Elaine Fido, "*The Road* and the Theatre of the Absurd," *Caribbean Journal of African Studies* 1 (Spring 1978), 75–94; Segun Adekoya, "Re-planting the

Tree of Life: *The Road* Retrodden," in *Soyinka: A Collection of Critical Essays*, Oyin Ogunda, ed., Ibadan, Nigeria: Syndicated Communications, 1994, 103–26.

49 This point has been given a major scholarly exploration in Femi Euba's *Archetypes, Imprecators and Victims of Fate: Origins and Development of Satire in Black Drama*, Westport, Connecticut: Greenwood Press, 1989. See also Ropo Sekoni in *Folk Poetics: A Sociosemiotic Study of Yoruba Trickster Tales*, Westport, Connecticut: Greenwood Press, 1994, especially Chapter 4, part of which is devoted to the analysis of some plays of Soyinka in the context of Sekoni's interesting theoretical distinctions between what he calls "mythic" and "secular" traditions of the trickster figure in Yoruba culture, the former represented by Esu, the latter by the tortoise persona of folktales.

50 See Ayodele Ogundipe's magisterial two-volume doctoral dissertation, *Esu Elegbara, the Yoruba God of Chance and Uncertainty: A Study in Yoruba Mythology*, unpublished PhD dissertation, Indiana University, 1978. Building on this work and the works of other scholars, H.L. Gates, Jr. has extended the complex significations of the Esu paradigm into an extended and original act of cultural theorizing and literary criticism in the Afro-American tradition in his *The Signifying Monkey: A Theory of Afro-American Literary Criticism*, New York: Oxford University Press, 1988.

51 One instance of this is Ato Quayson's "The Space of Transformations: Theory, Myth, and Ritual in the Work of Wole Soyinka" in Biodun Jeyifo (ed.), *Perspectives on Wole Soyinka: Freedom and Complexity*, Jackson, MI: University Press of Mississippi, 2001, 201–36. See also Isidore Okpewho, "Soyinka, Euripides and the Anxiety of Empire," *Research In African Literatures*, vol. 30, no. 4 (Winter 1999), 32–55.

52 Some of these scholars and critics are Femi Osofisan, Niyi Osundare, Ato Quayson, Michael Etherton and the author of this study. I have explored this issue in my Introduction to Soyinka's book of essays on literature and culture, *Art, Dialogue and Outrage*, Ibadan: New Horn Press, 1988, viii–xxxii. For Femi Osofisan and Niyi Osundare, see their contributions to the volume, *Wole Soyinka: An Appraisal*, Adewale Maja-Pearce (ed.), Heinemann, 1994, respectively "Wole Soyinka and a Living Dramatist: A Playwright's Encounter with Soyinka's Drama," 43–60 and "Wole Soyinka and the Atunda Ideal: A Reading of Soyinka's Poetry," 81–97. For Etherton see his *The Development of African Drama*, London: Hutchinson University Library for Africa, 1982, Chapter 6, "The Art Theatre: Soyinka's Protest Plays," 242–84. For Quayson see "The Space of Transformations: Theory, Myth, and Ritual in the Work of Wole Soyinka," in Jeyifo (ed.) *Perspectives on Wole Soyinka*.

2. TRAGIC MYTHOPOESIS AS POSTCOLONIAL DISCOURSE – CRITICAL AND THEORETICAL WRITINGS

1 Derek Wright, *Wole Soyinka Revisited*, New York: Twayne Publishers, 1993, 175.

2 Apart from the very widely quoted Preface to *Death and the King's Horseman*, other Prefaces to Soyinka's writings which contain major or thought-provoking theoretical and metacritical views on artistic representation and socio-historical crises are the Prefaces or "Author's Note" to *Poems of Black Africa*, *Myth, Literature and the African World*, *The Bacchae of Euripides*, *A Play of Giants*, *The Forest of a Thousand Daemons*, *Idanre and other Poems* and *A Shuttle in the Crypt*.

3 Among the more notable commentaries on Soyinka as a critic or theorist are essays or book chapters contained in the following titles: Obi Maduakor, *Wole Soyinka: An Introduction to His Writings*, New York: Garland Press, 1986; Ketu Katrak, *Wole Soyinka and Modern Tragedy: A Study of Dramatic Theory and Practice*, Westport, CO: Greenwood Press, 1986; Derek Wright, *Wole Soyinka Revisited*. Other notable essays on this topic are Ann B. Davis, "Dramatic Theory of Wole Soyinka" in *Critical Perspectives on Wole Soyinka* and Biodun Jeyifo, "Oguntoyinbo: Modernity and the 'Rediscovery' Phase of Postcolonial Literature," in *The Yearbook of Comparative and General Literature*, no. 43, 1995.

4 Louis Althusser remains of course the most influential theoretical proponent of this thesis of a fundamental "epistemological break" between the early "humanist" Marx and the "mature" and "scientific" Marx. See his *For Marx*, London: Allen Lane, 1969.

5 The following statement from Sagoe in a conversation with the African American homosexual, Joe Golder, could easily have come from some of Soyinka's early anti-Négritudist essays, especially "And After the Narcissist?": "Look, the truth is that I get rather sick of self-love. Even nationalism is a kind of self-love, but that can be defended. It is this cult of black beauty which sickens me. Are albinos supposed to go and drown themselves, for instance?" In *The Interpreters*, London: Andre Deutsch, 1965, 195–6.

6 Soyinka has said some interesting things on this subject in the "Foreword" to the Second Edition of his book of essays, *Art, Dialogue and Outrage*. Because the essays collected in the volume were never intended, Soyinka says, for compilation, he never hesitated, from time to time, "to cannibalize an essay which appeared, at the time, to have completed its tour of duty . . . This is therefore to acknowledge the initiative and labor of the publisher, Professor Irele and Dr. Jeyifo, editor of the collection, for embarking upon what must have been an infuriating and frustrating task. And also to absolve them of errors of attribution for awkward marriages in the volume. It must have been a daunting task, additionally, in the face of my stubborn insistence on retaining what they considered disposable idiosyncrasies of expression, including what one commentator has described as "linguistic anomy." (*ADO2*, vi)

7 Fanon, *The Wretched of the Earth*, 178–80.

8 There are useful extended discussions of Leopold S. Senghor and Alioune Diop and other theorists and pundits of Négritude in Robert July's *An African Voice: the Role of the Humanities in African Independence*, Durham: Duke University

Press, 1987. See also Bennetta Jules-Rosette, *Black Paris: the African Writer's Landscape*, Urbana: University of Illinois Press, 1998.

9 These abstract syntheses between Europe and Africa, considered as "racial" civilizations, are given their fullest elaboration in Senghor's writings. See, in particular, the essays "Towards a New African-Inspired Humanism," "The Struggle for Négritude" and "Reformed Négritude" in his *Prose and Poetry*, selected and translated by John Reed and Clive Wake, London: Oxford University Press, 1965.

10 The most notorious of such attacks on Soyinka is of course that of Chinweizu, Jemie and Madubuike in their *Towards the Decolonization of African Literature*, Washington, DC: Howard University Press, 1983.

11 The fullest elaboration of the construct or concept-metaphor of the *pharmakon* in Derrida's writings is to be found in his *Dissemination*, University of Chicago Press, 1981.

12 For a collection of essays which express this pessimism in ways somewhat similar to Soyinka's sentiments in "The Writer in a Modern African State" see R.H. Crossman (ed.), *The God That Failed*, New York: Harper, 1950.

13 Biodun Jeyifo, "Wole Soyinka and the Tropes of Disalienation," *Art, Dialogue and Outrage*, Ibadan: New Horn Press, 1988.

14 For one of the most authoritative scholarly studies of the Symbolists, see Anna Balakian, *The Symbolist Movement: A Critical Appraisal*, New York University Press, 1977.

15 This view is given an extended exploration in Florence Stratton's "Periodic Embodiments: A Ubiquitous Trope in African Men's Writing," *Research in African Literatures*, 21.1 (Spring 1990), 111–26.

16 Other notable bodies of critical writings from the period which have become influential, indeed almost canonical as the standard bearers of progressive literary-critical discourse in postcolonial African literature are Chinua Achebe, *Morning Yet on Creation Day*, Garden City, NY: Doubleday, 1975 and Ngugi wa Thiong'o, *Homecoming: Essays on African and Caribbean Literature, Culture and Politics*, New York: Hill, 1972.

17 Frantz Fanon, *Black Skin, White Masks*, (translated by Charles Lam Markmann) London: Pluto Press, 1986, Chapter 5, "The Fact of Blackness," especially 132–5.

18 I have briefly explored Soyinka's location in the tradition of Pan-African thinkers and pundits of an African order of knowledge of the nineteenth and twentieth centuries in my Introductory essay to Biodun Jeyifo (ed.), *Perspectives on Wole Soyinka: Freedom and Complexity*, Jackson, MI: University Press of Mississippi, 2001. See also J. Ayo Langley (ed.), *Ideologies of Liberation in Black Africa*, 1856–1970, London: Rex Collings, 1979.

19 Joel Adedeji, "Aesthetics of Soyinka's Theatre" in Dapo Adelugba (ed.), *Before Our Very Eyes*, 104–31, and Ketu Katrak, *Wole Soyinka and Modern Tragedy: A Study of Dramatic Theory and Practice*, Westport, CO: Greenwood Press, 1986.

20 M.H. Abrams, *Natural Supernaturalism: Tradition and Revolution in Romantic Literature*, New York: Norton, 1971.

21 See especially, Brian Crow, "Soyinka and the Romantic Tradition" in Dapo Adelugba (ed.), *Before Our Very Eyes*, 147–69, Robin Graham, "Wole Soyinka: Obscurity, Romanticism and Dylan Thomas" in Gibbs, *Critical Perspectives on Wole Soyinka*, 213–18, and Geoffrey Hunt, "Two African Aesthetics: Wole Soyinka Versus Amilcar Cabral" in *Marxism and African Literature*, Georg Gugelberger (ed.), Trenton, NJ: Africa World Press, 1985, 64–93.

22 Philip Brockbank, "Blood and Wine: Tragic Ritual from Aeschylus to Soyinka," *Shakespeare Survey* 36, no. 1 (1983), 15.

3. THE `DRAMA OF EXISTENCE´: SOURCES AND SCOPE

1 Some of the documentation can be found in James Gibbs, *Critical Perspectives on Wole Soyinka*, especially Chapters 2 and 3, 18–38, 39–53.

2 For an engrossing comparison of the dramaturgy of Soyinka with that of Heine Muller against the background of common Brechtian traces in both Soyinka and Muller, see Joachim Fiebach, "Wole Soyinka and Heine Muller: Different Cultural Contexts, Similar Approaches," in Biodun Jeyifo (ed.), *Perspectives on Wole Soyinka: Freedom and Complexity*, Jackson, MI: University Press of Mississippi, 2001.

3 In Soyinka, *Art, Dialogue and Outrage*.

4 Soyinka's most forthright statement of his deep interest in Cabral's ideas on culture, identity and revolution is to be found in the short statement, "Guinea-Bissau: An African Revolution" in *Transition* (Accra), 45, 9–11. But see also his reflections on Cabral in the polemical essay, "The Autistic Hunt; Or How To Marximize Mediocrity" in *Art, Dialogue and Outrage*, Ibadan: New Horn, 1988, New York: Pantheon, 1993.

5 While the influence of Soyinka on younger Nigerian playwrights like Femi Osofisan and Bode Sowande is very easily discernible in the form and subject matter of their dramatic works, the influence of Soyinka as a poet is far less obvious, far more subliminal in younger poets like Niyi Osundare and Odia Ofeimun, though both are great admirers of the older poet. For testimonies by Osofisan and Osundare on this point, see their contributions in the volume Jeyifo, *Perspectives on Wole Soyinka: Freedom and Complexity*.

6 I have explored the staging of Soyinka's *The Road* in three different regions of the English-speaking world, Port of Spain, Trinidad, Mysore, India and London in an essay, "Whose Theatre, Whose Africa?", forthcoming in the journal *Modern Drama*.

7 Derek Wright, in a not unsympathetic discussion of the novel, calls it "politically simplistic" in "its cartoon-like polarization of wicked, imbecilic potentates and impotent visionaries." In *Wole Soyinka Revisited*, New York: Twayne Publishers, 1993, 130. See also Abdulrazak Gunnar, "The Fiction of Wole Soyinka" in Adewale Maja-Pearce (ed.), *Wole Soyinka: An Appraisal*, London: Heinemann, 1994, 61–80, and Abiola Irele, "Parables of the African Condition: The New Realism in African Fiction" in his *The*

African Imagination: Literature in Africa and the Black Diaspora, New York: Oxford University Press, 2001, 212–45.

8 Gibbs, *Critical Perspectives on Wole Soyinka*. Significantly, the only play of Soyinka to have received publication as a text *before* any stage performance of it is *Death and the King's Horseman*.

9 Among Soyinka's more notable acting credits are his playing of Forest Head in his own staging of *A Dance of the Forests* for the Nigerian Independence celebrations in 1960; his playing of Kongi in the filming of *Kongi's Harvest* in 1969; and his playing of the role of Patrice Lumumba in Paris in a French-language version of Conor Cruise O'Brien's *Murderous Angels* in 1971.

10 "Interview with John Agetua," in Biodun Jeyifo (ed.), *Conversations with Wole Soyinka*, Jackson, MI: University Press of Mississippi, 2001, 37–8.

11 See Immanuel Wallerstein, *Africa and the Politics of Unity: An Analysis of a Contemporary Social Movement*, New York: Vintage Books, 1969.

12 See Femi Osofisan, "Wole Soyinka and a Living Dramatist: A Playwright's Encounter with Soyinka's Drama," in Maja-Pearce (ed.), *Wole Soyinka: An Appraisal*.

13 Annemarie Heywood, "The Fox's Dance: the Staging of Soyinka's Plays," in Gibbs, *Critical Perspectives on Wole Soyinka*.

14 Eldred Jones, *The Writings of Wole Soyinka*, London: Heinemann, 1973; Gerald Moore, *Wole Soyinka*, London: Evans, 1971; Adrian Roscoe, *Mother Is Gold: A Study of West African Literature*, Cambridge University Press, 1971.

15 In a private conversation with the author of this study.

16 I owe this perception of echoes of the John the Baptist-Salome story to Abiola Irele. This resonance is apparently so obvious that to date, it has simply gone unremarked in all critical and scholarly commentary on *Kongi's Harvest*.

17 Michel Foucault, *Language, Counter-Memory, Practice*, Ithaca, NY: Cornell University Press, 1977, especially Part Three, "Practice, Knowledge and Power"; Vaclav Havel, *The Power of the Powerless*, John Keane (ed.), Armonk, NY: M.E. Sharpe, 1985.

18 For a study of this aspect of Genet's dramaturgy, see Laura Oswald, *Jean Genet and the Semiotics of Performance*, Bloomington, Indiana: Indiana University Press, 1989.

19 Mary David, *Wole Soyinka: A Quest for Renewal*, Madras, India: B.I. Publications, 1995.

20 Among these are Florence Stratton, "Periodic Embodiments: A Ubiquitous Trope in African Men's Writing," Molara Ogundipe, "The Representation of Women: the Example of Soyinka's *Aké*," in Molara Ogundipe-Leslie, *Re-creating Ourselves: African Women and Critical Transformations*, Trenton, NJ: Africa World Press, 1994; and Carole Boyce Davis, "Maidens, Mistresses and Matrons: Feminine Images in Selected Soyinka Works," in *Ngambika: Studies of Women in African Literature*, Ann Adams Graves and Carole Boyce Davis (eds), Trenton, New Jersey: Africa World Press, 1986.

21 "Neo-Tarzanism: the Poetics of Pseudo-Tradition," in Soyinka, *Art, Dialogue and Outrage*.
22 Joachim Fiebach, "Wole Soyinka and Heine Muller: Different Cultural Contexts, Similar Approaches," in Jeyifo, *Perspectives on Wole Soyinka*, 129.
23 "Soyinka in Zimbabwe: A Question and Answer Session," in Jeyifo, *Conversations with Wole Soyinka*, 82.
24 There is an account of this event, together with Soyinka's role in it, in *West Africa*, April 22, 1985.
25 Ibid.
26 "BAI" – "Battle Against Indiscipline" – is Soyinka's satiric appropriation of "WAI" – "War Against Indiscipline" – the military regime's national project to rid Nigeria of "indiscipline," even as stories and reports circulated of great acts of corrupt abuse of office, mismanagement of public funds and bureaucratic inefficiency among the military and civilian scions of the regime.

4. RITUAL, ANTI-RITUAL AND THE FESTIVAL COMPLEX IN SOYINKA'S DRAMATIC PARABLES

1 Philip Brockbank, "Blood and Wine: Tragic Ritual from Aeschylus to Soyinka," *Shakespeare Survey* 36, no. 1 (1983).
2 Brian Crow, "Wole Soyinka and the Nigerian Theatre of Ritual Vision," in Brian Crow (with Chris Banfield), *An Introduction to Postcolonial Theatre*, Cambridge University Press, 1996.
3 Oyin Ogunba, *The Movement of Transition: A Study of the Plays of Wole Soyinka*, Ibadan University Press, 1975; Stephan Larsen, *A Writer and his Gods: A Study of the Importance of Myths and Religious Ideas to the Writings of Wole Soyinka*, University of Stockholm Department of History of Literature, 1983; Ketu Katrak, *Wole Soyinka and Modern Tragedy: A Study of Dramatic Theory and Practice*, Westport, CO: Greenwood Press, 1986; Mary David, *Wole Soyinka: A Quest for Renewal*; Derek Wright, *Wole Soyinka Revisited*; Philip Brockbank, "Blood and Wine," Brian Crow, "Wole Soyinka and the Nigerian Theatre of Ritual Vision," in Crow, *An Introduction*; Ato Quayson, "The Space of Transformations: Theory, Myth and Ritual in the Work of Wole Soyinka," in Jeyifo (ed.) *Perspectives on Wole Soyinka*; Adebayo Williams, "Ritual as Social Symbolism: Cultural Death and the King's Horseman," in Oyin Ogunba (ed.), *Soyinka: A Collection of Critical Essays*, Ibadan, Nigeria: Syndicated Communications, 1994; Isidore Okpewho, "Soyinka, Euripides, and the Anxiety of Empire," *Research in African Literatures*, vol. 30, no. 4 (Winter 1999), 32–55.
4 Wright, *Wole Soyinka Revisited*, 38–9.
5 Rene Girard, *Violence and the Sacred* (translated by Patrick Gregory), Baltimore: Johns Hopkins University Press, 1977.
6 "The Lysistrata of Aristophanes" (Aristophanes), "Shakespeare and the Living Dramatist" (Shakespeare), "Drama and the Idiom of Liberation" (Edward Albee), and "Between Self and System" (Brecht, Mnouchkine and

Frisch), all in Soyinka, *Art, Dialogue and Outrage*, Ibadan, Nigeria: New Horn Press, 1988.

7 In "Climates of Art," in Soyinka, *Art, Dialogue and Outrage*.

8 "Drama and the African World-view" (J.P. Clark and Duro Ladipo) and "Ideology and the Social Vision: the Religious Factor" (Achebe), both in *Myth, Literature and the African World*, Cambridge University Press, 1976; "The External Encounter: Ambivalence in African Arts and Literature" (Osofisan) in Soyinka, *Art, Dialogue and Outrage*.

9 Philip Brockbank, "Blood and Wine: Tragic Ritual from Aeschylus to Soyinka."

10 Oyin Ogunba, "Traditional African Festival Drama," in Oyin Ogunba and Abiola Irele (eds.), *Theatre in Africa*, Ibadan, Nigeria: University of Ibadan Press, 1978.

11 Peter Brook, "Introduction," Peter Weiss, *Marat-Sade*, New York: Atheneum, 1984.

12 Press Release, Swedish Academy, in *Black American Literature Forum*, vol. 2, no. 23 (Fall 1988).

13 Chinua Achebe, *Things Fall Apart*, (Expanded Edition with Notes), London: Heinemann, 1996 (1958), 66.

14 Peter Nazareth, *Literature and Society in Modern Africa*, Nairobi, Kenya: East African Literature Bureau, 1972, 64–5.

15 The point has to be made that the original Négritudists, because of the profound ideological perplexity caused by their peculiar situation, were uncritically extrapolating animist sentiments and tenets in their raptures over an intuitive oneness of black Africans with the rhythm of the cosmos, the dead and the earth. Some, like Cesaire wrote great poetry, *animist* poetry because the animist universe is a hall of mirrors throwing back reduplications of the image of the one essential unity. Let the metaphor stand: the reduplicated images are however, mere reflections, mere shadows and our willed animists compounded their *psychological* alienation as uprooted intellectuals blanched in the lycées and academies of Europe with the *ideological* alienation of erecting animism as a vehicle of racial politics.

16 Here is a contemporary philosophical statement of this point: "Carried far enough, the symbolic design of the factory as the basic framework of understanding our world and our actions within it leads us back, partly, to the recovery of the symbolic design of nature – that which "resists" being transformed to our specifications. We are in the process of shifting the symbolic designs of our civilization from the basic framework of the factory a little closer to the basic framework of nature. In this sense, and in this sense only, am I willing to accept the notion of "post-industrial society." Vytautas Kavolis, "Notes on Post-Industrial Culture," *Arts in Society*, vol. 11, no. 3 (Fall-Winter 1974), 415.

17 Wondrous tales are here remembered from my own childhood of forest ghommids, imps, etc., who flee and retreat from the laying of railroad tracks and highways through the forests, though not before allegedly making costly

exactions by way of causing fatal accidents, fevers and even insanity among the workers wreaking the "wound" of progress on the forests.

18 Christopher Caudwell, *Studies and Further Studies in a Dying Culture*, New York: Monthly Review Press, 1971, 19.

19 Lucy Mair, *New Nations*, University of Chicago Press, 1963.

20 Ronald Bryden, "The Asphalt God," in Gibbs, *Critical Perspectives on Wole Soyinka*, 104.

21 Joachim Fiebach, "Wole Soyinka and Heine Muller: Different Cultural Contexts, Similar Approaches," in Jeyifo, *Perspectives*, 129.

22 Ronald Bryden, "The Asphalt God," Gibbs, *Critical Perspectives on Wole Soyinka*, 104.

23 Biodun Jeyifo, "The Hidden Class War in *The Road*," in *The Truthful Lie: Essays in a Sociology of African Drama*, London: New Beacon, 1985, 11–22.

24 Oyin Ogunba, *The Movement of Transition: A Study of the Plays of Wole Soyinka*, Ibadan, Nigeria: Ibadan University Press, 1975, 125–64.

25 For an instance of this, see Derek Wright, *Wole Soyinka Revisited*, 99–101.

26 Albert Bates Lord, *The Singer of Tales*, Stephen Mitchell and Gregory Nagy, eds., Cambridge, MA: Harvard University Press, 2000.

27 "Interview with Soyinka," in Charles Mike, Jr., *Soyinka as a Director: the Example of Requiem for a Futurologist*, unpublished M. Phil. thesis, University of Ibadan, 1987.

28 Adebayo Williams, "Ritual as Social Symbolism: Cultural Death and the King's Horseman," in Oyin Ogunba, ed., *Soyinka: A Collection of Critical Essays*, Ibadan, Nigeria: Syndicated Communications, 1994, 89–102.

29 Olakunle George, "Cultural Criticism in Wole Soyinka's *Death and the King's Horseman*," *Representations* 67 (Summer 1999), 67–91.

30 Philip Brockbank, "Blood and Wine: Tragic Ritual from Aeschylus to Soyinka," *Shakespeare Survey* 36, no. 1 (1983), 11–19.

31 Longinus in Bernard F. Dukore (ed.), *Dramatic Theory and Criticism: Greeks to Grotowski*, New York: Holt, Rinehart and Winston, 1974, 79.

32 On the postmodernist conception of the sublime, see, among a vast body of critical and theoretical writings, Neil Hertz, *The End of the Line: Essays on Psychoanalysis and the Sublime*, New York: Columbia University Press, 1985; Slavoj Zizek, *The Sublime Object of Ideology*, London: Verso, 1989 and Jean-Francois Courtine *et al.*, *Of the Sublime: Presence in Question*, Albany, NY: SUNY Press, 1993. For an influential scholarly work on the sublime, see Thomas Weiskel, *The Romantic Sublime: Studies in the Structure and Psychology of Transcendence*, Baltimore: Johns Hopkins University Press, 1976.

33 Paul Gilroy, *The Black Atlantic: Modernity and Double Consciousness*, Cambridge, MA: Harvard University Press, 1993.

5. THE AMBIGUOUS FREIGHT OF VISIONARY MYTHOPOESIS: FICTIONAL AND NONFICTIONAL PROSE WORKS

1 Nothing shows the operation of this tacit regulative norm more than a comparison of critical attitudes towards linguistic exuberance in Yoruba and

African English-language writings respectively. In the former, it is almost something of a norm that the writer is not only expected to be an extraordinarily fluent user of the language, she or he is in fact expected to foreground her or his reflexive relationship to the language as an idiom of expression. In contrast, in the latter, the colonial complexes of the Caliban syndrome is thought to preclude any display of mastery, or playfulness in Prospero's language in and of itself, relatively freed of the burden of either cultural resistance or gratified celebration of the colonizer's language. For Soyinka's thoughts on the ramifications of this problem, see his Prefatory note to *Forest of A Thousand Daemons*, his translation from Yoruba of D.O. Fagunwa's *Ogboju Ode Ninu Igbo Irunmale*.

2 For important theoretical works on this problem, see Rosalind Coward and John Ellis, *Language and Materialism*, London: Routledge and Kegan Paul, 1997, and Michel Peucheux, *Language, Semantics and Ideology*, New York: St. Martins Press, 1981.

3 Charles Larson, *The Emergence of African Fiction*, Bloomington, IN: Indiana University Press, 1972.

4 One of the most acerbic critics of Soyinka as a novelist is Eustace Palmer in his *The Growth of the African Novel*, London: Heinemann Educational Books, 1979.

5 "Wole Soyinka," interview with Jane Wilkinson, in Jeyifo (ed.), *Conversations with Wole Soyinka*, 158.

6 That first sentence reads: "Although everybody in Dukana was happy at first." Ken Saro-Wiwa, *Sozaboy, A Novel in Rotten English*, White Plains, NY: Longman, 1994.

7 The reactions provoked by the book in Nigeria have been well-documented in John Agetua (ed.), *When the Man Died*.

8 One of the best books on the war and the period is John De St. Jorre, *The Nigerian Civil War*, London: Hodder and Stoughton, 1972.

9 Ngugi wa Thiong'o, *Detained: A Writer's Prison Diary*, London: Heinemann, 1981.

10 See in particular the pieces by Adamu Ciroma and Sobo Sowemimo in Agetua, *When the Man Died*.

11 Of these, see the pieces by Dan Izevbaye and Kole Omotoso in Agetua, *When the Man Died*.

12 Kole Omotoso has explored this issue in his book, *Achebe or Soyinka: A Study in Contrasts*, 79–96.

13 Derek Wright, *Wole Soyinka Revisited*, 133–45, especially insists on this point.

14 For important theoretical works on allegory which explore aspects of this issue, see H. Berger, Jr., *The Allegorical Temper*, 1957 and Angus Fletcher, *Allegory: The Theory of a Symbolic Mode*, 1964.

15 D.S. Izevbaye, "Soyinka's Black Orpheus," in Gibbs, *Critical Perspectives on Wole Soyinka*.

16 "The Representation of Women: the Example of Soyinka's *Aké*," in Molara Ogundipe-Leslie, *Re-creating Ourselves: African Women and Critical Transformations*, Trenton, New Jersey: Africa World Press, 1994.

17 It is noteworthy that except for Baroka in *The Lion and the Jewel*, marital couples in Soyinka's works are usually monogamous, the prime examples being the Reverend and Mrs. Erinjobi in *Camwood on the Leaves* and Makuri and Alu in *The Swamp Dwellers*.

18 Michel Foucault, *Madness and Civilization: A History of Insanity in the Age of Reason*, New York: Pantheon Books, 1965.

19 See Michel Peucheux, *Language, Semantics and Ideology*, New York: St. Martins Press, 1981.

20 Wande Abimbola, *Ifa: An Exposition of Ifa literary Corpus*, Ibadan University Press, 1976.

21 Biodun Jeyifo, "Wole Soyinka and the Tropes of Disalienation," in Soyinka, *Art, Dialogue and Outrage*.

22 These include, among others: the "Obitun Dancers" who are ascribed to Ado-Ekiti instead of Ondo (77); the NEPU female activist Gambo Sawaba (Gambo "Freedom") who is called Salawa Gambo (227); the Winneba Ideological Institute in Nkrumah's Ghana which is called Winneba School of Political Science (324).

23 On June 12, 1993, the government of the military dictator, Ibrahim Badamasi Babangida, annulled the decisive electoral victory of Mashood Kasimawo Abiola at the federal elections intended to usher in an elected civilian government after a mediocre and repressive military interregnum of twelve years. This act was massively resisted by huge mass protests and demonstrations in many parts of the country, especially in the southwest. Most of these protests and demonstrations were met with savagely brutal repression from Babangida's troops under the command of General Sani Abacha, the man who would later succeed Babangida and institute the most bloody and corrupt military rule in Nigeria's post-independence history. For these reasons, and also because Abiola later died under rather mysterious circumstances on the eve of his release from Abacha's dungeons, June 12, 1993 has since been memorialized in popular political consciousness as the ultimate marker of the tragedy of missed opportunities and an elusive destiny with humane, democratic governance in Nigeria.

6. POETRY, VERSIFICATION AND THE FRACTURED BURDENS OF COMMITMENT

1 The clearest statement of this view can be found in Chinweizu *et al.* in *Towards the Decolonization of African Literature*, Washington, DC: Howard University Press, 1983.

2 The essays in question are "And After the Narcissist?," *African Forum* vol. 1, no. 4 (Spring 1966), 53–64; "Neo-Tarzanism: the Poetics of Pseudo-Tradition" in Soyinka, *Art, Dialogue and Outrage*, "Aesthetic Illusions: Prescriptions for the Suicide of Poetry" in *Reading Black: Essays in the Criticism of African, Caribbean, and Black American Literature*, Houston A. Baker, Jr., (ed.), Ithaca: Cornell University Africana Studies and Research Center, 1976, 1–12, and "L.S. Senghor and Négritude: *J'accuse, mais, je pardonne*" and "Négritude and

the Gods of Equity," two of the three essays in *The Burden of Memory, the Muse of Forgiveness.*

3 For one essay which insightfully explores the place of verse in Soyinka's plays, see Alain Séverac, "The Verse of Soyinka's Plays: *A Dance of the Forests,*" *Research in African Literatures*, vol. 23, no. 3 (1992), 41–51. For a useful, though intellectually tendentious and aesthetically conservative summary of the positions of the accusers and defenders of Soyinka on the charge of the "difficulty" of his poetry, see James Booth, "Myth, Metaphor and Syntax in Soyinka's Poetry," *Research in African Literatures*, vol. 17, no. 1 (Spring 1986), 53–72.

4 See among others Jurgen Habermas, *The Philosophical Discourse of Modernity: Twelve Lectures*, (Translated by Fredric Lawrence), Cambridge, MA: MIT Press, 1987.

5 As quoted by Fraser, *West African Poetry: A Critical History*, 231.

6 "Climates of Art" in Soyinka, *Art, Dialogue and Outrage.*

7 On the place of the "ijuba" in traditional precolonial Yoruba performance, see Joel Adedeji in "'Alarinjo': the Traditional Yoruba Traveling Theatre," in Oyin Ogunba and Abiola Irele (eds.), *Theatre in Africa*, especially 45–6.

8 Fanon, *The Wretched of the Earth*, especially the chapter, "On National Culture," 167–99.

9 The notion of a "classical" or originary Négritude, as well as the corollary concept of a "revisionary" Négritude are Senghor's. See essays designated to these two formations of Négritude in *L.S. Senghor: Prose and Poetry*, John Reed and Clive Wake (translators and editors), Heinemann Educational Books, 1976. For authoritative English-language articles on Négritude see Abiola Irele "What Is Négritude?" and "Négritude and the African Personality" in his *The African Experience in Literature and Ideology*, 67–88, 89–116.

10 Walter Benjamin, "Theses on the Philosophy of History," in his *Illuminations: Essays and Reflections*, Hannah Arendt (ed.), New York: Schocken Books, 1968.

11 These are explored by Jacques Derrida in his "Racism's Last Word," in H.L. Gates, Jr. (ed.), *'Race,' Writing and Difference*, University of Chicago Press, 1985.

12 For a recent example of the postmodernist book-length discourse of non-racialism, see Paul Gilroy, *Against Race*, Cambridge, MA: Harvard University Press, 2000.

13 Nadine Gordimer, quoting Maxim Gorky, has the following sentence as one of the two epigraphs to her novel, *The Late Bourgeois World*: "The madness of the brave is the wisdom of life."

14 Among the most surprising defenders of Abacha and his regime were erstwhile highly respected intellectual champions of democracy like the economist, Sam Aluko and the journalist Peter Enahoro ("Peter Pan").

15 The list includes Roy Innis of the Congress of Racial Equality (CORE), Senator Carole Moseley Braun and Honorable Louis Farrakhan of the Nation of Islam.

7. "THINGS FALL TOGETHER": WOLE SOYINKA IN HIS OWN WRITE

1 Frank Kermode, *Forms of Attention*, Chicago and London: University of Chicago Press, 1985.

2 William Baer (ed.), *Conversations with Derek Walcott*, Jackson, MI: University Press of Mississippi, 1996.

3 For essays on Soyinka by Nadine Gordimer, Wilson Harris, Femi Osofisan and Niyi Osundare, see their respective contributions to *Wole Soyinka: An Appraisal*, Adewale Maja-Pearce (ed.), London: Heinemann Educational Books, 1994. For Achebe on Soyinka, see a brief comment in the book, *In Person: Achebe, Awoonor and Soyinka*, Karen L. Morell (ed.), African Studies Program, University of Washington, Seattle, 1975, 50–1; For Derek Walcott on Soyinka, see comments on *The Road* in "What the Twilight Says: An Overture" in *Dream on Monkey Mountain* and Other Plays, New York: Farrar, Strauss and Giroux, 1970, 3–40.

4 See Soyinka's "Aesthetic Illusions: Prescription for the Suicide of Poetry" in *Reading Black: Essays in the Criticism of African, Caribbean and Black American Literature*, Houston A. Baker (ed.), Ithaca: Cornell University Africana Studies and Research Center, 1976, 1–12.

5 I have explored the differences and common grounds of the two camps of Achebe-Ngugi "realism" and Soyinka "avantgardism" in modern African writing and their influences on younger African writers in an essay, "What Is the Will Of Ogun: Reflections on Soyinka's Nobel Prize and the African Literary Tradition" in *The Literary Half-yearly*, Mysore, India, vol. 28, no. 2 (July 1987), 142–60.

6 "Drama and the Idioms of Liberation," in Soyinka, *Art, Dialogue and Outrage*, 42–60.

7 Nadine Gordimer, "Soyinka the Tiger," in Maja-Pearce (ed.), *Wole Soyinka: An Appraisal*, 36–7.

8 Biodun Jeyifo, "Of Veils, Shrouds and Freedom: Soyinka and the Dialectics of Complexity and Simplicity" in *Perspectives on Wole Soyinka: Freedom and Complexity*, Jackson, MI: University Press of Mississippi, 2001, ix–xxii.

9 For an engaging exploration of "will" in the drama and literary career of Soyinka, see H.L. Gates, Jr., "Being, the Will and the Semantics of Death" in *Perspectives on Wole Soyinka: Freedom and Complexity*, 62–76.

10 I base this assertion on the totality of Soyinka's artistic works, theoretical and philosophical views and political journalism. Certainly, between such works as *A Play of Giants*, *The Road*, *Madmen and Specialists*, *Season of Anomy*, *The Man Died*, *Ibadan: the 'Penkelemes' Years*, *From Zia with Love* and *The Beatification of Area Boy* as well as essays like "The Fourth Stage," "And After the Narcissist?," "The Writer in a Modern African State" and "Cilmates of Art," it is possible to see strands of "Sorelian," "Fanonist" and anarcho-syndicalist traditions of revolutionary violence, as well as the sort of "sacred" sacrificial violence that Girard explores sympathetically if critically in his

influential monograph, *Violence and the Sacred*. Among Nigerian writers of a slightly younger generation, Festus Iyayi, Femi Osofisan and Niyi Osundare have also been deeply marked by this Soyinkan obsession with violence, the direct, repressive violence of the rulers, and the far more lethal violence *in* the political economy and social relations of dispossession, immiseration and disenfranchisement. For Georges Sorel, see his *Reflections on Violence* (authorized translation by T.E. Hulme), New York: B.W. Huebsch, 1914. For Fanon, see the chapter "Concerning Violence" in his *The Wretched of the Earth* (translated by Constance Farrington), New York: Grove Press, 1963. For René Girard, see his *Violence and the Sacred*, Baltimore: Johns Hopkins University Press, 1977.

Bibliography

PUBLISHED WORKS BY WOLE SOYINKA

The House of Banigeji (dramatic fragment) in *Reflections: Nigerian Prose and Verse*, Frances Ademola (ed.), Lagos, Nigeria: African Universities Press, 1962

The Lion and the Jewel (drama). London: Oxford University Press, 1963

A Dance of the Forests (drama). London: Oxford University Press, 1963

Five Plays: A Dance of the Forests, The Lion and the Jewels, The Swamp Dwellers, The Trials of Brother Jero and *The Strong Breed*. London: Oxford University Press, 1964

The Interpreters (novel). London: Andre Deutsch, 1965

The Road (drama). London: Oxford University Press, 1965

Kongi's Harvest (drama). London: Oxford University Press, 1967

Idanre and Other Poems. London: Methuen, 1967

The Forest of a Thousand Daemons. Translation of Yoruba novel, *Ogboju Ode Ninu Igbo Irunmale* by D.O. Fagunwa. London: Nelson, 1968

Three Plays: The Swamp Dwellers, The Trials of Brother Jero and *The Strong Breed*. Ibadan, Nigeria: Mbari Publications. Republished as *Three Short Plays*, London: Oxford University Press, 1969

Poems from Prison. London: Rex Collings, 1969

Before the Blackout (revue sketches). Ibadan: Orisun Editions, 1971

A Shuttle in the Crypt (poetry). London: Rex Collings/Metheun, 1971

Madmen and Specialists (drama). London: Metheun, 1971

The Man Died (prison memoir). London: Rex Collings, 1972

The Bacchae of Euripides: A Communion Rite (drama). London: Methuen, 1973

Camwood on the Leaves (radio drama). London: Metheun, 1973

Collected Plays, Vol 1. London: Oxford University Press, 1973

The Jero Plays (The Trials of Brother Jero and *Jero's Metamorphosis)*. London: Methuen, 1973

Season of Anomy (novel). London: Rex Collings, 1973

Collected Plays, Vol 2. London: Oxford University Press, 1974

Death and the King's Horseman (drama). London: Methuen, 1975

Poems of Black Africa (edited anthology). London: Secker and Warburg, 1975

Myth, Literature and the African World (criticism). Cambridge University Press, 1976

Ogun Abibiman (poetry). London: Rex Collings, 1976

Aké: The Years of Childhood (autobiography). London: Rex Collings, 1981
Opera Wonyosi (drama). London: Rex Collings, 1981
A Play of Giants (drama). London: Methuen, 1984
Six Plays (The Trials of Brother Jero; Jero's Metamorphosis; Camwood on the Leaves; Death and the King's Horseman; Madmen and Specialists; Opera Wonyosi). London: Methuen, 1984
Requiem for a Futurologist (drama). London: Rex Collings, 1985
Mandela's Earth and Other Poems. New York: Random House, 1988
Isara: A Voyage Around 'Essay' (memoir). New York: Random House, 1989
From Zia with Love and *A Scourge of Hyacinths* (dramas). London: Metheun, 1992
Art, Dialogue and Outrage: Essays on Literature and Culture. [Edited by Biodun Jeyifo] Ibadan: New Horn Press, 1988. Expanded and Revised. Edition published by Methuen, 1993
Ibadan: The 'Penkelemes' Years (memoir). London: Methuen, 1994
The Beatification of Area Boy: A Lagosian Kaleidoscope (drama). London: Methuen, 1995
The Open Sore of a Continent: A Personal Narrative of the Nigerian Crisis (political and philosophical reflection). New York: Oxford University Press, 1996
The Burden of Memory, the Muse of Forgiveness (literary criticism, political and philosophical reflection). New York: Oxford University Press, 1999
Outsiders (poetry). Canton, GA: Wisteria Press, 1999

UNCOLLECTED ESSAYS AND ARTICLES

"And After the Narcissist?." *African Forum* 1.4, 1966, 53–64
"The Nigerian Stage: A Study in Tyranny and Individual Survival." In *Colloquium on Negro Art*. Paris: Presence Africaine, 1968, 538–49
"Ethics, Ideology and the Critic." In *Criticism and Ideology*, Kirsten Holst Petersen (ed.), Uppsala: Scandinavian Institute of African Studies, 1988, 26–51
"This Past Must Address Its Present" (Nobel Prize Lecture). In *Black American Literature Forum* 22.3, 1988, 429–46
"Twice Bitten: The Fate of Africa's Culture Producers." In *PLMA* 105, no. 1, 1990, 110–20
"Of Power and Change." *African Statesman* 1.3, 1999, 17–19
"From Ghetto to Garrison: A Chronic Case of *Orisunitis*," *Research in African Literatures*, vol. 30 no. 4, (Winter 1999), 6–23

WORKS CITED

Abrams, M.H., *Natural Supernaturalism: Tradition and Revolution in Romantic Literature*, New York: Norton, 1971
Abimbola, Wande, *Ifa: An Exposition of the Ifa Literary Corpus*, Ibadan, Nigeria: Ibadan University Press, 1976
Achebe, Chinua, *Things Fall Apart* [Expanded Edition with Notes], London: Heinemann, 1966[1958]

Morning Yet on Creation Day, Garden City, NY: Doubleday, 1975

Adedeji, Joel, "Alarinjo: The Traditional Yoruba Traveling Theatre," in Oyin Ogunba and Abiola Irele (eds.), *Theatre in Africa*, Ibadan University Press, 1978

"Aesthetics of Soyinka's Theatre," in Dapo Adelugba (ed.), *Before Our Very Eyes*, Ibadan, Nigeria: Spectrum Books, 1988

Adekoya, Segun, "Re-planting the Tree of Life: *The Road* Re-trodden," *Soyinka: A Collection of Critical Essays*, Oyin Ogunba, ed., Ibadan: Syndicated Communications, 1994, 103–26

Adeniran, Tunde, *The Politics of Wole Soyinka*, Ibadan: Fountain Publications, 1994

Agetua, John (ed.), *When the Man Died*, Benin City, Nigeria: Bendel Newspapers Corporation, 1975

Althusser, Louis, *For Marx*, London: Allen Lane, 1969

Aristotle, *The Poetics*, in Bernard F. Dukore (ed.), Dramatic Theory: from Greeks to Grotowski, New York: Holt, Rinehart and Winston, 1974

Armah, Ayi Kwei, *The Beautyful Ones Are Not Yet Born*, London: Heinemann, 1968

Austin, J.L., *How to Do Things with Words*, Cambridge, MA: Harvard University Press, 1962

Awoonor, Kofi, *The Breast of the Earth: A Survey of the History, Culture and Literature of Africa South of the Sahara*, Garden City, NY: Anchor Press, 1975

Baker, Houston A. Jr., (ed.), *Reading Black: Essays in the Criticism of African, Caribbean, and Black American Literature*, Ithaca: Cornell University Africana Studies and Research Center, 1976

Balakian, Anna, *The Symbolist Movement: A Critical Appraisal*, New York: New York University Press, 1977

Barber, Karen, *I Could Speak Until Tomorrow: 'Oriki', Women and the Past in a Yoruba Town*, Washington, DC: Smithsonian Institution Press, 1991

Beier, Ulli (ed.), "Review of *A Dance of the Forests*," in *Black Orpheus* 8, 1960

Orisa Liberates the Mind: Wole Soyinka in Conversation with Ulli Beier on Yoruba Religion, Bayreuth, Germany: Iwalewa, 1992

Benjamin, Walter, "Theses on the Philosophy of History," in *Illuminations*, ed. Hannah Arendt, New York: Schocken Books, 1968

Berger, Jr., Harry, *The Allegorical Temper*, New Haven: Yale University Press, 1957

Boal, Augusto, *The Theatre of the Oppressed* (translated by Charles and Maria-Odilia Leal McBride), New York: Theatre Communications, 1985

Bryden, Ronald, "The Asphalt God," in James Gibbs (ed.), *Critical Perspectives on Wole Soyinka*, Washington, DC: Three Continents Press, 1980

Booth, James, *Writers and Politics in Nigeria*, London: Hodder and Stoughton, 1981

"Myth, Metaphor and Syntax in Soyinka's Poetry" in *Research in African Literatures* 17, no. 1 (Spring 1986)

Brockbank, Philip, "Blood and Wine: Tragic Ritual from Aeschylus to Soyinka," *Shakespeare Survey* 36, no. 1 (1983)

Cabral, Amilcar, *Unity and Struggle*, London: Heinemann Educational Books, 1980

Caudwell, Christopher, *Studies and Further Studies in A Dying Culture*, New York: Monthly Review Press, 1971

Chinweizu, *et al.*, *Towards the Decolonization of African Literature*, Washington, DC: Howard University Press, 1983

Churchill, Caryl, *Serious Money*, London: Methuen, 1987

Clark, J.P., *America, Their America*, London: Andre Deutsch, 1964

Cockshott, Una, "*A Dance of the Forests*" (Review), *Ibadan* 10 (November 1960)

Courtine, Jean-Fracois, *et al.*, *Of the Sublime: Presence in Question*, translated by Jeffrey S. Librett, Albany, NY: SUNY Press, 1993

Coward, Rosalind and John Ellis, *Language and Materialism*, London: Routledge and Kegan Paul, 1977

Crossman, R.H. (ed.), *The God that Failed*, New York: Harper, 1950

Crow, Brian, "Soyinka and the Romantic Tradition," in *Before Our Very Eyes*, ed. Dapo Adelugba, Ibadan, Nigeria: Spectrum Books, 1987, 147–69

 "Wole Soyinka and the Nigerian Theatre of Ritual Vision" in Brian Crow (with Chris Banfield), *An Introduction to Postcolonial Theatre*, Cambridge University Press, 1996

Cruise O'Brien, Conor, *Murderous Angels: A Political Tragedy in Black and White*, Boston: Little, Brown, 1968

David, Mary, *Wole Soyinka: A Quest for Renewal*, Madras, India: B.I. Publications, 1995

Davis, Anne B., "The Dramatic Theory of Wole Soyinka," in *Critical Perspectives on Wole Soyinka*, ed. James Gibbs, London: Heinemann, 1981, 147–57

Davis, Carole Boyce, "Maidens, Mistresses and Matrons: Feminine Images in Selected Soyinka Works," in Ann Adams Graves and Carole Boyce Davis (eds.), *Ngambika: Studies of Women in African Literature*, Trenton, NJ: Africa World Press, 1986, 75–88

Derrida, Jacques, *Dissemination*, University of Chicago Press, 1981

 "Racism's Last Word", in H.L. Gates, Jr. (ed.), '*Race*', *Writing and Difference*, University of Chicago Press, 1985, 329–38

De St. Jorre, John, *The Nigerian Civil War*, London: Hodder and Stoughton, 1972

Dunton, Chris, *Make Man Talk True: Nigerian Drama in English Since 1970*, London and New York: Hans Zell Publishers, 1992

Enahoro, Peter, "*A Dance of the Forests*: Wole Soyinka Has Overdone It This Time," *Daily Times* (Lagos, Nigeria), October 7, 1960

Eso, Kayode, *The Mystery Gunman: History, Politics, Power-Play, Justice*, Ibadan, Nigeria: Spectrum Books, 1996

Etherton, Michael, *The Development of African Drama*, London: Hutchinson University Library for Africa, 1982

 "Tribute to Wole Soyinka," in *Before Our Very Eyes*, ed. Dapo Adelugba, Ibadan, Nigeria: Spectrum Books, 1987, 33–7

Euba, Femi, *Archetypes, Imprecators and Victims of Fate: Origins and Development of Satire in Black Drama*, Westport, Co: Greenwood Press, 1989

Euripides, *The Bacchae and Other Plays*, New York: Viking Penguin, 1954

Falola, Toyin and Julius Ihonvbere, *The Rise and the Fall of Nigeria's Second Republic,* 1978–84, London: Zed Press Books, 1985

Fanon, Frantz, *The Wretched of the Earth,* New York: Grove Press, 1963
   Towards the African Revolution, New York: Grove Press, 1967
   Black Skin, White Masks, New York: Grove Press, 1986 [New Edition with Foreword by Homi Bhabha]

Fido, Elaine, "*The Road* and the Theatre of the Absurd," *Caribbean Journal of African Studies* 1 (Spring 1978), 75–94

Fiebach, Joachim, "Wole Soyinka and Heine Muller: Different Cultural Contexts, Similar Approaches," in Biodun Jeyifo (ed), *Perspectives on Wole Soyinka: Freedom and Complexity,* Jackson, MI: University Press of Mississippi, 2001, 128–39

Fletcher, Angus, *Allegory: The Theory of a Symbolic Mode,* Ithaca, NY: Cornell University Press, 1964

Foucault, Michel, *Madness and Civilization: A History of Insanity in the Age of Reason,* New York, Pantheon Books, 1965
   Language, Counter-Memory, Practice, Ithaca, NY: Cornell University Press, 1977

Fraser, Robert, *West African Poetry: A Critical History,* Cambridge University Press, 1986

Gates, Jr., H.L., "Being, the Will and the Semantics of Death," in *Perspectives on Wole Soyinka: Freedom and Complexity,* 62–76
   The Signifying Monkey: A Theory of Afro-American Literary Criticism, New York: Oxford University Press, 1988

Genet, Jean, *The Balcony,* New York: Grove Press, 1966

George, Olakunle, "Cultural Criticism in Wole Soyinka's *Death and the King's Horseman,*" *Representations* 67 (Summer 1999), 67–91

Gibbs, James, ed., *Critical Perspectives on Wole Soyinka,* London: Heinemann, 1981
   Wole Soyinka, New York: Grove Press, 1986
   and Bernth Lindfors (eds.), *Research on Wole Soyinka,* Trenton, NJ: Africa World Press, 1993

Gilliat, Penelope, "A Nigerian Original," in *Critical Perspectives on Wole Soyinka,* 106–7

Gilroy, Paul, *The Black Atlantic: Modernity and Double Consciousness,* Cambridge, MA: Harvard University Press, 1993
   Against Race, Cambridge, MA: Harvard University Press, 2000

Girard, René, *Violence and the Sacred,* Baltimore: Johns Hopkins University Press, 1977

Graham, Robin, "Wole Soyinka: Obscurity, Romanticism and Dylan Thomas," in *Critical Perspectives on Wole Soyinka,* ed. James Gibbs, London: Heinemann, 1981, 213–18

Greenblatt, Stephen, *Renaissance Self-fashioning from More to Shakespeare,* University of Chicago Press, 1980

Gunnar, Abdulrazak, "The Fiction of Wole Soyinka," in Adewale Maja-Pearce (ed.), *Wole Soyinka: An Appraisal,* London: Heinemann Educational Books, 1994, 61–80

Habermas, Jurgen, *The Philosophical Discourse of Modernity: Twelve Lectures*, Cambridge: MIT Press, 1987

Havel, Vaclav, *The Power of the Powerless* (John Keane, ed.), Armonk, NY: M.E. Sharpe, 1985

Haynes, John, *African Poetry and the English Language*, London: Macmillan, 1987

Heidegger, Martin, *On the Way to Language*, New York: Harper and Row, 1971

Hertz, Neil, *The End of the Line: Essays on Psychoanalysis and the Sublime*, New York: Columbia University Press, 1985

Heywood, Annemarie, "The Fox's Dance: the Staging of Soyinka's Plays," in *Critical Perspectives on Wole Soyinka*, 130–8

Hunt, Geoffrey, "Two African Aesthetics: Wole Soyinka Versus Amilcar Cabral" in *Marxism and African Literature*, Georg Gugelberger (ed.), Trenton, NJ: Africa World Press, 1985, 64–93

Irele, Abiola, "The Season of a Mind: Wole Soyinka and the Nigerian Crisis," in his *The African Experience in Literature and Ideology*, Bloomington, IN: Indiana University Press, 1990

  "Tradition and the Yoruba Writer: D.O. Fagunwa, Amos Tutuola and Wole Soyinka," in *The African Experience in Literature and Ideology*, 174–97, 1990

  "What Is Negritude?," in *The African Experience in Literature and Ideology*, 67–88, 1990

  "Negritude and the African Personality," in *The African Experience in Literature and Ideology*, 89–116, 1990

  "Parables of the African Condition: The New Realism in African Fiction," in *The African Imagination: Literature in Africa and the Black Diaspora*, New York: Oxford University Press, 2001, 212–45

Izevbaye, D.S., "Soyinka's Black Orpheus," in *Critical Perspectives on Wole Soyinka*

James, C.L.R., *Mariners, Renegades and Castaways*, Detroit: Beckwick/Ed, 1978

Jeyifo, Biodun, "The Hidden Class War in The Road," in *The Truthful Lie*, London: New Beacon Books, 1985, 11–22

  "Wole Soyinka and the Tropes of Disalienation," in Wole Soyinka, *Art, Dialogue and Outrage*, Ibadan, Nigeria: New Horn Press, 1988, viii–xxxii

  "What Is the Will of Ogun: Reflections on Soyinka's Nobel Prize and the African Literary Tradition," in Yemi Ogunbiyi (ed.), *Perspectives on Nigerian Literature, 1700 to the Present*, Lagos, Nigeria: Guardian Books, 1988, 169–85

  "The Nature of Things: Arrested Decolonization and Critical Theory," in *Research in African Literatures* 21 (1990)

  "Oguntoyinbo: Modernity and the 'Rediscovery' Phase of Postcolonial Literature," *The Yearbook of Comparative and General Literature*, no. 43, 1995, 98–109

  "Of Veils, Shrouds and Freedom: Soyinka and the Dialectics of Complexity and Simplicity in Postcolonial Discourse," in *Perspectives on Wole Soyinka: Freedom and Complexity*, ed. Biodun Jeyifo, Jackson, MI: University Press of Mississippi, 2001, ix–xxii

Jones, Eldred, *The Writings of Wole Soyinka*, London: Heinemann, 1973

Jonson, Ben, *The Alchemist*, New York: Hill and Wang, 1965

Joyce, James, *The Portrait of the Artist as a Young Man*, New York: B.W. Huebsch, 1916

Jules-Rosette, Bennetta, *Black Paris: the African Writer's Landscape*, Urbana: University of Illinois Press, 1998

July, Robert, *An African Voice: the Role of the Humanities in African Independence*, Durham, NC: Duke University Press, 1987

Katrak, Ketu, *Wole Soyinka and Modern Tragedy: A Study of Dramatic Theory and Practice*, Westport, CO: Greenwood Press, 1986

Kavolis, Vytautas, "Notes on Postindustrial Culture," in *Arts in Society*, vol. 11, no. 3 [Fall-Winter 1974], 415–17

Kermode, Frank, *Forms of Attention*, University of Chicago Press, 1985

Koestler, Arthur, *Darkness at Noon*, New York: Modern Library, 1941

Laclau, Ernesto and Chantal Mouffe, *Hegemony and Socialist Strategy: Towards a Radical Democratic Politics*, London: Verso, 1985

Langley, J. Ayo, *Ideologies of Liberation in Black Africa, 1856–1970*, London: Rex Collings, 1979

Larsen, Stephan, *A Writer and His Gods: A Study of the Importance of Myths and Religious Ideas to the Writings of Wole Soyinka*, Stockholm: University of Stockholm Department of the History of Literature, 1983

Larson, Charles, *The Emergence of African Fiction*, Bloomington, IN: University of Indiana Press, 1972

Lewis, Philip, "The Poststructuralist Condition," in *Diacritics*, vol. 12 (Spring 1982), 2–24

Lindfors, Bernth, "Wole Soyinka, When Are You Coming Home?," *Yale French Studies* 53 (1976), 197–210

"The Early Writings of Wole Soyinka," in *Critical Perspectives on Wole Soyinka*, James Gibbs, ed., London: Heinemann, 1981, 19–44

Longinus, "On the Sublime," in Bernard F. Dukore (ed.), *Dramatic Theory and Criticism*, New York: Holt, Rinehart and Winston, 1974, 76–82

Lord, Albert Bates, *The Singer of Tales*, Stephen Mitchell and Gregory Nagy (eds.), Cambridge, MA: Harvard University Press, 2000

Macebuh, Stanley, "Poetics and the Mythic Imagination," in *Critical Perspectives on Wole Soyinka.*, 200–12

Macherey, Pierre, *A Theory of Literary Production*, London: Routledge and Kegan Paul, 1978

Maduakor, Obi, *Wole Soyinka: An Introduction to his Writings*, New York: Garland Press, 1986

Madunagu, Edwin, *Nigeria: the Economy and the People*, London: New Beacon Books, 1984

Mair, Lucy, *New Nations*, University of Chicago Press, 1963

Maja-Pearce, Adewale (ed.), *A Mask Dancing: Nigerian Novelists of the Eighties*, London and New York: Hans Zell Publishers, 1992

Wole Soyinka: An Appraisal, London: Heinemann, 1994

Marx, Karl, *The German Ideology*, New York: International Publishers, 1947

Mbembe, Achille, *On the Postcolony*, Berkeley, CA: University of California Press, 2001

Mike, Jr., Charles, *Soyinka as a Director: the Example of Requiem for a Futurologist*, unpublished M. Phil thesis, University of Ibadan, 1987

Moore, Gerald, *Wole Soyinka*, London: Evans, 1971

Msiska, Mpalive-Hangson, *Wole Soyinka*, Plymouth, UK: Northcote House Publishers, 1998

Naipaul, V.S., *A House for Mr. Biswas*, London: Andre Deutsch, 1961

Nandy, Ashis, *The Intimate Enemy: the Loss and Recovery of the Self Under Colonialism*, Delhi, India: Oxford University Press, 1983

Naylor, Gloria, *Linden Hills*, New York: Ticknor and Fields, 1985

Nazareth, Peter, *Literature and Society in Modern Africa*, Nairobi, Kenya: East Africa Literature Bureau, 1972

Ngugi wa Thiong'o, *Homecoming: Essays on African and Caribbean Literature, Culture and Politics*, New York: Hill, 1972

    Detained: A Writer's Prison Diary, London: Heinemann, 1981

    Decolonizing the Mind: the Politics of Language in African Literature, London: James Currey, 1986

Norris, Christopher, *Truth and the Ethics of Criticism*, Manchester and New York: Manchester University Press, 1994

Ogunba, Oyin, *Soyinka: A Collection of Critical Essays*, Ibadan, Nigeria: Syndicated Communications Ltd, 1994

    The Movement of Transition: A Study of the Plays of Wole Soyinka, Ibadan University Press, 1975

    "Traditional African Festival Drama," in Oyin Ogunba and Abiola Irele (eds.), *Theatre in Africa*, Ibadan University Press, 1978, 3–26

Ogundipe, Ayodele, *Esu Elegbara, the Yoruba God of Chance and Uncertainty: A Study in Yoruba Mythology*, unpublished PhD dissertation, Indiana University, 1978

Ogundipe, Molara, "The Representation of Women: the Example of Soyinka's *Ake*," in her *Re-creating Ourselves: African Women and Critical Transformations*, Trenton, NJ: Africa World Press, 1994, 101–10

Ojaide, Tanure, *The Poetry of Wole Soyinka*, Lagos: Malthouse Press, 1994

Okigbo, Christopher, *Labyrinths; with Path of Thunder*, London: Heinemann, 1971

Okpewho, Isidore, *Myth in Africa*, New York: Cambridge University Press, 1983

    "Soyinka, Euripides, and the Anxiety of Empire," *Research in African Literatures*, vol. 30, no. 4 (Winter 1999), 32–55

Olaniyan, Tejumola, *Scars of Conquest, Masks of Resistance: the Invention of Cultural Identities in African, African-American and Caribbean Drama*, New York: Oxford University Press, 1995

Omotoso, Kole, *Achebe or Soyinka: A Study in Contrasts*, London, New York: Hans Zell Publishers, 1996

Osofisan, Femi, "Wole Soyinka and a Living Dramatist: A Playwright's Encounter with Soyinka's Drama," in *Wole Soyinka: An Appraisal*, Adewale Maja-Pearce, ed., London: Heinemann, 1994, 43–60

Playing Dangerously: Drama at the Frontiers of Terror in a Postcolonial State, Ibadan University Press, 1997

Oswald, Laura, *Jean Genet and the Semiotics of Performance*, Bloomington, IN: Indiana University Press, 1989

Palmer, Eustace, *The Growth of the African Novel*, London: Heinemann, 1979

Peucheux, Michel, *Language, Semantics and Ideology*, New York: St. Martin's Press, 1981

Quayson, Ato, *Strategic Transformations in Nigerian Writing: Orality and History in the Work of the Reverend Samuel Johnson, Amos Tutuola, Wole Soyinka and Ben Okri*, Bloomington, IN: Indiana University Press, 1997

Roscoe, Adrian, *Mother Is Gold: A Study of West African Literature*, Cambridge University Press, 1971

Rothenberg, Albert, *Creativity and Madness*, Baltimore: Johns Hopkins University Press, 1990

Ruitenbeck, Hendrik (ed.), *The Creative Imagination: Psychoanalysis and the Genius of Inspiration*, Chicago: Quadrangle Books, 1965

Saro-Wiwa, Ken, *Sozaboy: A Novel in Rotten English*, New York: Longman, 1994

Sedar Senghor, Leopold, *Prose and Poetry*, Selected and translated by John Reed and Clive Wake, London: Oxford University Press, 1965

Sekoni, Ropo, *Folk Poetics: A Sociosemiotic Study of Yoruba Trickster Tales*, Westport, CO: Greenwood Press, 1994

Séverac, Alain, "The Verse of Soyinka's Plays: *A Dance of the Forests*," *Research in African Literatures*, vol. 23, no. 3 (1992), 41–51

Shakespeare, William, *The Tempest*, New York: Signet Classic, 1987

A Midsummer Night's Dream, New York: St. Martin Press, 1996

Solzhenitsyn, Aleksander, *The Gulag Archipelago*, trans. by Thomas Whitney, New York: Harper and Row, 1974

Sorel, Georges, *Reflections on Violence* (authorized translation by T.E. Hulme), New York: B.W. Huebsch, 1914

Stratton, Florence, "Periodic Embodiments: A Ubiquitous Trope in African Men's Writing," *Research in African Literatures* 21, (1990), 111–26

Swift, Jonathan, *Gulliver's Travels*, New York: Garland Publishing Co., 1975

Thomson, George Derwent, *Marxism and Poetry*, London: Lawrence and Wishart, 1945

Usman, Yusufu Bala, *For the Liberation of Nigeria*, London: New Beacon Books, 1984

Wali, Obi, "The Dead-end of African Literature," Kampala, *Transition* no. 11, (September 1963), 13–18

Wallerstein, Immanuel, *Africa and the Politics of Unity: An Analysis of a Contemporary Social Movement*, New York: Vintage Books, 1969

Wauthier, Claude, *The Literature and Thought of Modern Africa*, trans. by Shirley Kay, Washington, DC: Three Continents Press, 1979

Weiskel, Thomas, *The Romantic Sublime: Studies in the Structure and Psychology of Transcendence*, Baltimore: Johns Hopkins University Press, 1976

Weiss, Peter, *Marat-Sade*, New York: Atheneum, 1984

Wilkinson, Jane, "Interview with Wole Soyinka," in Biodun Jeyifo (ed.), *Conversations with Wole Soyinka*, Jackson, MS: University Press of Mississippi, 2001, 143–66

Williams, Adebayo, "Ritual as Social Symbolism: Cultural Death and the King's Horseman," in Oyin Ogunba (ed.), *Soyinka: A Collection of Critical Essays*, 89–102

Wilson, Roderick, "Complexity and Confusion in Soyinka's Shorter Poems," in *Critical Perspectives on Wole Soyinka*, 158–69

Wren, Robert, *Those Magical Years: the Making of Nigerian Literature at Ibadan, 1948–1966*, Washington, DC: 1991

Wright, Derek, *Wole Soyinka Revisited*, New York: Twayne Publishers, 1993

Yerima, Ahmed and Ayo Akinwale, eds., *Theatre and Democracy in Nigeria*, Ibadan: Kraft Books, 2002

Zizek, Slavoj, *The Sublime Object of Ideology*, London: Verso, 1989

Index

Abacha, Sani, 9, 207, 216, 267, 303
Abimbola, Wande, 303 (*Ifa: An Exposition of Ifa Literary Corpus*)
Abiola, M.K.O., 303
Abrams, M.H., 80
Achebe, Chinua, xv, 1, 2, 4, 5, 15, 20, 50, 68, 69 (*Arrow of God*); 124, 141 (*Things Fall Apart*); 167, 277, 280, 296 (*Morning Yet On Creation Day*)
Adamu,Ciroma, 302
Adekoya, Segun, 35
Adelabu, Adegoke, 208
Adeniran, Tunde, xii (*The Politics of Wole Soyinka*)
African socialism, 252
Aidoo, Ama Ata, xvii, 5, 280
Aiyejina, Funso, xvii, 6
Akinrinade, Alani, 207
Akintola, S.L., 215, 246
Albee, Edward, 124 (*Who's Afraid of Virginia Woolf*)
Alkali, Zeinab, xvii
Althusser, Louis, 295
Aluko, Sam, 304
Amin, Idi, xii, 7, 72, 96
Anagnorisis, 238
Anikulapo-Kuti, Fela, 6, 115
Apartheid, 7, 256
Arden, John, 158, 277
Aristophanes, 83, 124 (*Lysistrata*); 153 (*The Clouds*)
Aristotle, 19 (*Poetics*); 19
Armah, Ayi Kwei, 5, 68, 69 (*Two Thousand Seasons*); 68, 169, 173 (*The Beautyful Ones Are Not Yet Born*)
Austin, J.L., 33
Awolowo, Obafemi, xvi, 213
Awoonor, Kofi, 5, 289 (*The Breast of the Earth*)
Ayindoho, Kofi, xvii
Azikiwe, Nnamdi, xvi

Ba, Ahmadou Hampate, 67
Ba, Mariama, xvii, 280
Babangida, Ibrahim Badamasi, 10, 207, 216, 303
Bacon, Francis, 73, 124
Baer, William, 305
Balakian, Anna, 296 (*The Symbolist Movement*)
Balewa, Tafawa, 9
Banda, Hastings, 7, 96
Banham, Martin, 4
Bappa, Saliu, 6
Barber, Karin, 14, 291
Beehan, Brendan, 2
Beier, Ulli, 4, 27, 28, 291
Bello, Ahmadu, xvi
Benjamin, Walter, 304 ("Theses on the Philosophy of History")
Beowulf, 236
Berger, Jr, H., 302
Beti, Mongo, 5, 7, 50, 69
Beyala, Calithxe, xvii
Blyden, Edward Wilmot, 65
Boal, Augusto, 83 (*The Theatre of the Oppressed*)
Bokasa, Jean-Bedel, 96
Booth, James, 290, 304
Borges, Jorge Luis, 277
Bosch, Hieronymous, 73
Botha, Pik, 264
Brecht, Bertolt, xiv (*Herr Puntilla and his Man Matti*); 91, 95 (*The Threepenny Opera*); 124 (*Baal*); 158, 282
Brockbank, Philip, 81, 123, 160
Brodsky, Josef, 268, 274
Brook, Peter, 124, 137
Brutus, Dennis, 68
Buhari, Muhammadu, 111, 216
Burundi, 247
Busia, Abena, xvii
Byrd, Rudolph, 269, 271

Cabral, Amilcar, xii, 15, 297
Camboida, 247
Casely-Hayford, J.E., 65
Castro, Fidel, xvi
Cauldwell, Christopher, 137
Chaplin, Charlie, 22 (Modern Times); 107
Cheney-Coker, Syl, xvii
Chinweizu, 15, 303
Churchill, Caryl, 103 (*Serious Money*);
    158
Clark, J.P., xv, xxiii, 2, 4, 5, 69, 124, 289
class approach to literary criticism, xiii
Cockshot, Una, 291
Coetzee, J.M., 281
Commonwealth Arts Festival 1965, 121
Conton, William, 68
Cooper, Brenda, xvii
Courtine, Jean-Francois, 301 (*Of the Sublime*)
Coward, Rosalind, 302 (*Language and
    Materialism*)
Crossman, R.H., 296 (*The God that Failed*)
Crow, Brian, 123, 125, 297
Crowther, Ajai, 193

Dangarembga, Tsitsi, xvii
Dante, Allegheri, 254
David, Mary, 99, 123
Davis, Ann B., 295
Davis, Carole Boyce, 298
De St. Jorre, John, 302 (*The Nigerian Civil War*)
Derrida, Jacques, 304
Descartes, Rene, 66
Djebar, Assia, xvii
Dunton, Chris, 290

Eliot, T.S., 148–149, 154, 236 (*The Wasteland*)
Emecheta, Buchi, xvii
Emokpae, Erabor, 4
Enahoro, Anthony, 207
Enahoro, Peter, 291, 304
Enwonwu, Ben, 4
Eso, Kayode, 290 (*The Mystery Gunman*)
Etherton, Michael, 14, 291, 294
Euba, Femi, 294
Euripides, 83, 161 (*The Bacchae*)

Fagunwa, D.O., 4
Fall, Aminata Sow, xvii
Fanon, Frantz, 21, 47–48, 64, 90, 256
Farrakhan, Louis, 304
Fasina, Dipo, 6
Fatoba, Femi, 6, 12
Fatunde, Tunde, 6
Fawehinmi, Gani, 6

Festival of Black Arts and Culture(Festac) 1977,
    10
Fido, Elaine, 35
Fiebach, Joachim, 105, 297
Fletcher, Angus, 302
Foucault, Michel, 96, 194
Fraser, Robert, 224–225, 234
Frisch, Max, 124 (*Count Oederland*)
Fry, Christopher, 49
Fugard, Athol, 88, 91

Garland, Colin, 73
Gates, Jr., H.L., 16, 294, 305
Gay, John, 95 (*The Beggar's Opera*)
Genet, Jean, 96 (*The Balcony*) 158
George, Olakunde, 159
Gibbs, James, 11, 17, 88, 282, 290, 291
Gilliat, Penelope, 2
Gilroy, Paul, 164–165, 304
Girard, Rene, 124, 306
Gordimer, Nadine, xvii, 15, 268, 277, 279, 304
Government College, Ibadan, 215
Gowon, Yakubu, xii, 180, 181, 251
Graham, Robin, 297
Gramsci, Antonio, xvii
Greenblatt, Stephen, 293
Guevarra, Che, xvi
Gunnar, Abdulrazak, 297

Habermas, Jurgen, 304
Hagher, Irowuese, 6
Harris, Wilson, 15, 277
Havel, Vaclav, 96, 120, 183
Head, Bessie, xvii, 21
Hegel, G.W.F., 60, 164
Heidegger, Martin, 31
Hertz, Neil, 301
Hess, Rudolph, 264
Heywood, Annemarie, 92
Ho Chi Minh, xvi
Hume, David, 60
Hunt, Geoffrey, 297

Ibadan-Ife group, xii, xiii
Ibsen, Henrik, 91
Idiagbon, Tunde, 111
Imbuga, Francis, 278
Innis, Roy, 304
Irele, Abiola, xv, xxiii, 4, 297, 304
Irobi, Esiaba, 6
Iyayi, Festus, xvii, 6, 306
Izevbaye, D.S., 189, 302

Jacobean drama, 83
James, C.L.R., 183

Jeyifo, Biodun, 292, 293, 295
Johnson, Femi, 12, 269
Johnson, Samuel, 167, 189
Jolly, Rosemary, xvii
Jones, Eldred, 93, 141
Jonson, Ben, 101–102, 103 (*The Alchemist*); 103
Joyce, James, 1, 209 (*Portrait of the Artist as a Young Man*); 249 (*Ulysses*)
Jules-Rosette, Benetta, 296
July, Robert, 290

Kabuki Theatre, 155
Kafka, Frantz, 22
Kandinsky, Vassily, 71, 124
Kane, Cheikh Hamidou, 5, 67, 68
Kavolis, Vytautas, 300
Katrak, Ketu, 123, 295
Kenyatta, Jomo, xvi
Kermode, Frank, 276
Khayyam, Omar, 76
Koestler, Arthur, 183
Kokoschka, Oscar, 71
Kosovo, 247

La Rose, John, xxiii
Labou Tansi, Sonny, xvii
Laclau, Ernesto, 293
Ladipo, Duro, 4, 69, 124, 170–171 (*Oba Koso*)
Langley, J. Ayo, 296
Larsen, Stephan, 123
Larson, Charles, 214
Latin American "boom literature," 15
Laye, Camara, 68
Lee, Bruce, 215
Lindfors, Bernth, 1, 15, 92, 280, 289, 292
Locke, John, 60
Lord, Albert, 154 (*The Singer of Tales*)

Macebuh, Stanley, 220, 292
Machel, Samora, 257
Macherey, Pierre, 292
Maduakor, Obi, 295
Madunagu, Eddie, 6, 290
Mahood, Molly, 4
Mair, Lucy, 141
Mandela, Nelson, 261–263, 264
Mangakis, George, 182
Marechera, Dambudzo, 278, 281
Marinetti, Filipo Tomaso, 71
Marx, Karl, 42 (*The German Ideology*); 42 (*Capital*)
Marxian labor theory of value, 252
Mbembe, Achille, 289
Mbowa, Rose, xvii
McFarlane, James, 276

Maja-Pearce, Adewele, 290
Mike, Charles, 301
Mishima, Yukio, 23
Mitterand, Francois, 269
Mnouchkine, Ariadne, 124
Mobutu, Sese Soko, 7
Mohammed, Bala, 6
Mohammed, Murtala, xii
Moore, Gerald, 4, 93
Moseley-Braun, Carole, 304
Mouffe, Chantal, 293
Msiska, Mpalive-Hangson, xii
Mugo, Micere, xvii

Naipaul, V.S., 23, 201 (*A House for Mr. Biswas*)
Nandy, Ashis, 21, 293
Nasser, Gamal Abdel, xvi
Naylor, Gloria, 278 (*Linden Hills*)
Nazareth, Peter, 131
Négritude, 2, 51, 64, 257, 300, 304
Nehru, Pandit, xvi
Nguema, Macias, 7, 96
Ngugi wa Thiongo, 7, 15, 18, 21, 185 (*Detained: A Writer's Diary*); 280, 296 (*Homecoming*)
Nichol, Abioseh, 5
Nietzsche, Friedrich Wilhelm, 37 (*The Birth of Tragedy*)
Nigeria,
    Agbekoya revolt, 182, 214
    civil war, 7, 59, 178, 181–183, 243
    crisis of 1962–65, 213
    General Strike 1964, 213
    "independence generation of writers," 5
    January 15, 1966 military coup, 246
    June 12, 1963 Elections, 218, 303
    Massacre of Igbos, 1966, 243, 246
    Nigerian Labor Congress, 9
    "pre-independence generation of writers," 4
Njemanze, Israel, 8, 9
Nkosi, Lewis, 68
Nkrumah, Kwame, xvi, 94
Noh Theatre, 155
Nwapa, Flora, xvii
Nwoko, Demas, 4
Nyerere, Julius, 252

Obafemi, Olu, 6
Obileye, Yomi, 12
Obumselu, Ben, 4
Ofeimun, Odia, 297
Ogah, Aba, 6
Ogunba, Oyin, 123, 144
Ogunde, Hubert, 4, 85–86, 115, 291, 298
Ogundipe, Ayodele, 294
Ogundipe, Molara, xvii, 6, 193

Ogunmola, Kola, 4
Ogunyemi, Chikwenye, xvii
Ogunyemi, Wale, 12
Ojaide, Tanure, xii, xvii
Okai, Atukwei, xvii
Okigbo, Chris, xv, xxiii, 4, 5, 246 ("Path of Thunder")
Okosun, Sunny, 6
Okoye, Mokwugo, 6
Okpewho, Isidore, 29–30, 123, 294
Okri, Ben, 278
Olaniyan, Tejumola, xi, 16
Omotoso, Kole, xii, xvii, 290, 302
Onabrakpeya, Bruce, 4
O'Neill, Eugene, 83, 158
Oni, Ola, 6
Onoge, Omafume, 6
Onwueme, Tess, xvii, 6
Orwell, George, 183 (*Animal Farm*)
Osofisan, Femi, xv, xxiii, 6, 12, 16, 83, 124, 277, 291, 294, 297, 306
Osundare, Niyi, xvii, 6, 277, 278, 294, 297, 306
Oswald, Laura, 298
Ouloguem, Yambo, 68, 190 (*Bound to Violence*)
Oyelana, Tunji, 12

Palmer, Eustace, 302
Pecheux, Michel, 302 (*Language, Semantics and Ideology*)
Peters, Jonathan, xi
Peters, Shina, 115
Phillips, Caryl, 277
postmodernist discourse of race, 267
poststructuralism, 20, 23
Pound, Ezra, 23, 236 (*The Cantos*)

Quayson, Ato, 16, 123, 294

Radin, Paul, 167
Ransome-Kuti, Beko, 6
Ransome-Kuti, Funmilayo, 197
Rive, Richard, 68
Roscoe, Adrian, 93
Rothberg, Albert, 293
Rotimi, Ola, 6
Royal Court Theatre, 230
Ruitenbeck, 293

Saadawi, Nawal el-, xvii, 7
Saro-Wiwa, Ken, 172 (*Sozaboy*); 216, 217, 267, 272, 274
Sartre, Jean-Paul, 41, 64 ("Orphée Noir")
Sekoni, Ropo, 277
Sekyi, Kobina, 65

Sembene, Ousmane, 5, 20, 68, 69 (*God's Bits of Wood*); 280
Senghor, Leopold Sedar, xvi, 48, 55 (*Chaka*)
Severac, Alain, 304
Shagari, Shehu, 8, 216
Shaka, 258–261
Shakespeare, William, 11, 83, 124 (*Anthony and Cleopatra*); 249 (*Hamlet*); 11, 128 (*Midsummer Night's Dream*); 128–129 (*The Tempest*)
Solarin, Tai, 217
Solanke, Jimi, 12
Solzhenitsyn, Aleksander, 183 (*The Gulag Archipelago*)
Sorel, Georges, 306 (*Reflections on Violence*)
Sowande, Bode, 6, 278
Sowemimo, Segun, 181
Sowemimo, Sobo, 302
Wole Soyinka,
   and aesthetic radicalism in developing world, 15–16
   African influences in dramatic works of, 83–86
   animism, thought in works of, 134–136
   avantgardism of, xviii, xxii, 10
   and the Bakhtinian grotesque realism, 106
   "complexity" and "obscurity" in poetry of, 223, 279
   the "Coriolanus complex," 249, 263
   cosmopolitanism in works of, 287
   and the dilemma of pure anteriority, 67, 79
   dogmatic application of Marxism, xiv
   and the duality of creation and destruction, 225–226, 283
   and the Eurocentric discourse on Africa, 65
   exile, xii–xiii, 9
   first phase of critical thought, 46, 48–60
   and gender, 58, 97–101
   and the "great man" theory of history and politics, xviii
   heroic mythos in prose works of, 172
   and the "literature of rediscovery," 48, 53
   the "Kongi" appellation, 293
   and the metanarratives of emancipation, 280–281
   nativism in works of, 287
   and the national-masculine tradition, xv, xvii, xix, xx, 58
   nature objectified in works of, 133–136
   on Négritude cult of blackness, 51–52
   Nobel prize, 10, 20, 21, 86
   on numinous being and consciousness, 34–35
   and Ogun archetype, 35–37, 285
   and the Orisanla-Atunda myth, 132
   overvalorization of will in works of, 285–286

and the "pharmakon," 281
on poetic solipsism of Négritude, 51
political activism, xiv, 6
radical break in critical thought of, 42–45
resistance and oppositionality in works
  of, 287
and the Romantics, 80–81
ritual festivity in plays of, 122
ritual matrix as interpretive construct in
  critical thought, 124–125
ritual problematic in plays of, 123–128
scope of scholarly works on, xi–xii
seclusion as spiritual
  enhancement, 240–255
second phase of critical thought, 46–47,
  60–70
self-writing in works of, 22–23
on social malaise of village life in colonial
  Africa, 206
solitary confinement in prison, 253
as a student in Britain, 3
and the sublime, xviii, xx
and the Symbolists, 57
taking political and artistic risks, 5–14
thematic patterns in dramatic works
  of, 93–94
third phase of critical thought, 47, 70–80
tragic mythopoesis in works of, 80–82
and transnational capitalism, 283
use of language in prose works of, 168–171
version of the leftist script of Nigerian crisis
  of 1962–65, 213–214
and violence, 283–284
and voluntarism, 219
"And after the Narcissist?," 50–51
"Climates of Art," 72–73
"The Credo of Being and
  Nothingness," 75–77
"The Critic and Society," 63
"Drama and the Idioms of Liberation,"
  279
"The External Encounter," 70–72
"The Fourth Stage," 39, 56–58, 166
"From a Common Black Cloth," 49–50
"Neo-Tarzanism and the Poetics of
  Pseudo-tradition," 256
"New Frontiers for Old," 73–75
Nobel lecture, 60, 61
"Theatre in Traditional African
  Societies," 84–86, 126
"Towards a True Theatre," 48–49
"The Writer in a Modern African
  State," 52–53, 55–56, 59
Prose Works:
Aké, 24–25, 26, 27, 192–197, 214

Art, Dialogue and Outrage, xiv, xxi
*The Burden of Memory and the Muse of
  Forgiveness*, 77–79
Ibadan, 19, 22, 26, 207–216
The Interpreters, 2, 10, 24, 27, 36, 87, 169,
  172–178
Isara, 198–207
The Man Died, 23, 27, 178–188, 289
Myth and Literature and the African World, 60,
  62, 66–69, 83
The Open Sore of a Continent, 216–219
Season of Anomy, 87, 169, 178–179, 188–192
Plays:
The Bacchae of Euripides, 121, 154, 161–163
The Beatification of Area Boy, 12, 91
Before the Blackout, 12
A Dance of the Forests, 10, 11, 87, 120, 122,
  128–141
Death and the King's Horseman, 87, 98, 121,
  122, 154–160, 165, 262, 281
From Zia with Love, 12, 91, 103, 111–119
The Invention, 256
Kongi's Harvest, 12, 94–95, 101–102, 103
The Lion and the Jewel, 87, 106–111
Madmen and Specialists, 22, 89–90, 105, 121,
  122, 141–144, 148–149, 154, 233, 248
Opera Wonyosi, 12, 95
A Play of Giants, 96–97
Requiem for a Futurologist, 12
The Road, 2, 10, 11, 22, 30–38, 103–105, 121,
  141–149, 228–229, 241, 289
A Scourge of Hyacinths, 91
The Strong Breed, 22
The Swamp Dwellers, 22
Poetry:
Idanre and Other Poems, 220–222, 224–240
Mandela's Earth, 261–267
Ogun Abibiman, 256–261
Outsiders, 267–275
A Shuttle in the Crypt, 240–255
"Telephone Conversation," 292
Film:
"Blues for a Prodigal," 8
St. John Perse, 277
Stratton, Florence, 298
Sublime, the, 164–166, 301
Sukarno, Achmed, xvi
Sundiata epic, 236
Sutherland, Efua, xvii, 5
Swift, Jonathan, 249 (*Gulliver's Travels*)

Toyo, Eskor, 6
Transition magazine, xii, xv
transnational capitalism, 283
Tutuola, Amos, 4, 50

U'Tamsi, Tchicaya, 68
University of Ife, xiii
Usman, Bala Yusufu, 4, 6, 290 (For the
    Liberation of Nigeria)

Vera, Yvonne, xvii
violence, 305–306
violence of representation, 20–21
Voltaire, 60

Walcott, Derek, 15, 41, 123, 125, 185, 234, 295,
    297
Wali, Obi, 18
Wallerstein, Immanuel, 298
Wauthier, Claude, 290
Weiss, Peter, 127 (*Marat-Sade*); 158
Williams, Adebayo, 123, 156

Williams, Eric, xvi
Wilson-Tagoe, Nana, xvii
Wren, Robert, 5
Wright, Derek, 15, 41, 123, 125, 185, 234, 295,
    297

Yerima, Ahmed, 290
Yoruba,
    Eshu, 36–37, 111
    Ifa, 1
    Ogun, 23, 26, 27–30, 54, 55, 161, 221,
        236–239, 258
    Orisanla-Atunda myth, 26–28,
        240

Zia ul-Haq, 113
Zizek, Slavoj, 301